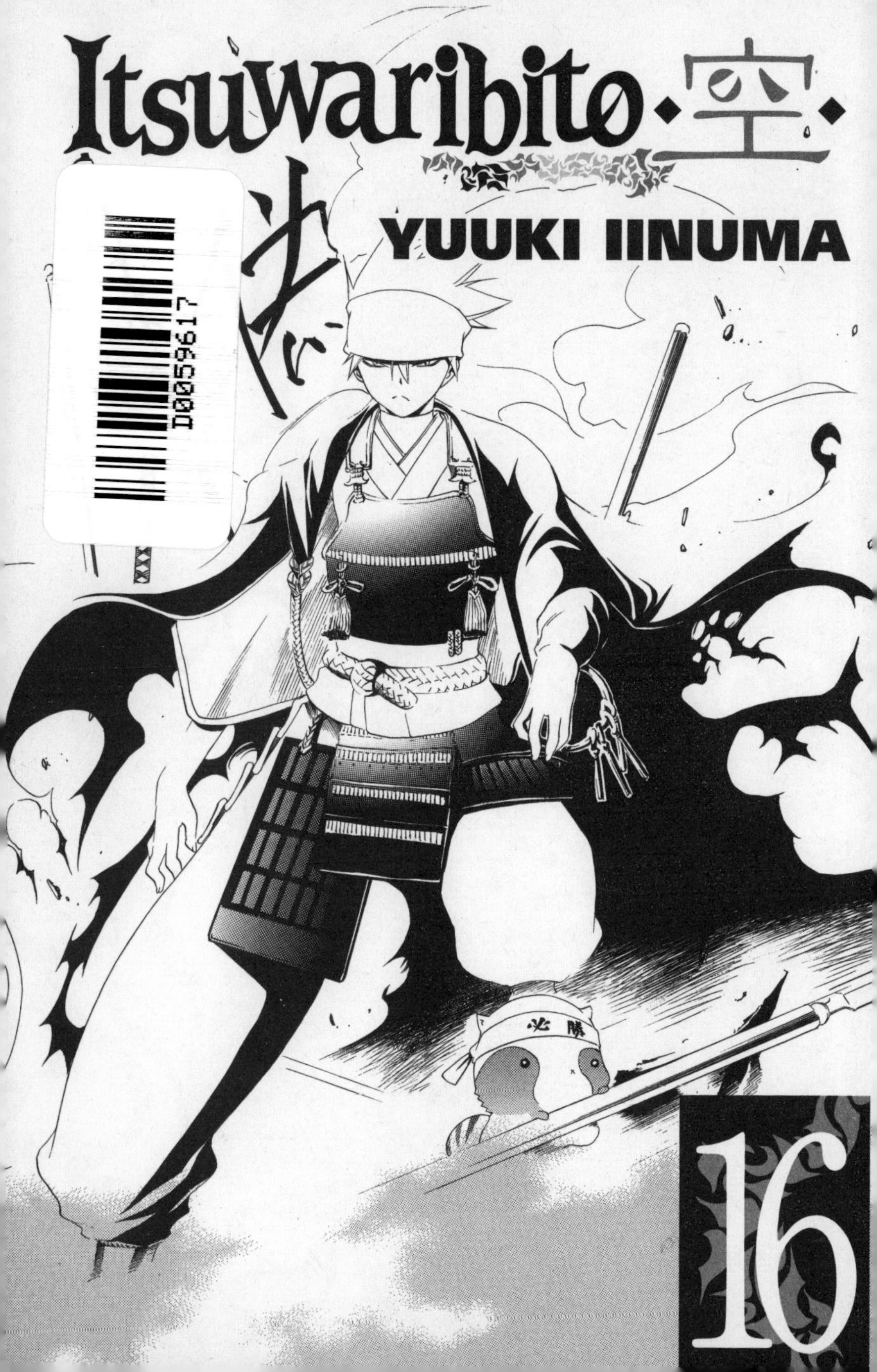
Itsuwaribito・空・
YUUKI IINUMA
必勝
16

Contents

Chapter 148: Utsuho and Tsukumo

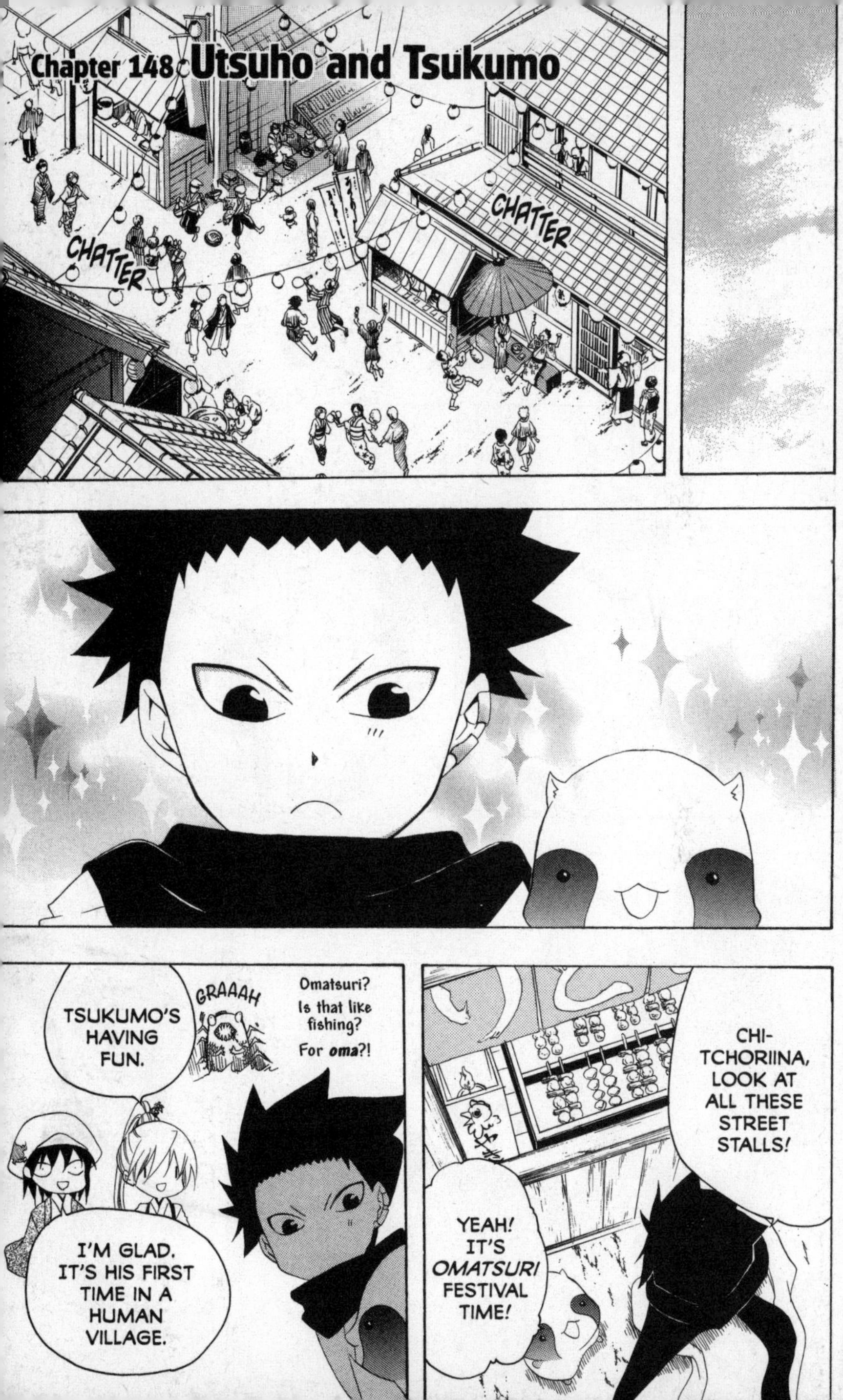
CHATTER
CHATTER
CHI-TCHORIINA, LOOK AT ALL THESE STREET STALLS!
YEAH! IT'S *OMATSURI* FESTIVAL TIME!
Omatsuri? Is that like fishing? For *oma*?!
GRAAAH
TSUKUMO'S HAVING FUN.
I'M GLAD. IT'S HIS FIRST TIME IN A HUMAN VILLAGE.

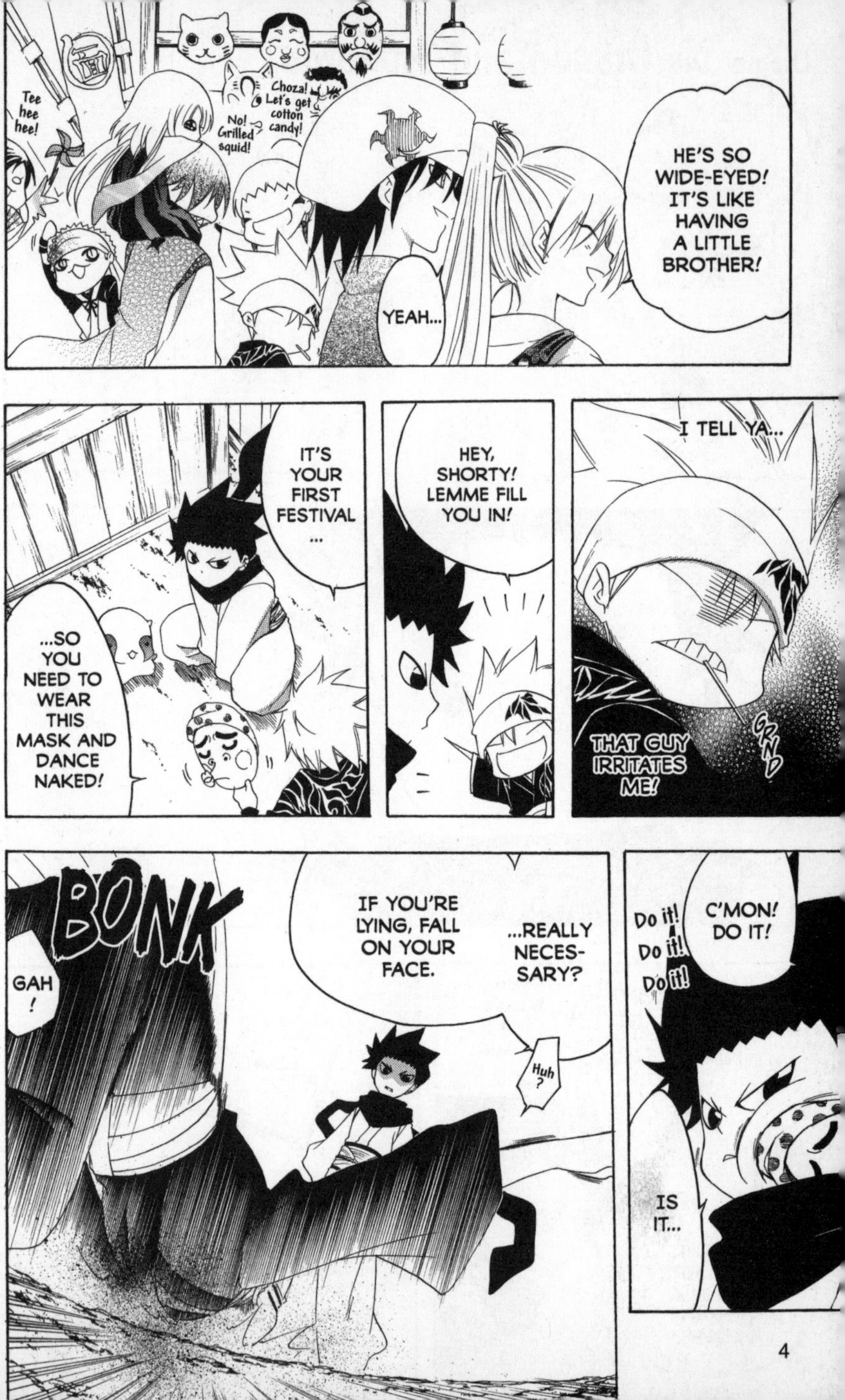
HE'S SO WIDE-EYED! IT'S LIKE HAVING A LITTLE BROTHER!
YEAH...
Choza! Let's get cotton candy!
No! Grilled squid!
Tee hee hee!
I TELL YA...
THAT GUY IRRITATES ME!
GRND
HEY, SHORTY! LEMME FILL YOU IN!
IT'S YOUR FIRST FESTIVAL ...
...SO YOU NEED TO WEAR THIS MASK AND DANCE NAKED!
C'MON! DO IT!
Do it! Do it! Do it!
IS IT...
...REALLY NECES-SARY?
IF YOU'RE LYING, FALL ON YOUR FACE.
Huh?
BONK
GAH!

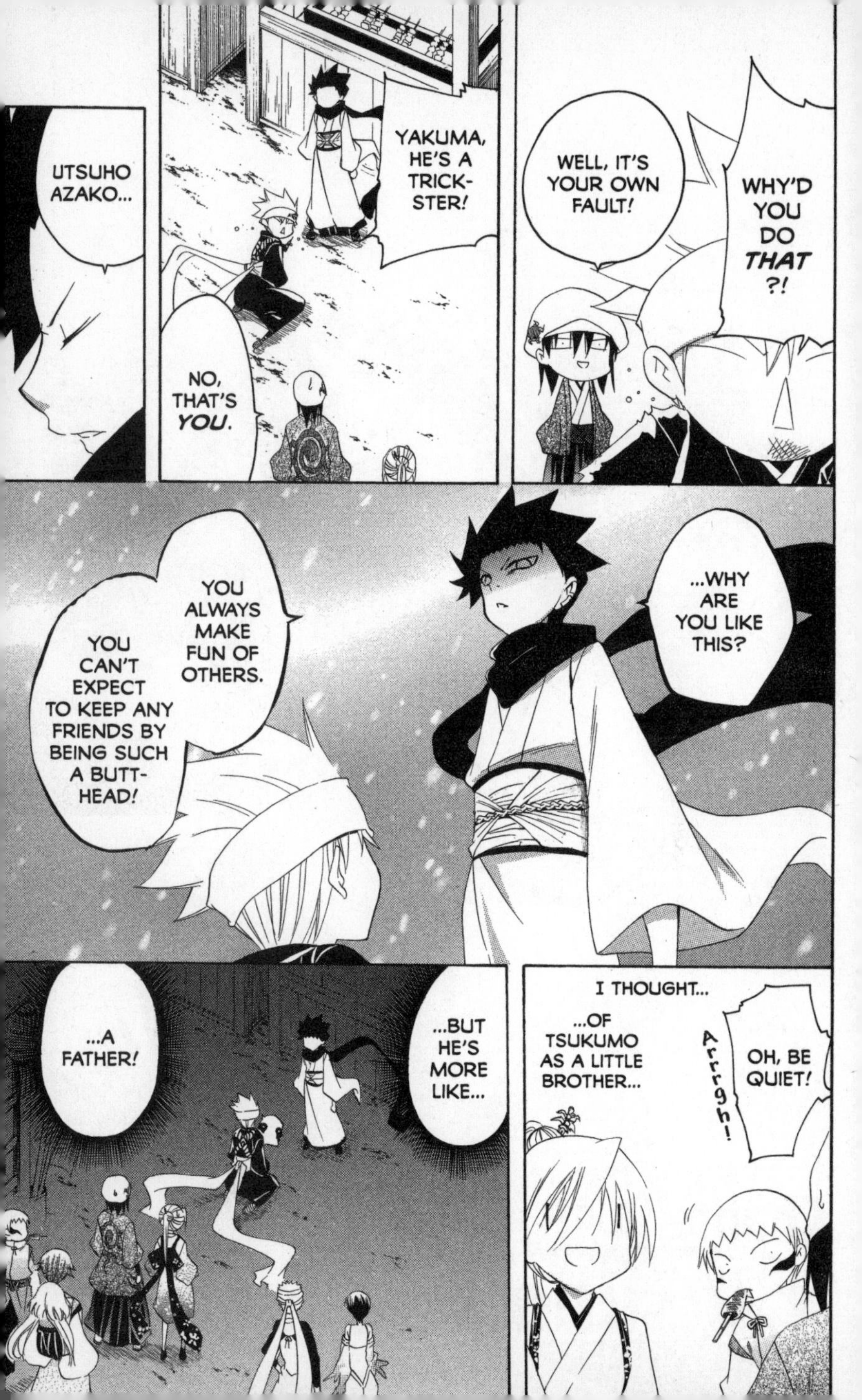
WHY'D YOU DO THAT?!
WELL, IT'S YOUR OWN FAULT!
YAKUMA, HE'S A TRICK-STER!
NO, THAT'S YOU.
UTSUHO AZAKO...
...WHY ARE YOU LIKE THIS?
YOU ALWAYS MAKE FUN OF OTHERS.
YOU CAN'T EXPECT TO KEEP ANY FRIENDS BY BEING SUCH A BUTT-HEAD!
OH, BE QUIET!
Arrrgh!
I THOUGHT...
...OF TSUKUMO AS A LITTLE BROTHER...
...BUT HE'S MORE LIKE...
...A FATHER!

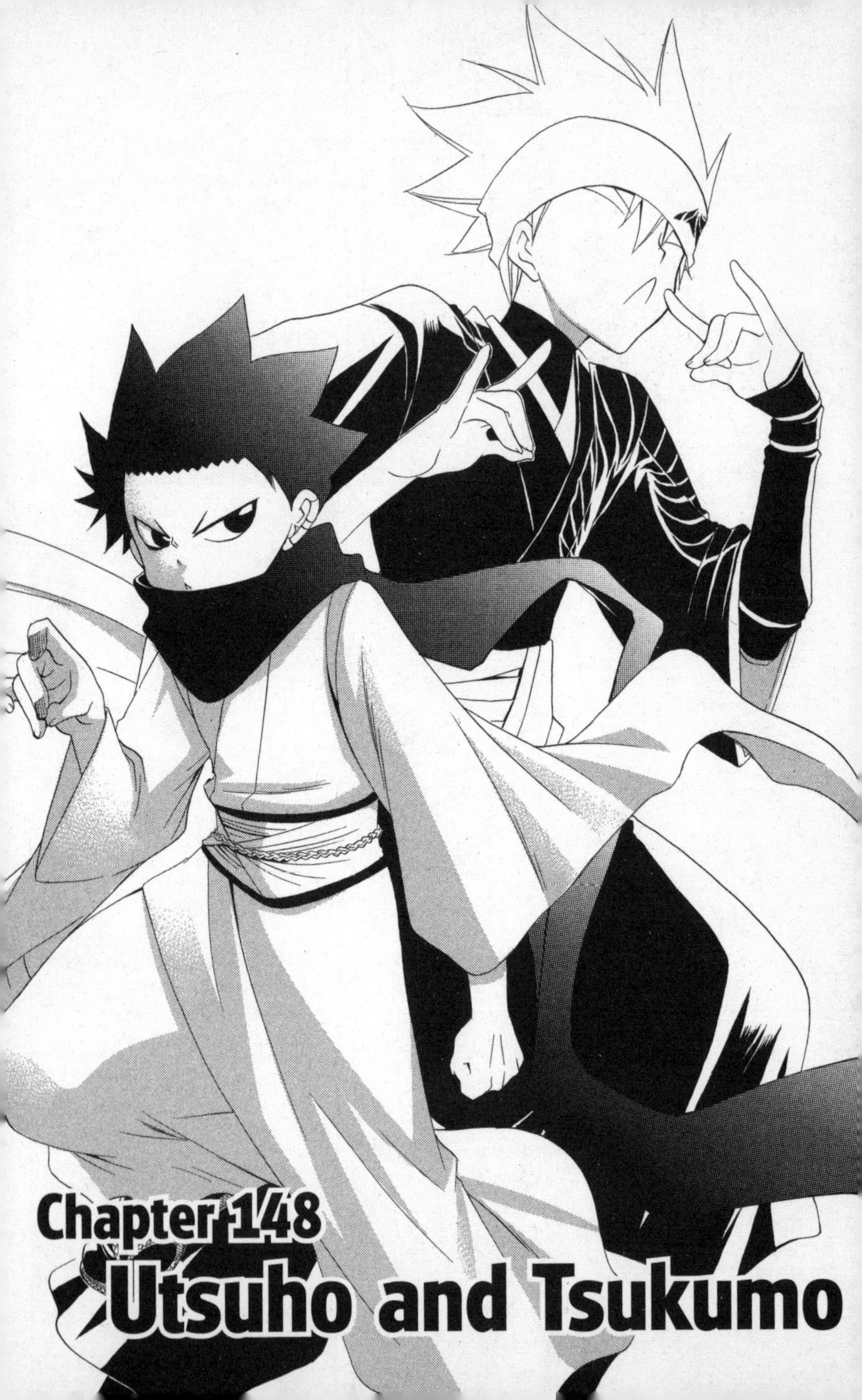

Chapter 148
Utsuho and Tsukumo

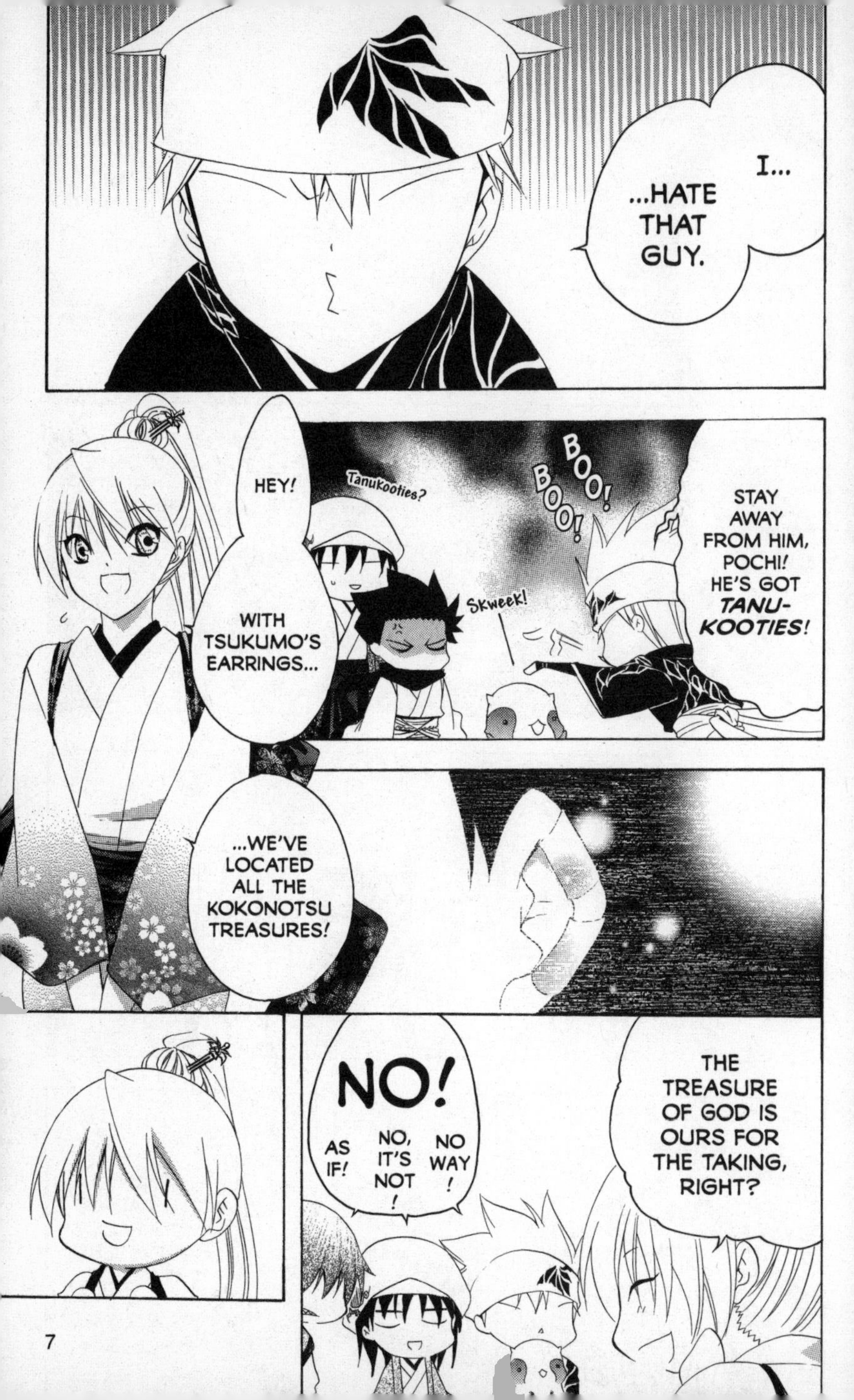
I...
...HATE THAT GUY.
STAY AWAY FROM HIM, POCHI! HE'S GOT *TANU-KOOTIES*!
BOO! BOO!
Skweek!
Tanukooties?
HEY!
WITH TSUKUMO'S EARRINGS...
...WE'VE LOCATED ALL THE KOKONOTSU TREASURES!
THE TREASURE OF GOD IS OURS FOR THE TAKING, RIGHT?
NO!
NO WAY!
NO, IT'S NOT!
AS IF!

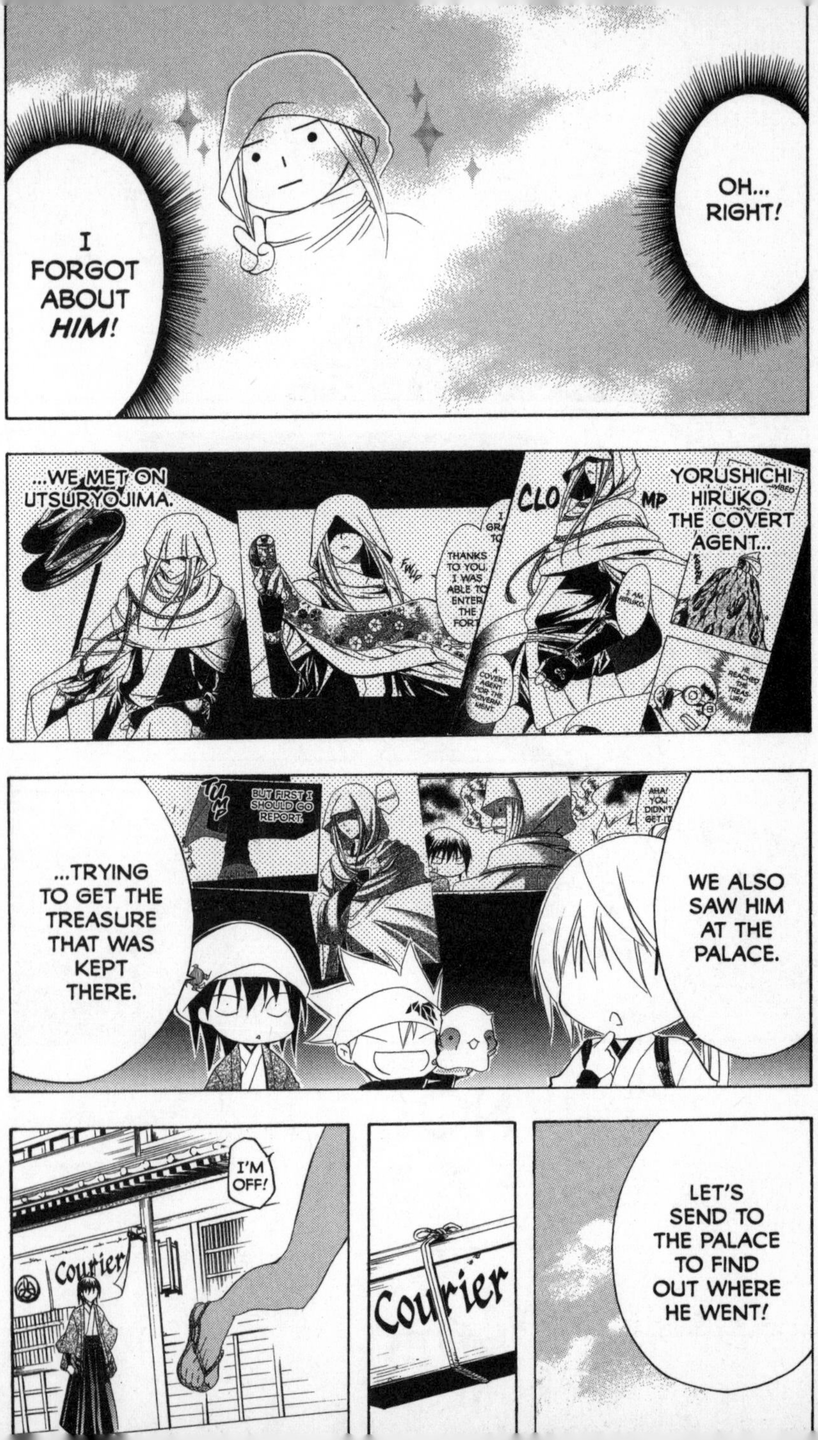

OH... RIGHT!
I FORGOT ABOUT *HIM!*
YORUSHICHI HIRUKO, THE COVERT AGENT...
CLOMP
I AM HIRUKO.
HE REACHED THE TREASURE!
A COVERT AGENT FOR THE GOVERNMENT.
THANKS TO YOU, I WAS ABLE TO ENTER THE FORT
...WE MET ON UTSURYOJIMA.
WE ALSO SAW HIM AT THE PALACE.
AHA! YOU DIDN'T GET IT
BUT FIRST I SHOULD GO REPORT.
...TRYING TO GET THE TREASURE THAT WAS KEPT THERE.
LET'S SEND TO THE PALACE TO FIND OUT WHERE HE WENT!
Courier
I'M OFF!
Courier

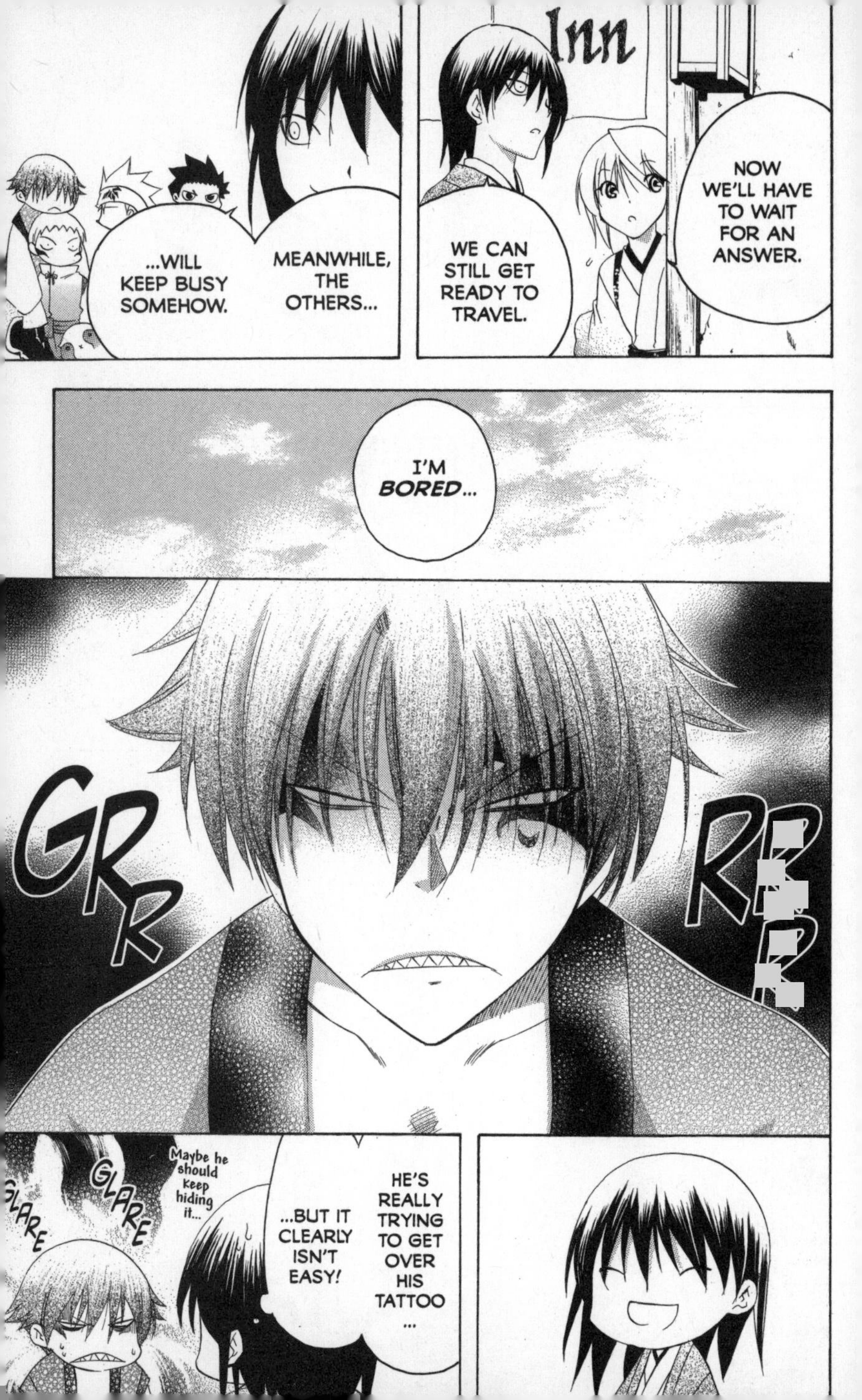
Inn
NOW WE'LL HAVE TO WAIT FOR AN ANSWER.
WE CAN STILL GET READY TO TRAVEL.
MEANWHILE, THE OTHERS...
...WILL KEEP BUSY SOMEHOW.
I'M *BORED*...
GRR
RRR
HE'S REALLY TRYING TO GET OVER HIS TATTOO...
...BUT IT CLEARLY ISN'T EASY!
Maybe he should keep hiding it...
GLARE
GLARE

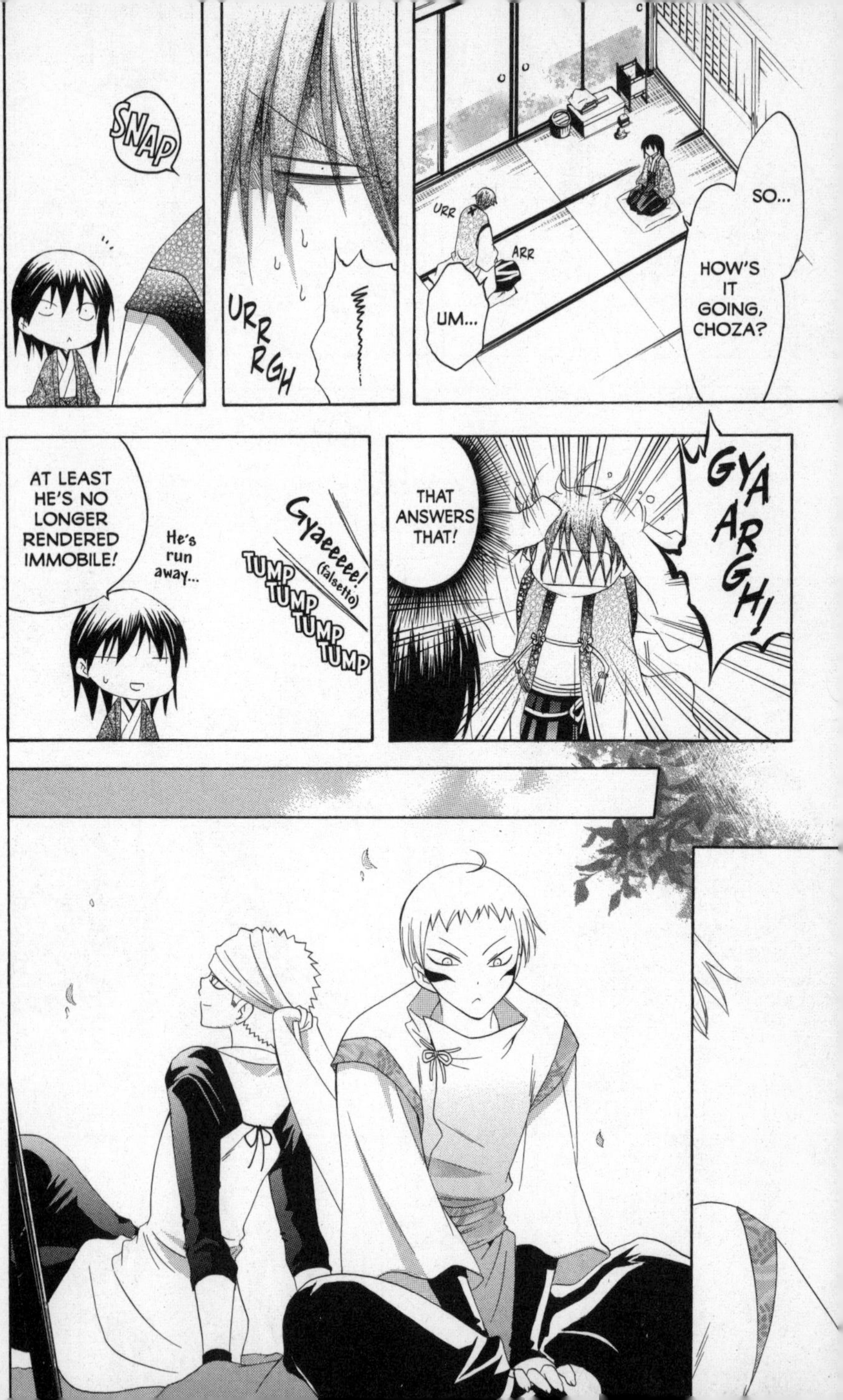
SO... HOW'S IT GOING, CHOZA?
URR
ARR
UM...
URRRGH
SNAP
GYAARGH!
THAT ANSWERS THAT!
Gyaeeeee! (falsetto)
TUMP TUMP TUMP TUMP
He's run away...
AT LEAST HE'S NO LONGER RENDERED IMMOBILE!

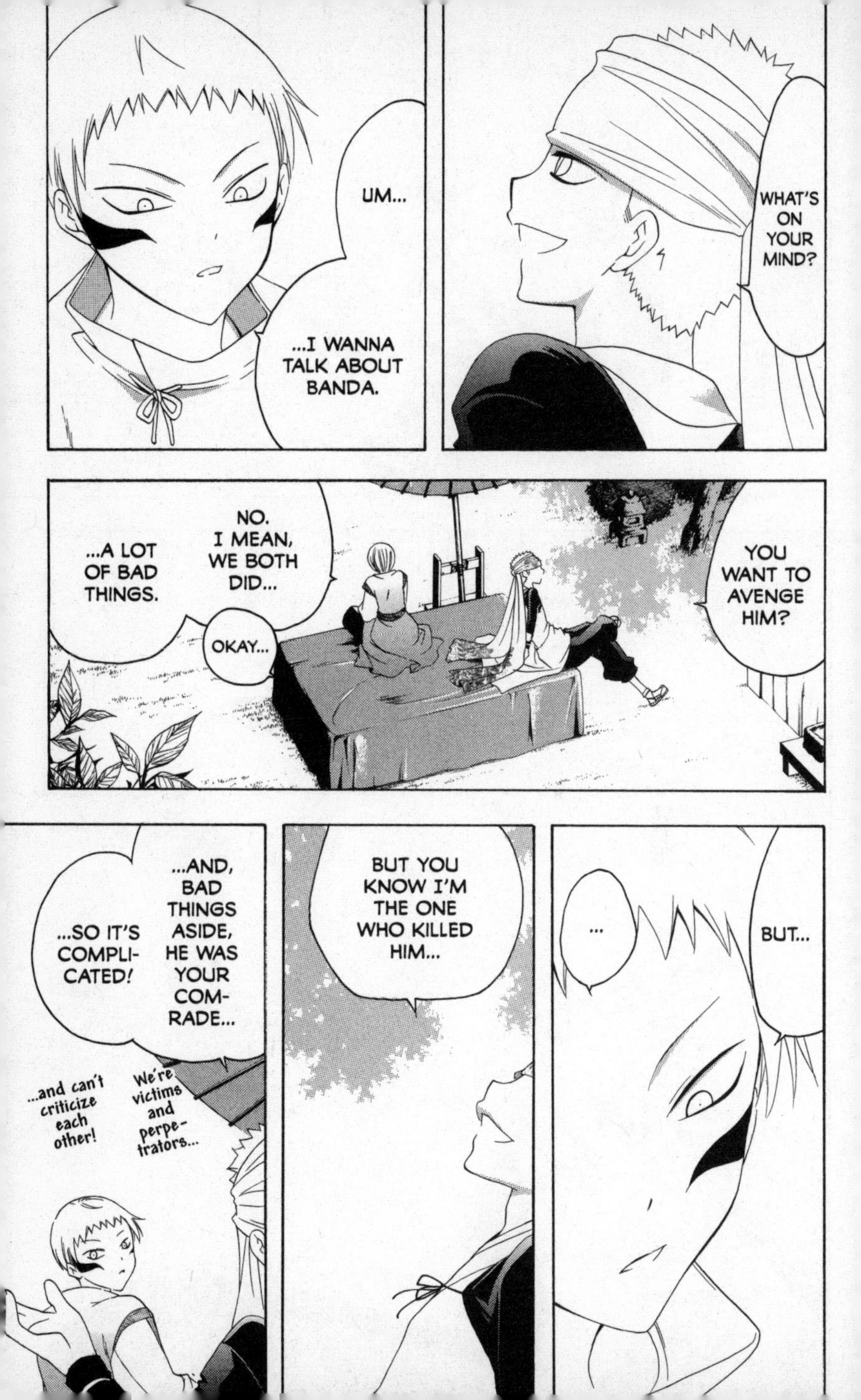
WHAT'S ON YOUR MIND?
UM...
...I WANNA TALK ABOUT BANDA.
YOU WANT TO AVENGE HIM?
NO. I MEAN, WE BOTH DID...
...A LOT OF BAD THINGS.
OKAY...
BUT...
...
BUT YOU KNOW I'M THE ONE WHO KILLED HIM...
...AND, BAD THINGS ASIDE, HE WAS YOUR COM-RADE...
...SO IT'S COMPLI-CATED!
We're victims and perpe-trators...
...and can't criticize each other!

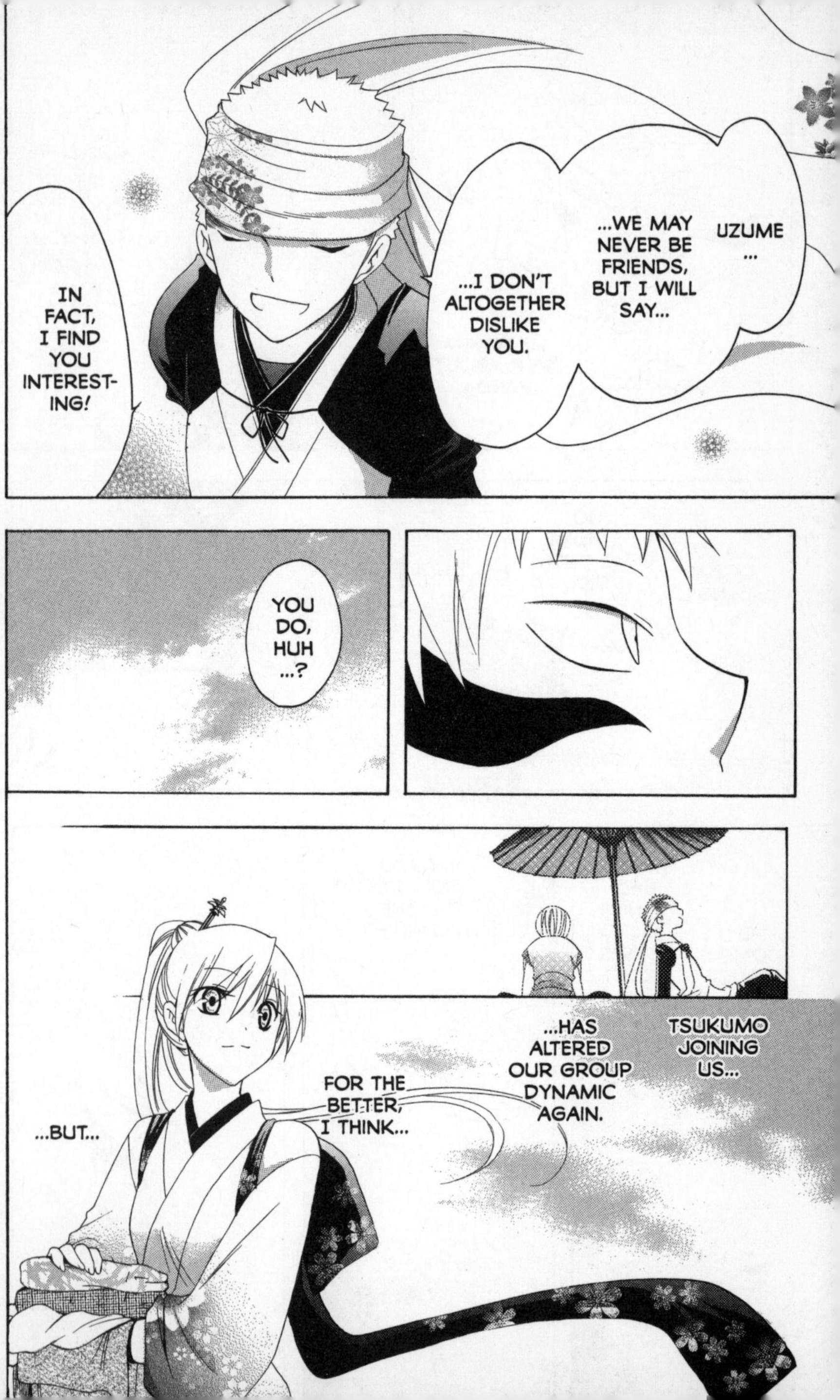
UZUME ...
...WE MAY NEVER BE FRIENDS, BUT I WILL SAY...
...I DON'T ALTOGETHER DISLIKE YOU.
IN FACT, I FIND YOU INTERESTING!
YOU DO, HUH ...?
TSUKUMO JOINING US...
...HAS ALTERED OUR GROUP DYNAMIC AGAIN.
FOR THE BETTER, I THINK...
...BUT...

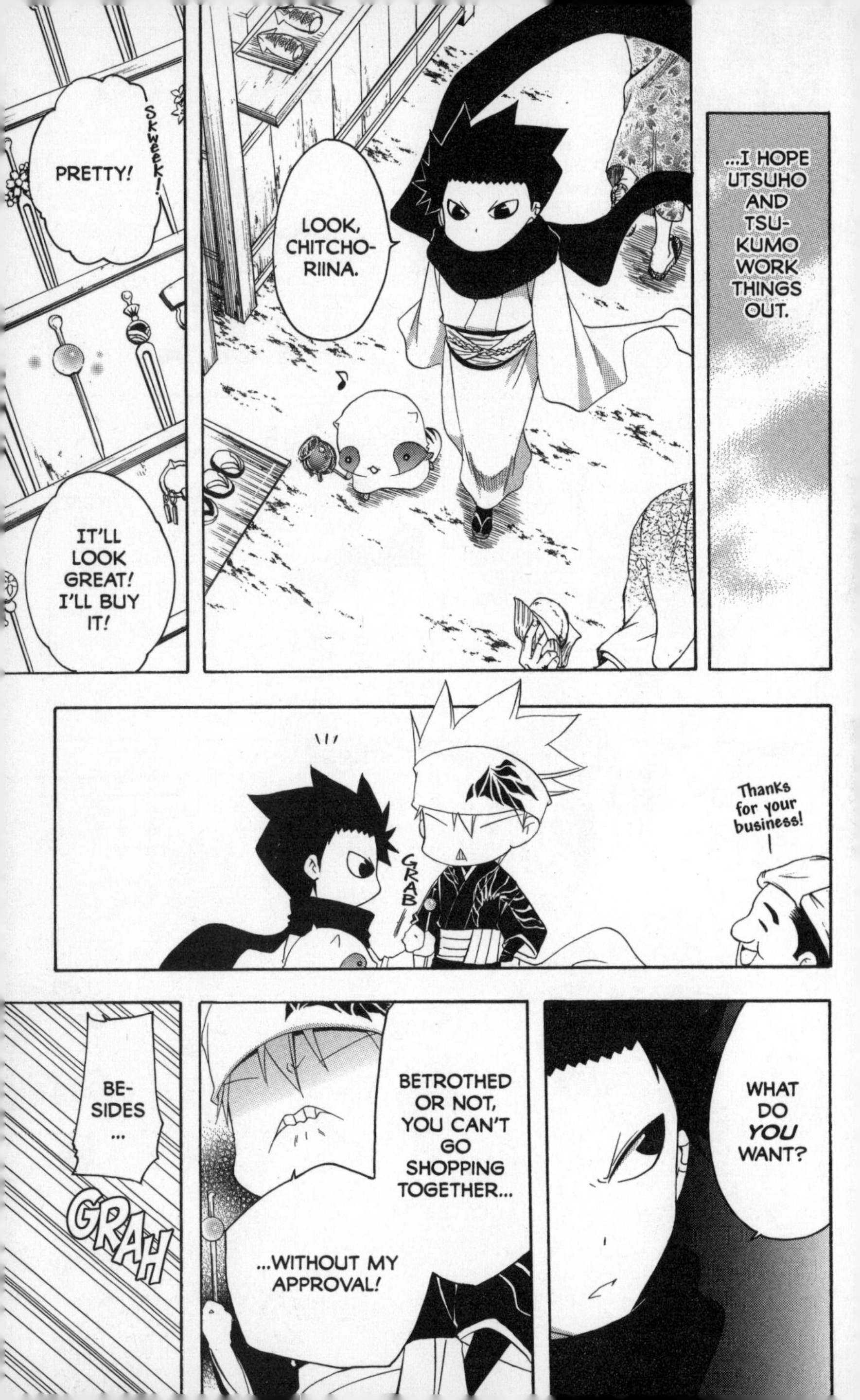
...I HOPE UTSUHO AND TSU-KUMO WORK THINGS OUT.
LOOK, CHITCHO-RIINA.
Skweek!
PRETTY!
IT'LL LOOK GREAT! I'LL BUY IT!
Thanks for your business!
GRAB
WHAT DO *YOU* WANT?
BETROTHED OR NOT, YOU CAN'T GO SHOPPING TOGETHER...
...WITHOUT MY APPROVAL!
BE-SIDES ...
GRAH

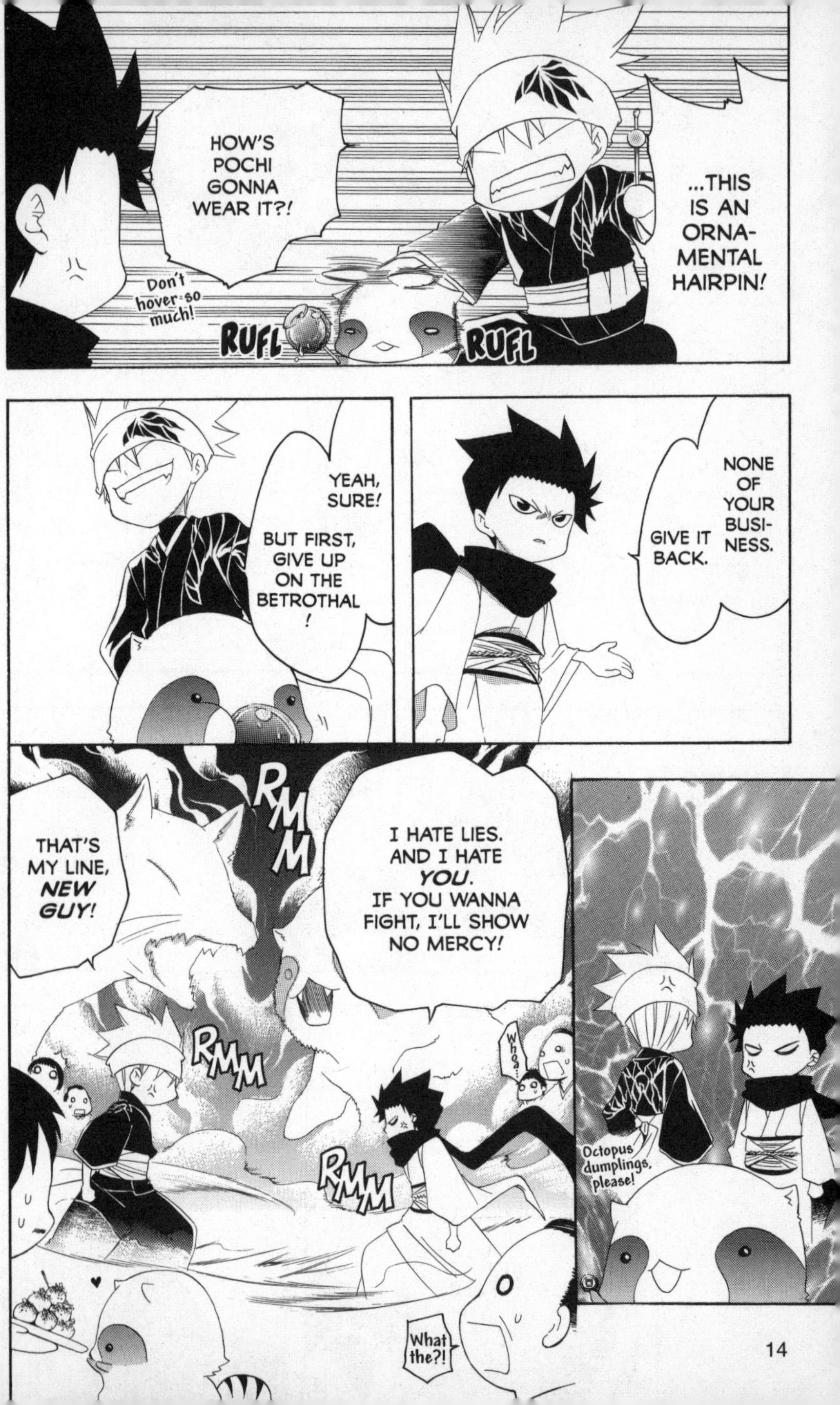
...THIS IS AN ORNA-MENTAL HAIRPIN!
HOW'S POCHI GONNA WEAR IT?!
Don't hover so much!
RUFL
RUFL
NONE OF YOUR BUSI-NESS.
GIVE IT BACK.
YEAH, SURE!
BUT FIRST, GIVE UP ON THE BETROTHAL!
Octopus dumplings, please!
RMM
I HATE LIES. AND I HATE *YOU*. IF YOU WANNA FIGHT, I'LL SHOW NO MERCY!
THAT'S MY LINE, ***NEW GUY***!
RMM
Whoa...
RMM
What the?!

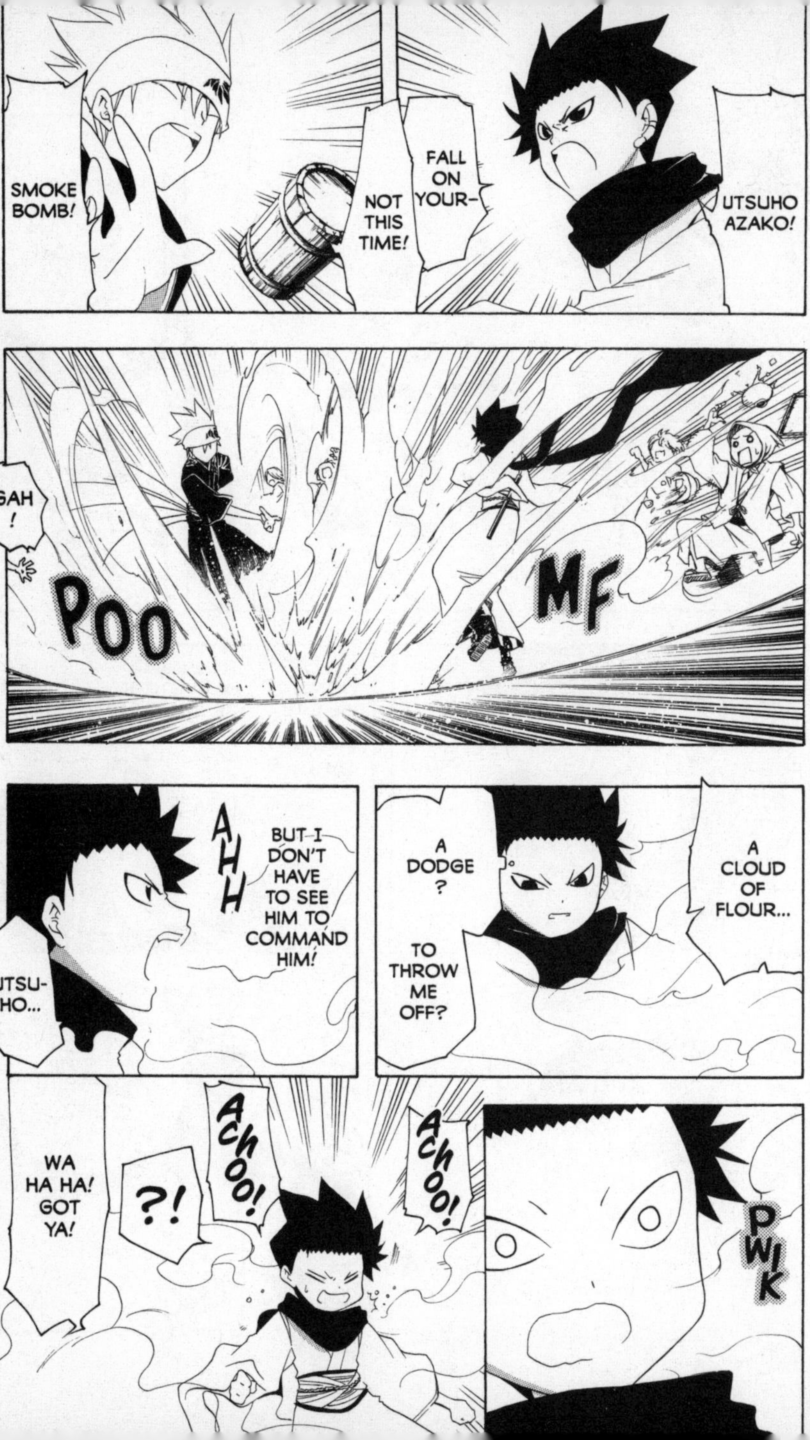
UTSUHO AZAKO!
FALL ON YOUR–
NOT THIS TIME!
SMOKE BOMB!
GAH!
POOMF
A CLOUD OF FLOUR...
A DODGE?
TO THROW ME OFF?
BUT I DON'T HAVE TO SEE HIM TO COMMAND HIM!
AHH
UTSU-HO...
PWIK
ACHOO!
ACHOO!
?!
WA HA HA! GOT YA!

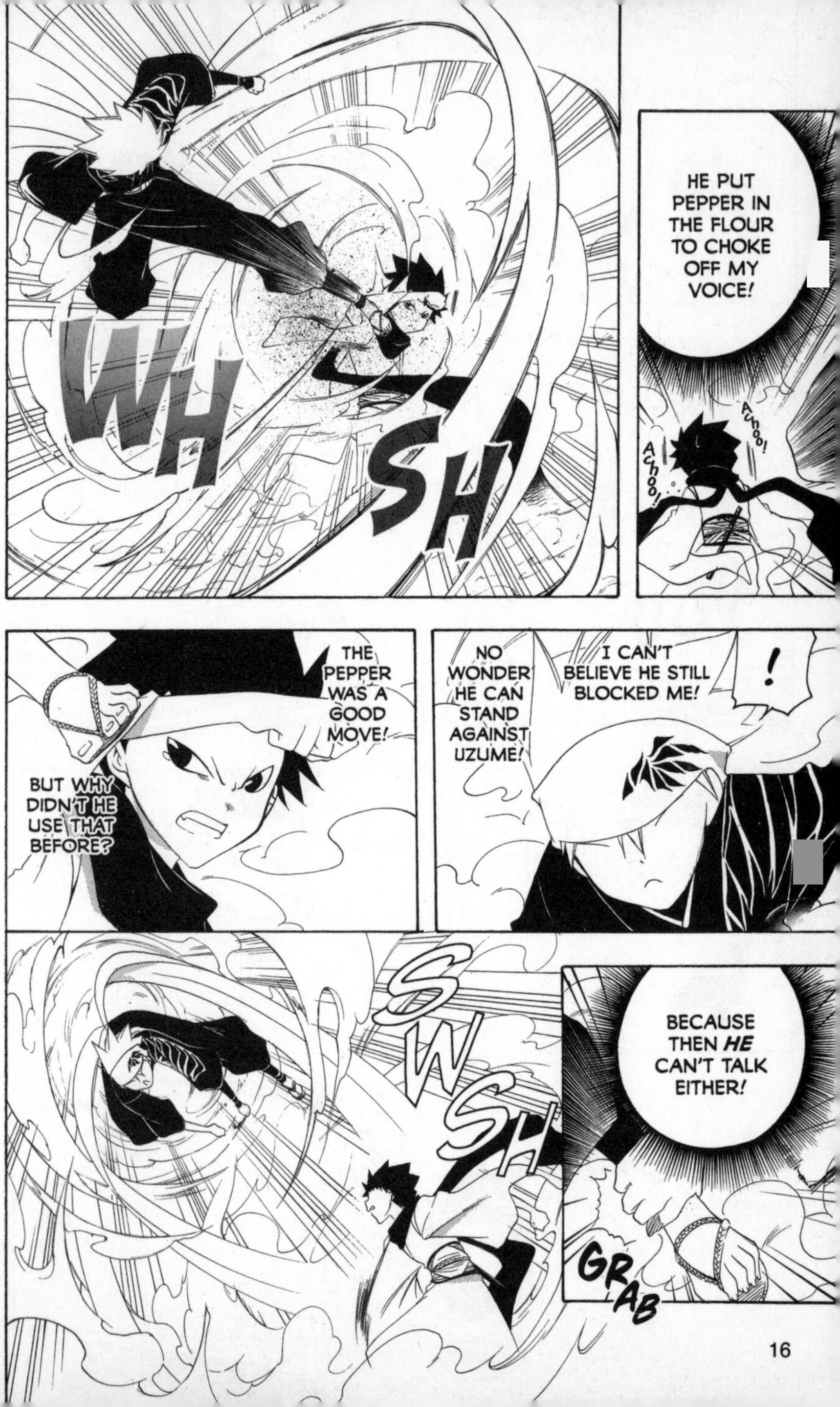
HE PUT PEPPER IN THE FLOUR TO CHOKE OFF MY VOICE!
Achoo!
Achoo!
WHSH
!
I CAN'T BELIEVE HE STILL BLOCKED ME!
NO WONDER HE CAN STAND AGAINST UZUME!
THE PEPPER WAS A GOOD MOVE!
BUT WHY DIDN'T HE USE THAT BEFORE?
BECAUSE THEN *HE* CAN'T TALK EITHER!
GRAB
SWSH

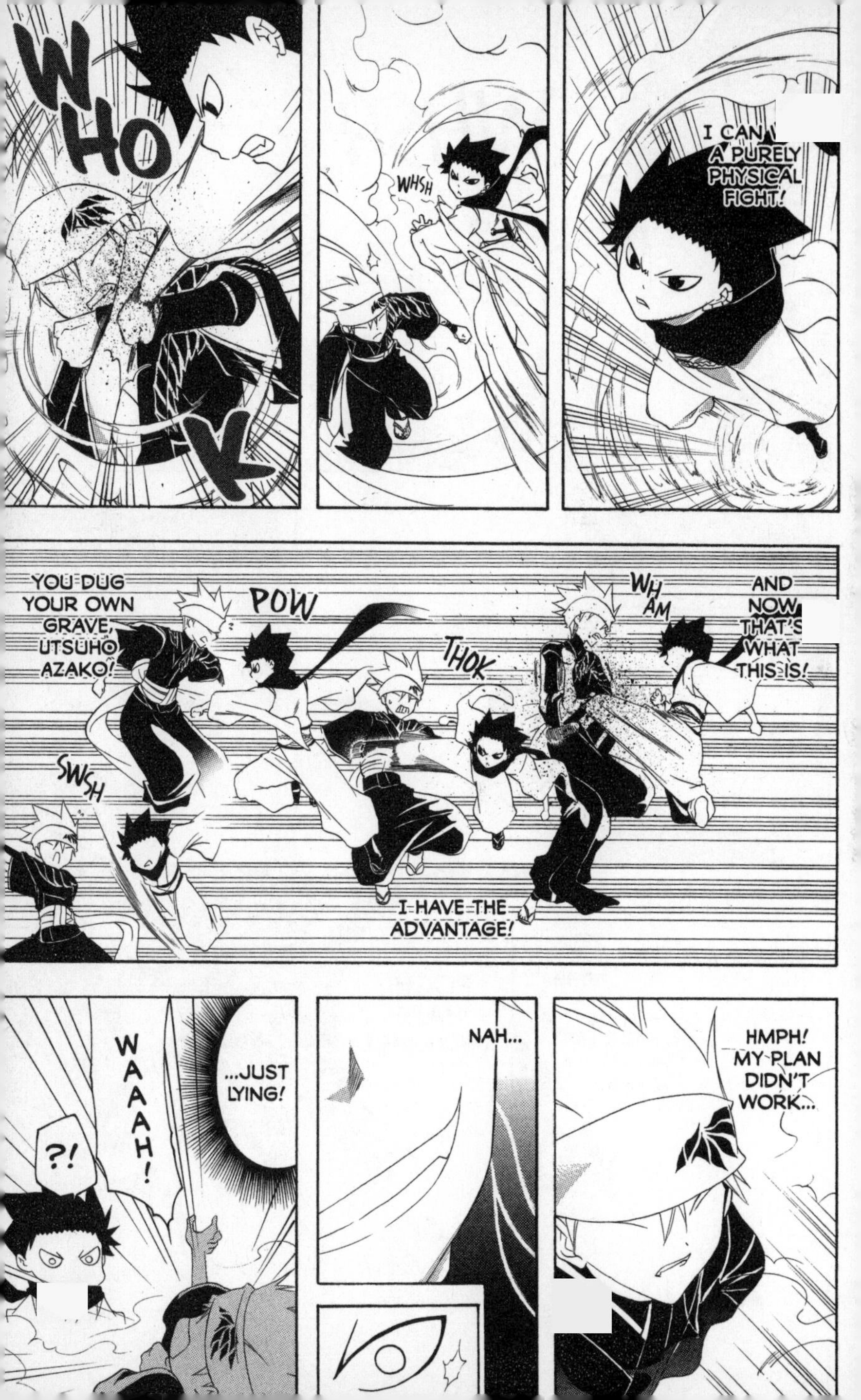
I CAN
A PURELY PHYSICAL FIGHT!
WHSH
WHOK
AND NOW THAT'S WHAT THIS IS!
WHAM
THOK
POW
YOU DUG YOUR OWN GRAVE, UTSUHO AZAKO!
I HAVE THE ADVANTAGE!
SWSH
HMPH! MY PLAN DIDN'T WORK...
NAH...
...JUST LYING!
WAAAAH!
?!

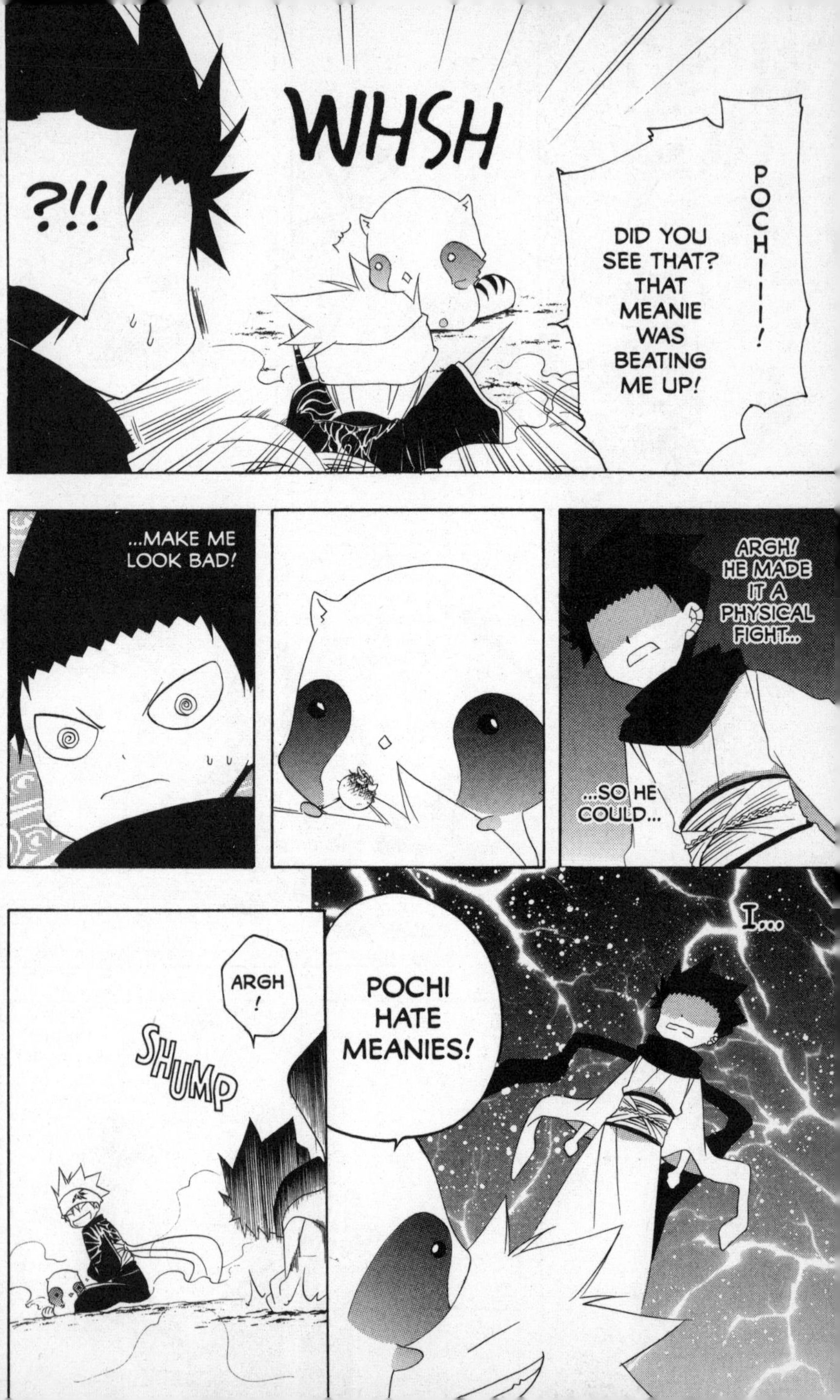
POCHIIII!
DID YOU SEE THAT? THAT MEANIE WAS BEATING ME UP!
WHSH
?!!
ARGH! HE MADE IT A PHYSICAL FIGHT...
...SO HE COULD...
...MAKE ME LOOK BAD!
I...
POCHI HATE MEANIES!
ARGH!
SHUMP

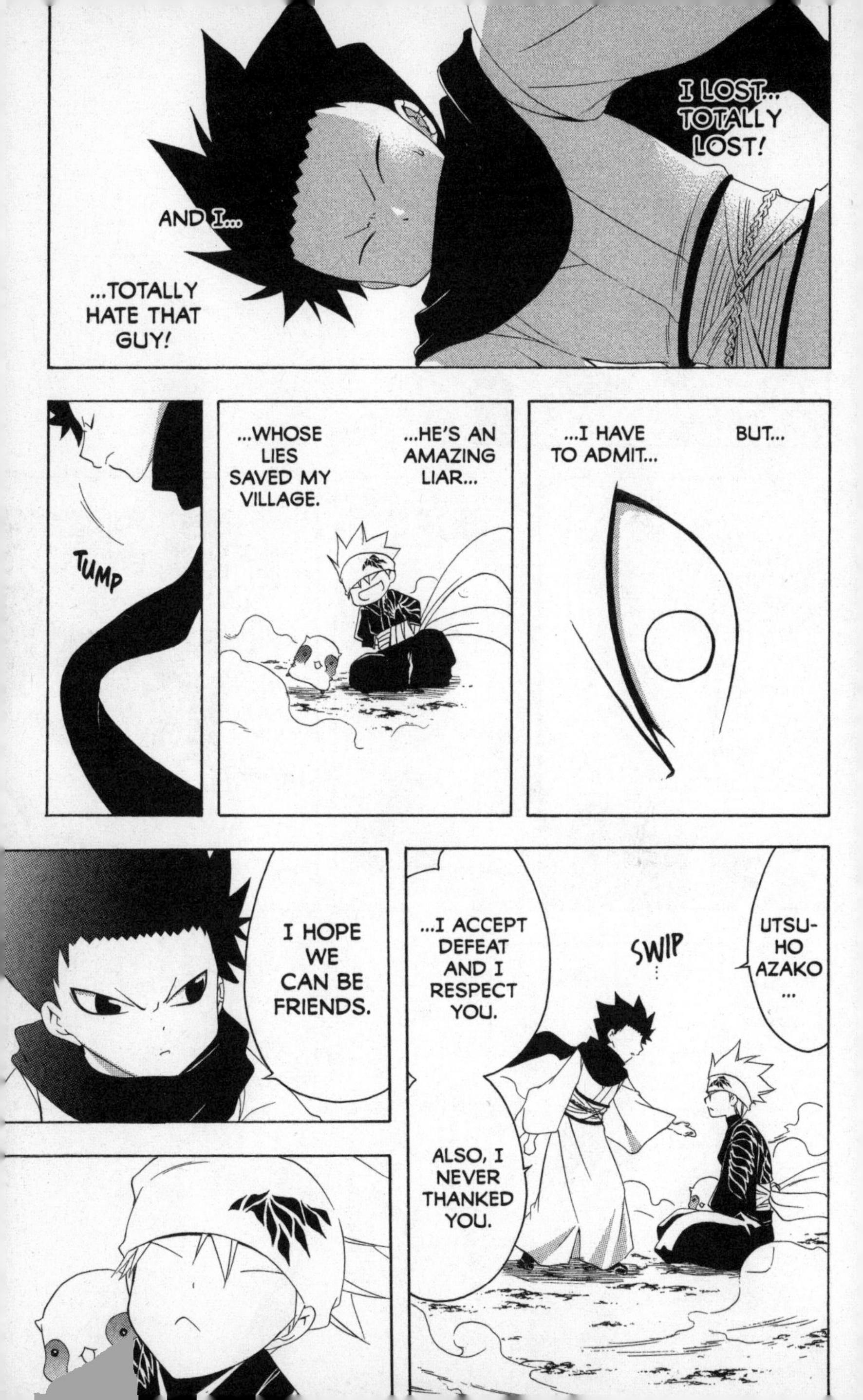
I LOST... TOTALLY LOST!
AND I...
...TOTALLY HATE THAT GUY!
BUT...
...I HAVE TO ADMIT...
...HE'S AN AMAZING LIAR...
...WHOSE LIES SAVED MY VILLAGE.
TUMP
UTSU-HO AZAKO ...
SWIP
...I ACCEPT DEFEAT AND I RESPECT YOU.
ALSO, I NEVER THANKED YOU.
I HOPE WE CAN BE FRIENDS.

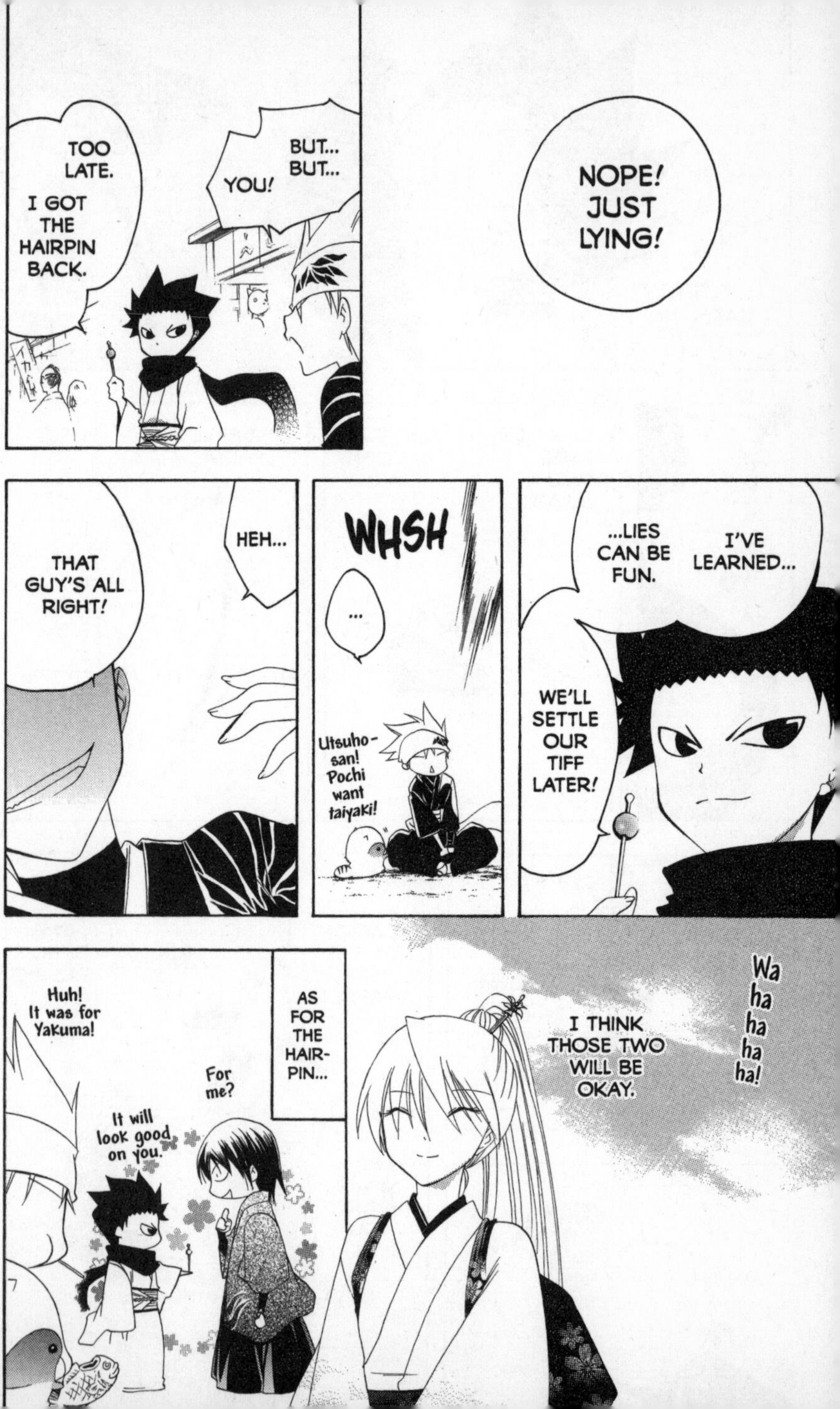
NOPE! JUST LYING!
BUT... BUT...
YOU!
TOO LATE.
I GOT THE HAIRPIN BACK.
I'VE LEARNED...
...LIES CAN BE FUN.
WE'LL SETTLE OUR TIFF LATER!
WHSH
...
Utsuho-san! Pochi want taiyaki!
HEH...
THAT GUY'S ALL RIGHT!
Wa ha ha ha ha!
I THINK THOSE TWO WILL BE OKAY.
AS FOR THE HAIRPIN...
For me?
Huh! It was for Yakuma!
It will look good on you.

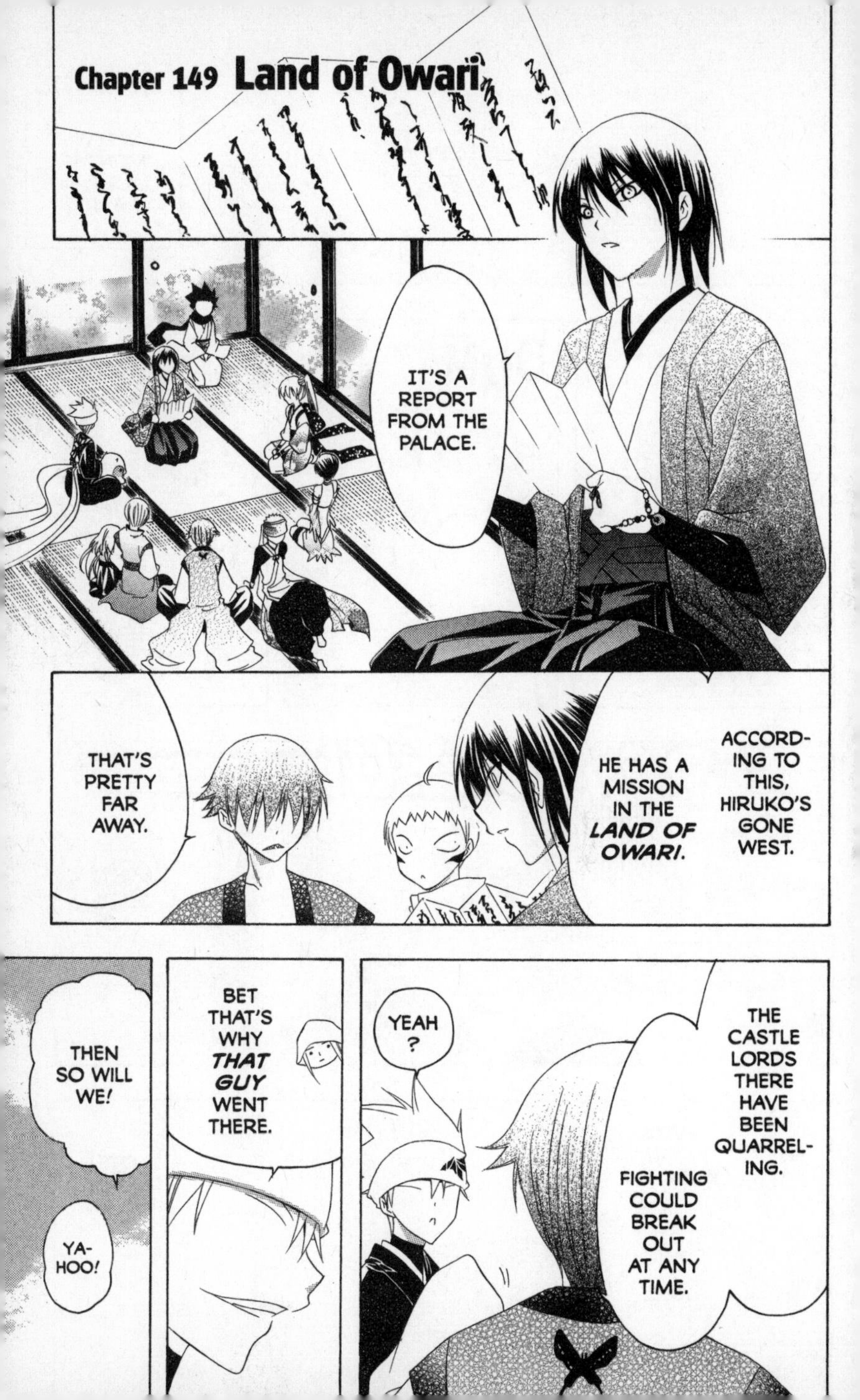
Chapter 149 Land of Owari
IT'S A REPORT FROM THE PALACE.
ACCORDING TO THIS, HIRUKO'S GONE WEST.
HE HAS A MISSION IN THE *LAND OF OWARI*.
THAT'S PRETTY FAR AWAY.
THE CASTLE LORDS THERE HAVE BEEN QUARRELING.
FIGHTING COULD BREAK OUT AT ANY TIME.
YEAH?
BET THAT'S WHY *THAT GUY* WENT THERE.
THEN SO WILL WE!
YA-HOO!

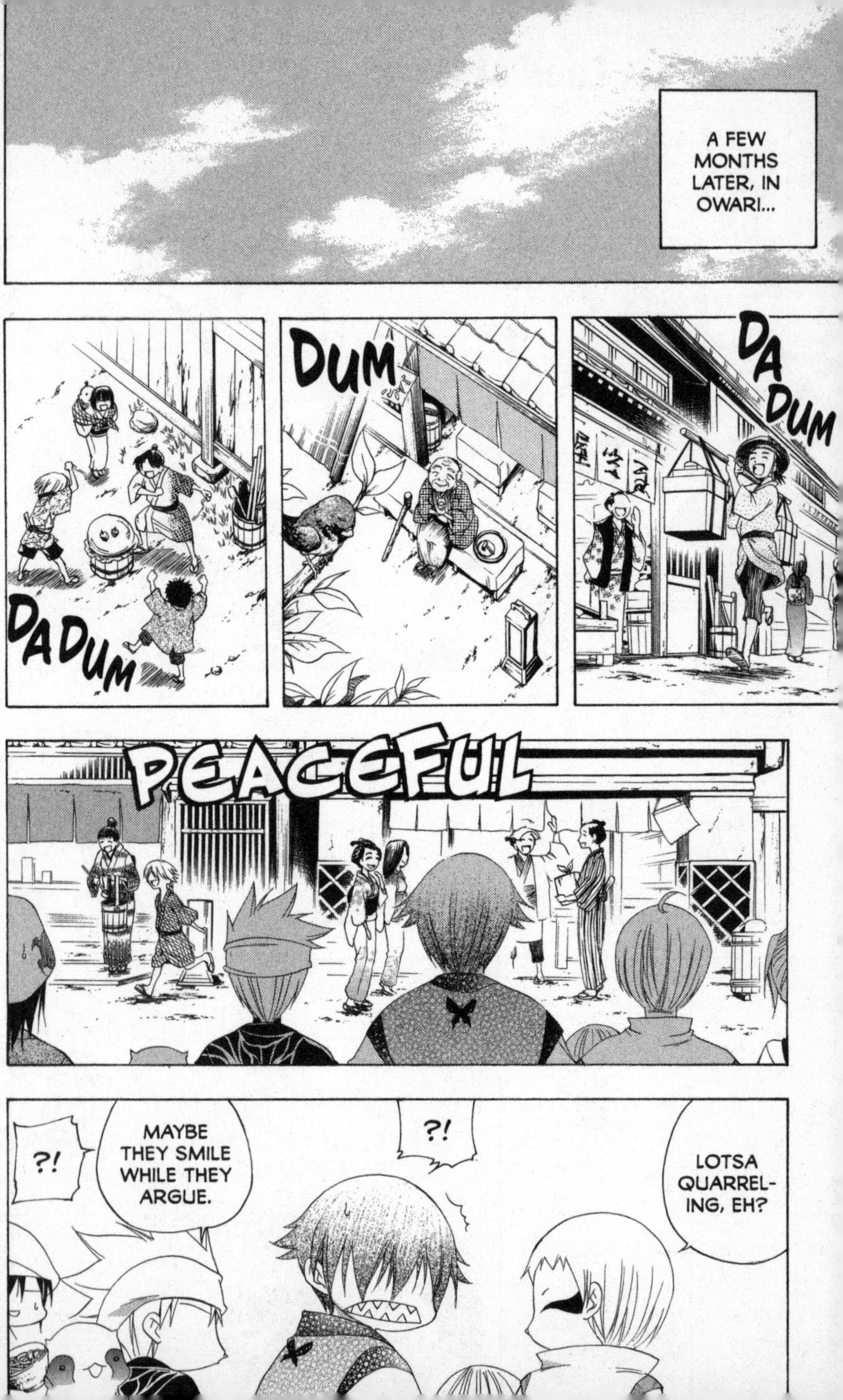
A FEW MONTHS LATER, IN OWARI...
DA DUM
DUM
DADUM
PEACEFUL
LOTSA QUARREL-ING, EH?
?!
MAYBE THEY SMILE WHILE THEY ARGUE.
?!

Chapter 149
Land of Owari

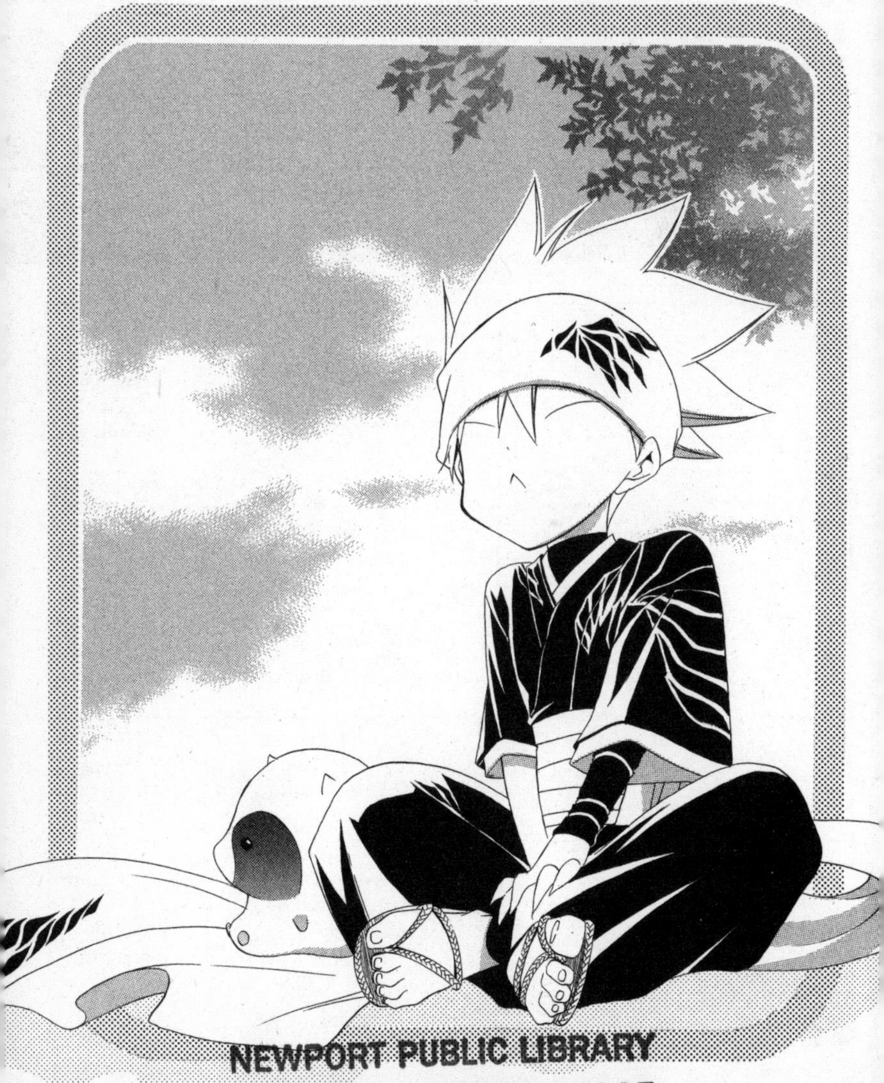

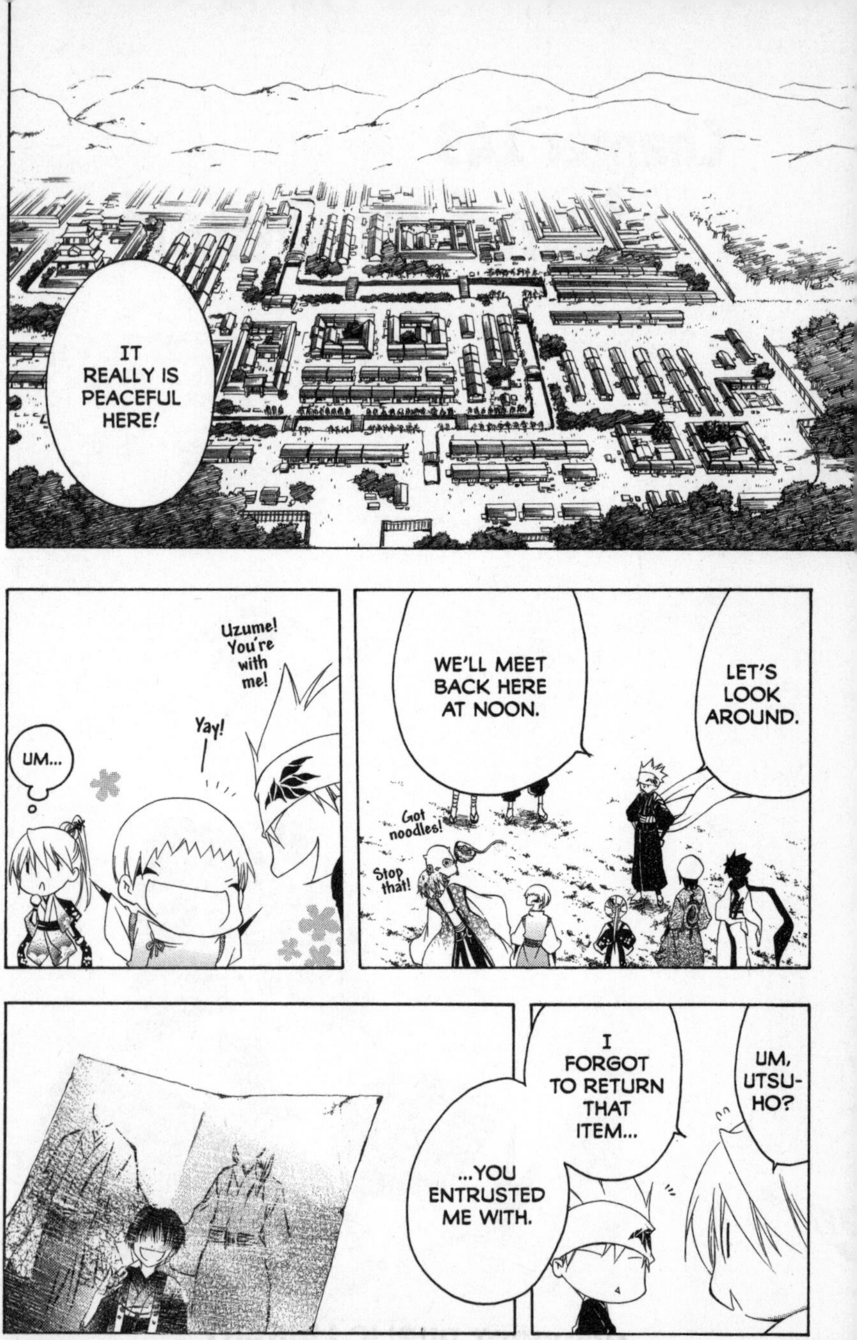
IT REALLY IS PEACEFUL HERE!
LET'S LOOK AROUND.
WE'LL MEET BACK HERE AT NOON.
Got noodles!
Stop that!
Uzume! You're with me!
Yay!
UM...
UM, UTSU-HO?
I FORGOT TO RETURN THAT ITEM...
...YOU ENTRUSTED ME WITH.

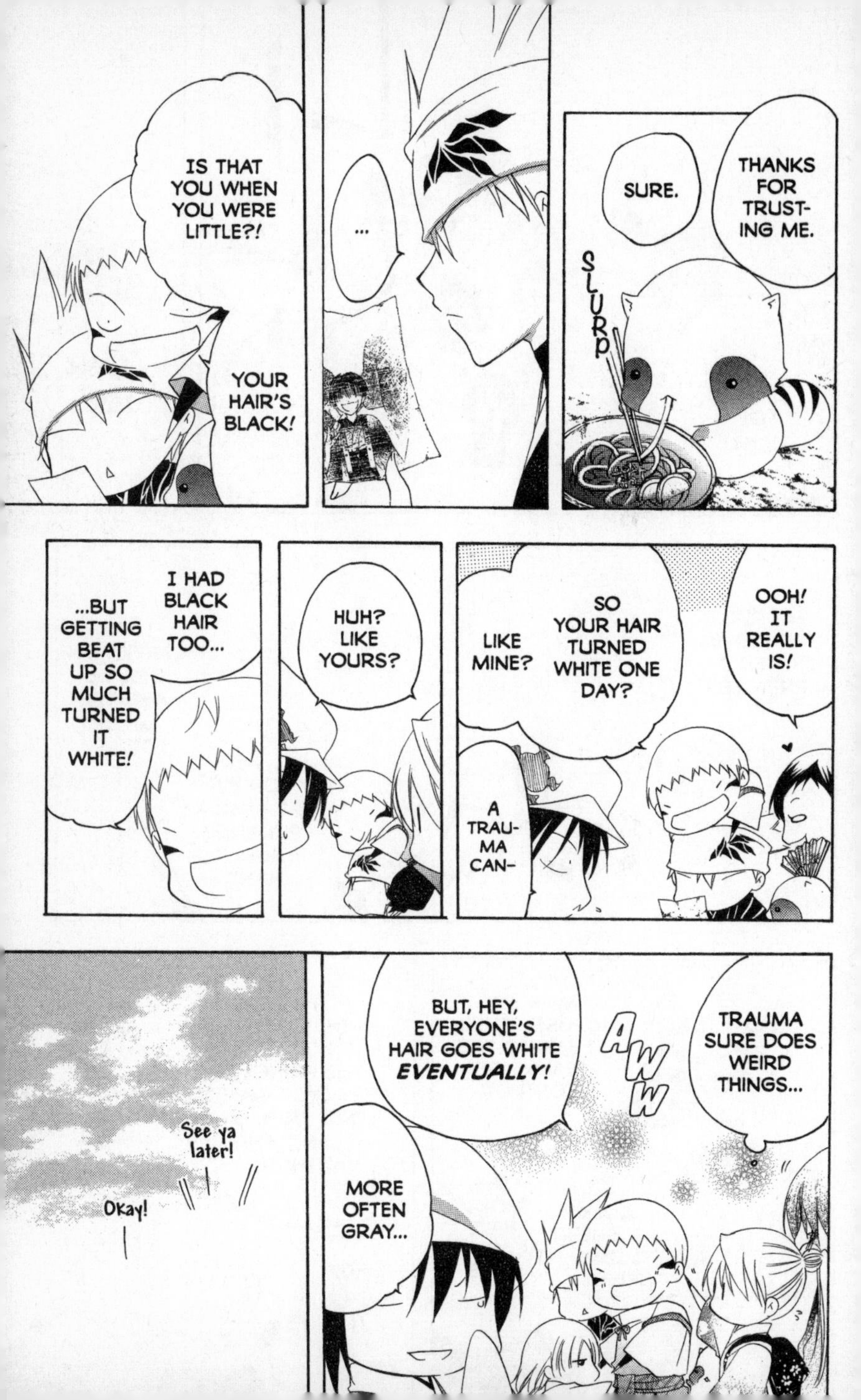
THANKS FOR TRUSTING ME.
SURE.
SLURP
...
IS THAT YOU WHEN YOU WERE LITTLE?!
YOUR HAIR'S BLACK!
OOH! IT REALLY IS!
SO YOUR HAIR TURNED WHITE ONE DAY?
LIKE MINE?
A TRAUMA CAN-
HUH? LIKE YOURS?
I HAD BLACK HAIR TOO...
...BUT GETTING BEAT UP SO MUCH TURNED IT WHITE!
TRAUMA SURE DOES WEIRD THINGS...
AWW
BUT, HEY, EVERYONE'S HAIR GOES WHITE *EVENTUALLY*!
MORE OFTEN GRAY...
See ya later!
Okay!

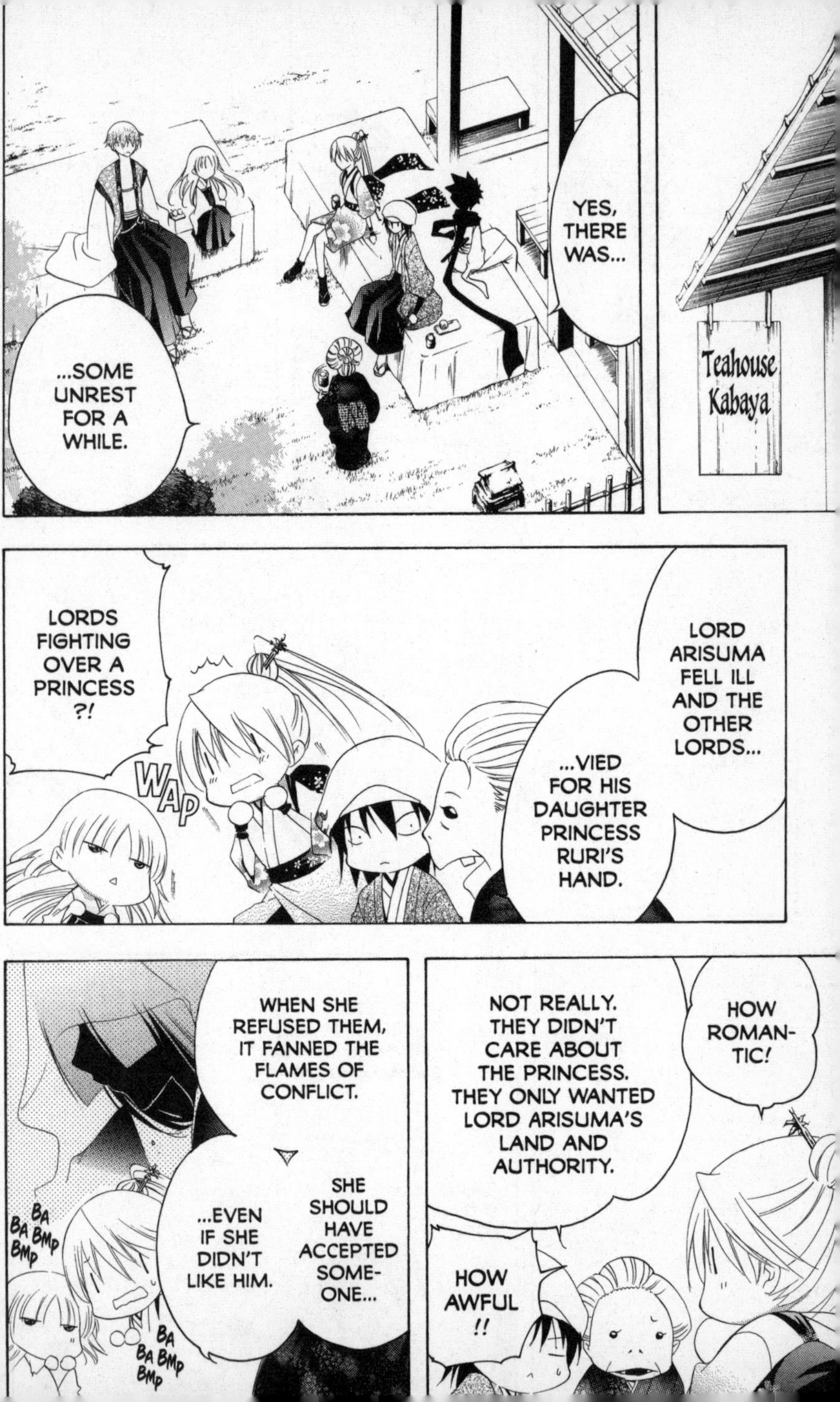
Teahouse Kabaya
YES, THERE WAS...
...SOME UNREST FOR A WHILE.
LORD ARISUMA FELL ILL AND THE OTHER LORDS...
...VIED FOR HIS DAUGHTER PRINCESS RURI'S HAND.
WAP
LORDS FIGHTING OVER A PRINCESS ?!
HOW ROMAN-TIC!
NOT REALLY. THEY DIDN'T CARE ABOUT THE PRINCESS. THEY ONLY WANTED LORD ARISUMA'S LAND AND AUTHORITY.
HOW AWFUL !!
WHEN SHE REFUSED THEM, IT FANNED THE FLAMES OF CONFLICT.
SHE SHOULD HAVE ACCEPTED SOME-ONE...
...EVEN IF SHE DIDN'T LIKE HIM.
BA BA BMP BMP
BA BA BMP BMP

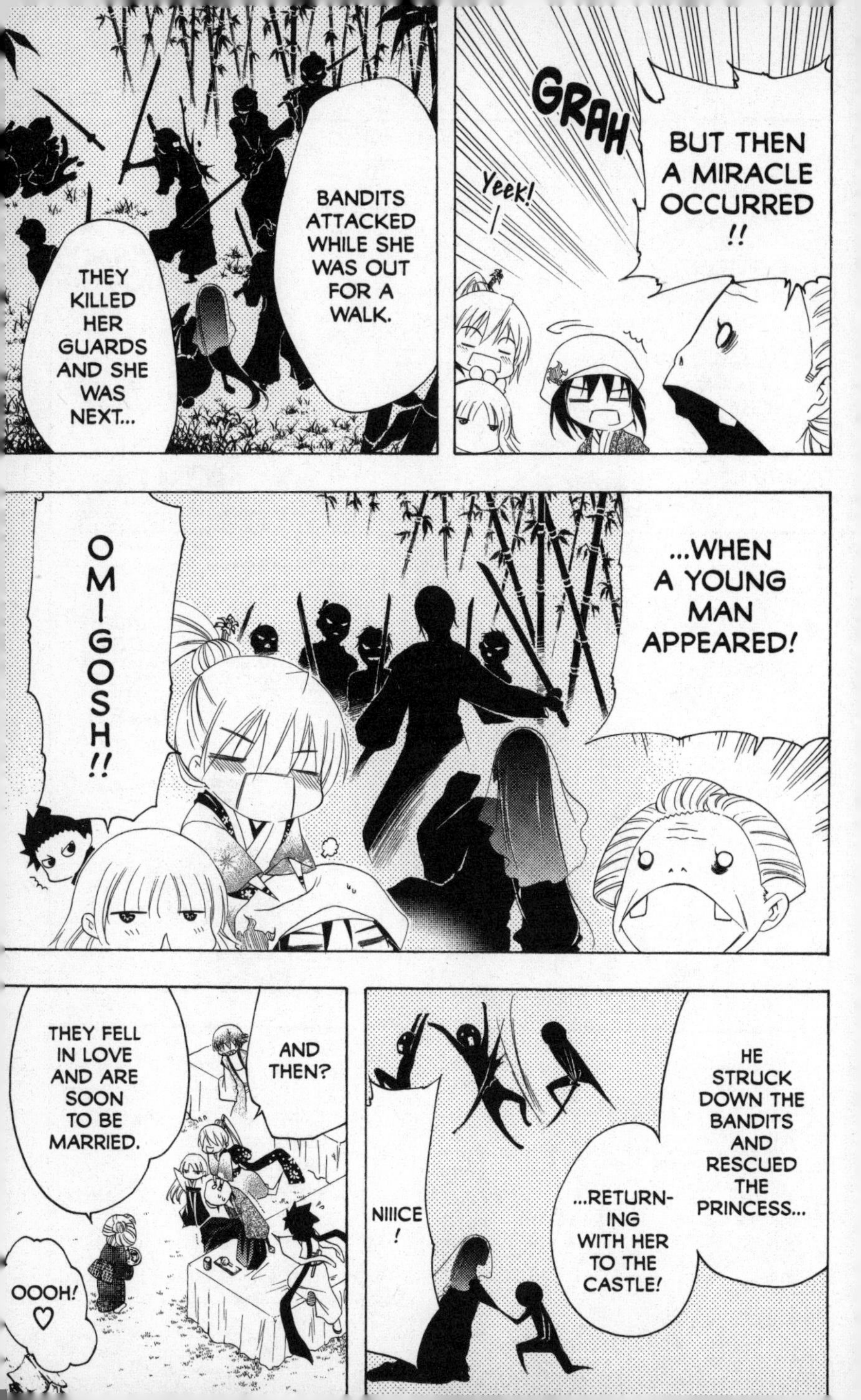
BUT THEN A MIRACLE OCCURRED!!
GRAH
Yeek!
BANDITS ATTACKED WHILE SHE WAS OUT FOR A WALK.
THEY KILLED HER GUARDS AND SHE WAS NEXT...
...WHEN A YOUNG MAN APPEARED!
OMIGOSH!!
HE STRUCK DOWN THE BANDITS AND RESCUED THE PRINCESS...
...RETURNING WITH HER TO THE CASTLE!
NIIICE!
AND THEN?
THEY FELL IN LOVE AND ARE SOON TO BE MARRIED.
OOOH! ♡

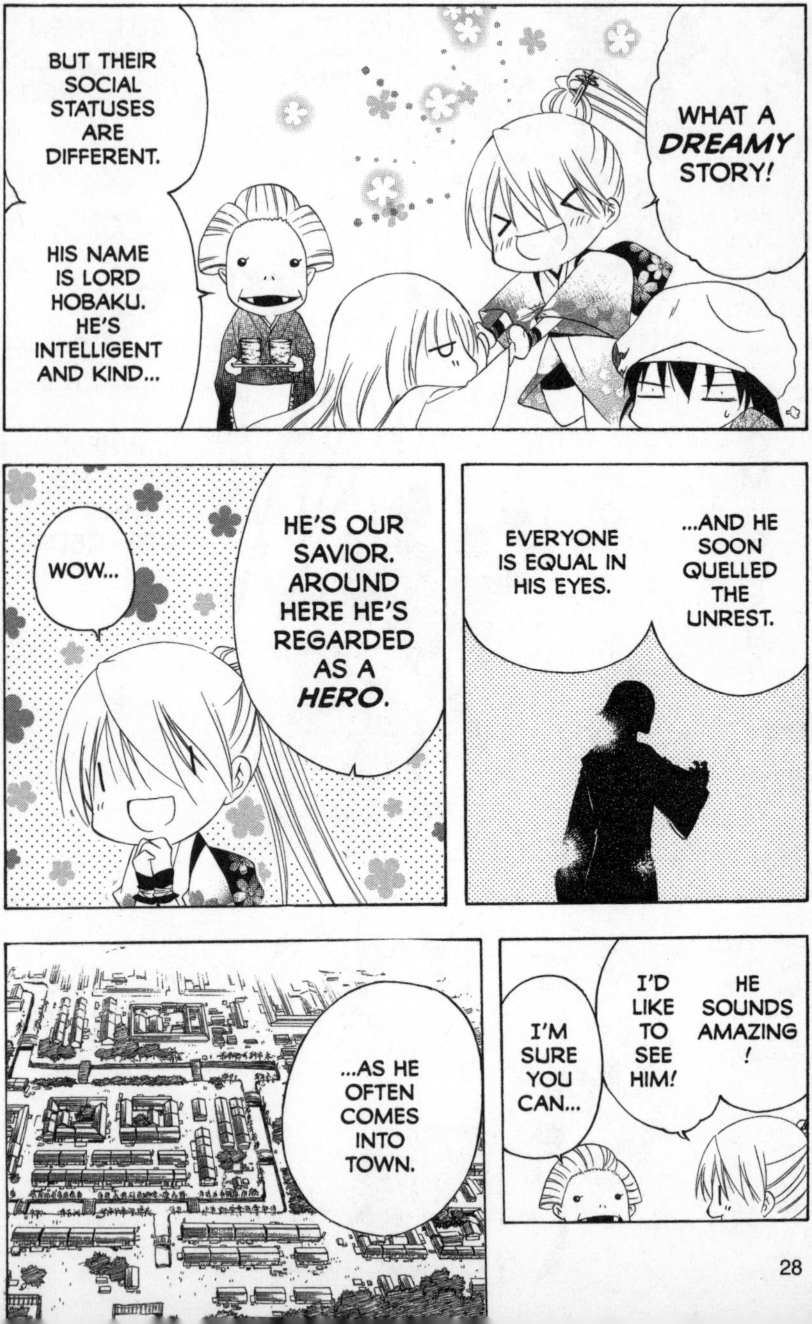
WHAT A *DREAMY* STORY!
BUT THEIR SOCIAL STATUSES ARE DIFFERENT.
HIS NAME IS LORD HOBAKU. HE'S INTELLIGENT AND KIND...
...AND HE SOON QUELLED THE UNREST.
EVERYONE IS EQUAL IN HIS EYES.
HE'S OUR SAVIOR. AROUND HERE HE'S REGARDED AS A ***HERO***.
WOW...
HE SOUNDS AMAZING!
I'D LIKE TO SEE HIM!
I'M SURE YOU CAN...
...AS HE OFTEN COMES INTO TOWN.

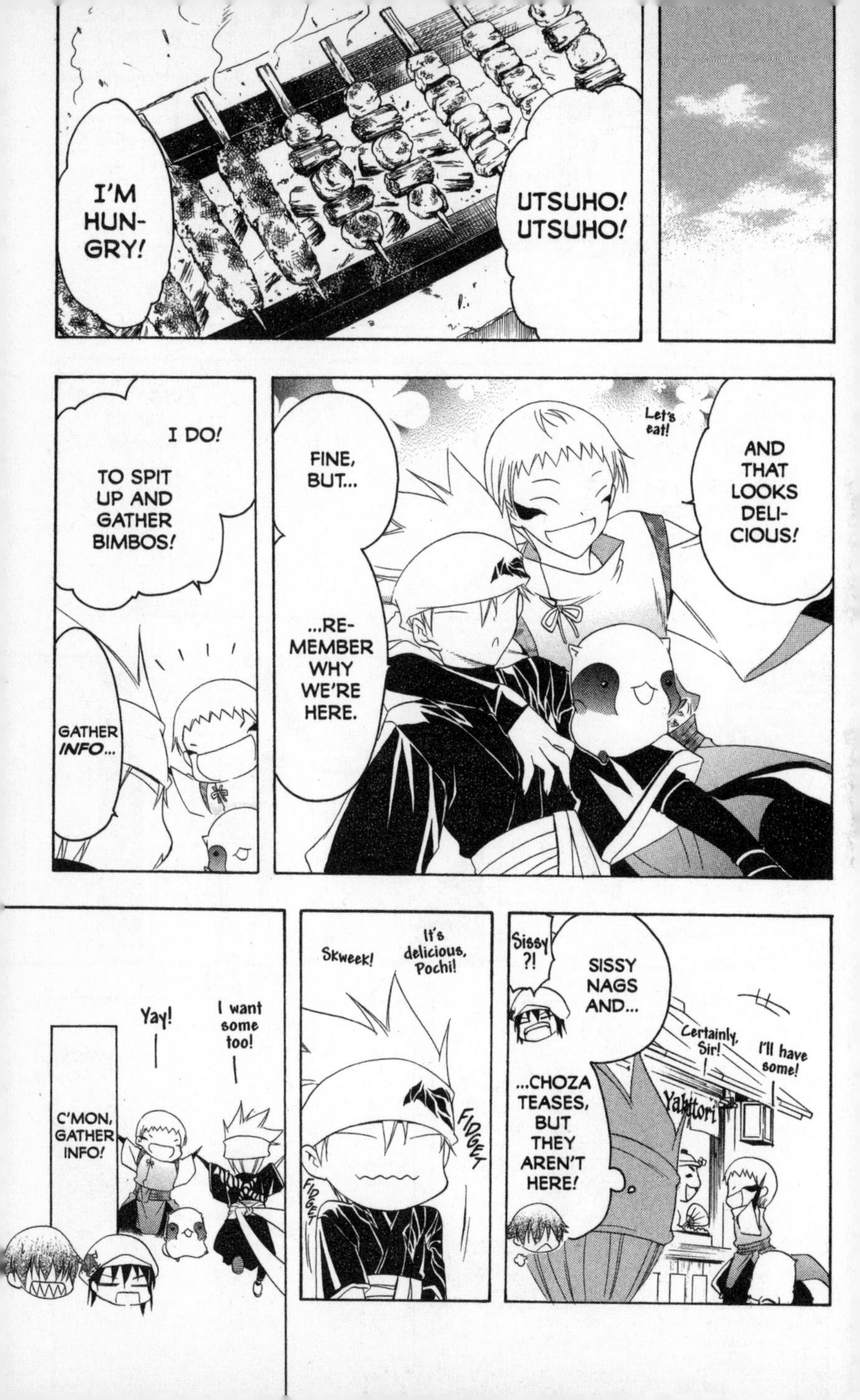
UTSUHO! UTSUHO!
I'M HUN-GRY!
Let's eat!
AND THAT LOOKS DELI-CIOUS!
FINE, BUT...
...RE-MEMBER WHY WE'RE HERE.
I DO!
TO SPIT UP AND GATHER BIMBOS!
GATHER *INFO*...
Sissy ?!
SISSY NAGS AND...
...CHOZA TEASES, BUT THEY AREN'T HERE!
I'll have some!
Certainly, Sir!
Yakitori
It's delicious, Pochi!
Skweek!
FIDGET
FIDGET
I want some too!
Yay!
C'MON, GATHER INFO!

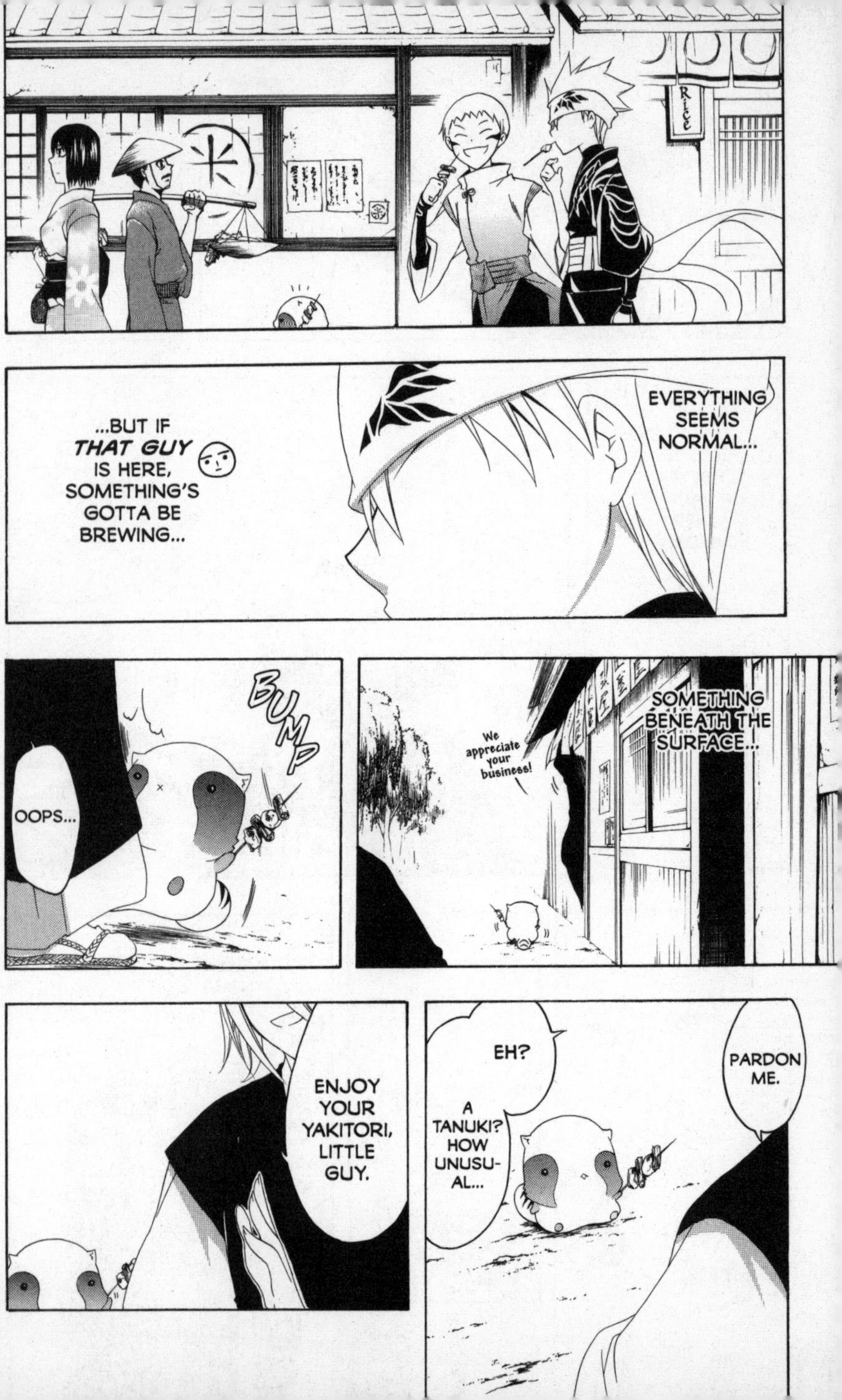
RICE
EVERYTHING SEEMS NORMAL...
...BUT IF *THAT GUY* IS HERE, SOMETHING'S GOTTA BE BREWING...
SOMETHING BENEATH THE SURFACE...
We appreciate your business!
BUMP
OOPS...
PARDON ME.
EH?
A TANUKI? HOW UNUSU-AL...
ENJOY YOUR YAKITORI, LITTLE GUY.

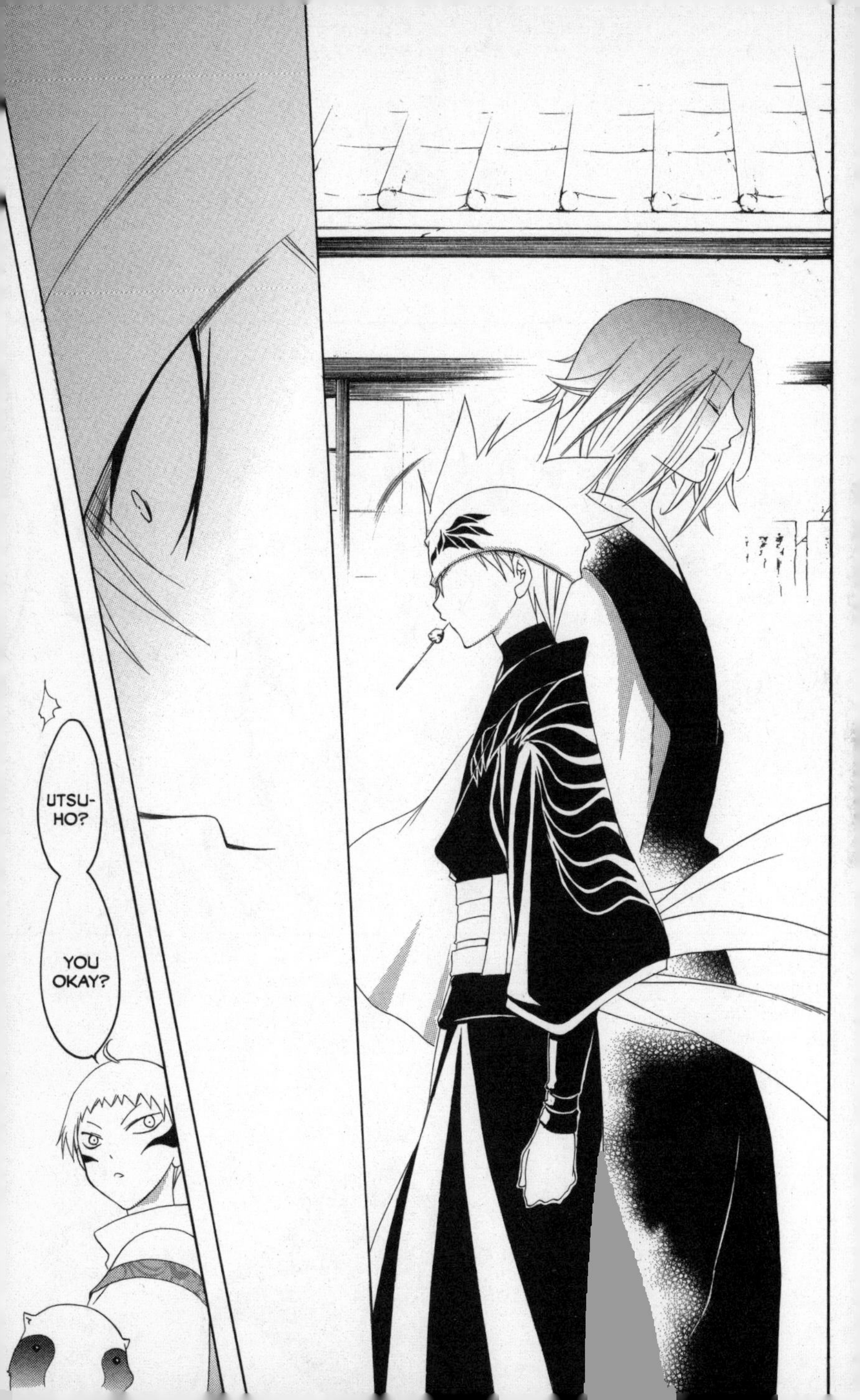
UTSU-HO?
YOU OKAY?

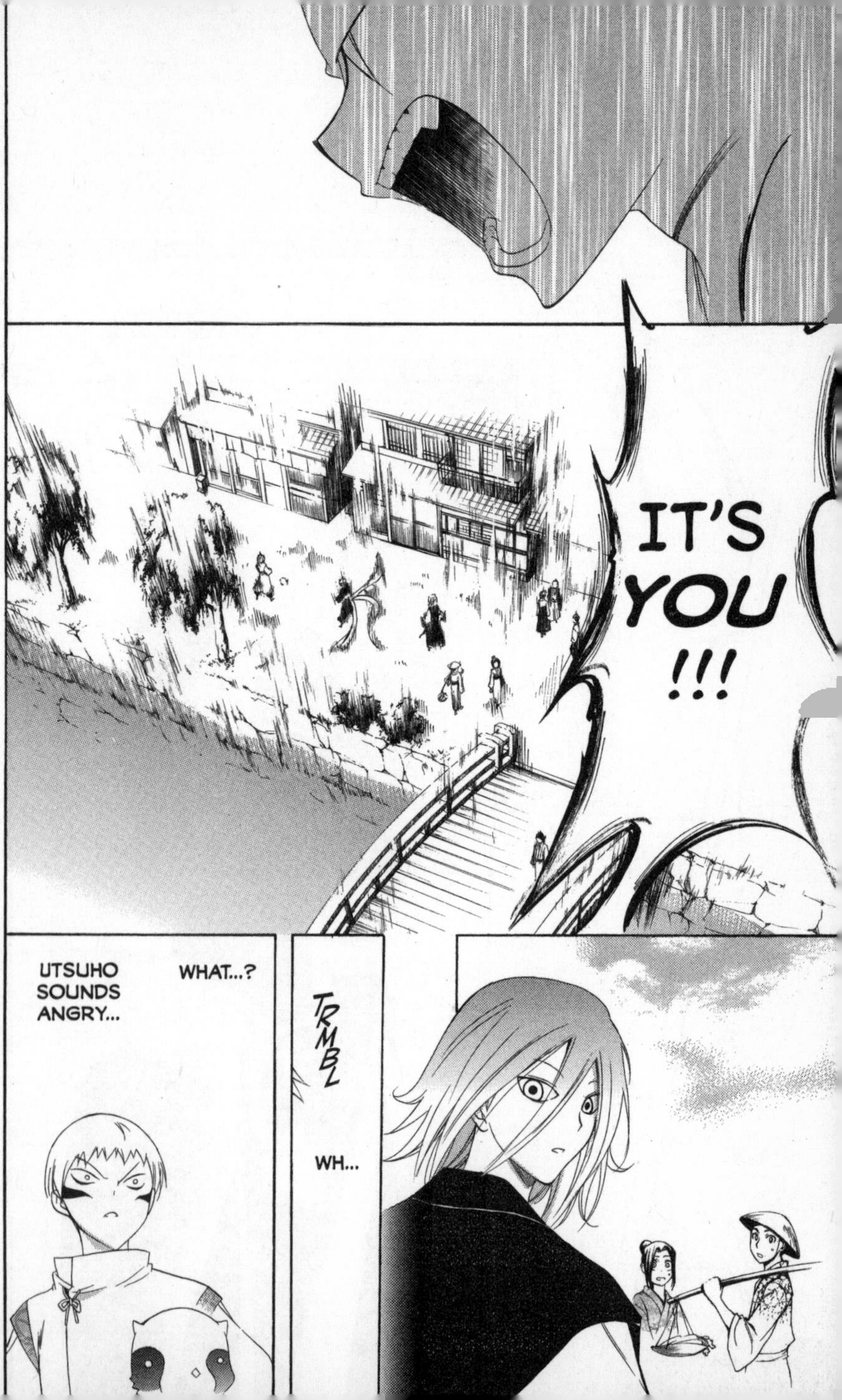
IT'S YOU !!!
TRMBL
WH...
WHAT...?
UTSUHO SOUNDS ANGRY...

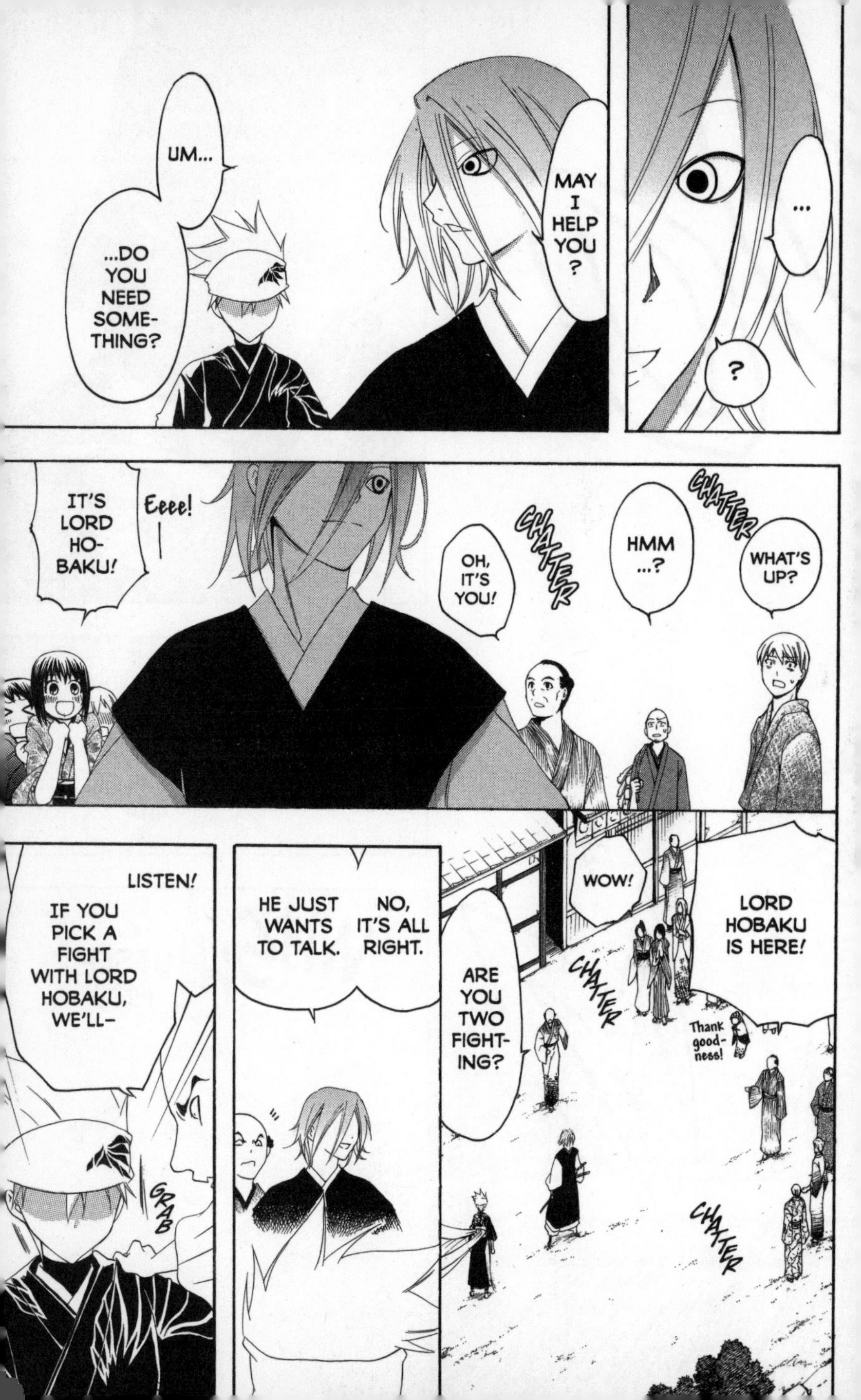
...
?
MAY I HELP YOU?
UM...
...DO YOU NEED SOMETHING?
CHATTER
WHAT'S UP?
HMM...?
CHATTER
OH, IT'S YOU!
Eeee!
IT'S LORD HOBAKU!
LORD HOBAKU IS HERE!
Thank goodness!
WOW!
CHATTER
ARE YOU TWO FIGHTING?
CHATTER
NO, IT'S ALL RIGHT.
HE JUST WANTS TO TALK.
LISTEN!
IF YOU PICK A FIGHT WITH LORD HOBAKU, WE'LL—
GRAB

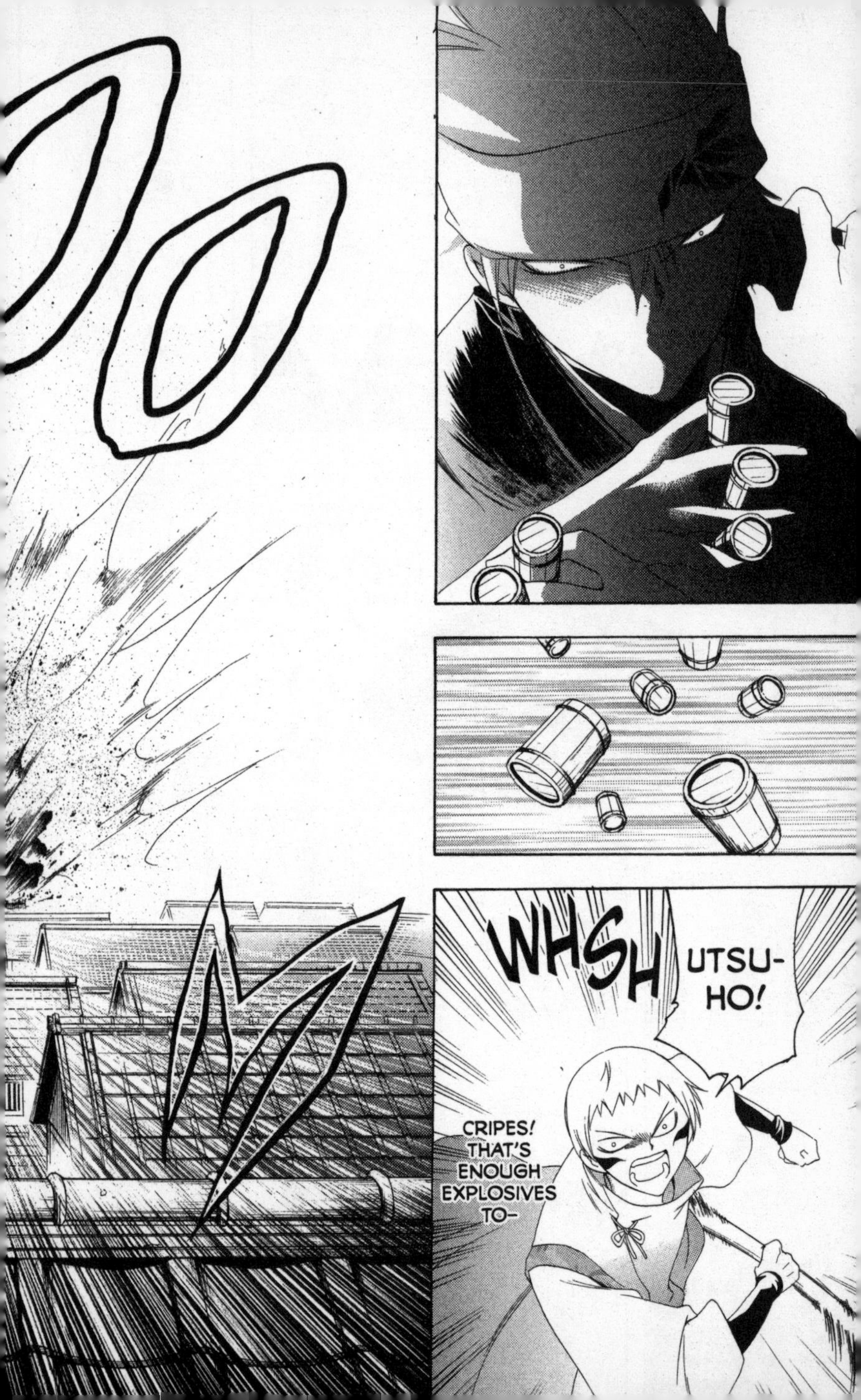
WHSH
UTSU-HO!
CRIPES! THAT'S ENOUGH EXPLOSIVES TO–

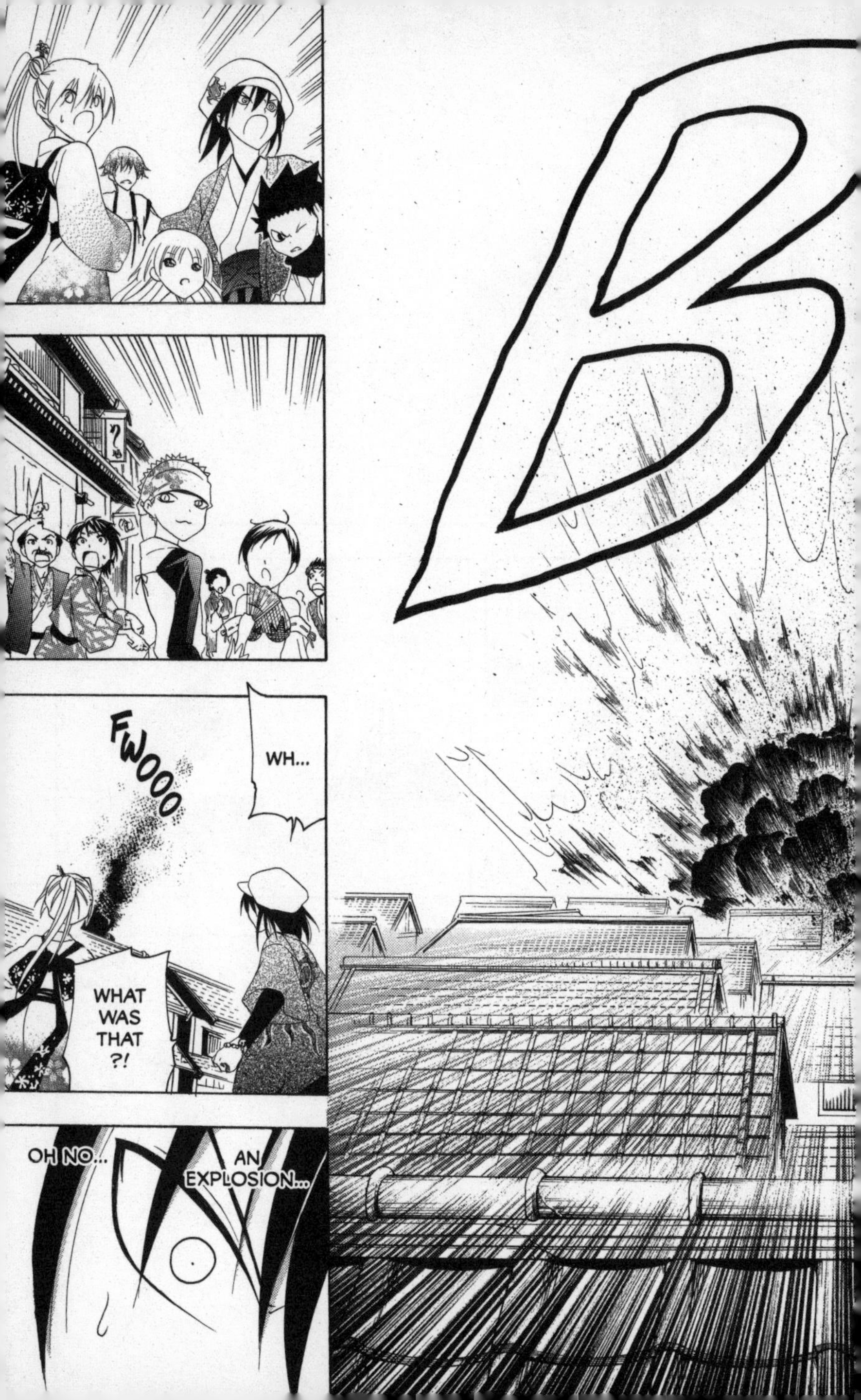
B
WH...
FWOOO
WHAT WAS THAT?!
OH NO...
AN EXPLOSION...

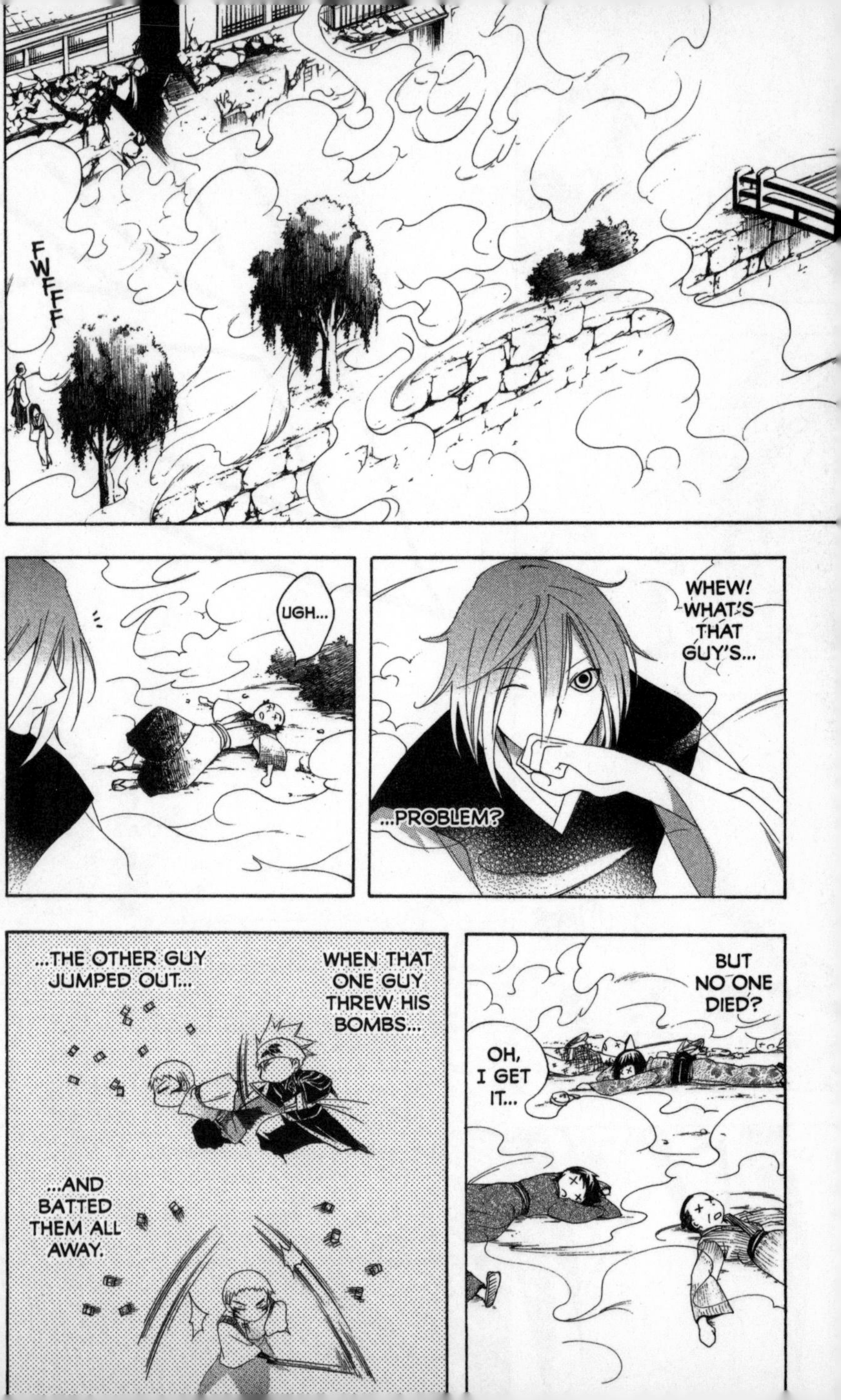
FWFFF
WHEW! WHAT'S THAT GUY'S...
...PROBLEM?
UGH...
BUT NO ONE DIED?
OH, I GET IT...
WHEN THAT ONE GUY THREW HIS BOMBS...
...THE OTHER GUY JUMPED OUT...
...AND BATTED THEM ALL AWAY.

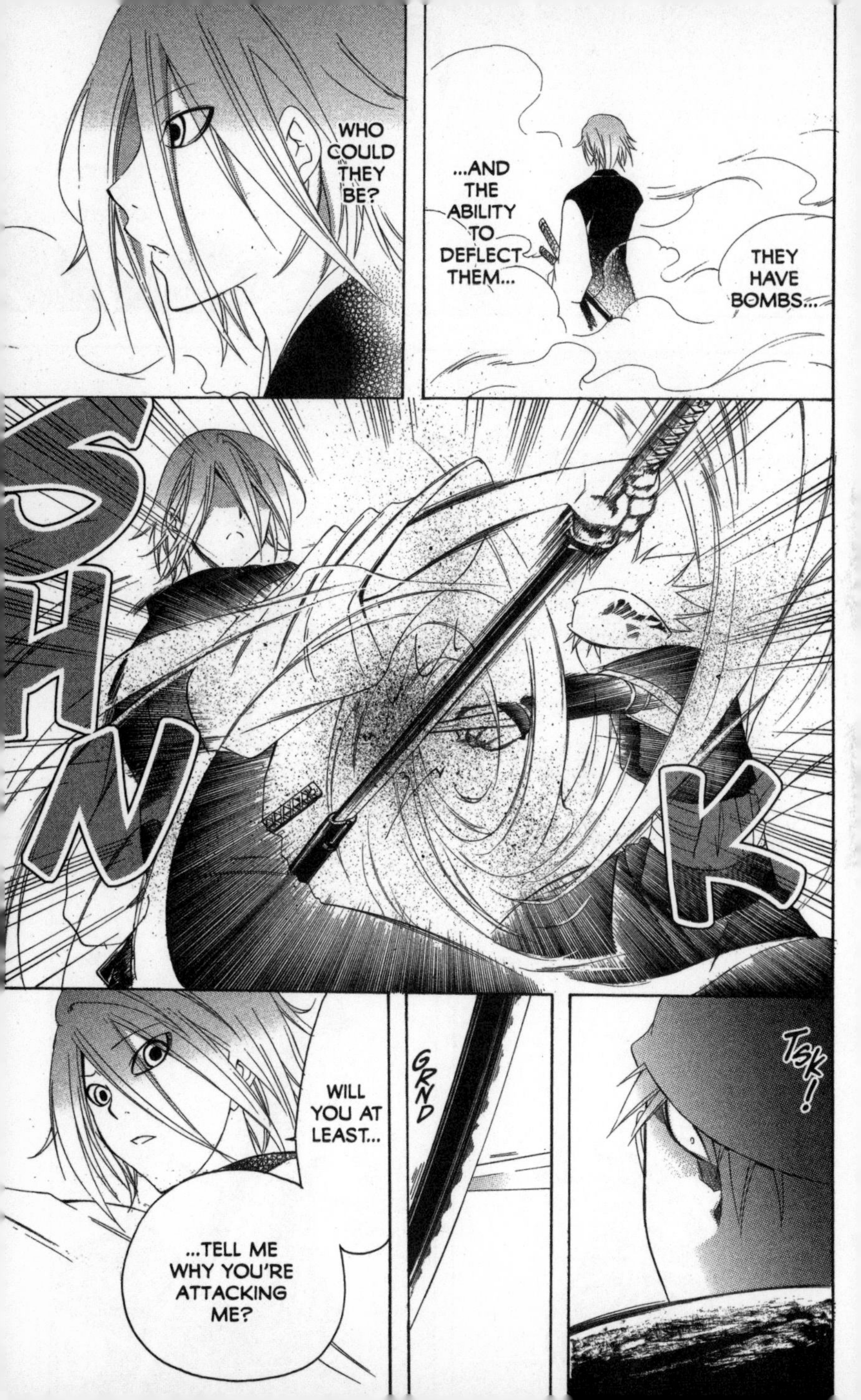
THEY HAVE BOMBS...
...AND THE ABILITY TO DEFLECT THEM...
WHO COULD THEY BE?
CHNK
TSK!
GRND
WILL YOU AT LEAST...
...TELL ME WHY YOU'RE ATTACKING ME?

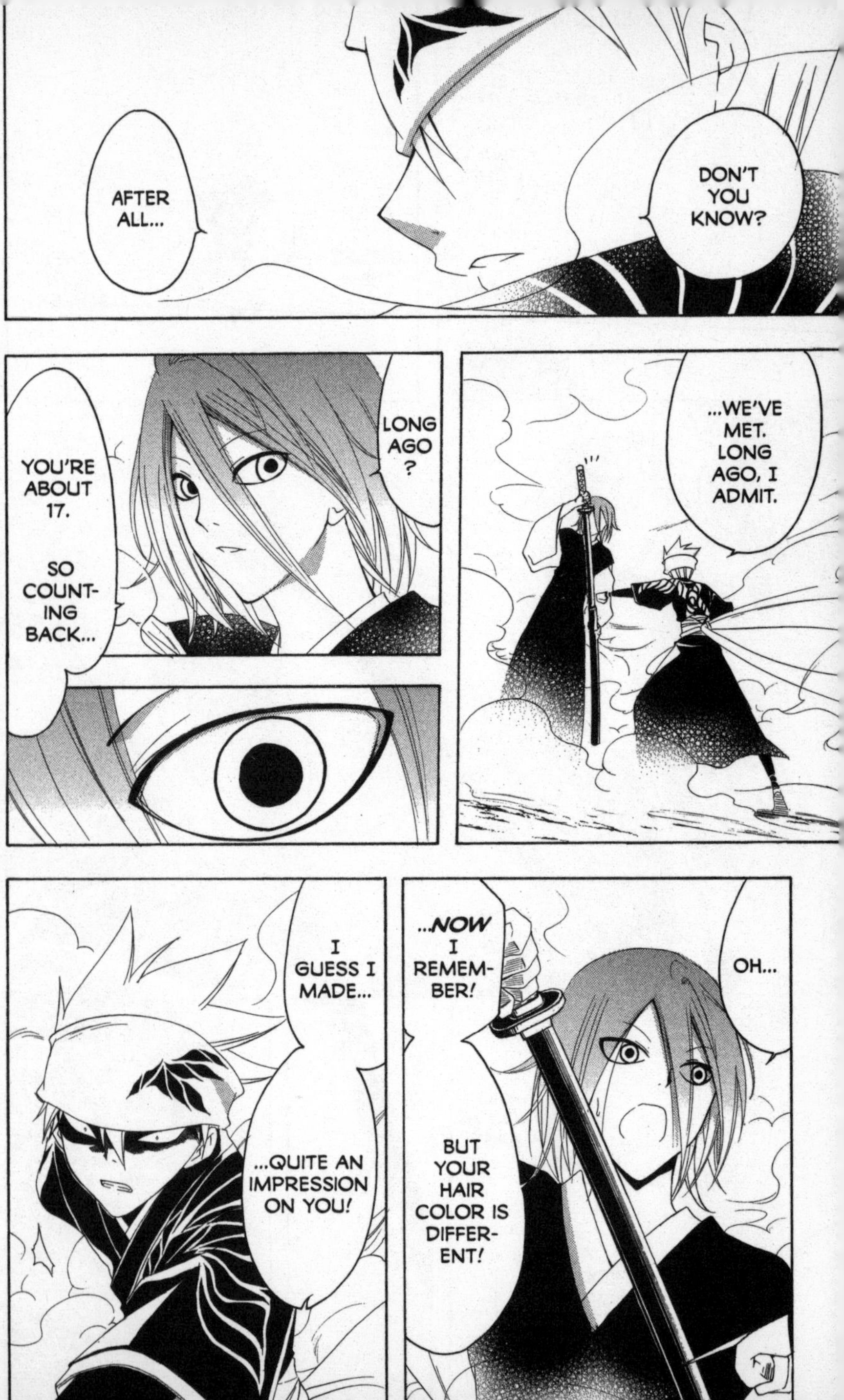
DON'T YOU KNOW?
AFTER ALL...
...WE'VE MET. LONG AGO, I ADMIT.
LONG AGO?
YOU'RE ABOUT 17.
SO COUNTING BACK...
OH...
...*NOW* I REMEMBER!
BUT YOUR HAIR COLOR IS DIFFERENT!
I GUESS I MADE...
...QUITE AN IMPRESSION ON YOU!

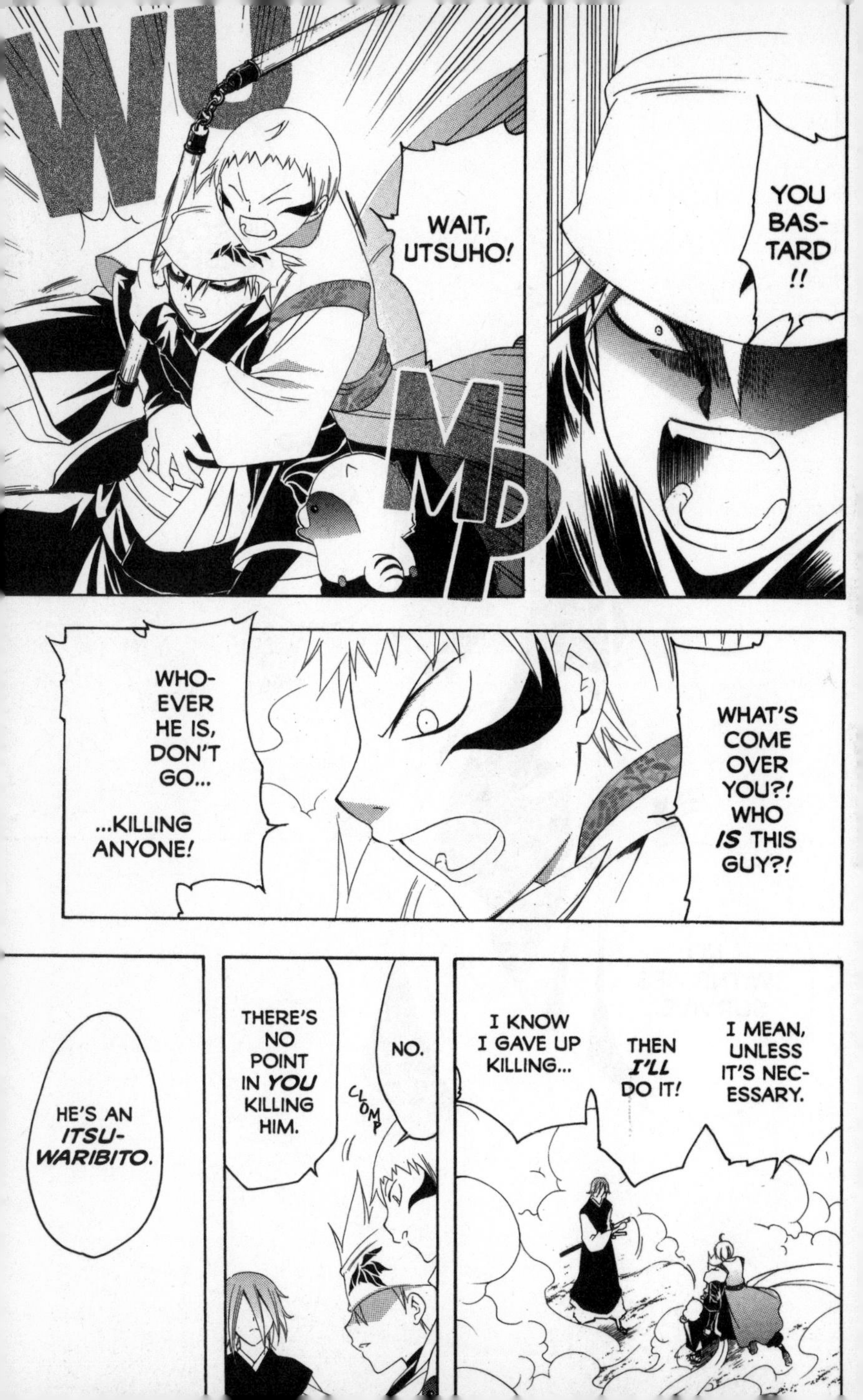
YOU BASTARD!!
WAIT, UTSUHO!
WU
MMP
WHAT'S COME OVER YOU?! WHO *IS* THIS GUY?!
WHOEVER HE IS, DON'T GO...
...KILLING ANYONE!
I MEAN, UNLESS IT'S NECESSARY.
THEN *I'LL* DO IT!
I KNOW I GAVE UP KILLING...
NO.
CLOMP
THERE'S NO POINT IN *YOU* KILLING HIM.
HE'S AN *ITSUWARIBITO*.

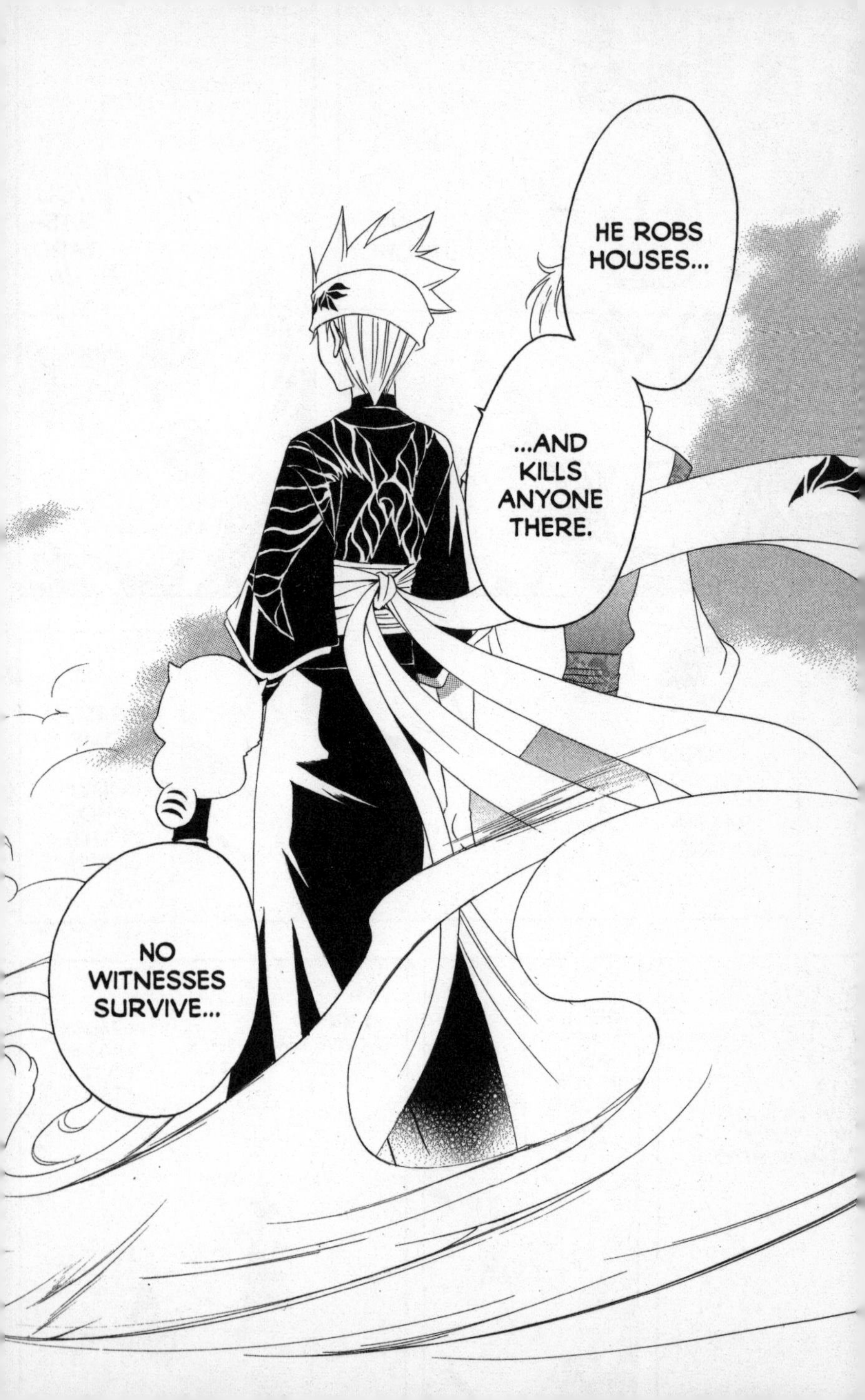
HE ROBS HOUSES...
...AND KILLS ANYONE THERE.
NO WITNESSES SURVIVE...

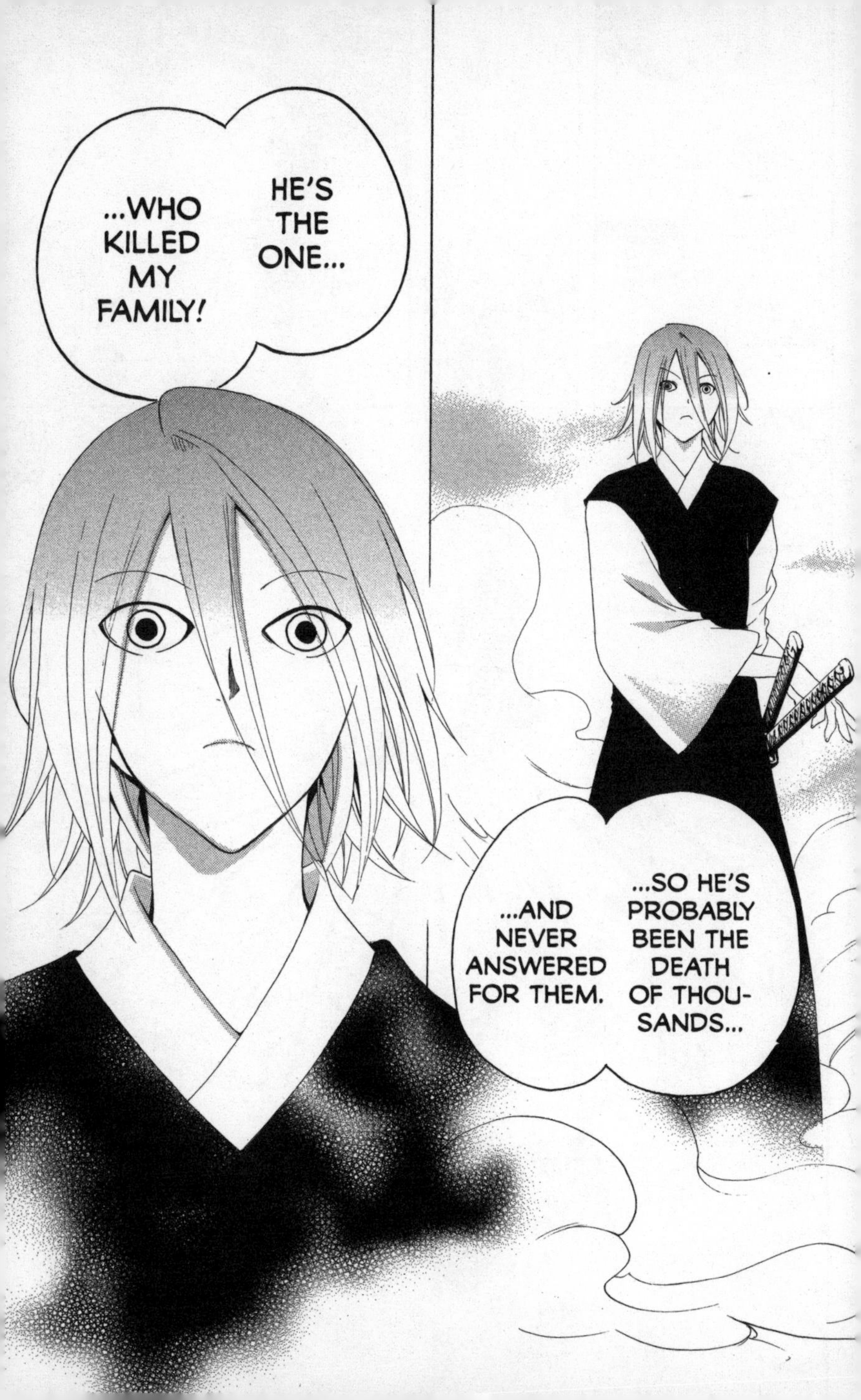
...SO HE'S PROBABLY BEEN THE DEATH OF THOUSANDS...
...AND NEVER ANSWERED FOR THEM.
HE'S THE ONE...
...WHO KILLED MY FAMILY!

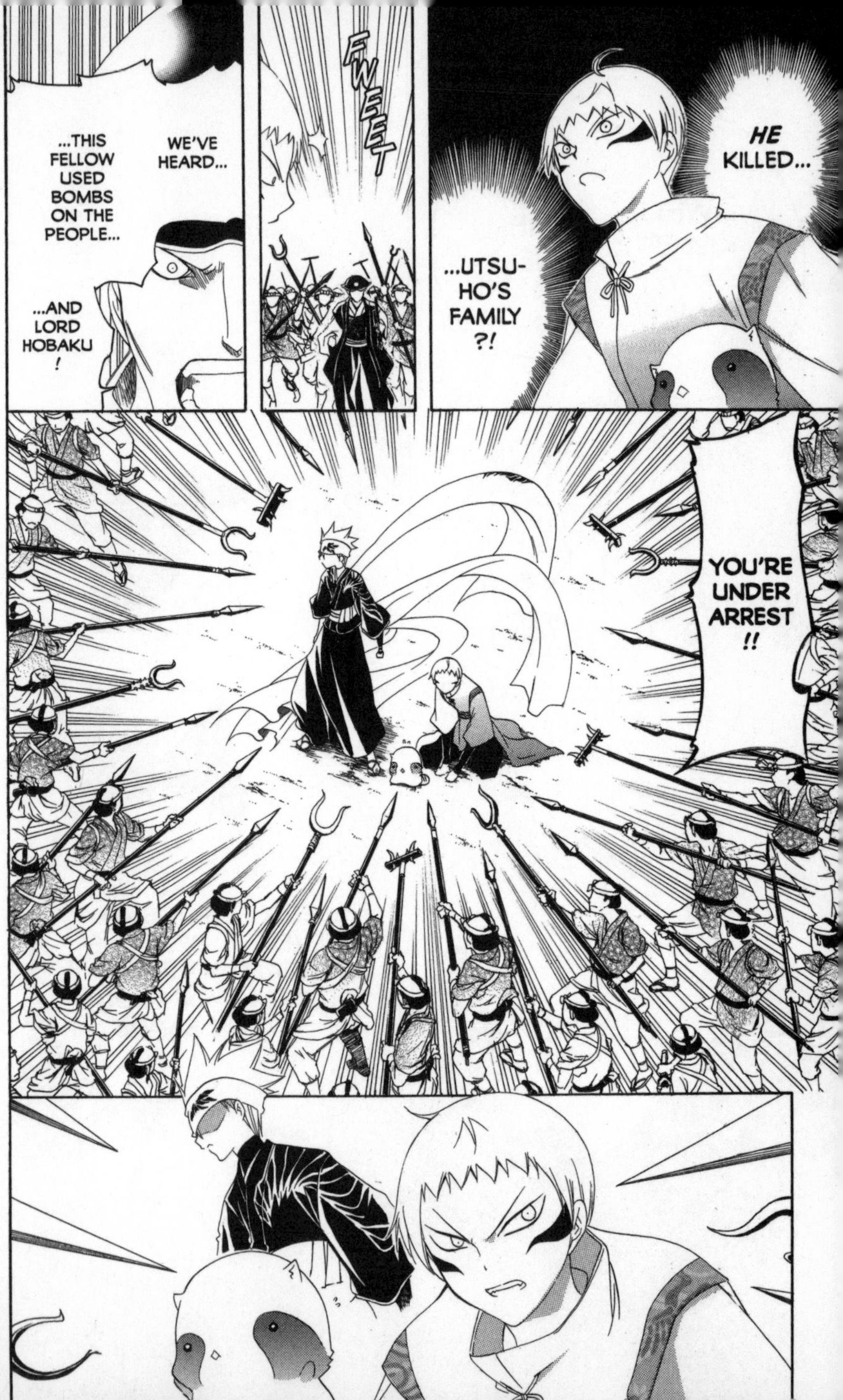
HE KILLED...
...UTSU-HO'S FAMILY?!
FWEET
WE'VE HEARD...
...THIS FELLOW USED BOMBS ON THE PEOPLE...
...AND LORD HOBAKU!
YOU'RE UNDER ARREST!!

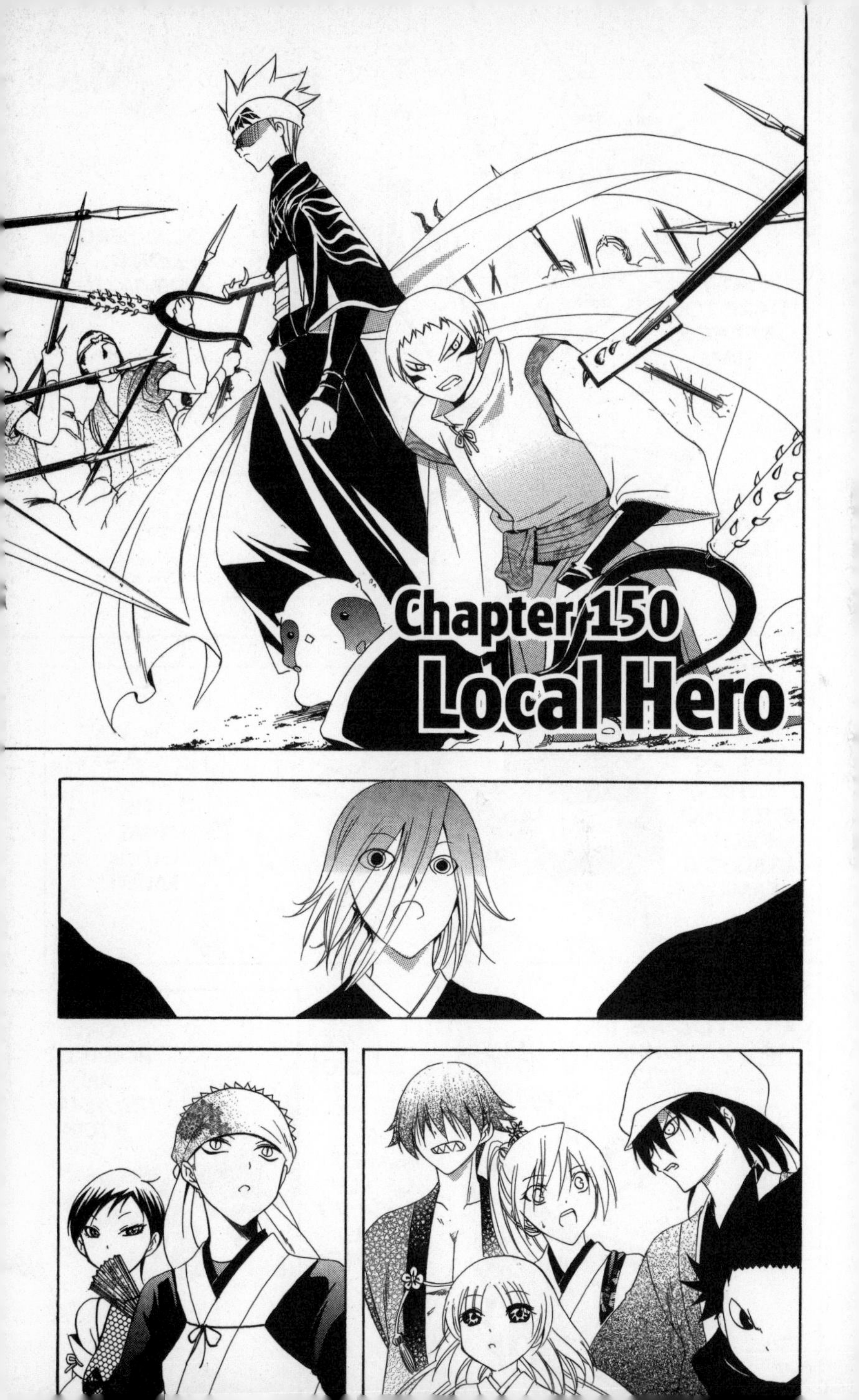
Chapter 150
Local Hero

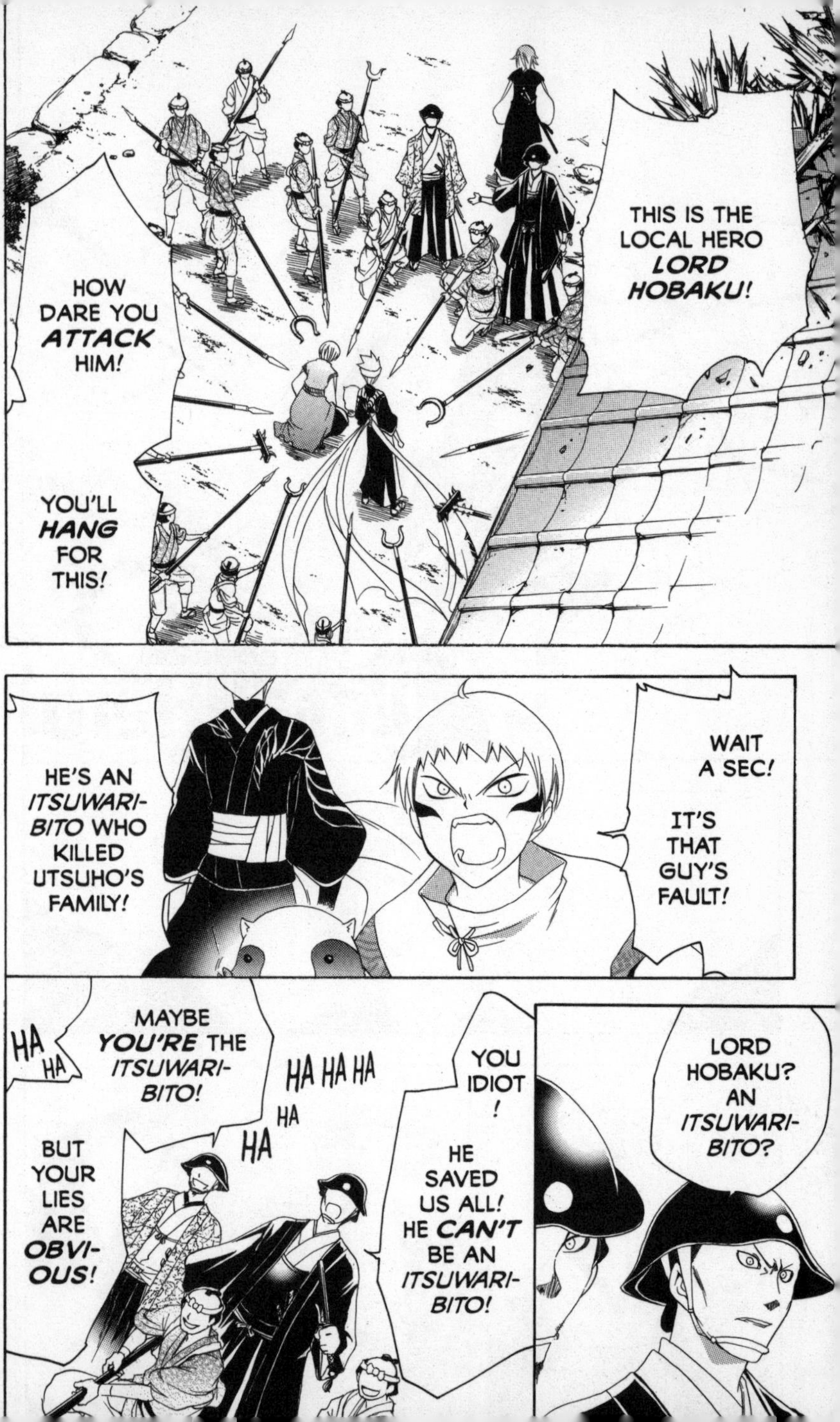
THIS IS THE LOCAL HERO LORD HOBAKU!
HOW DARE YOU ATTACK HIM!
YOU'LL HANG FOR THIS!
WAIT A SEC!
IT'S THAT GUY'S FAULT!
HE'S AN ITSUWARI-BITO WHO KILLED UTSUHO'S FAMILY!
LORD HOBAKU? AN ITSUWARI-BITO?
YOU IDIOT!
HE SAVED US ALL! HE CAN'T BE AN ITSUWARI-BITO!
HA HA HA
HA HA
MAYBE YOU'RE THE ITSUWARI-BITO!
HA HA
BUT YOUR LIES ARE OBVIOUS!

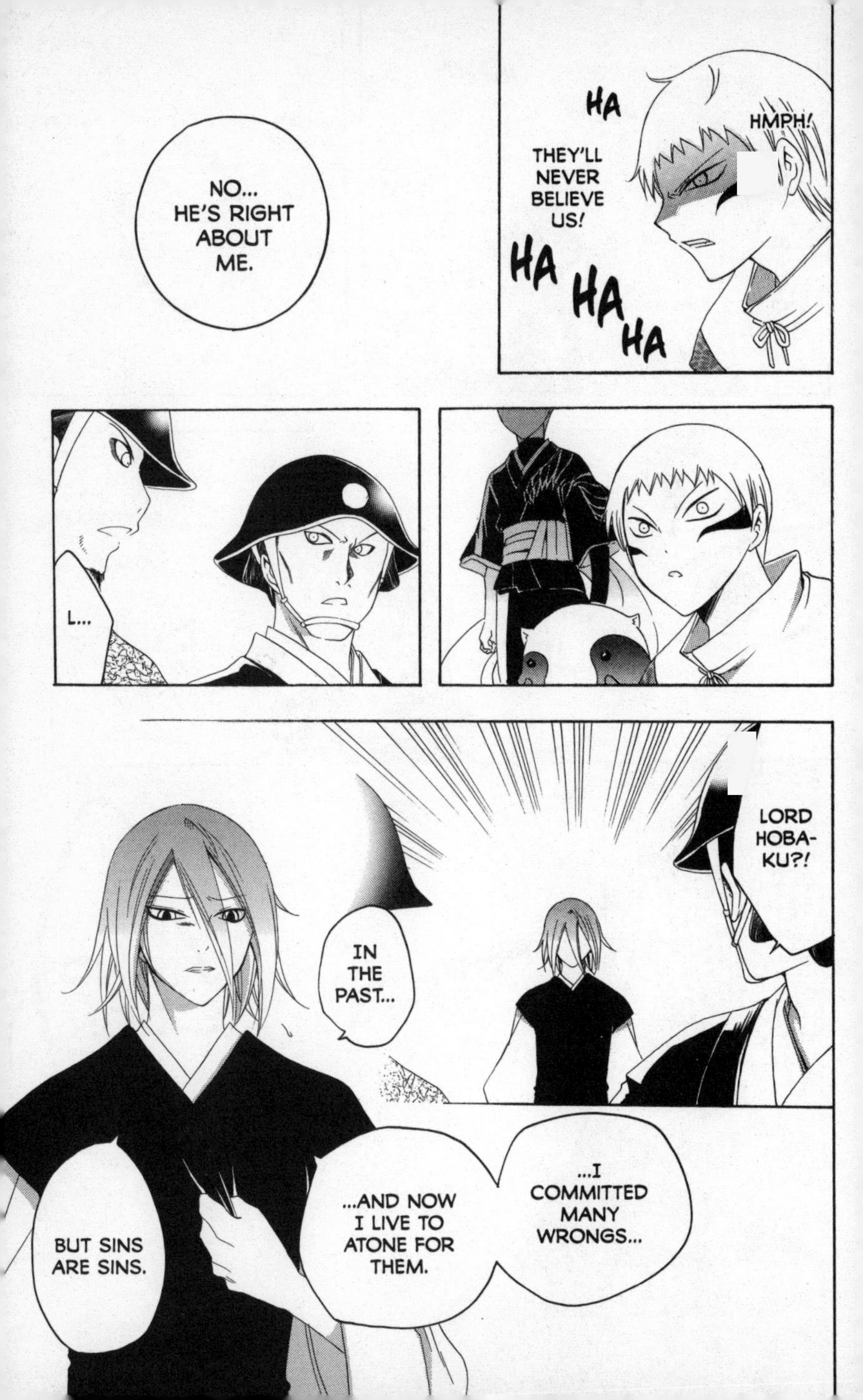
HMPH!
HA
THEY'LL NEVER BELIEVE US!
HA HA HA
NO... HE'S RIGHT ABOUT ME.
I...
LORD HOBA-KU?!
IN THE PAST...
...I COMMITTED MANY WRONGS...
...AND NOW I LIVE TO ATONE FOR THEM.
BUT SINS ARE SINS.

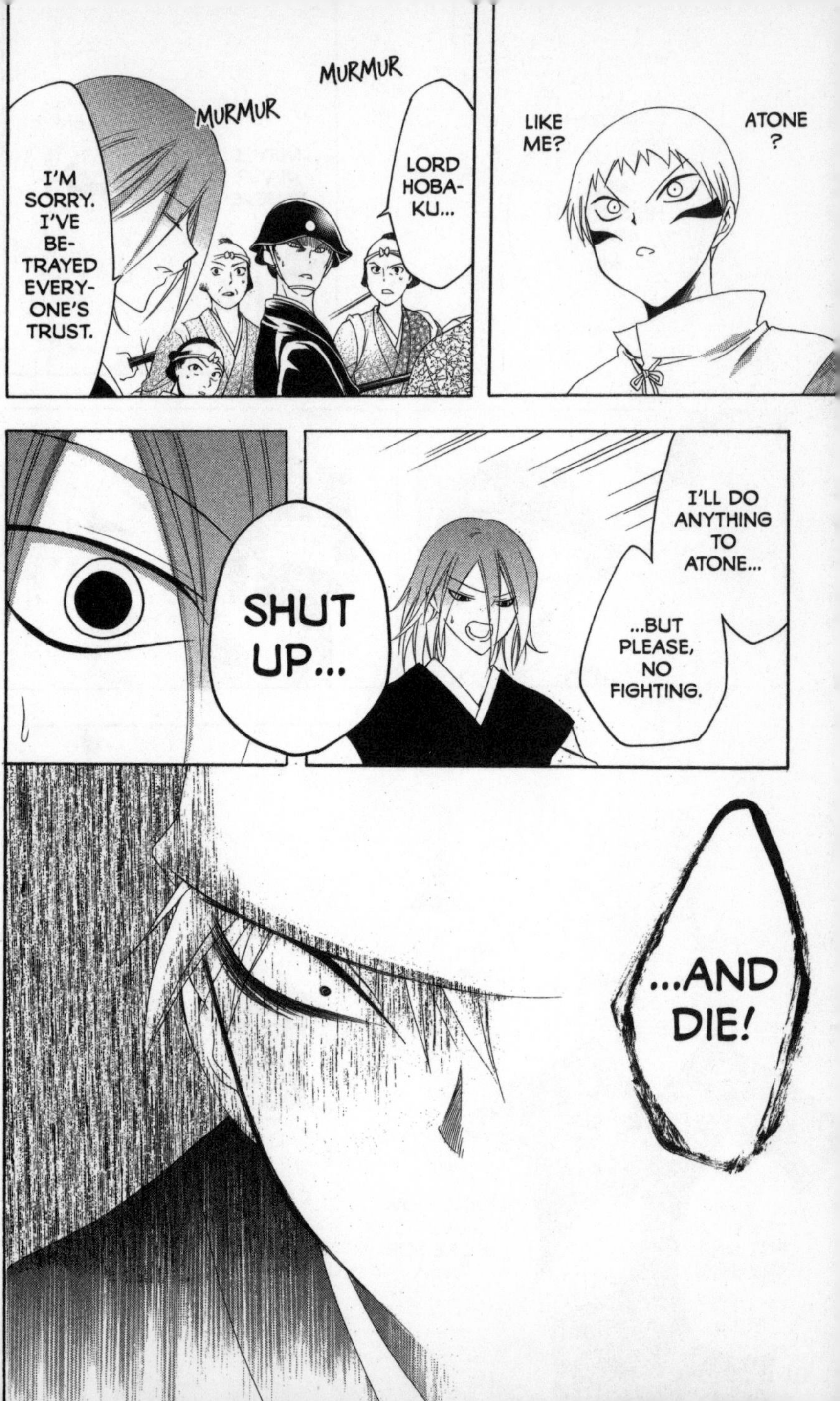
ATONE ?
LIKE ME?
MURMUR
LORD HOBAKU...
MURMUR
I'M SORRY. I'VE BETRAYED EVERYONE'S TRUST.
I'LL DO ANYTHING TO ATONE...
...BUT PLEASE, NO FIGHTING.
SHUT UP...
...AND DIE!

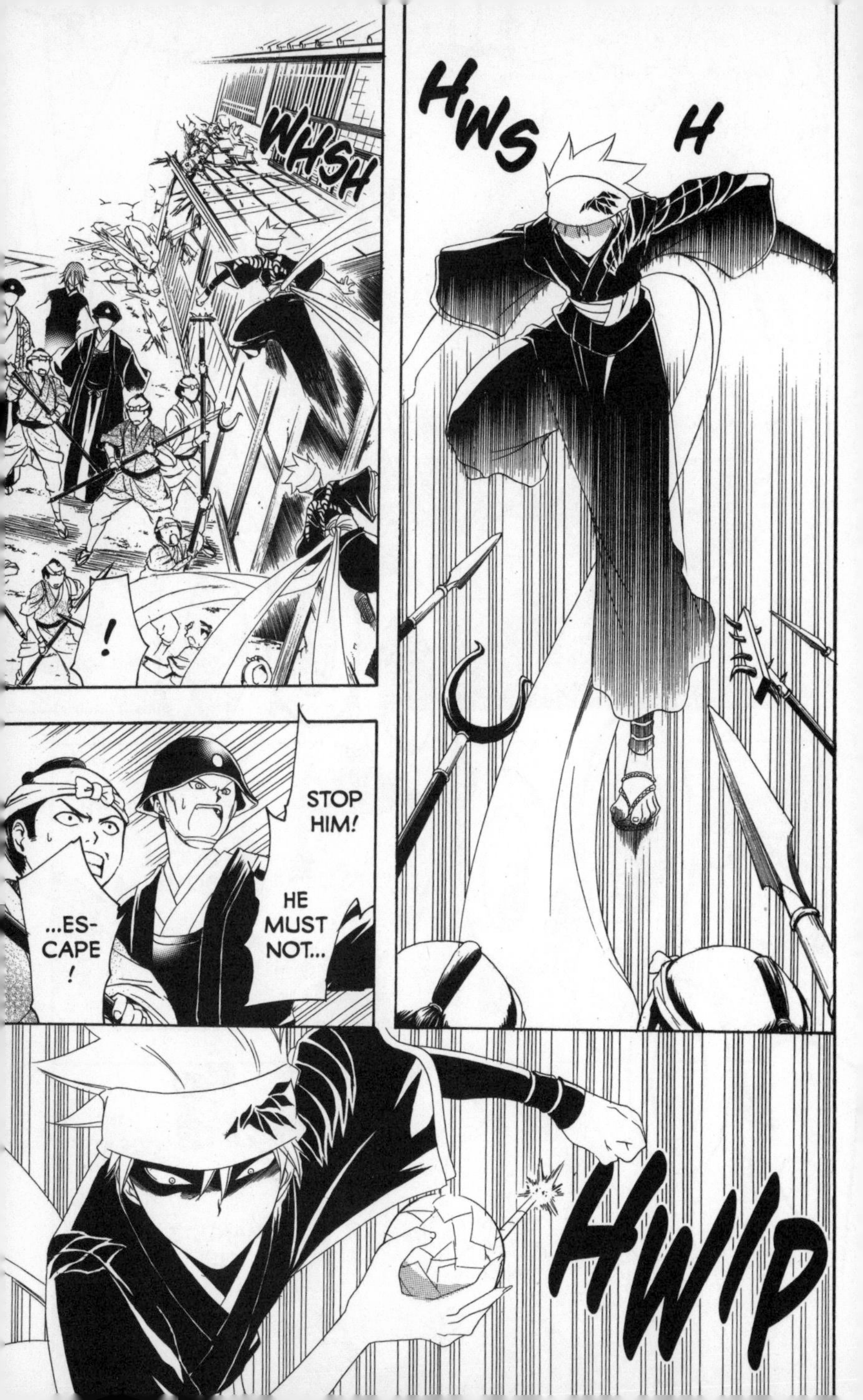
HWSH
WHSH
!
STOP HIM!
HE MUST NOT...
...ES-CAPE!
HWIP

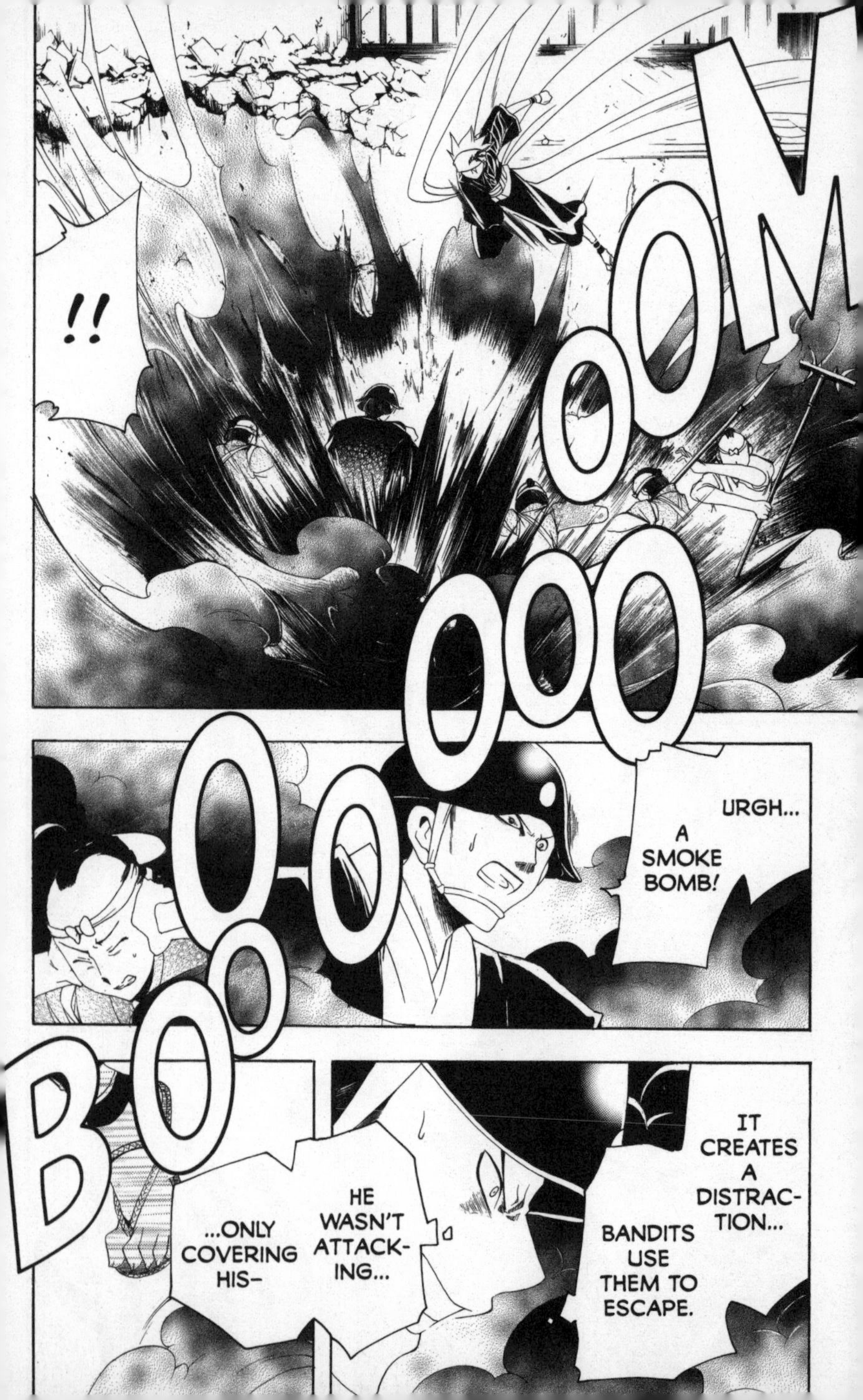
!!
BOOOOOOOOOOOM
URGH...
A SMOKE BOMB!
IT CREATES A DISTRACTION...
BANDITS USE THEM TO ESCAPE.
HE WASN'T ATTACKING...
...ONLY COVERING HIS–

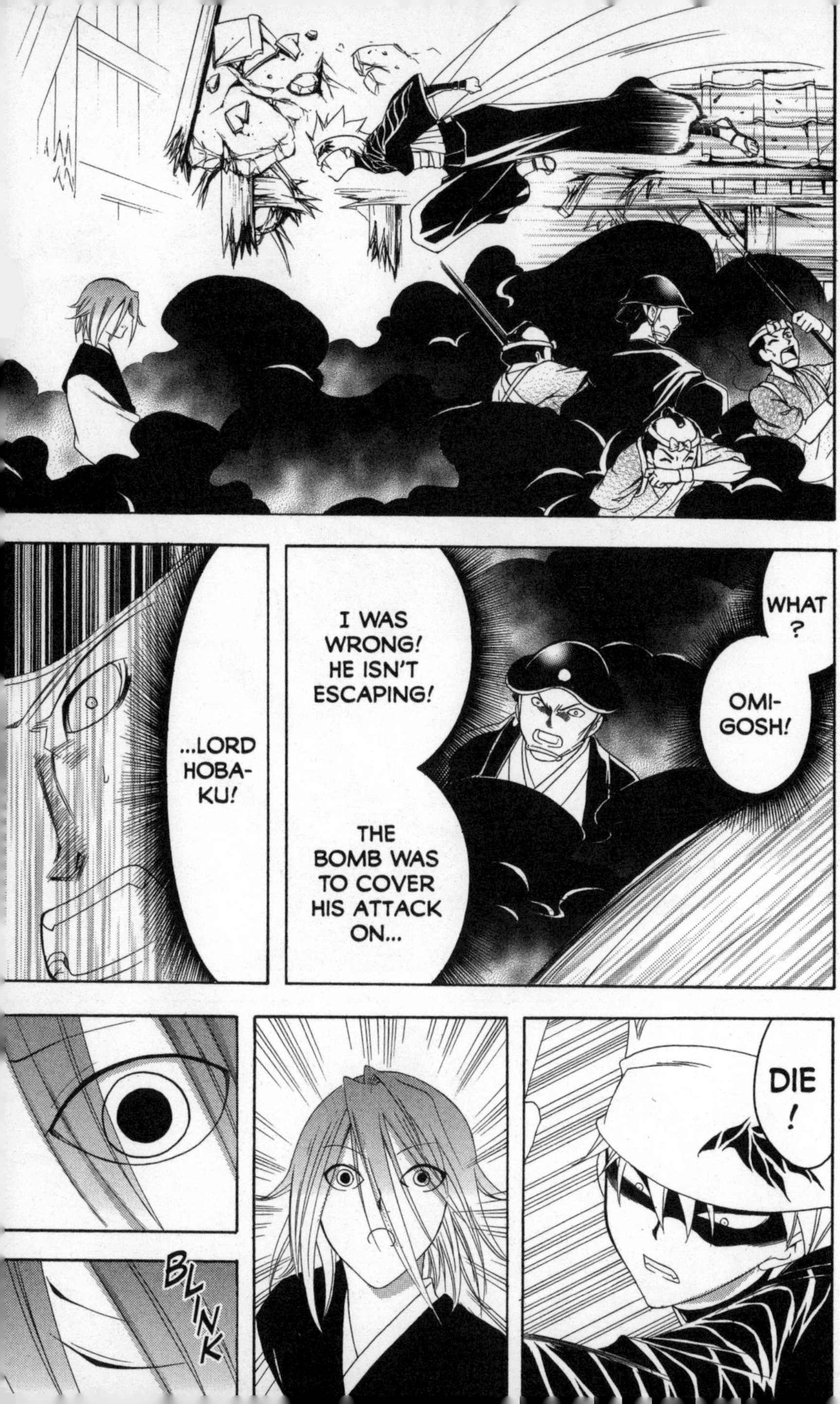
WHAT?
OMI-GOSH!
I WAS WRONG! HE ISN'T ESCAPING!
THE BOMB WAS TO COVER HIS ATTACK ON...
...LORD HOBA-KU!
DIE!
BLINK

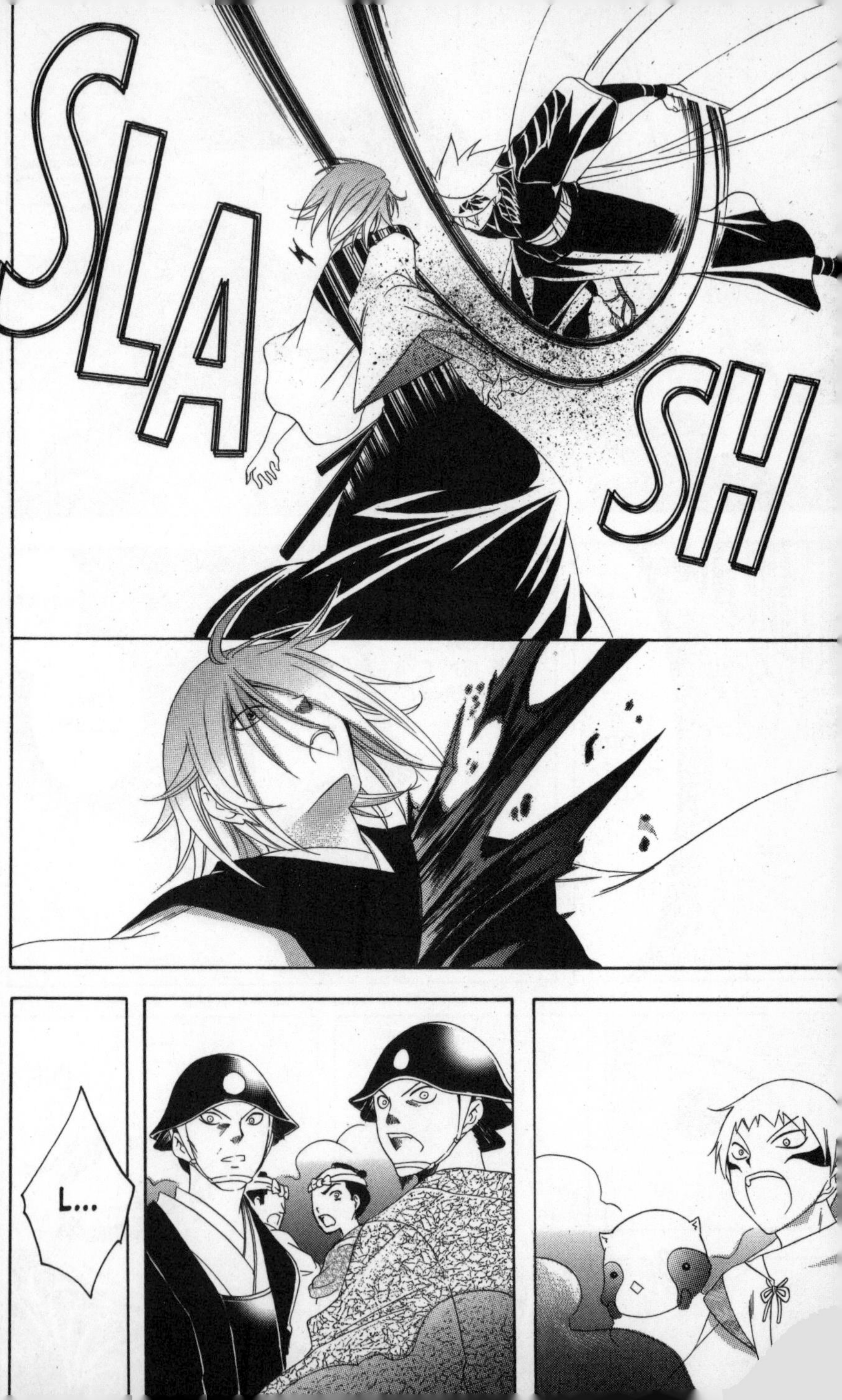
SLASH
L...

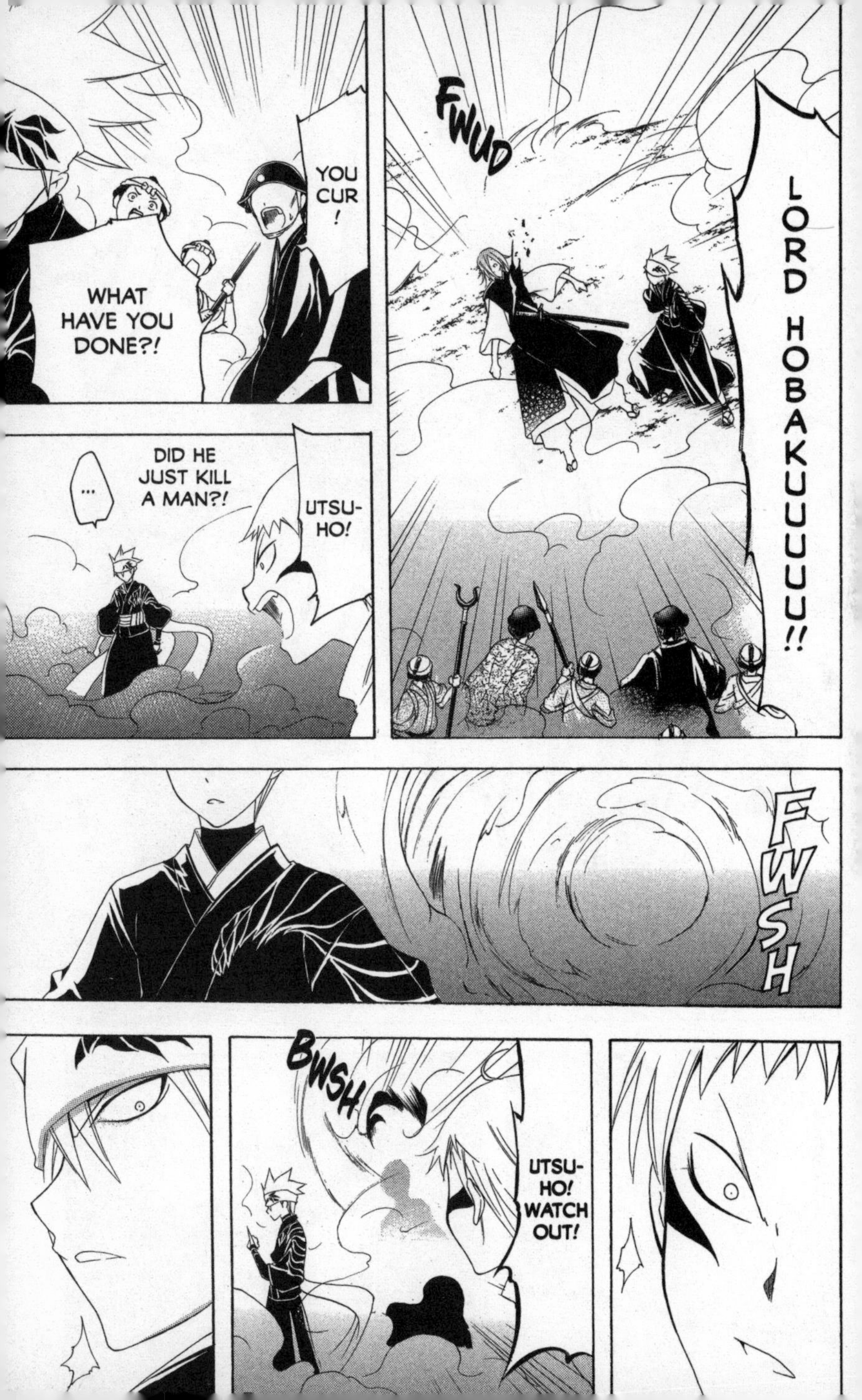
FWUD
LORD HOBAKUUUUUU!!
YOU CUR!
WHAT HAVE YOU DONE?!
UTSU-HO!
DID HE JUST KILL A MAN?!
...
FWSH
BWSH
UTSU-HO! WATCH OUT!

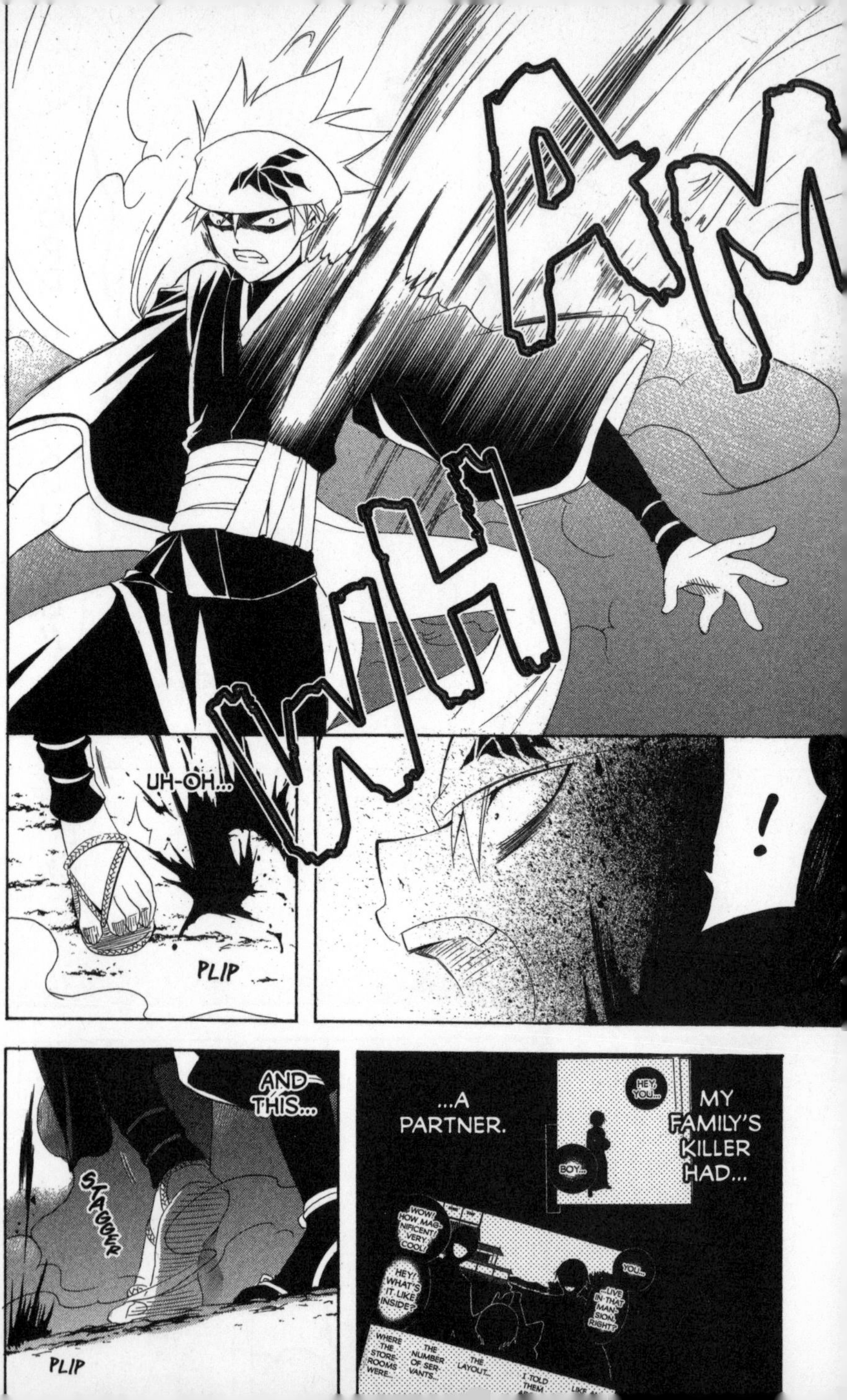
WHAM
!
UH-OH...
PLIP
MY FAMILY'S KILLER HAD...
HEY, YOU...
BOY...
...A PARTNER.
YOU...
...LIVE IN THAT MANSION, RIGHT?
WOW! HOW MAGNIFICENT! VERY COOL!
HEY! WHAT'S IT LIKE INSIDE?
WHERE THE STOREROOMS WERE...
THE NUMBER OF SERVANTS...
THE LAYOUT...
I TOLD THEM
AND THIS...
STAGGER
PLIP

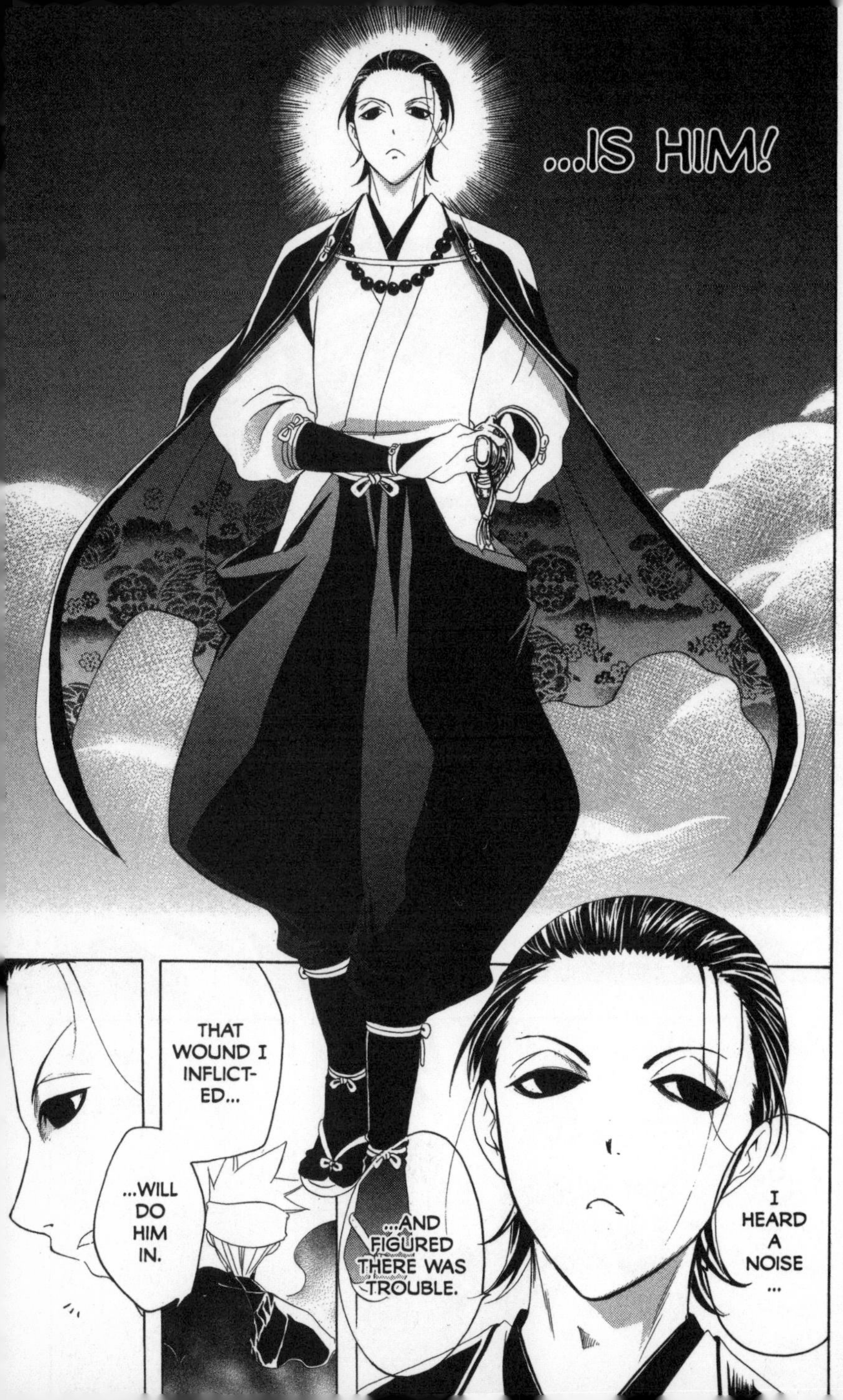
...IS HIM!
I HEARD A NOISE ...
...AND FIGURED THERE WAS TROUBLE.
THAT WOUND I INFLICT-ED...
...WILL DO HIM IN.

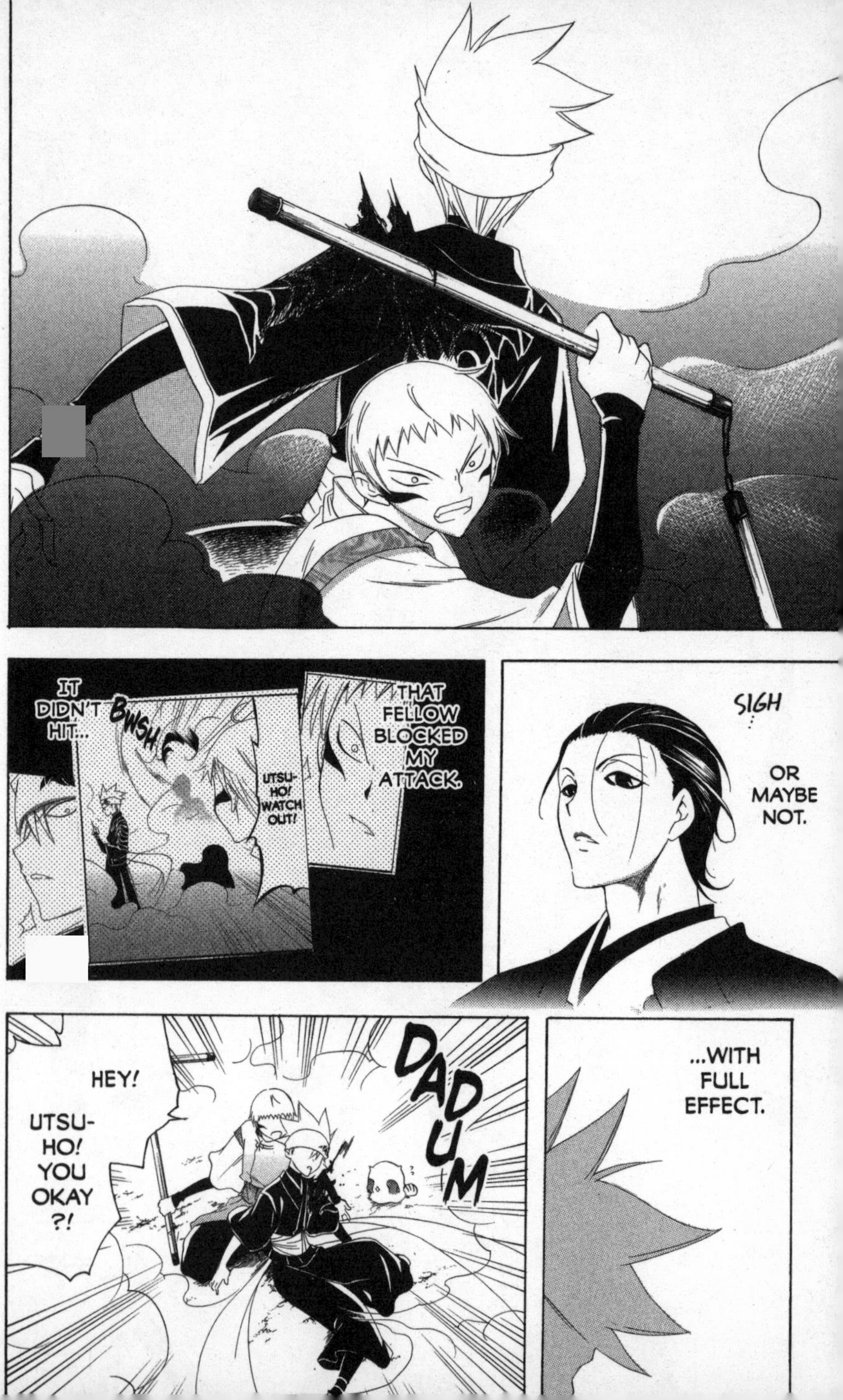
SIGH
OR MAYBE NOT.
THAT FELLOW BLOCKED MY ATTACK.
IT DIDN'T HIT...
BWSH
UTSU-HO! WATCH OUT!
...WITH FULL EFFECT.
DADUM
HEY!
UTSU-HO! YOU OKAY?!

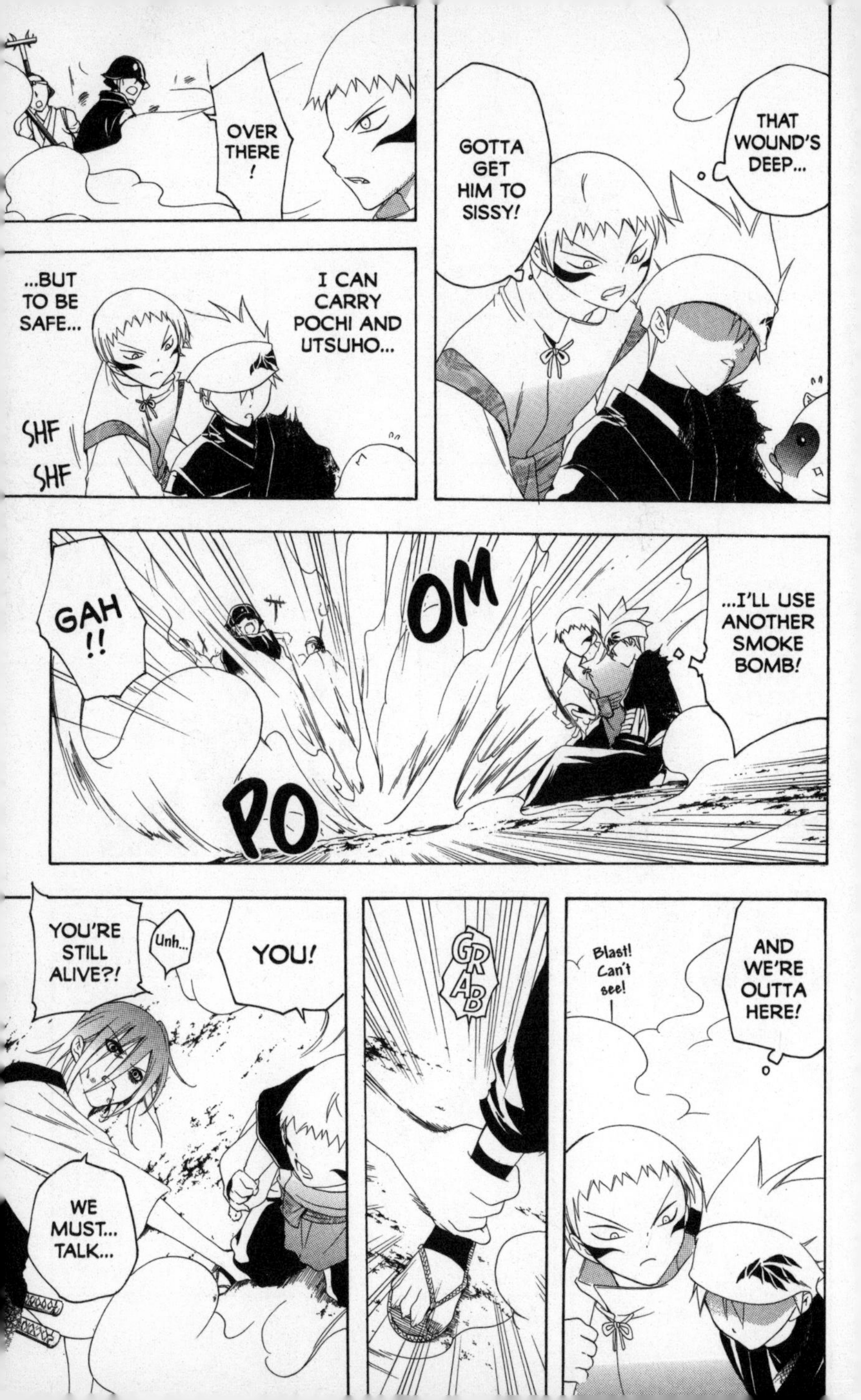
THAT WOUND'S DEEP...
GOTTA GET HIM TO SISSY!
OVER THERE!
I CAN CARRY POCHI AND UTSUHO...
...BUT TO BE SAFE...
SHF
SHF
...I'LL USE ANOTHER SMOKE BOMB!
PO
OM
GAH!!
AND WE'RE OUTTA HERE!
Blast! Can't see!
GRAB
YOU!
Unh...
YOU'RE STILL ALIVE?!
WE MUST... TALK...

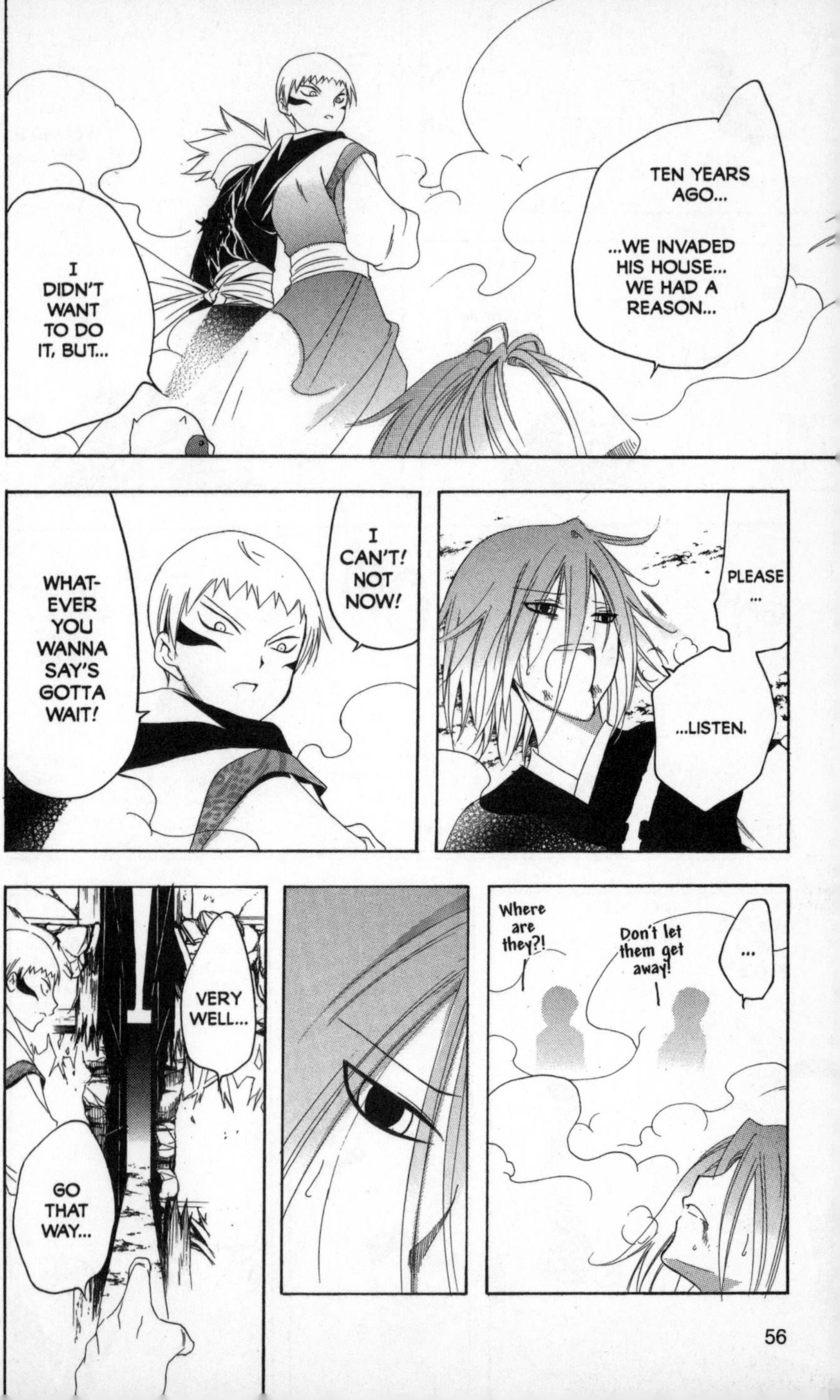
TEN YEARS AGO...
...WE INVADED HIS HOUSE... WE HAD A REASON...
I DIDN'T WANT TO DO IT, BUT...
PLEASE ...
...LISTEN.
I CAN'T! NOT NOW!
WHAT-EVER YOU WANNA SAY'S GOTTA WAIT!
...
Don't let them get away!
Where are they?!
VERY WELL...
GO THAT WAY...

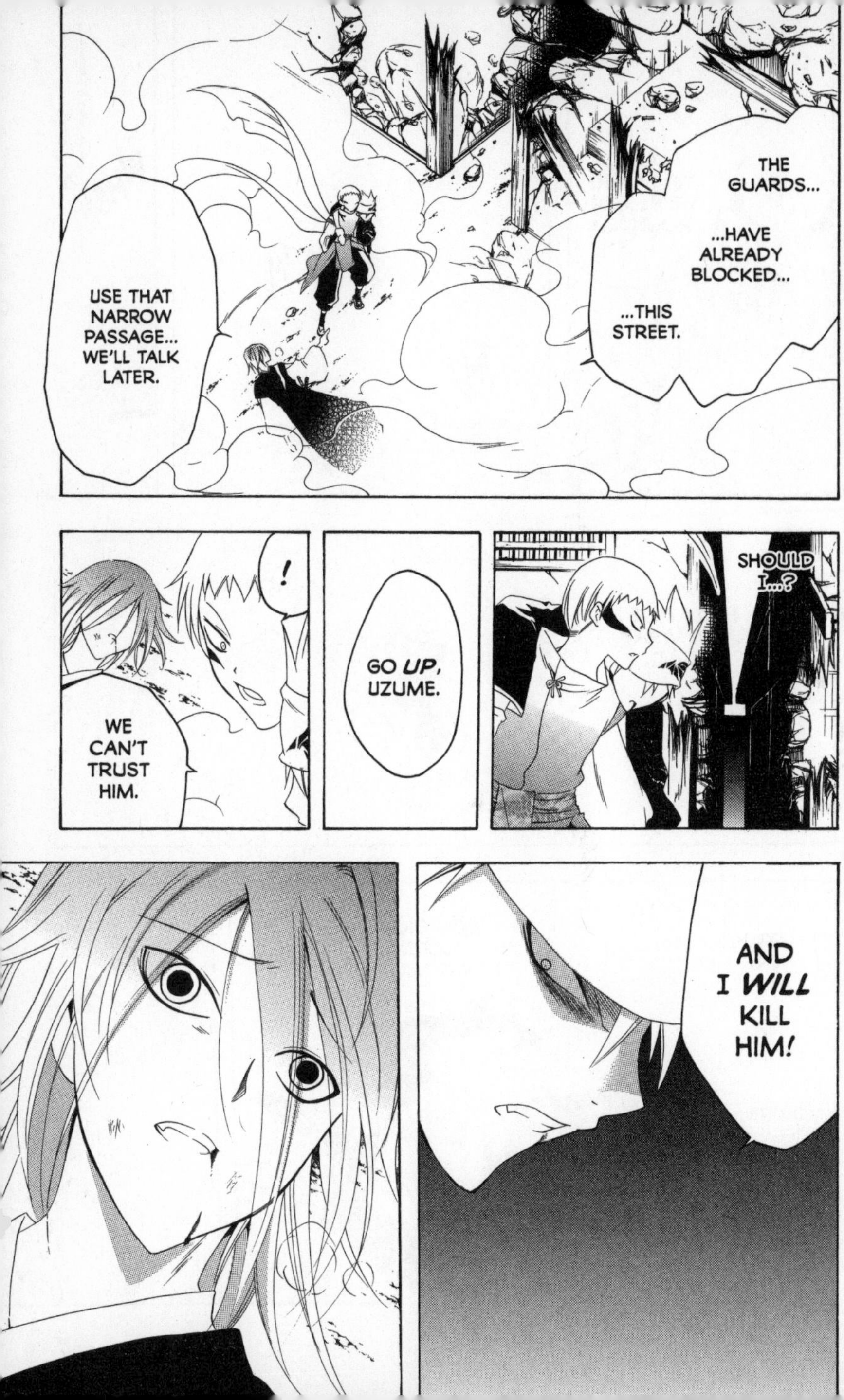
THE GUARDS...
...HAVE ALREADY BLOCKED...
...THIS STREET.
USE THAT NARROW PASSAGE... WE'LL TALK LATER.
SHOULD I...?
GO *UP*, UZUME.
!
WE CAN'T TRUST HIM.
AND I *WILL* KILL HIM!

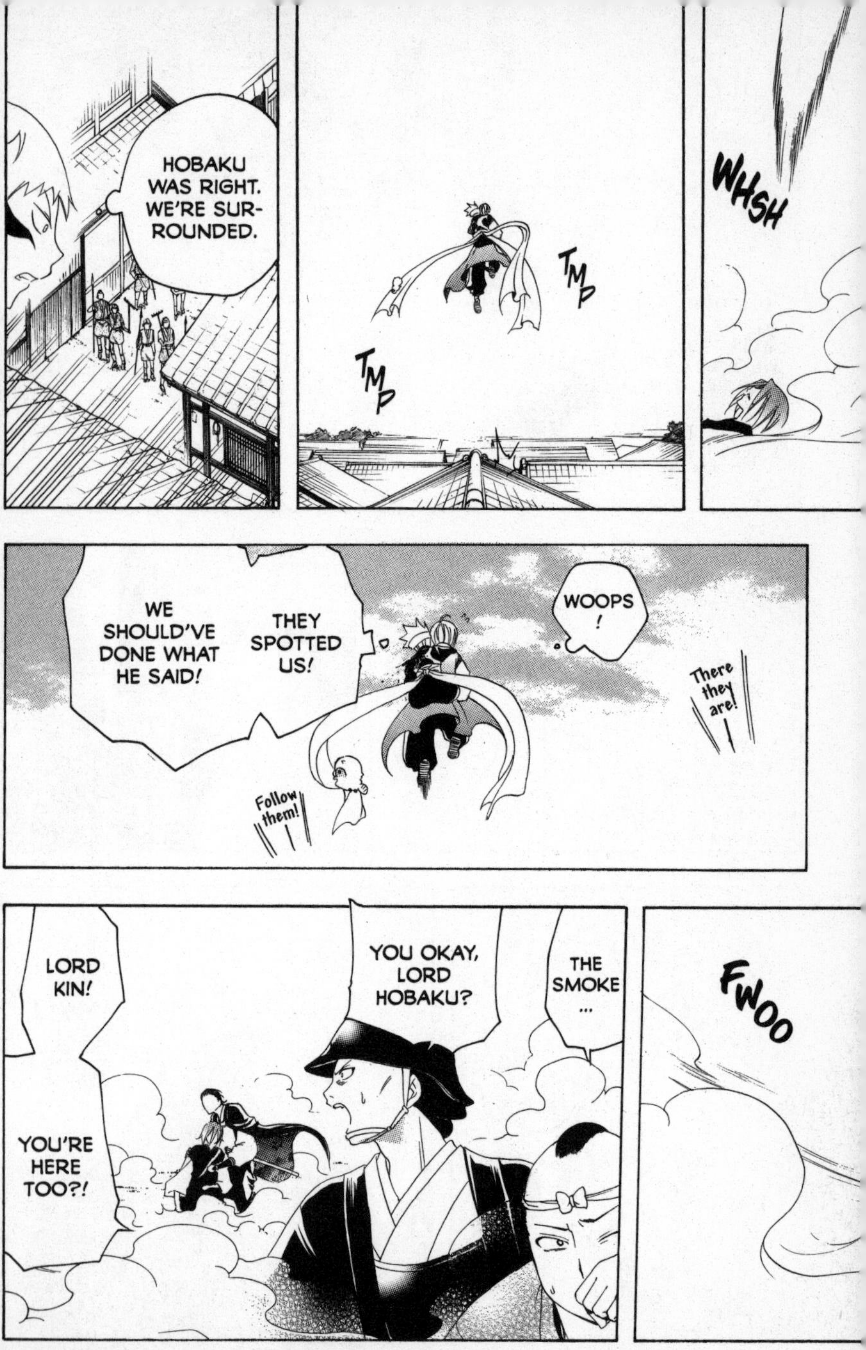
WHSH
TMP
TMP
HOBAKU WAS RIGHT. WE'RE SUR-ROUNDED.
WOOPS!
There they are!
THEY SPOTTED US!
WE SHOULD'VE DONE WHAT HE SAID!
Follow them!
FWOO
THE SMOKE...
YOU OKAY, LORD HOBAKU?
LORD KIN!
YOU'RE HERE TOO?!

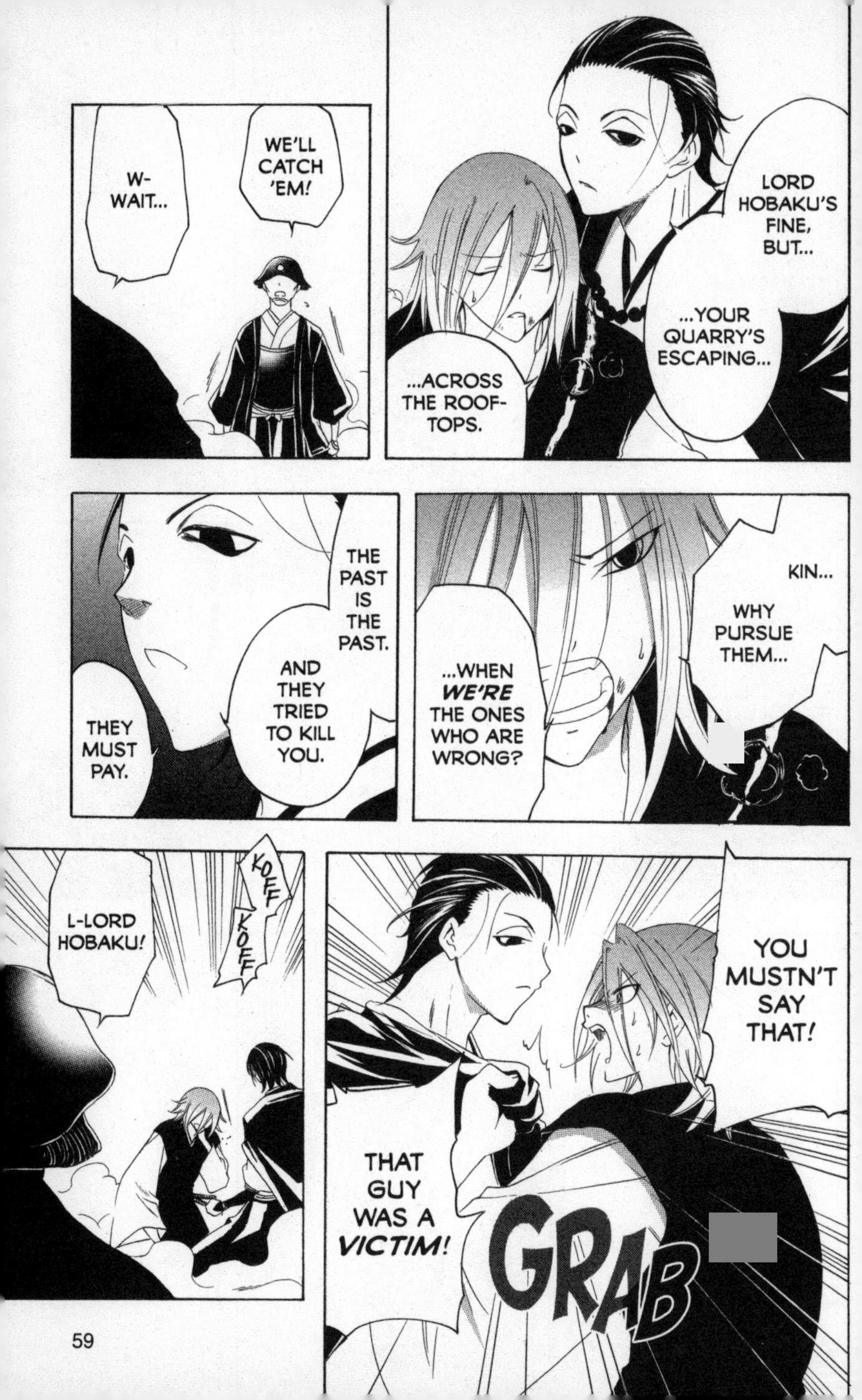
LORD HOBAKU'S FINE, BUT...
...YOUR QUARRY'S ESCAPING...
...ACROSS THE ROOF-TOPS.
WE'LL CATCH 'EM!
W-WAIT...
KIN...
WHY PURSUE THEM...
...WHEN *WE'RE* THE ONES WHO ARE WRONG?
THE PAST IS THE PAST.
AND THEY TRIED TO KILL YOU.
THEY MUST PAY.
YOU MUSTN'T SAY THAT!
THAT GUY WAS A *VICTIM*!
GRAB
KOFF
KOFF
L-LORD HOBAKU!

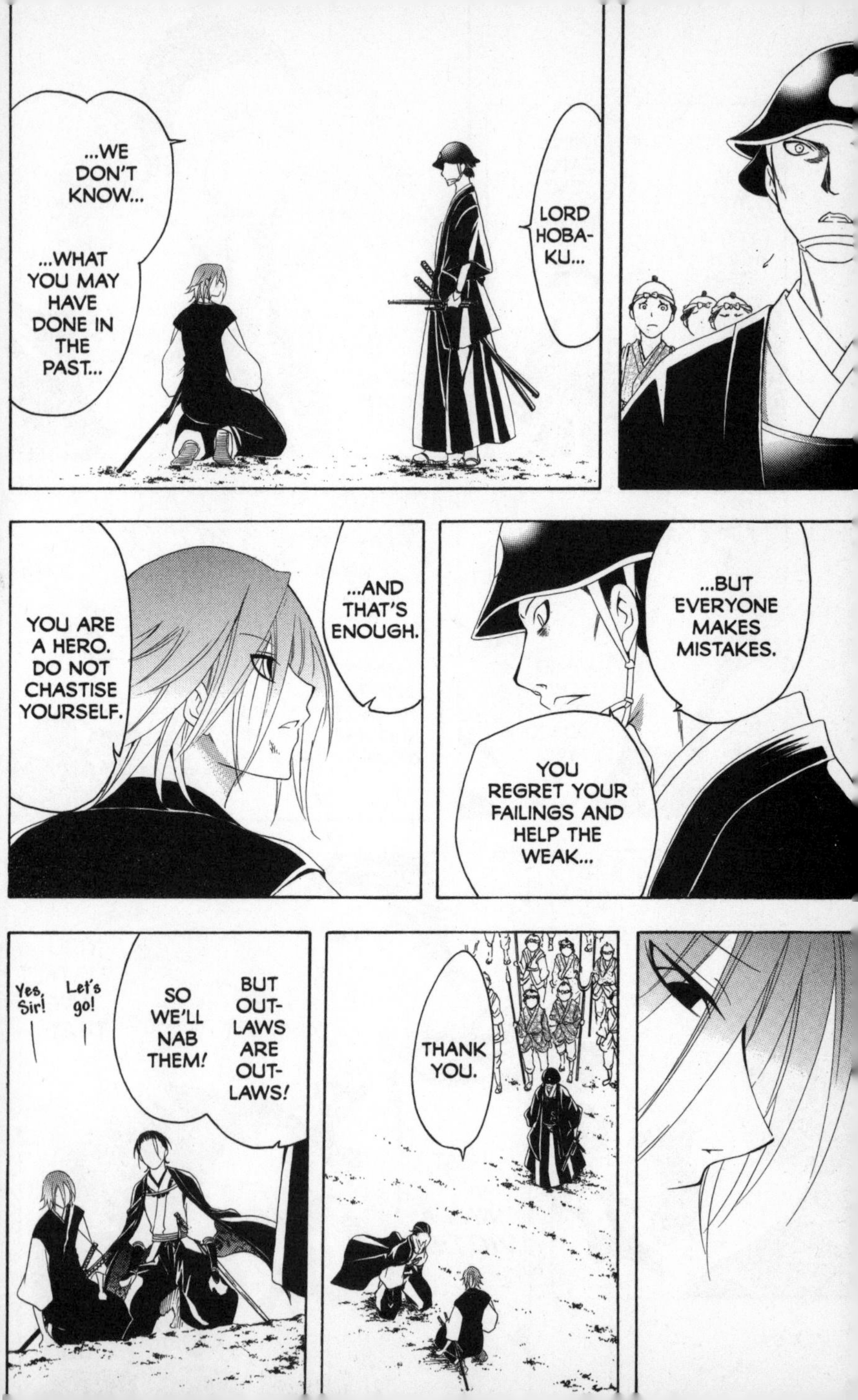
LORD HOBAKU...
...WE DON'T KNOW...
...WHAT YOU MAY HAVE DONE IN THE PAST...
...BUT EVERYONE MAKES MISTAKES.
YOU REGRET YOUR FAILINGS AND HELP THE WEAK...
...AND THAT'S ENOUGH.
YOU ARE A HERO. DO NOT CHASTISE YOURSELF.
THANK YOU.
BUT OUTLAWS ARE OUTLAWS!
SO WE'LL NAB THEM!
Let's go!
Yes, Sir!

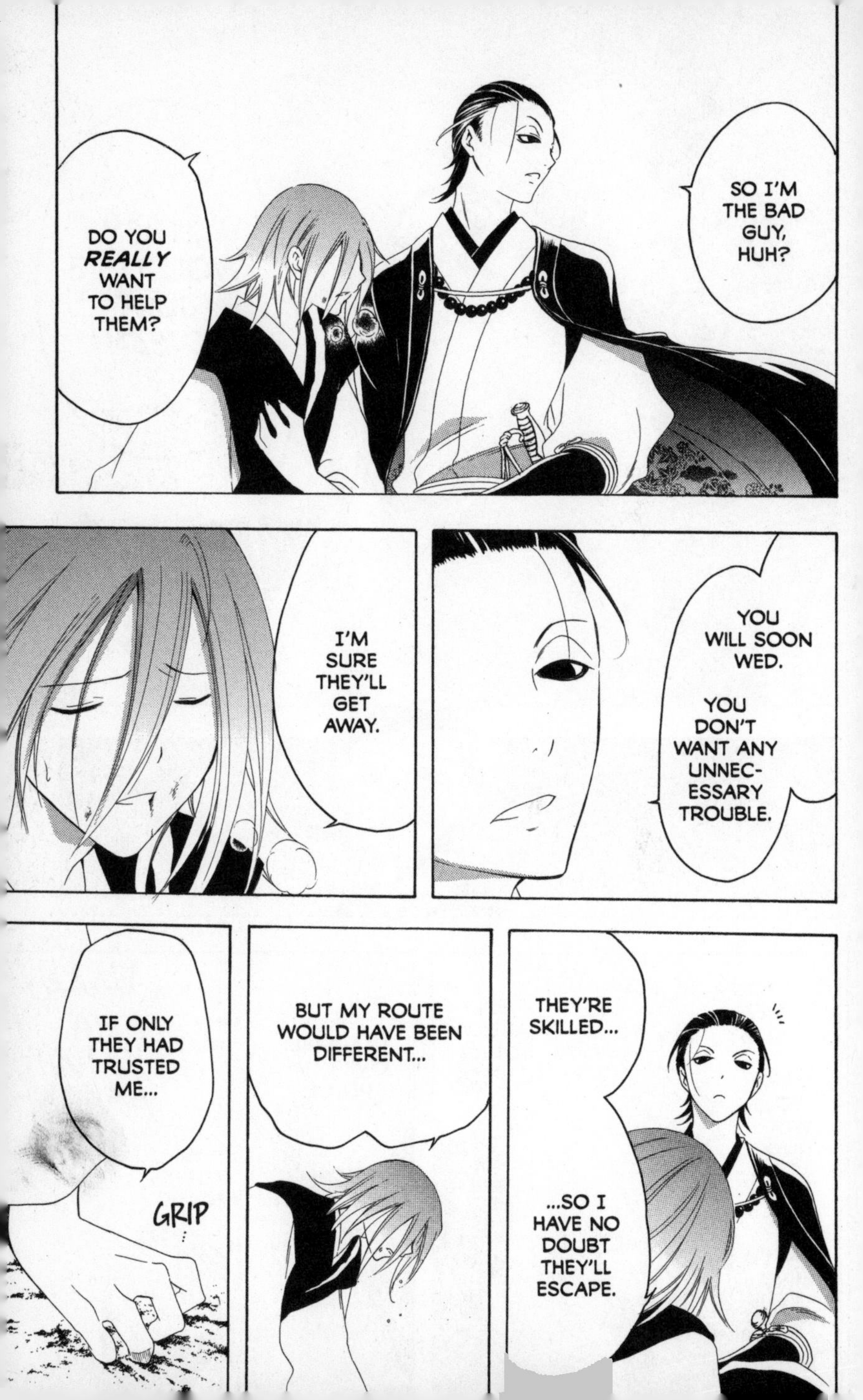
SO I'M THE BAD GUY, HUH?
DO YOU *REALLY* WANT TO HELP THEM?
YOU WILL SOON WED.
YOU DON'T WANT ANY UNNEC-ESSARY TROUBLE.
I'M SURE THEY'LL GET AWAY.
THEY'RE SKILLED...
...SO I HAVE NO DOUBT THEY'LL ESCAPE.
BUT MY ROUTE WOULD HAVE BEEN DIFFERENT...
IF ONLY THEY HAD TRUSTED ME...
GRIP

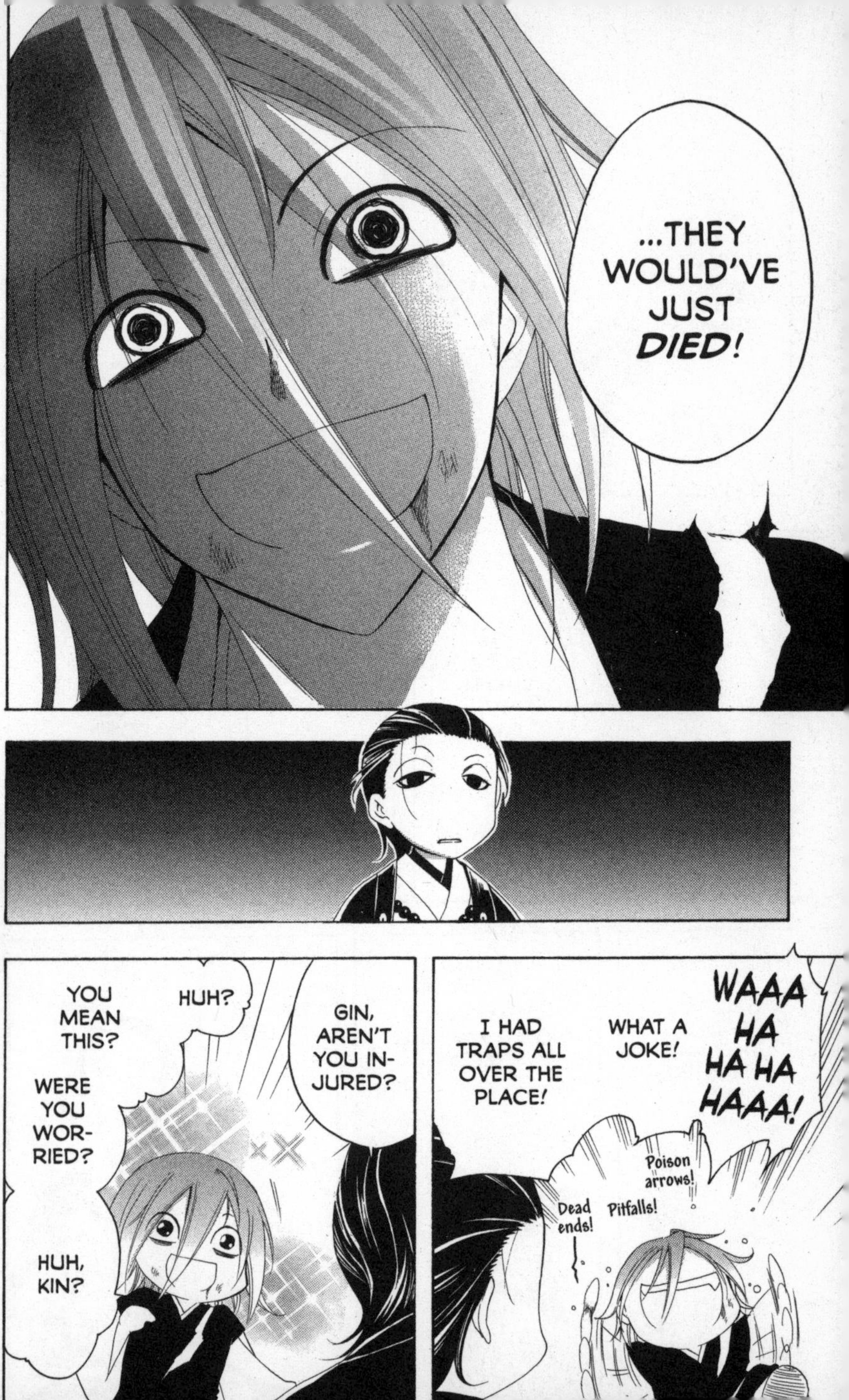
...THEY WOULD'VE JUST *DIED*!
WAAA HA HA HA HAAA!
WHAT A JOKE!
I HAD TRAPS ALL OVER THE PLACE!
Poison arrows!
Pitfalls!
Dead ends!
GIN, AREN'T YOU IN-JURED?
HUH?
YOU MEAN THIS?
WERE YOU WOR-RIED?
HUH, KIN?

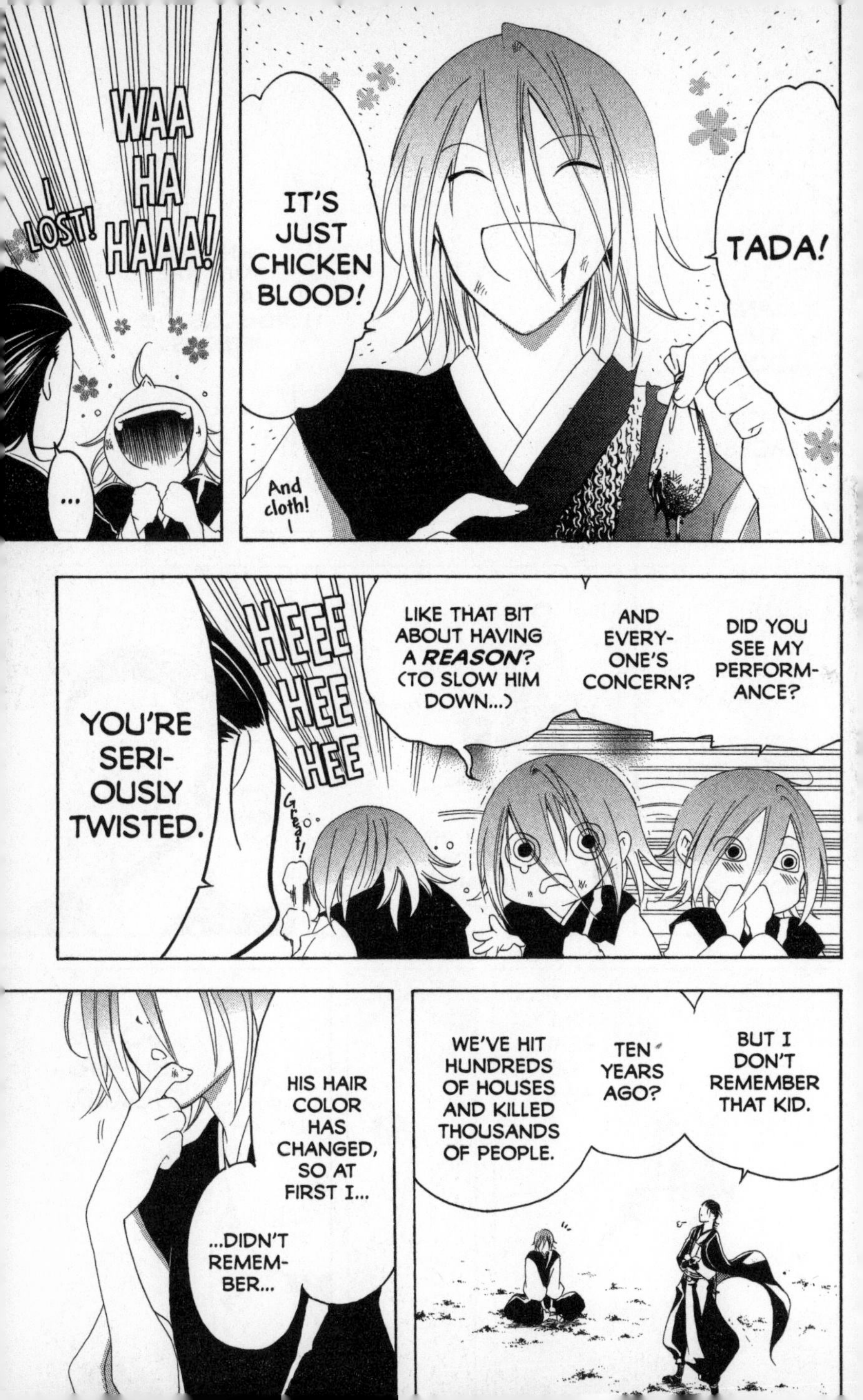
TADA!
IT'S JUST CHICKEN BLOOD!
And cloth!
WAA HA HAAAA!
I LOST!
...
DID YOU SEE MY PERFORMANCE?
AND EVERYONE'S CONCERN?
LIKE THAT BIT ABOUT HAVING A *REASON*? (TO SLOW HIM DOWN...)
HEEE HEE HEE
Great!
YOU'RE SERIOUSLY TWISTED.
BUT I DON'T REMEMBER THAT KID.
TEN YEARS AGO?
WE'VE HIT HUNDREDS OF HOUSES AND KILLED THOUSANDS OF PEOPLE.
HIS HAIR COLOR HAS CHANGED, SO AT FIRST I...
...DIDN'T REMEMBER...

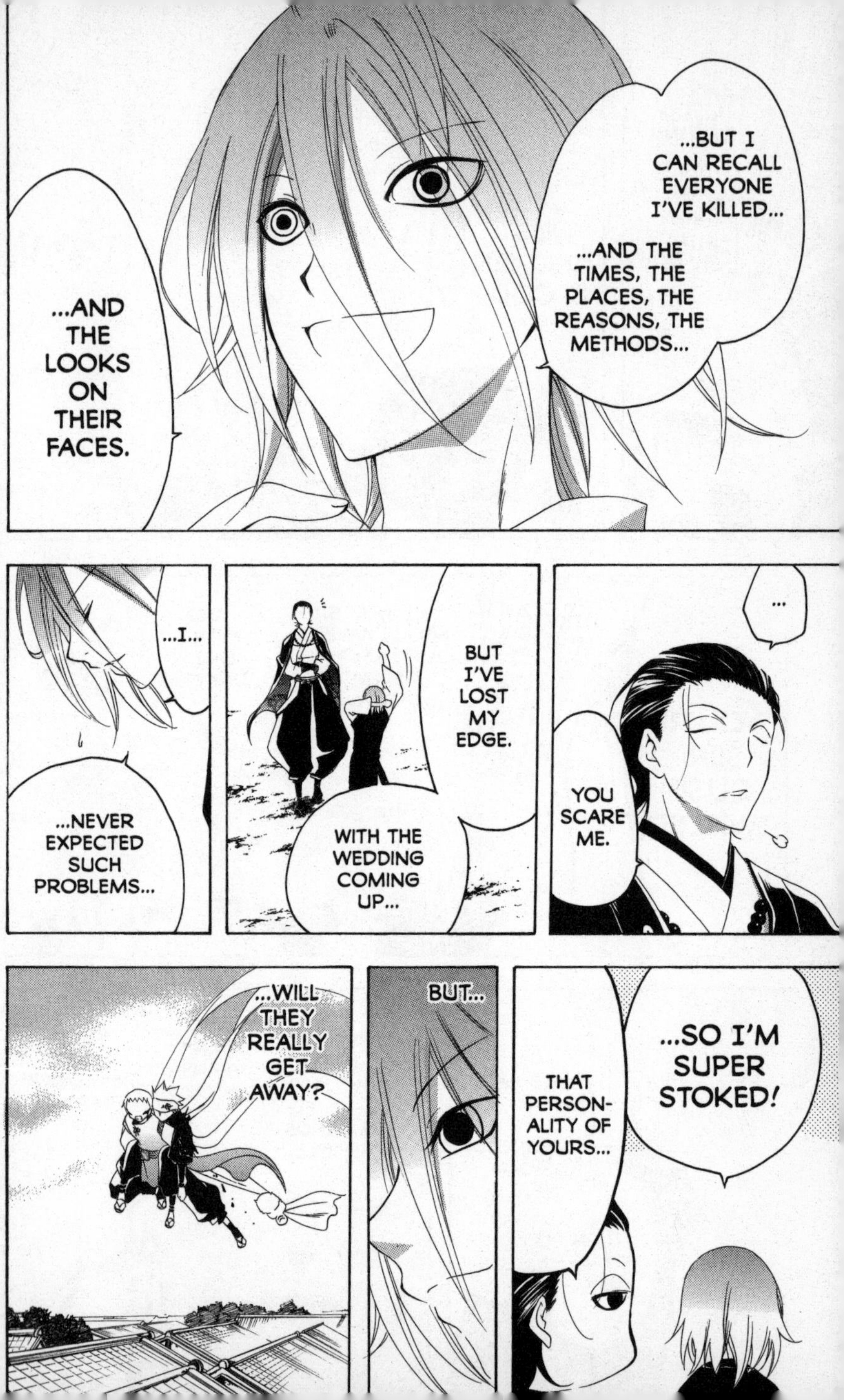
...BUT I CAN RECALL EVERYONE I'VE KILLED...
...AND THE TIMES, THE PLACES, THE REASONS, THE METHODS...
...AND THE LOOKS ON THEIR FACES.
...
YOU SCARE ME.
BUT I'VE LOST MY EDGE.
WITH THE WEDDING COMING UP...
...I...
...NEVER EXPECTED SUCH PROBLEMS...
...SO I'M SUPER STOKED!
THAT PERSON-ALITY OF YOURS...
BUT...
...WILL THEY REALLY GET AWAY?

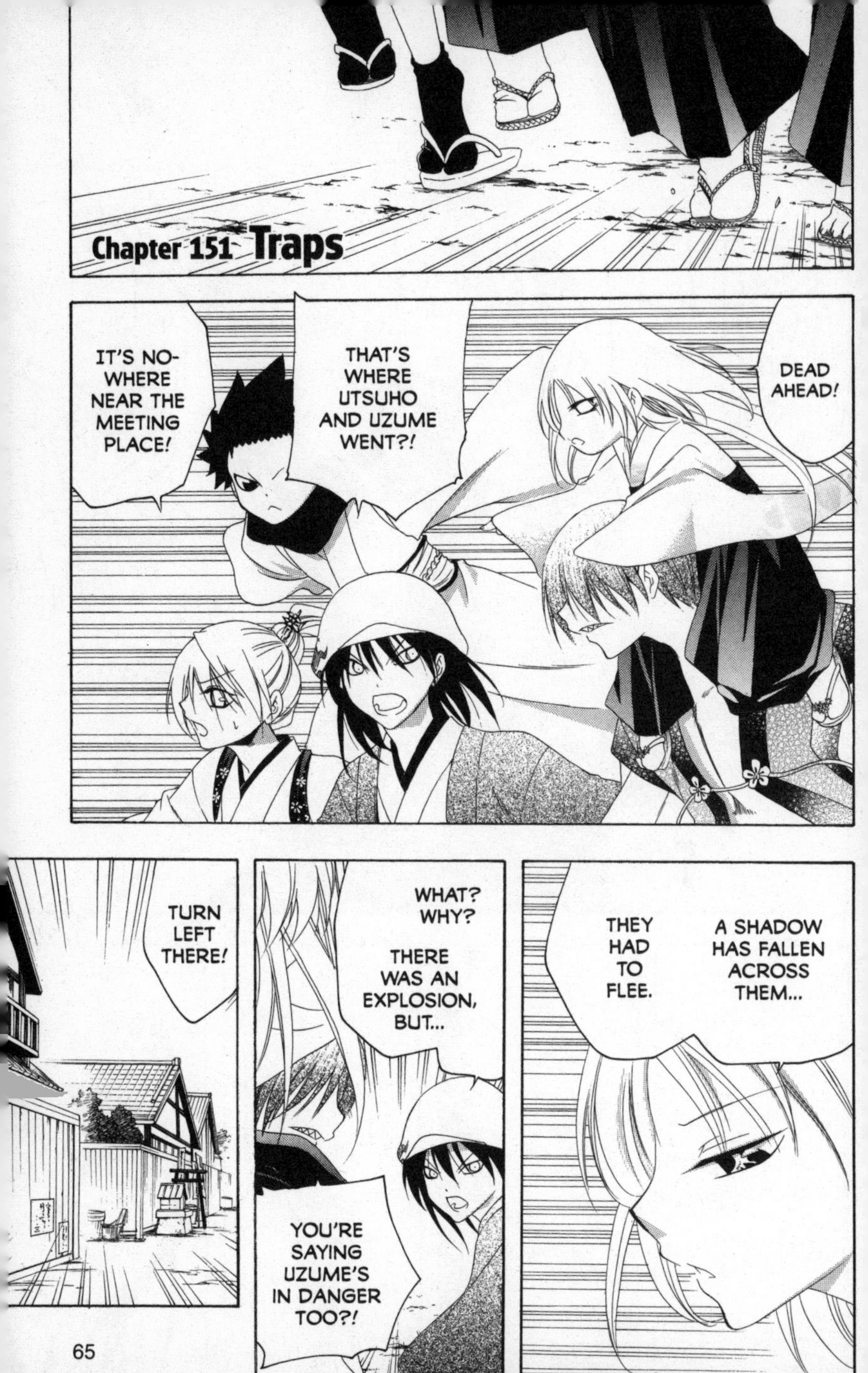
Chapter 151 Traps
DEAD AHEAD!
THAT'S WHERE UTSUHO AND UZUME WENT?!
IT'S NO-WHERE NEAR THE MEETING PLACE!
A SHADOW HAS FALLEN ACROSS THEM...
THEY HAD TO FLEE.
WHAT? WHY?
THERE WAS AN EXPLOSION, BUT...
YOU'RE SAYING UZUME'S IN DANGER TOO?!
TURN LEFT THERE!

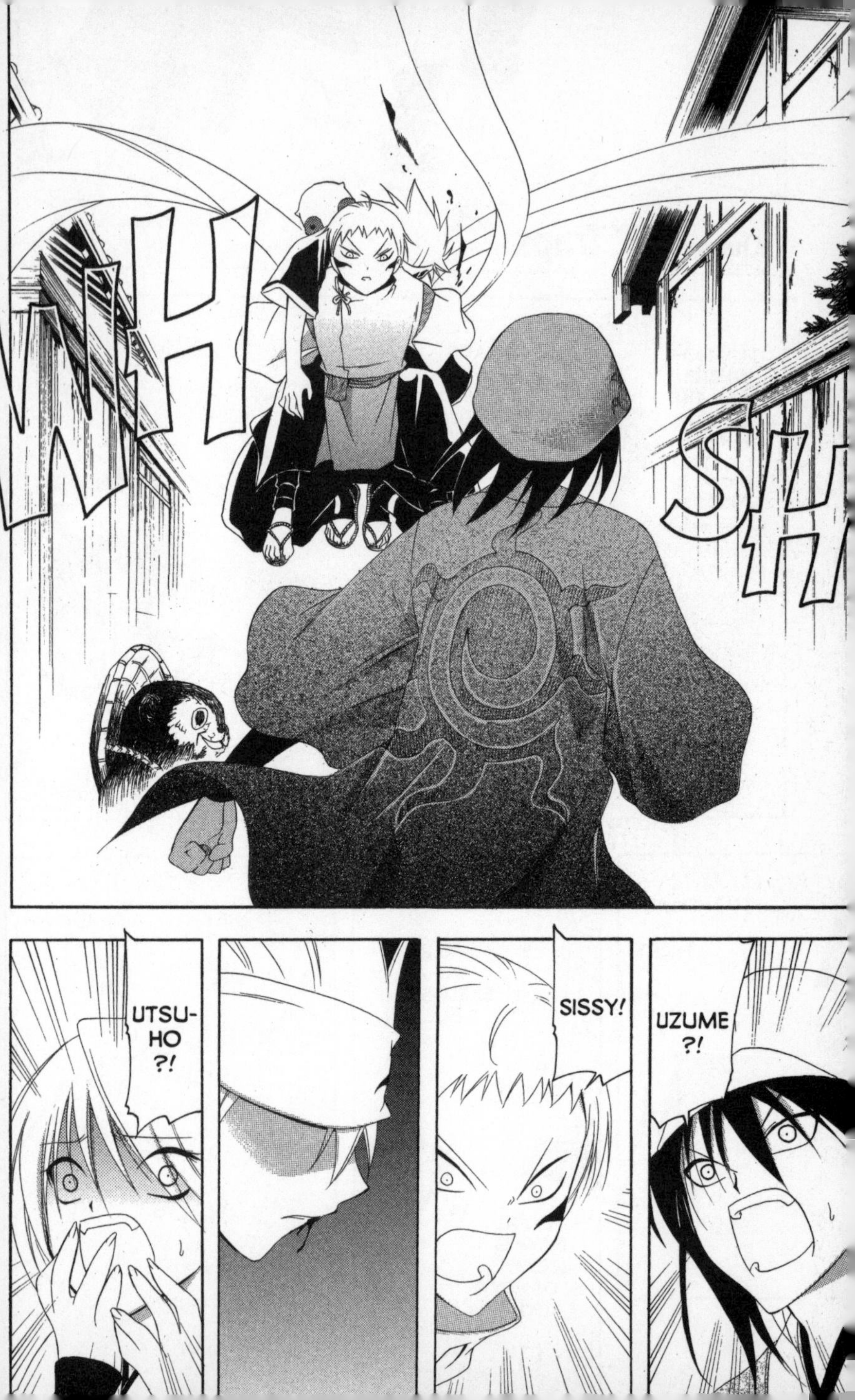
UZUME ?!
SISSY!
UTSU-HO ?!

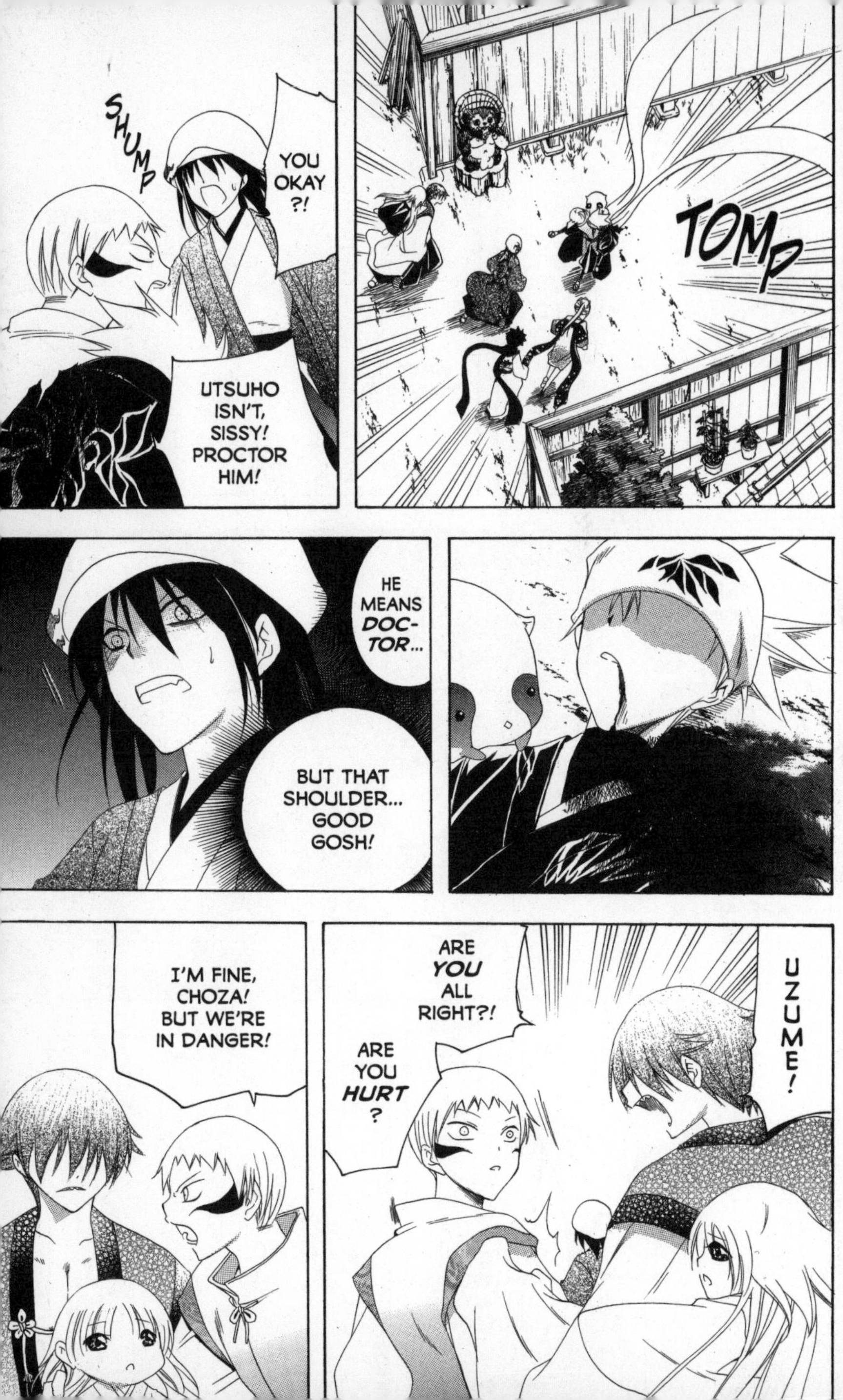
TOMP
SHUMP
YOU OKAY ?!
UTSUHO ISN'T, SISSY! PROCTOR HIM!
HE MEANS DOCTOR...
BUT THAT SHOULDER... GOOD GOSH!
UZUME!
ARE YOU ALL RIGHT?!
ARE YOU HURT?
I'M FINE, CHOZA! BUT WE'RE IN DANGER!

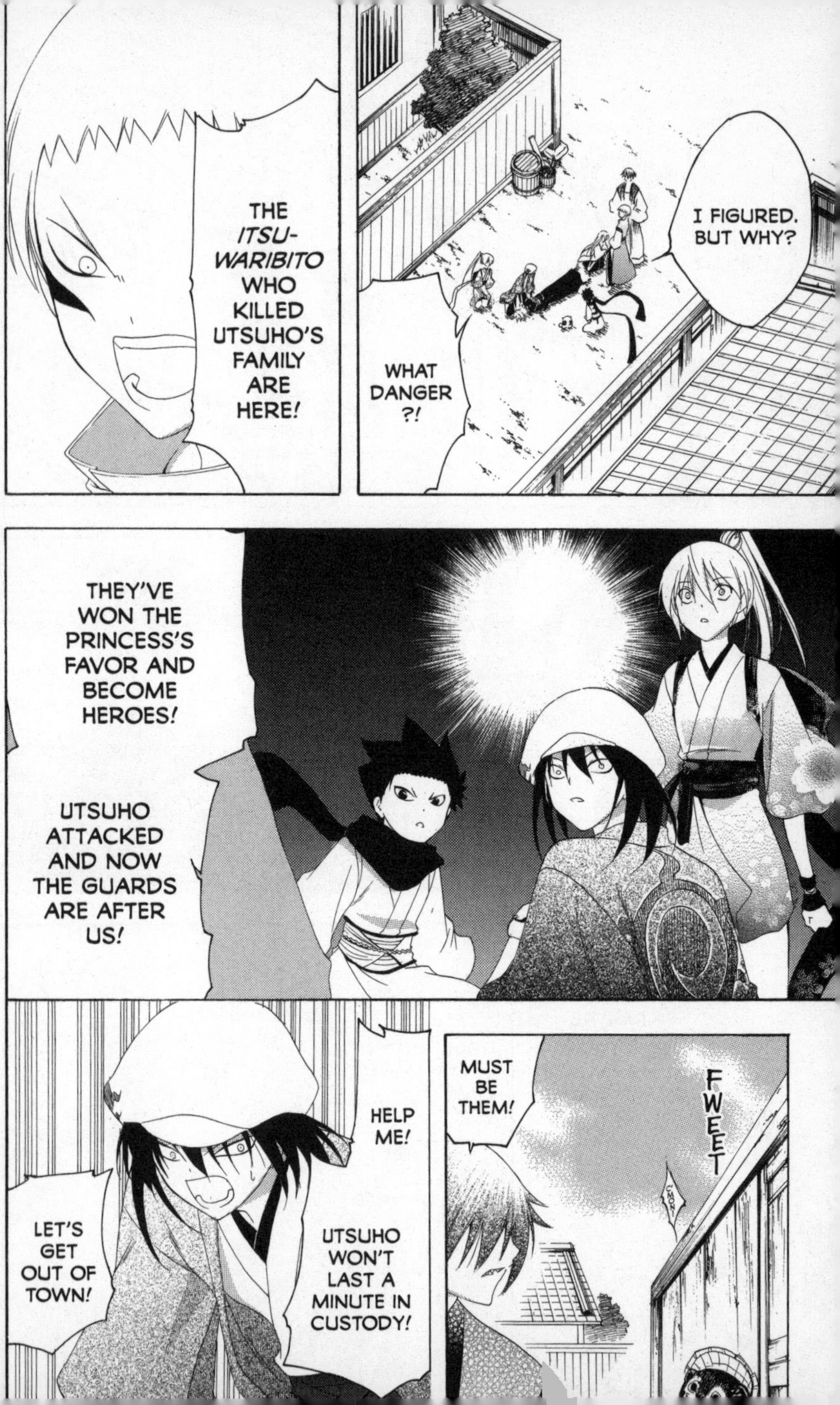
I FIGURED. BUT WHY?
WHAT DANGER ?!
THE ITSU-WARIBITO WHO KILLED UTSUHO'S FAMILY ARE HERE!
THEY'VE WON THE PRINCESS'S FAVOR AND BECOME HEROES!
UTSUHO ATTACKED AND NOW THE GUARDS ARE AFTER US!
MUST BE THEM!
FWEET
C'MON
HELP ME!
UTSUHO WON'T LAST A MINUTE IN CUSTODY!
LET'S GET OUT OF TOWN!

Chapter 151
Traps

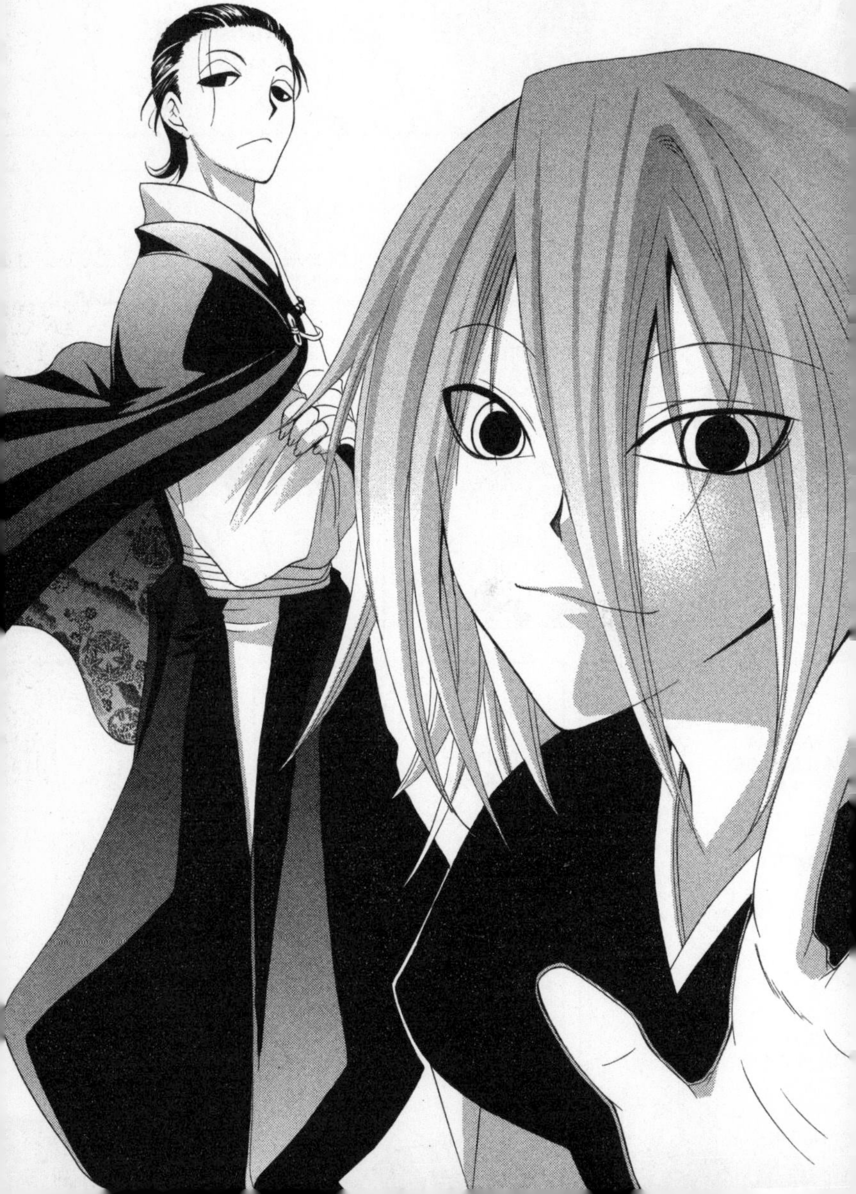

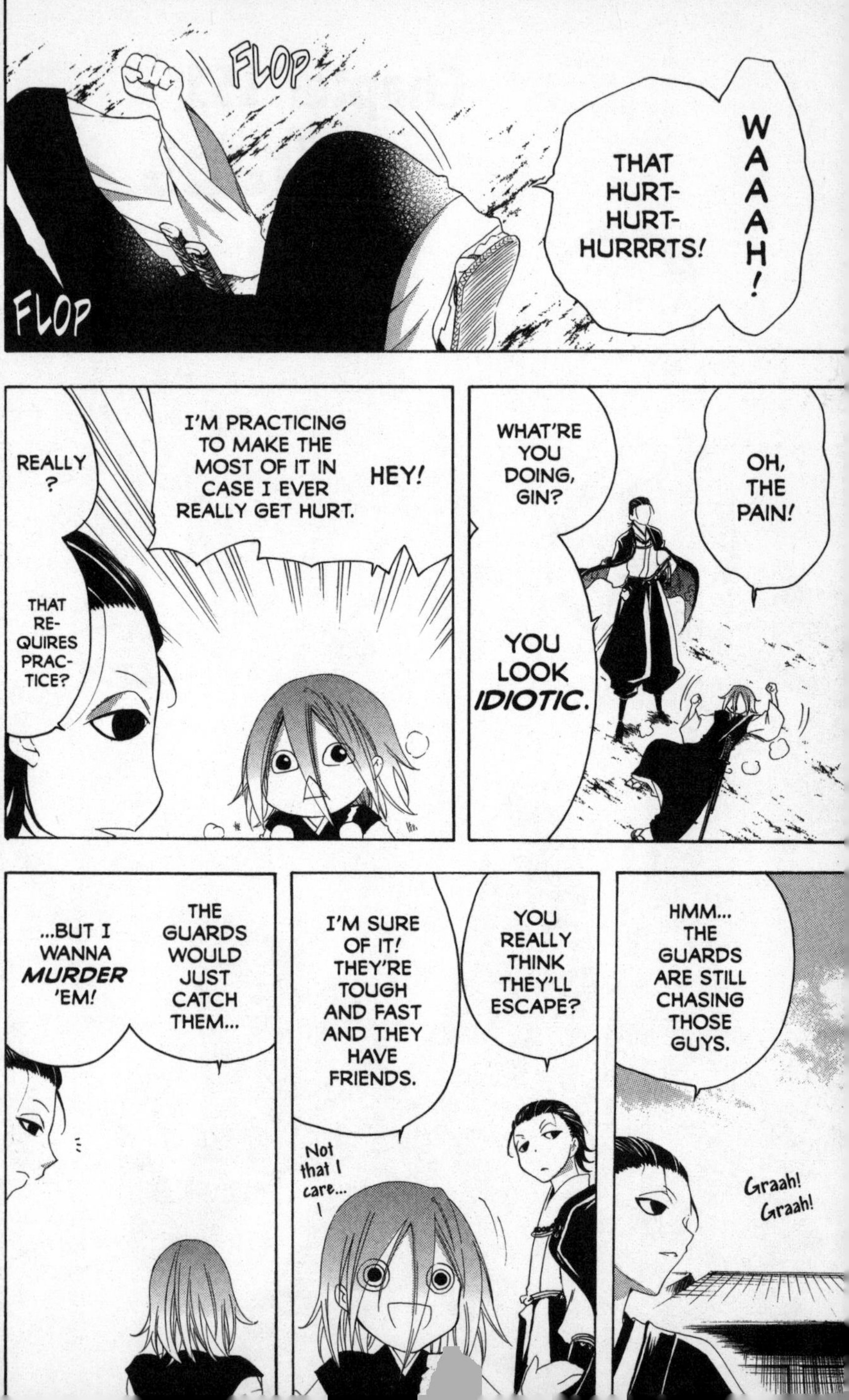
WAAAH!
THAT HURT-HURT-HURRRTS!
FLOP
FLOP
OH, THE PAIN!
WHAT'RE YOU DOING, GIN?
YOU LOOK *IDIOTIC*.
HEY!
I'M PRACTICING TO MAKE THE MOST OF IT IN CASE I EVER REALLY GET HURT.
REALLY?
THAT RE-QUIRES PRAC-TICE?
HMM... THE GUARDS ARE STILL CHASING THOSE GUYS.
Graah! Graah!
YOU REALLY THINK THEY'LL ESCAPE?
I'M SURE OF IT! THEY'RE TOUGH AND FAST AND THEY HAVE FRIENDS.
Not that I care...!
THE GUARDS WOULD JUST CATCH THEM...
...BUT I WANNA *MURDER* 'EM!

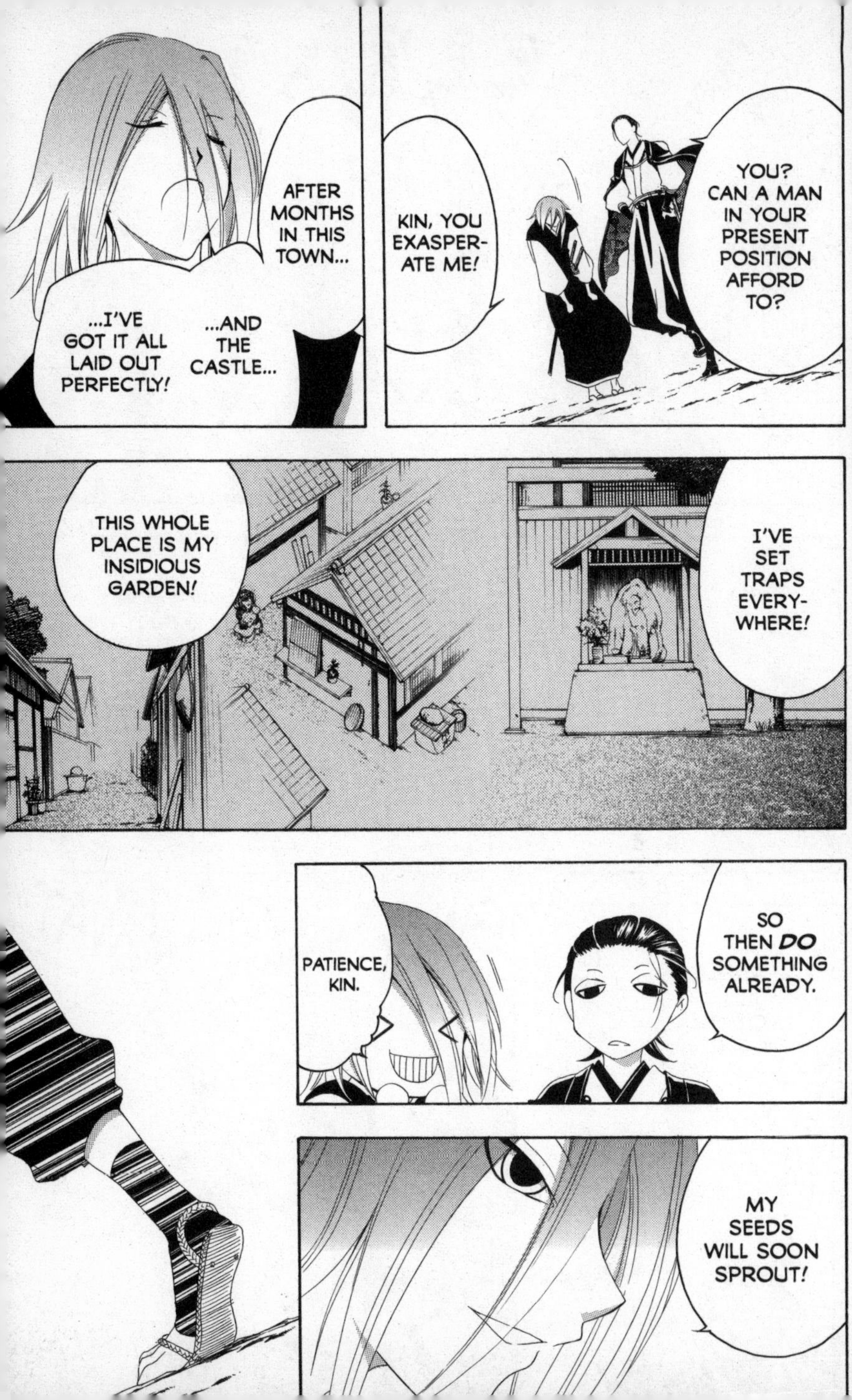
YOU? CAN A MAN IN YOUR PRESENT POSITION AFFORD TO?
KIN, YOU EXASPERATE ME!
AFTER MONTHS IN THIS TOWN...
...AND THE CASTLE...
...I'VE GOT IT ALL LAID OUT PERFECTLY!
I'VE SET TRAPS EVERYWHERE!
THIS WHOLE PLACE IS MY INSIDIOUS GARDEN!
SO THEN *DO* SOMETHING ALREADY.
PATIENCE, KIN.
MY SEEDS WILL SOON SPROUT!

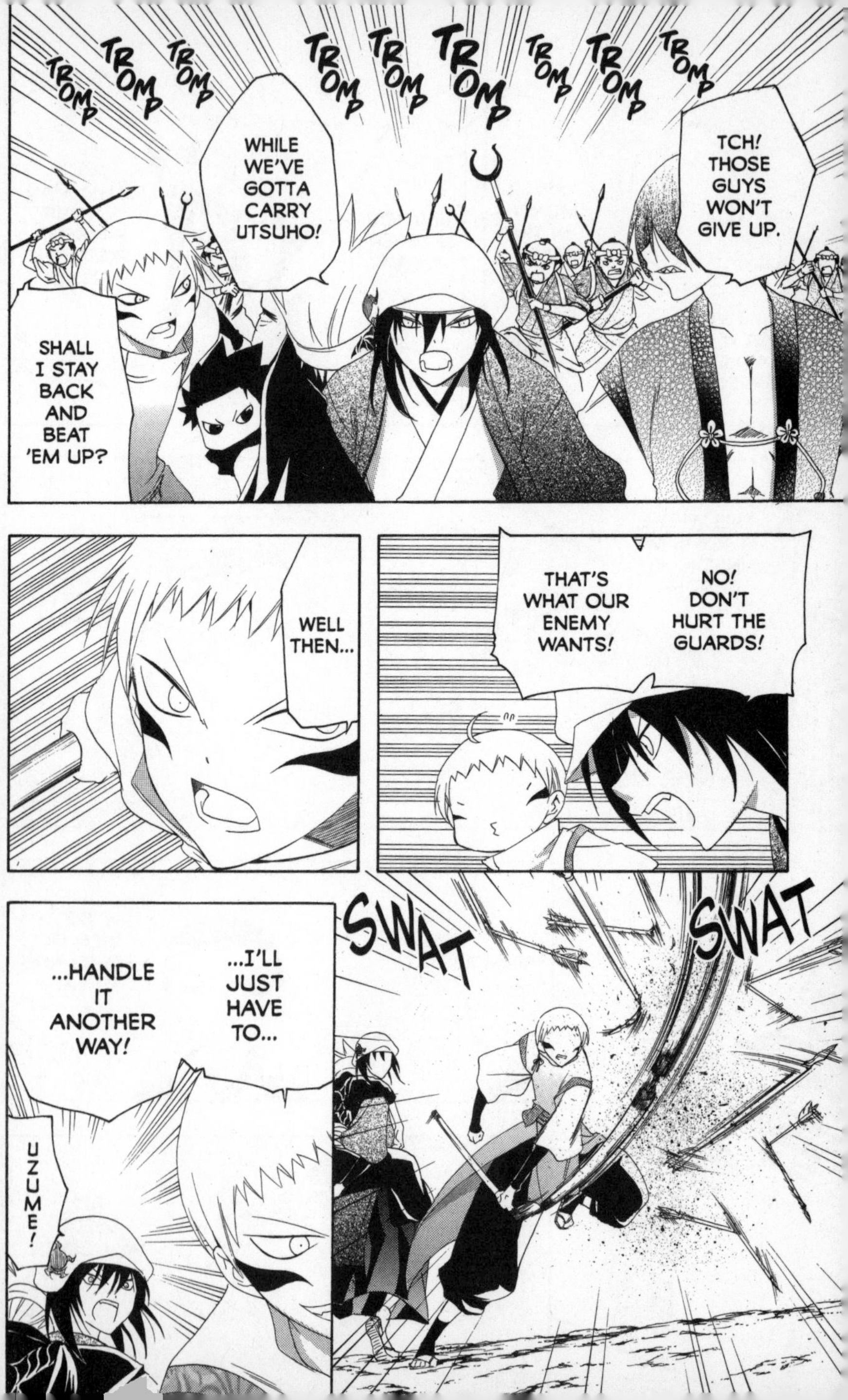
TROMP TROMP TROMP TROMP TROMP TROMP
TROMP TROMP TROMP
TCH! THOSE GUYS WON'T GIVE UP.
WHILE WE'VE GOTTA CARRY UTSUHO!
SHALL I STAY BACK AND BEAT 'EM UP?
NO! DON'T HURT THE GUARDS!
THAT'S WHAT OUR ENEMY WANTS!
WELL THEN...
SWAT
SWAT
...I'LL JUST HAVE TO...
...HANDLE IT ANOTHER WAY!
UZUME!

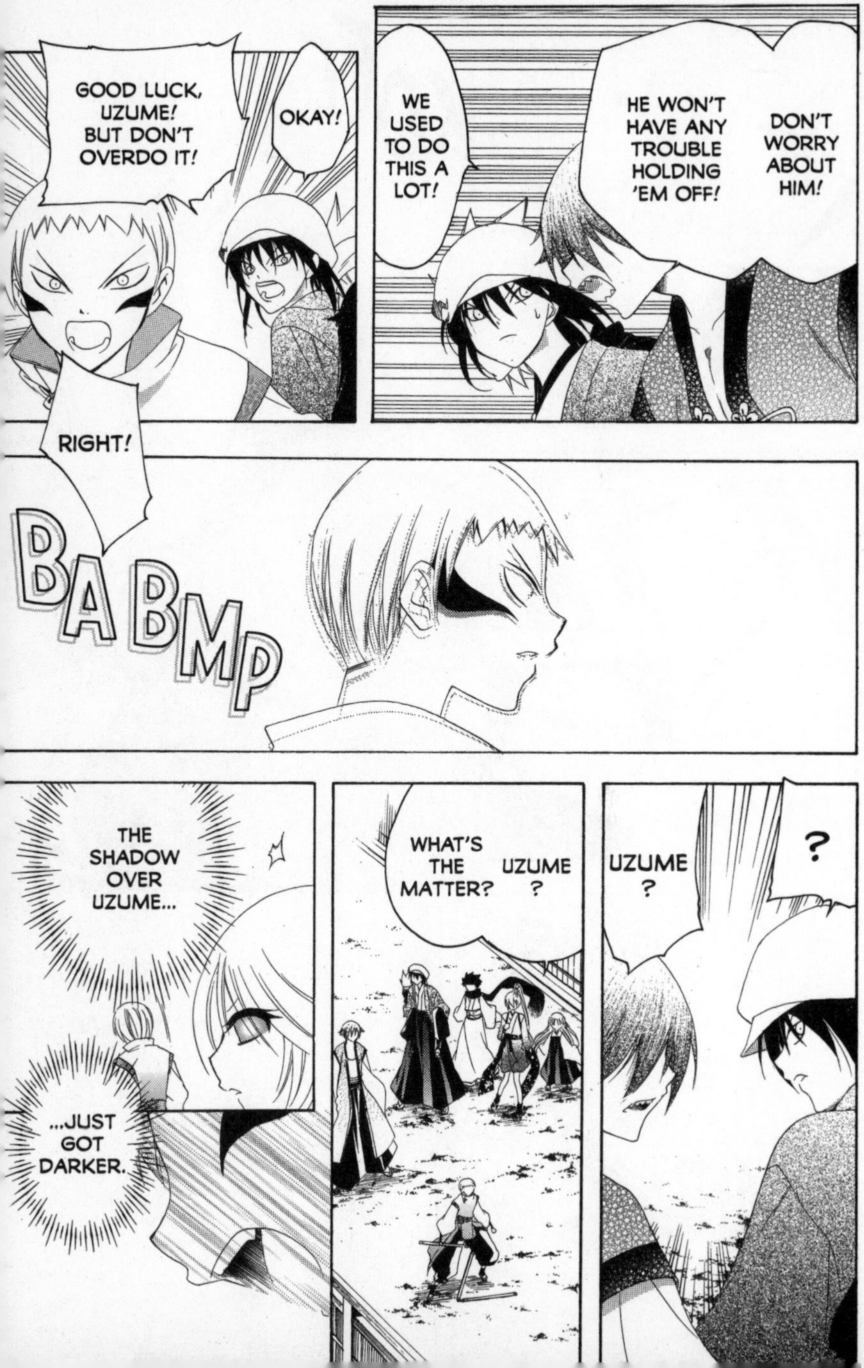
DON'T WORRY ABOUT HIM!
HE WON'T HAVE ANY TROUBLE HOLDING 'EM OFF!
WE USED TO DO THIS A LOT!
OKAY!
GOOD LUCK, UZUME! BUT DON'T OVERDO IT!
RIGHT!
BABMP
?
UZUME ?
UZUME ?
WHAT'S THE MATTER?
THE SHADOW OVER UZUME...
...JUST GOT DARKER.

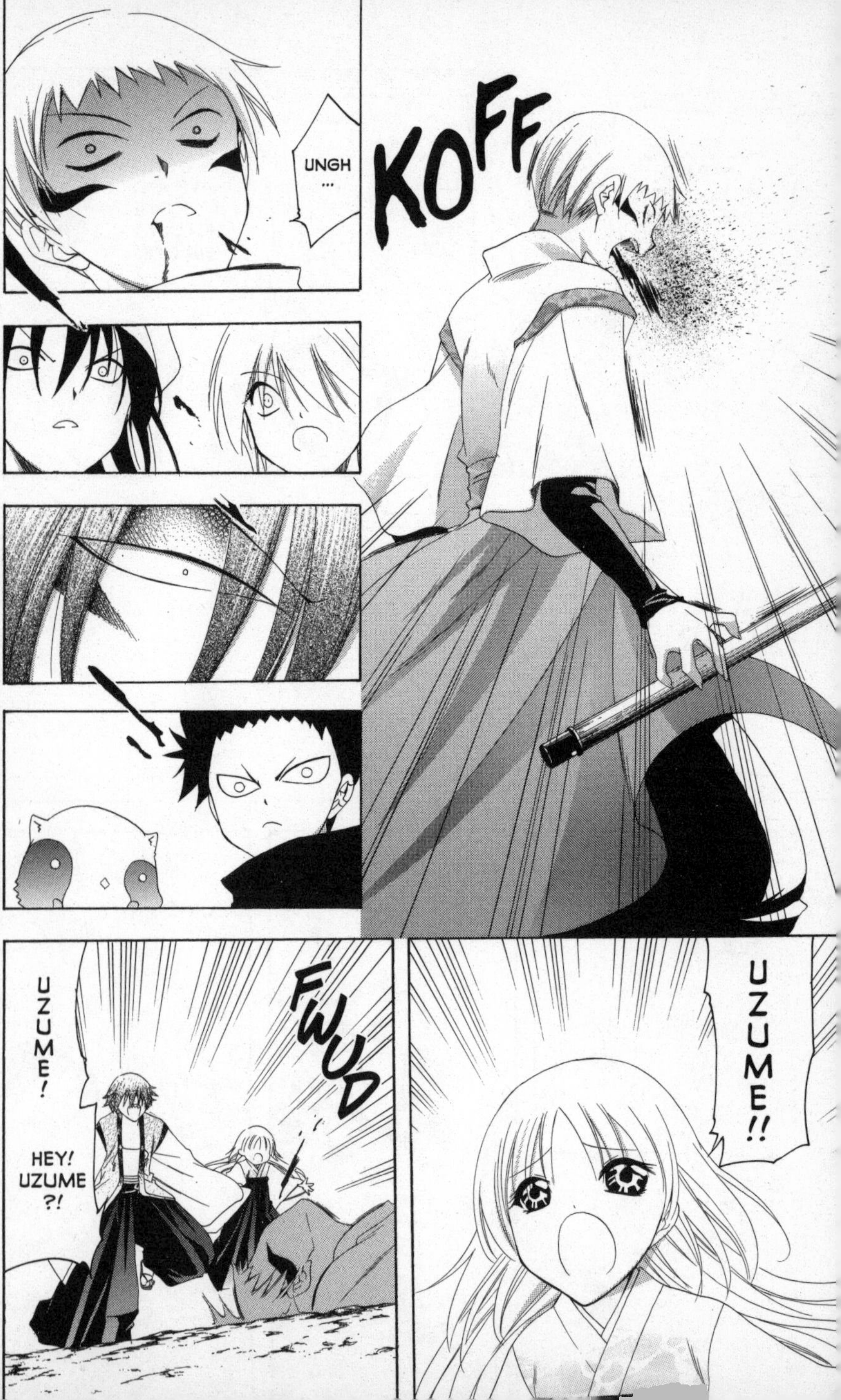
KOFF
UNGH ...
UZUME!!
FWUD
UZUME!
HEY! UZUME ?!

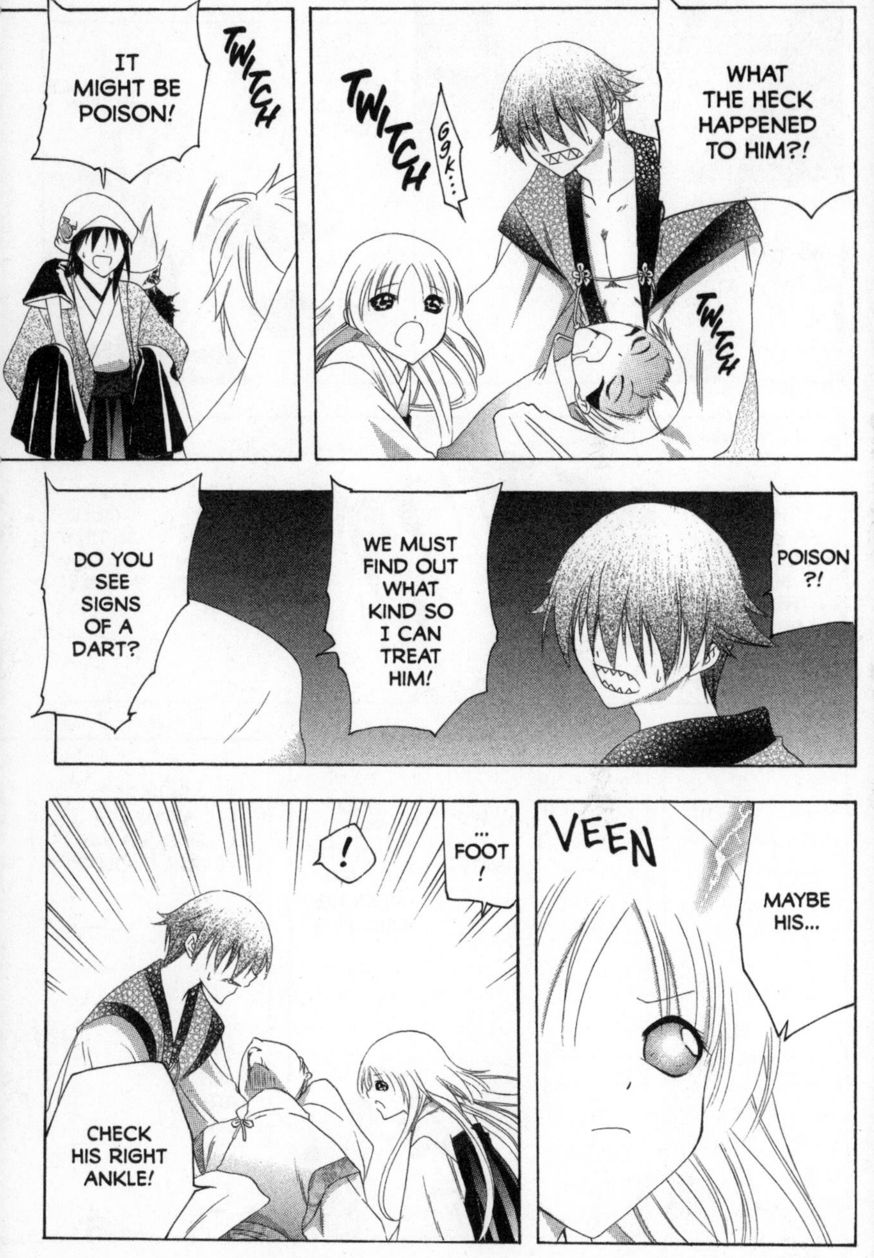
WHAT THE HECK HAPPENED TO HIM?!
TWITCH
Ggk...
TWITCH
IT MIGHT BE POISON!
TWITCH
POISON?!
WE MUST FIND OUT WHAT KIND SO I CAN TREAT HIM!
DO YOU SEE SIGNS OF A DART?
VEEN
MAYBE HIS...
...FOOT!
!
CHECK HIS RIGHT ANKLE!

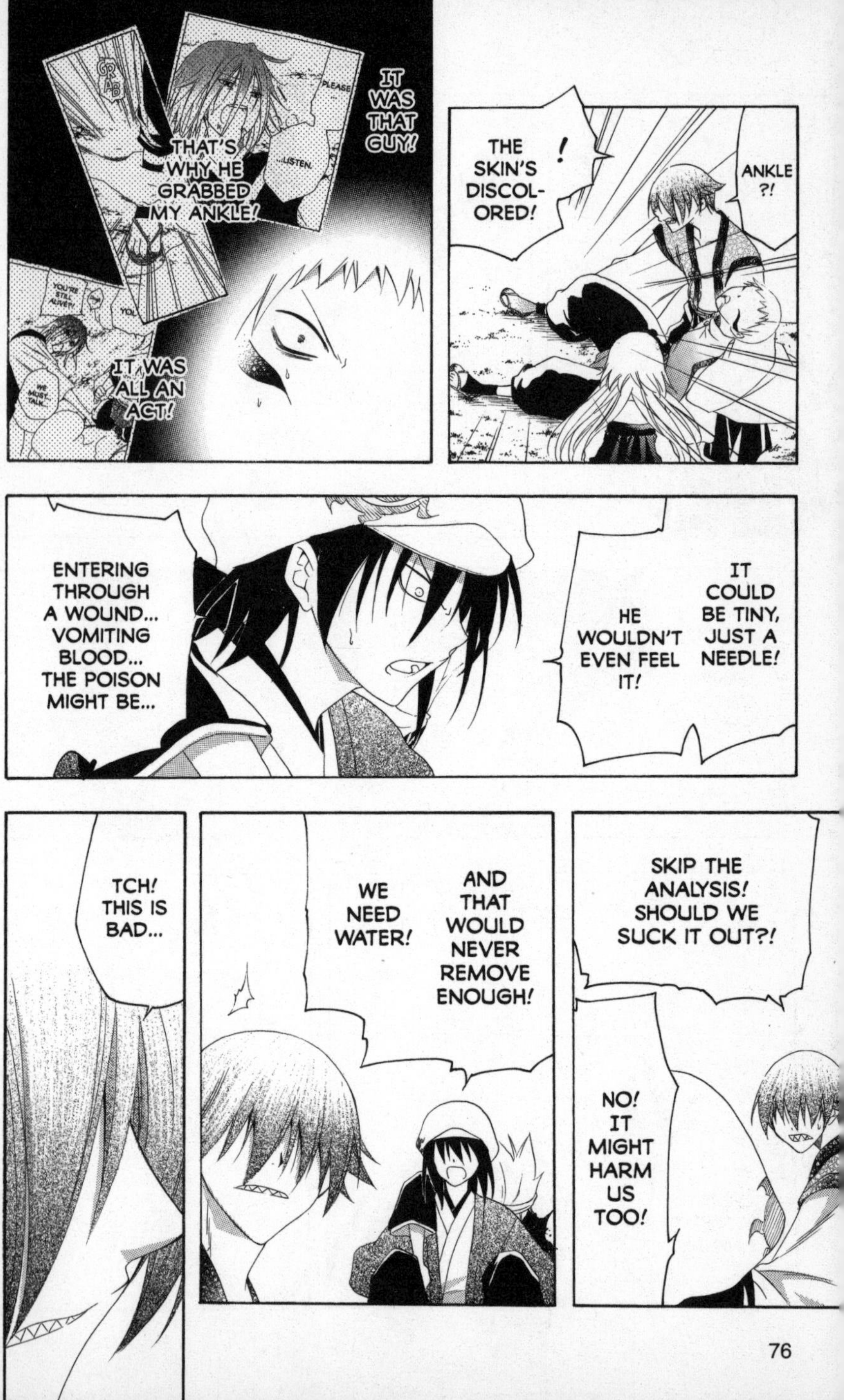
ANKLE ?!
!
THE SKIN'S DISCOL-ORED!
IT WAS THAT GUY!
PLEASE
...LISTEN.
GRAB
THAT'S WHY HE GRABBED MY ANKLE!
YOU'RE STILL ALIVE?!
YOU
WE MUST... TALK...
IT WAS ALL AN ACT!
IT COULD BE TINY, JUST A NEEDLE!
HE WOULDN'T EVEN FEEL IT!
ENTERING THROUGH A WOUND... VOMITING BLOOD... THE POISON MIGHT BE...
SKIP THE ANALYSIS! SHOULD WE SUCK IT OUT?!
NO! IT MIGHT HARM US TOO!
AND THAT WOULD NEVER REMOVE ENOUGH!
WE NEED WATER!
TCH! THIS IS BAD...

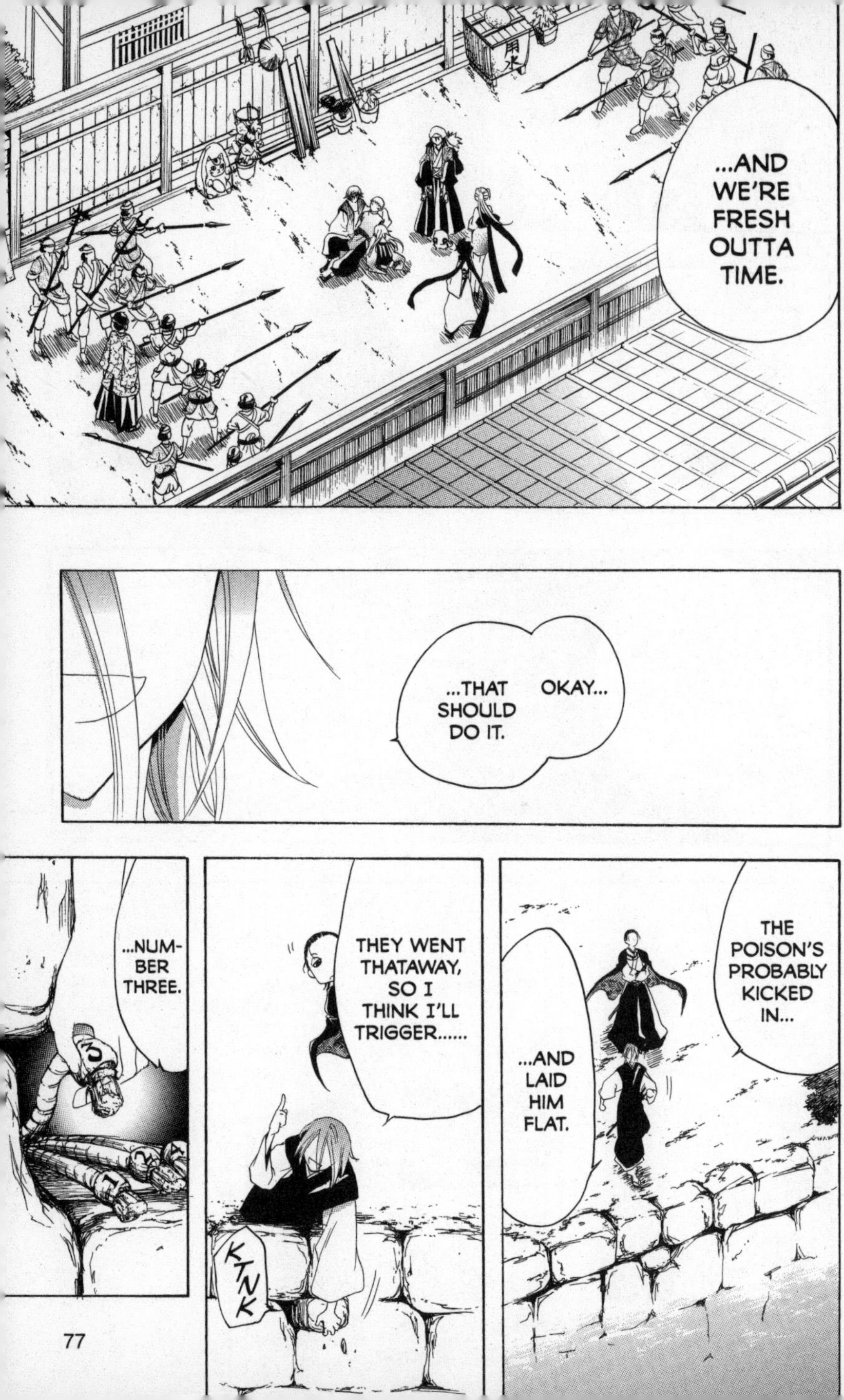
...AND WE'RE FRESH OUTTA TIME.
OKAY...
...THAT SHOULD DO IT.
THE POISON'S PROBABLY KICKED IN...
...AND LAID HIM FLAT.
THEY WENT THATAWAY, SO I THINK I'LL TRIGGER......
KTNK
...NUMBER THREE.

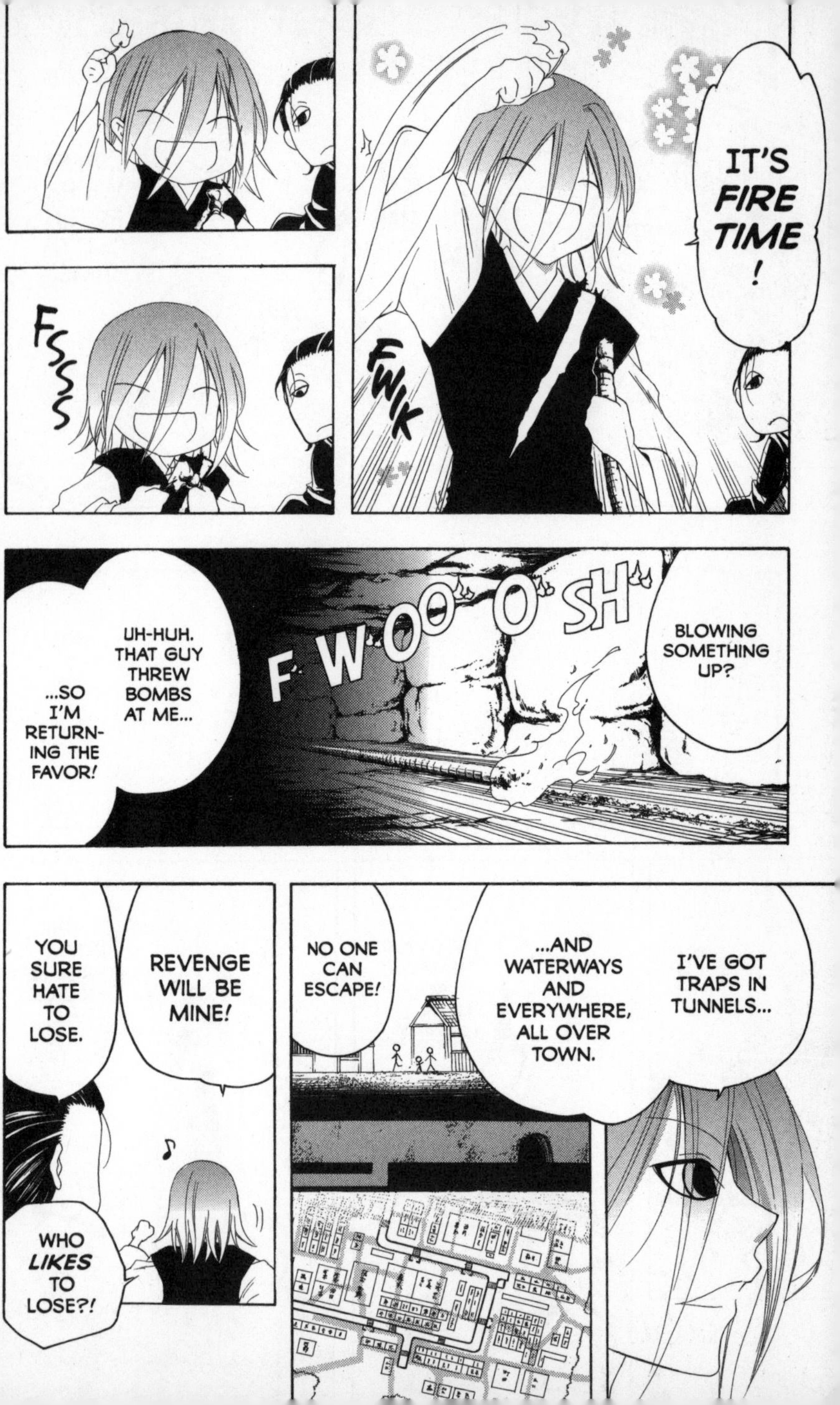
IT'S FIRE TIME!
FWIK
FSSS
BLOWING SOMETHING UP?
FWOOOOSH
UH-HUH. THAT GUY THREW BOMBS AT ME...
...SO I'M RETURNING THE FAVOR!
I'VE GOT TRAPS IN TUNNELS...
...AND WATERWAYS AND EVERYWHERE, ALL OVER TOWN.
NO ONE CAN ESCAPE!
REVENGE WILL BE MINE!
YOU SURE HATE TO LOSE.
WHO LIKES TO LOSE?!

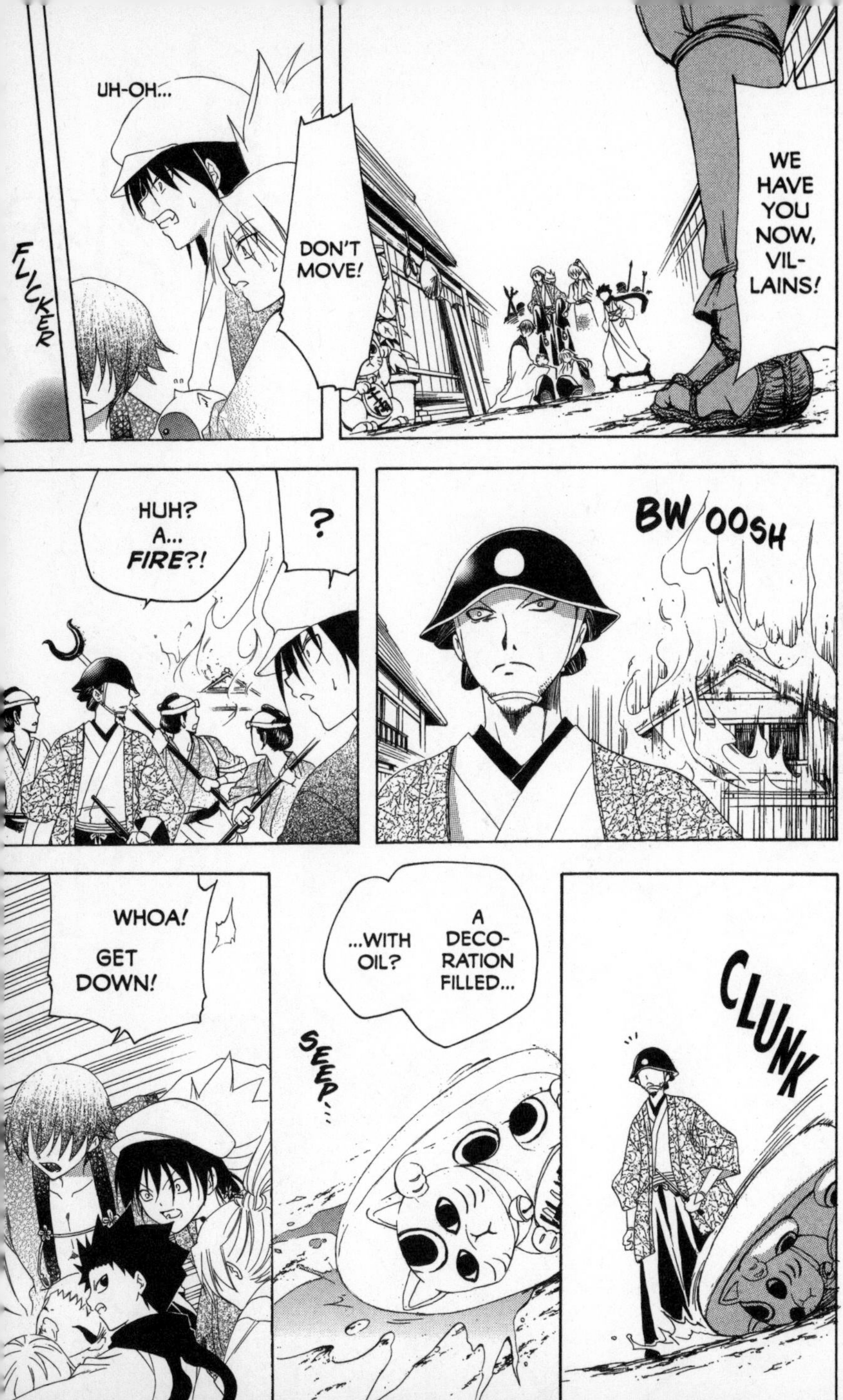

WE HAVE YOU NOW, VIL-LAINS!
DON'T MOVE!
UH-OH...
FLICKER
BWOOSH
?
HUH? A... *FIRE*?!
CLUNK
A DECO-RATION FILLED...
...WITH OIL?
SEEP...
WHOA!
GET DOWN!

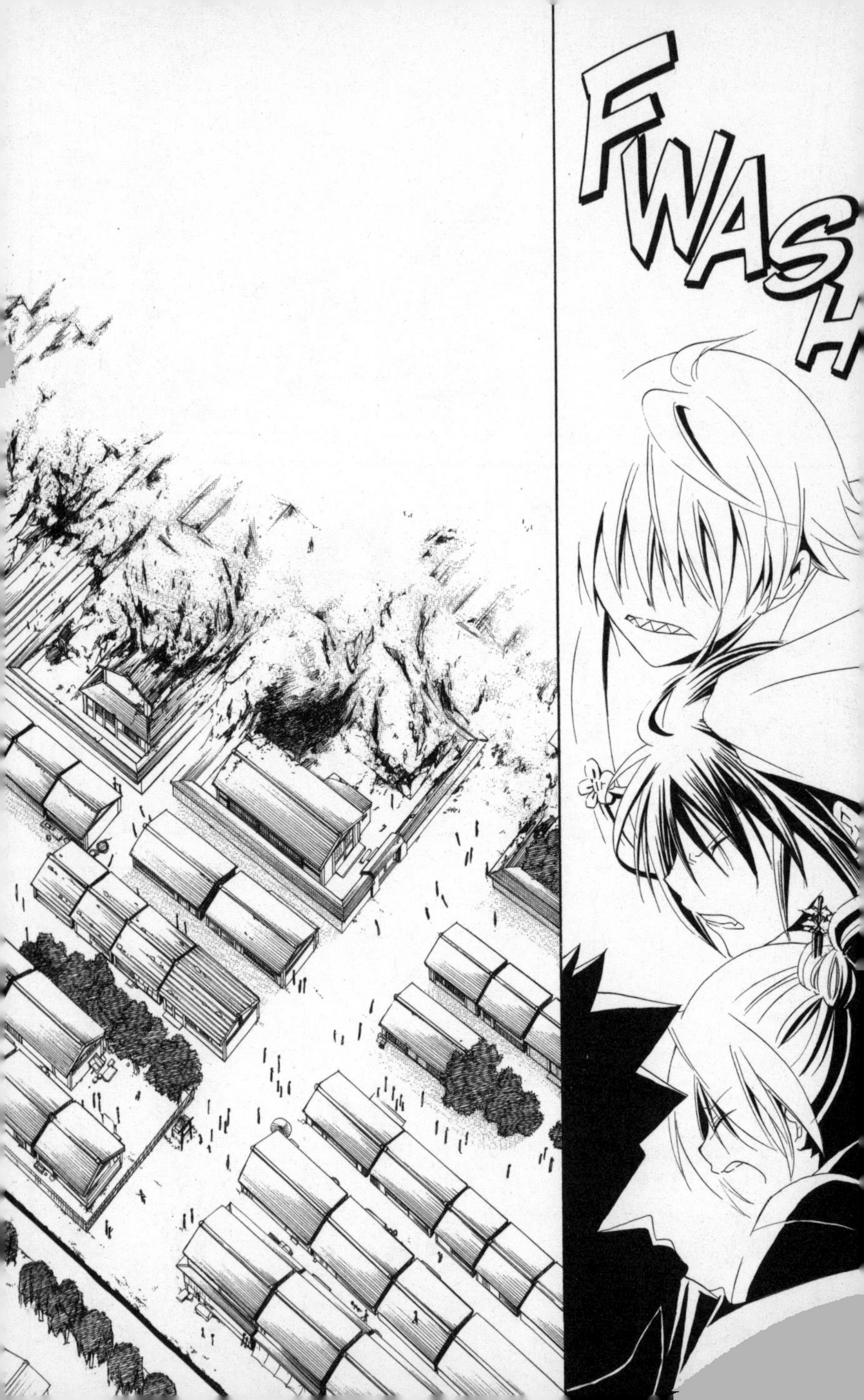
FWASH

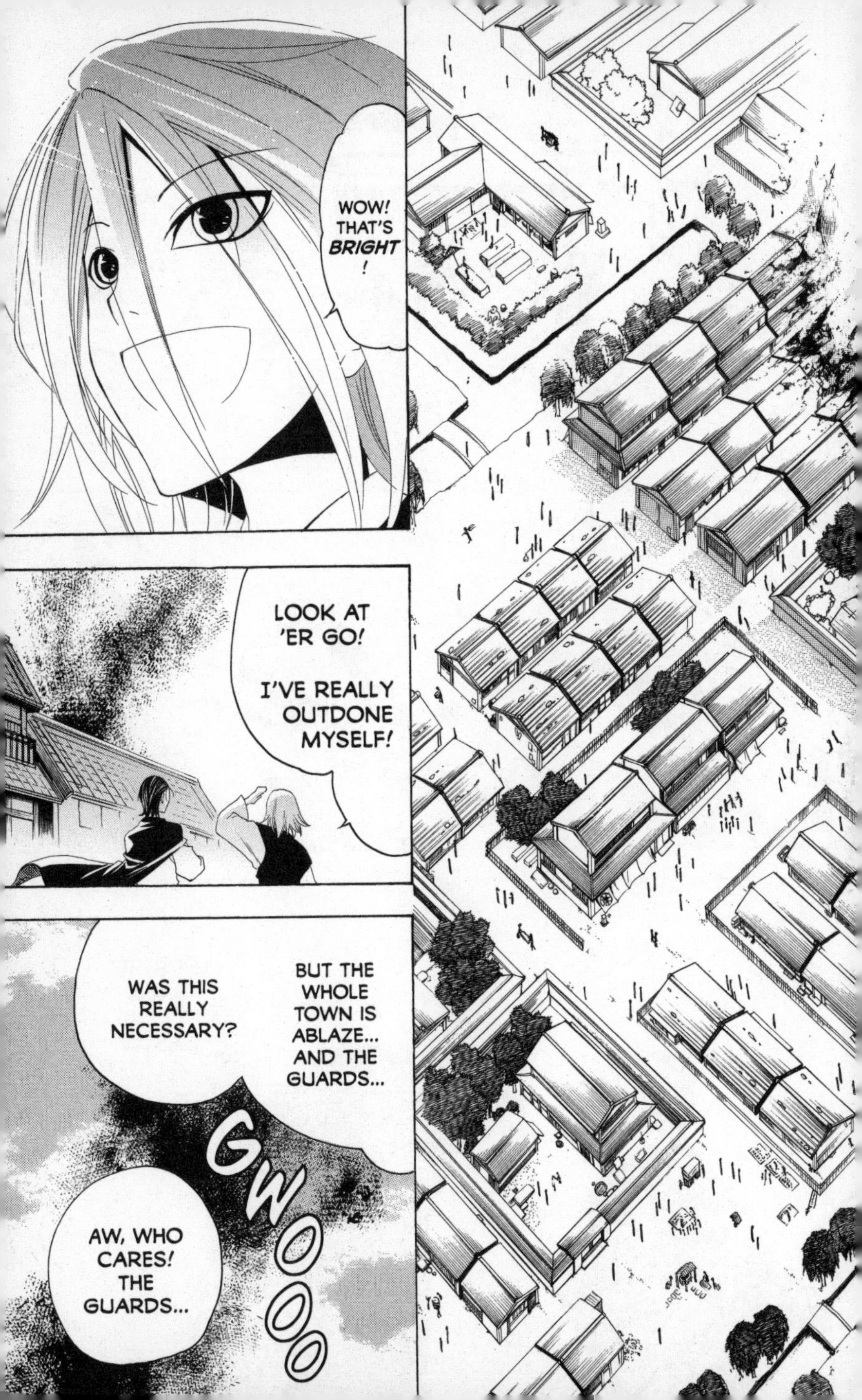
WOW! THAT'S BRIGHT!
LOOK AT 'ER GO!
I'VE REALLY OUTDONE MYSELF!
BUT THE WHOLE TOWN IS ABLAZE... AND THE GUARDS...
WAS THIS REALLY NECESSARY?
GWOOO
AW, WHO CARES! THE GUARDS...

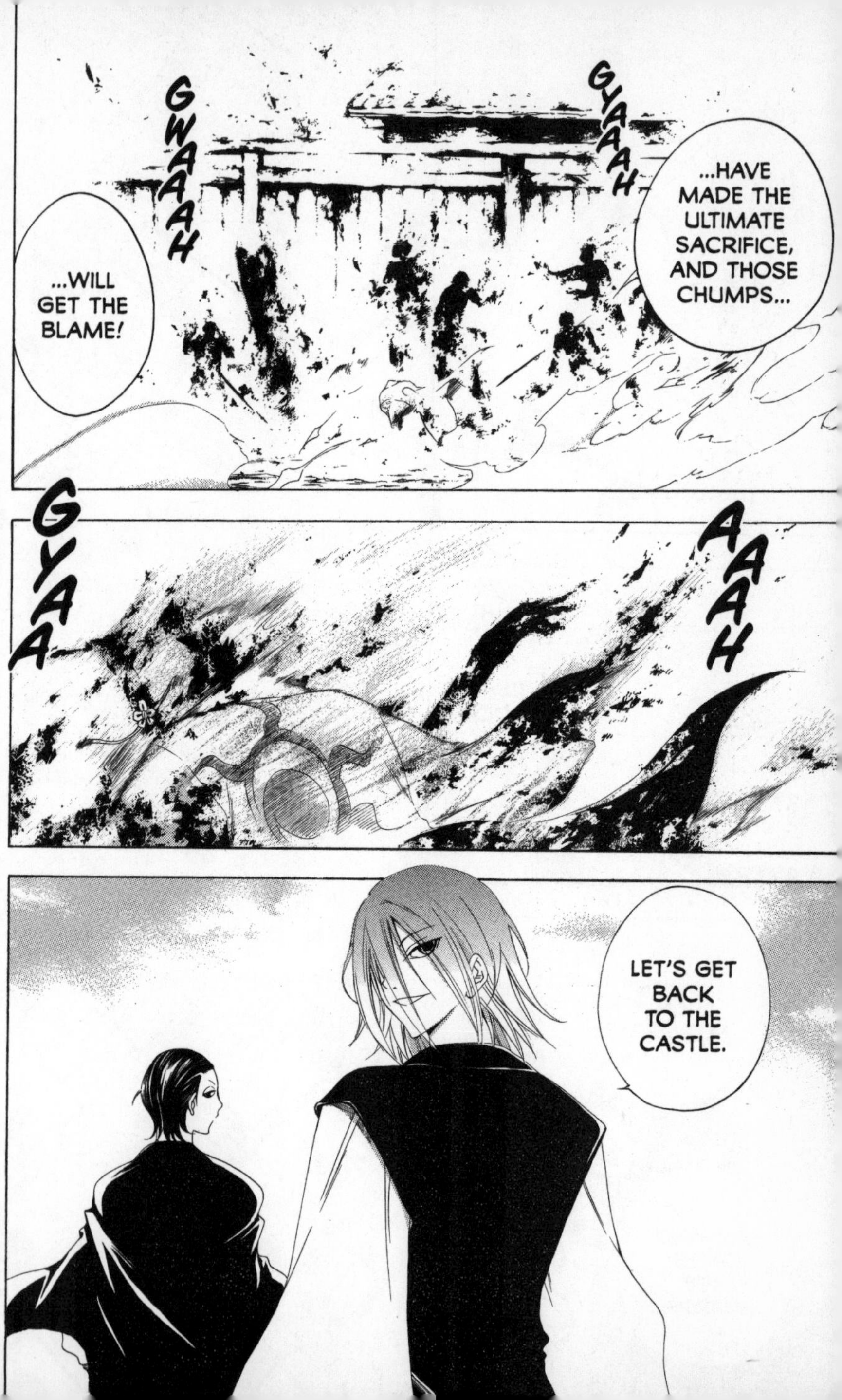
GYAAAH
...HAVE MADE THE ULTIMATE SACRIFICE, AND THOSE CHUMPS...
GWAAAH
...WILL GET THE BLAME!
GYAAA
AAAH
LET'S GET BACK TO THE CASTLE.

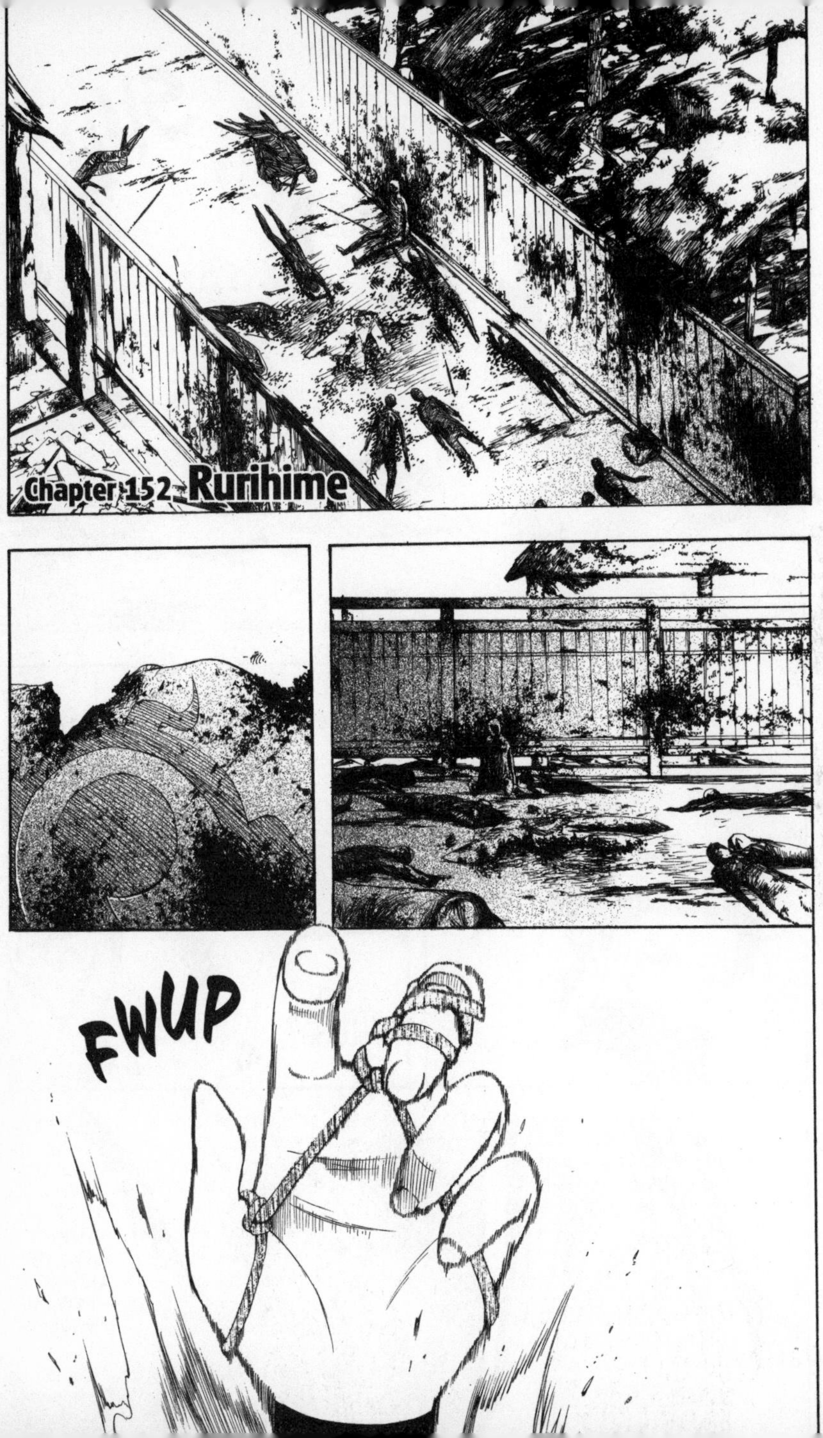
Chapter 152 Rurihime
FWUP

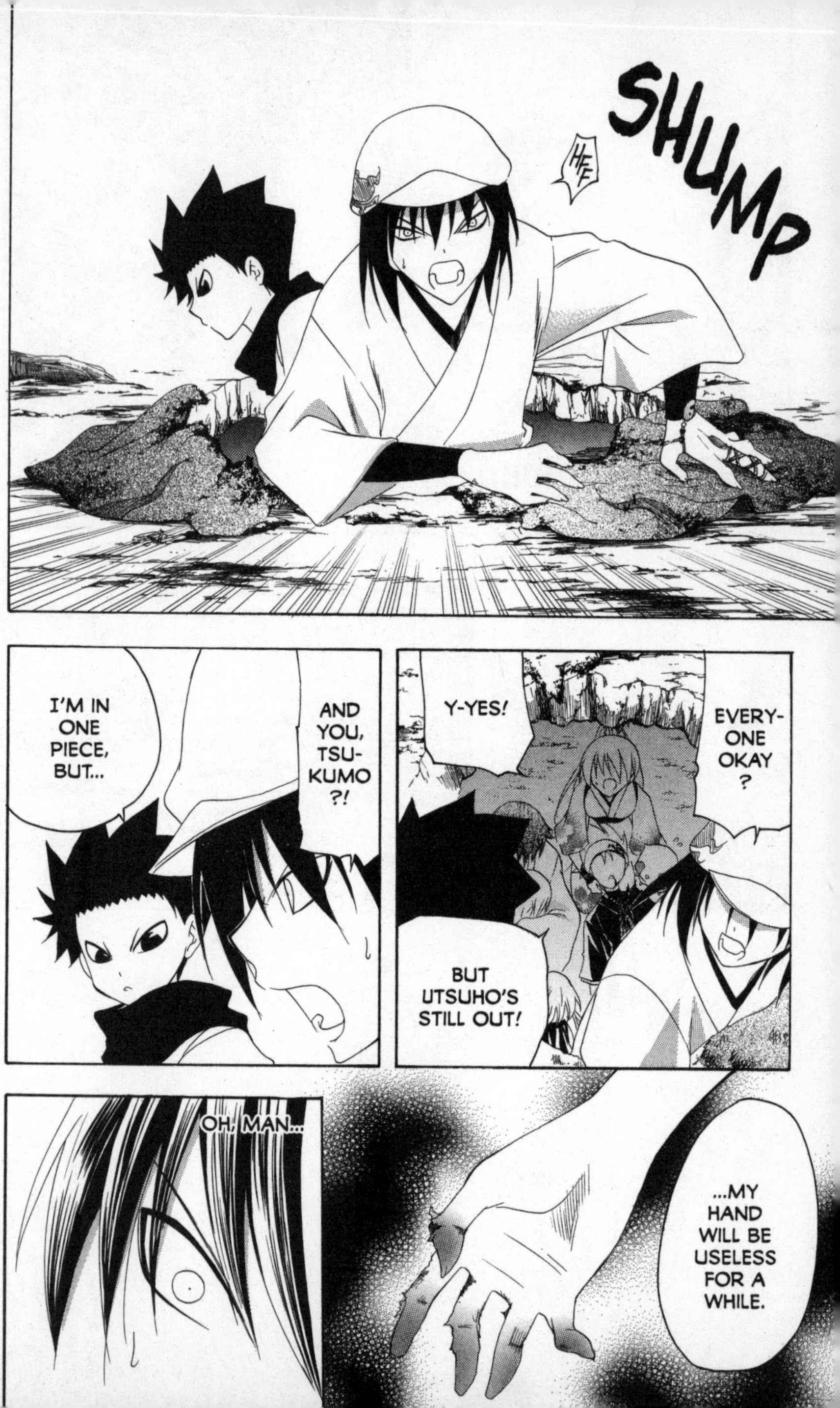
SHUMP
HEF
EVERY-ONE OKAY?
Y-YES!
BUT UTSUHO'S STILL OUT!
AND YOU, TSU-KUMO?!
I'M IN ONE PIECE, BUT...
...MY HAND WILL BE USELESS FOR A WHILE.
OH, MAN...

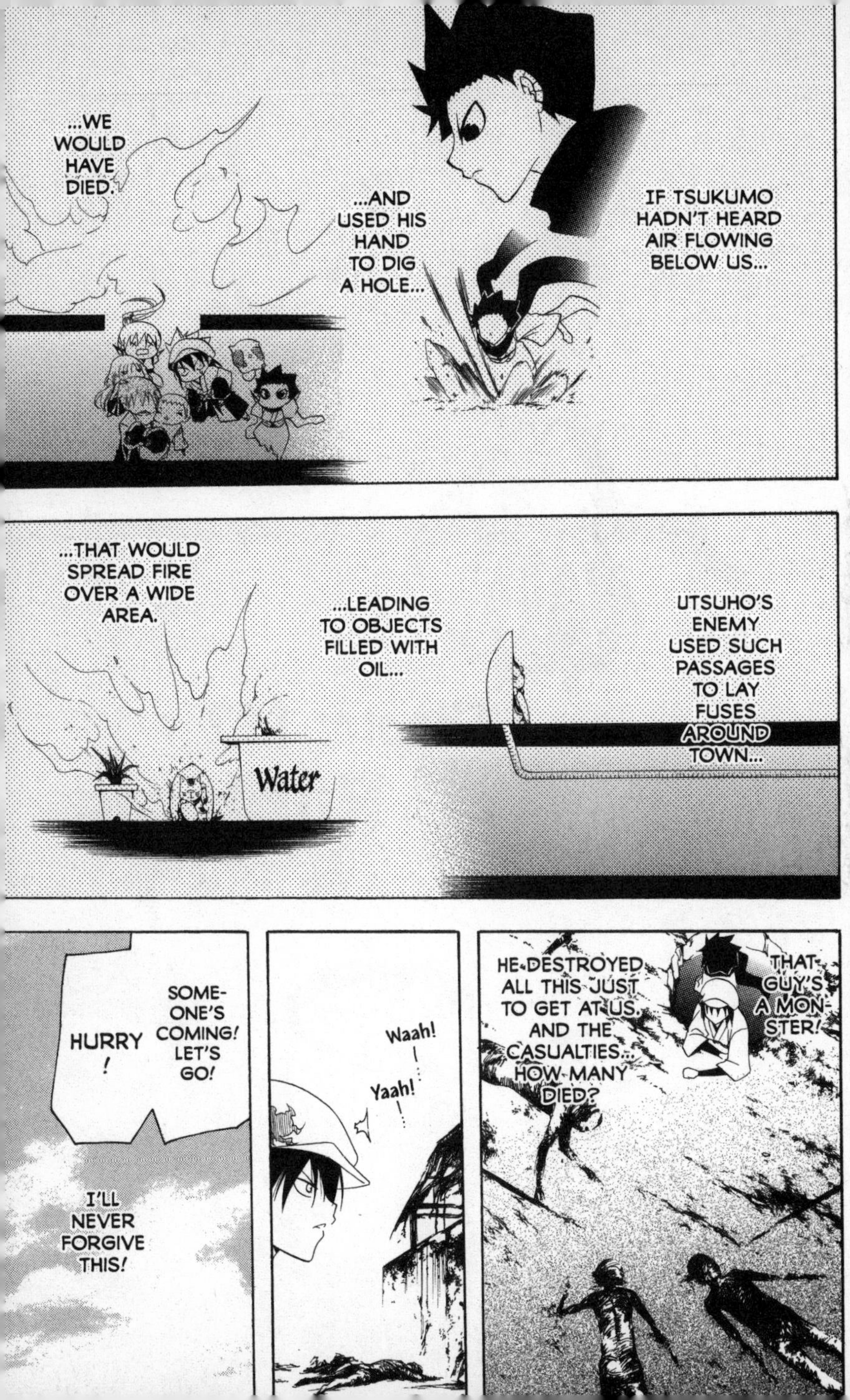
IF TSUKUMO HADN'T HEARD AIR FLOWING BELOW US...
...AND USED HIS HAND TO DIG A HOLE...
...WE WOULD HAVE DIED.
UTSUHO'S ENEMY USED SUCH PASSAGES TO LAY FUSES AROUND TOWN...
...LEADING TO OBJECTS FILLED WITH OIL...
...THAT WOULD SPREAD FIRE OVER A WIDE AREA.
Water
THAT GUY'S A MONSTER!
HE DESTROYED ALL THIS JUST TO GET AT US. AND THE CASUALTIES... HOW MANY DIED?
Waah!
Yaah!
SOME-ONE'S COMING! LET'S GO!
HURRY!
I'LL NEVER FORGIVE THIS!

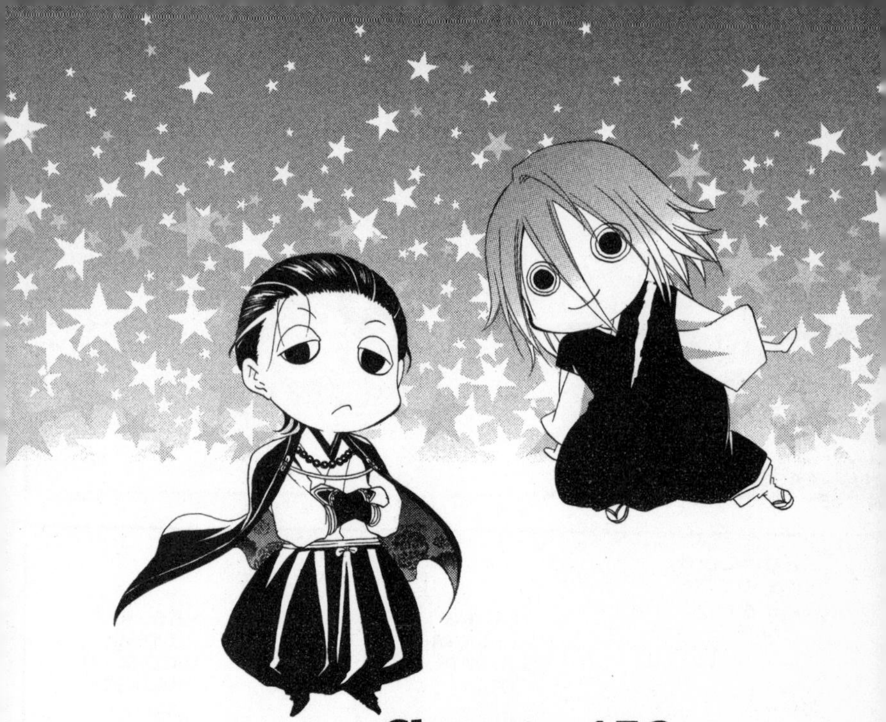

Chapter 152
Rurihime

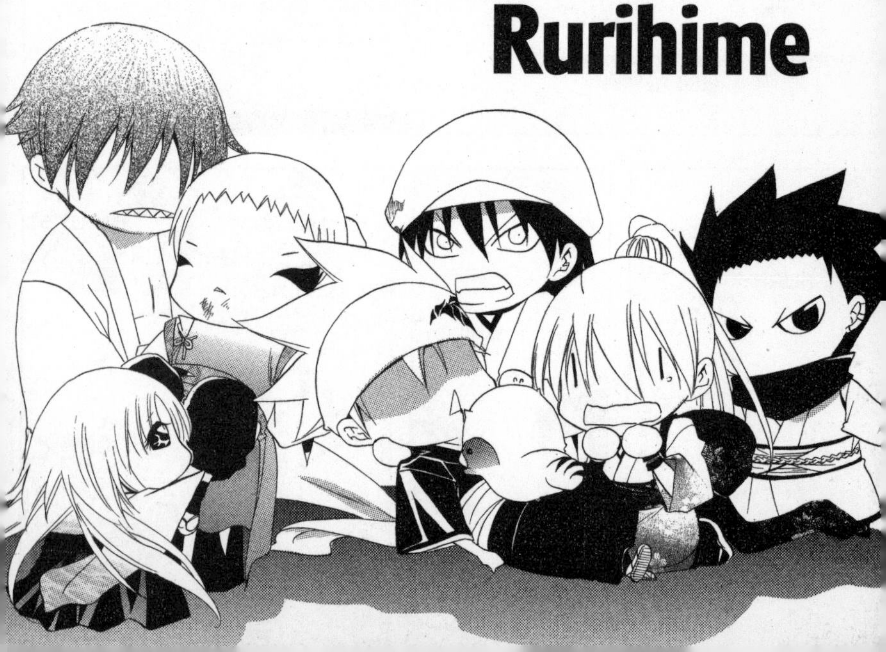

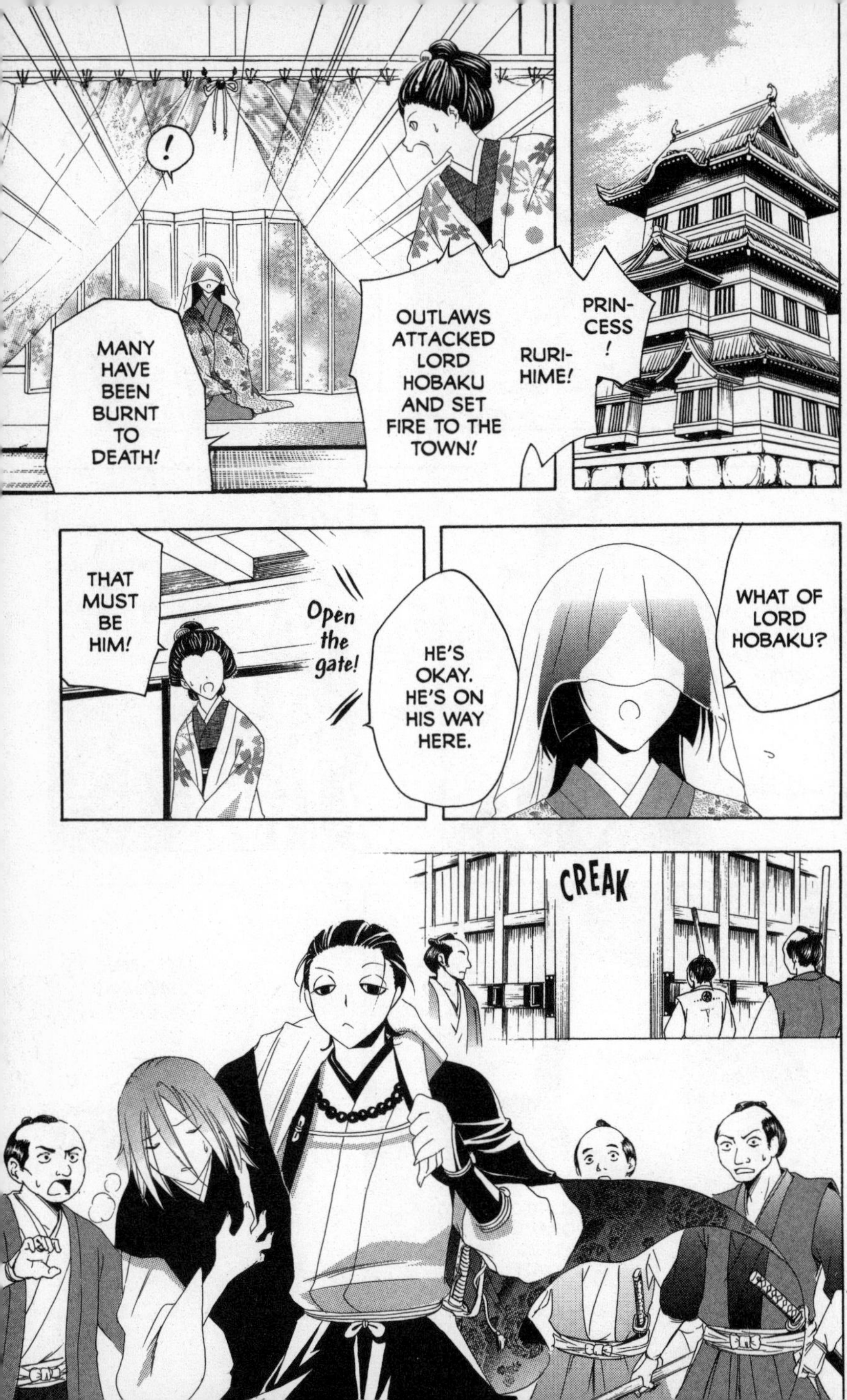
PRIN-CESS!
RURI-HIME!
OUTLAWS ATTACKED LORD HOBAKU AND SET FIRE TO THE TOWN!
!
MANY HAVE BEEN BURNT TO DEATH!
WHAT OF LORD HOBAKU?
HE'S OKAY. HE'S ON HIS WAY HERE.
Open the gate!
THAT MUST BE HIM!
CREAK

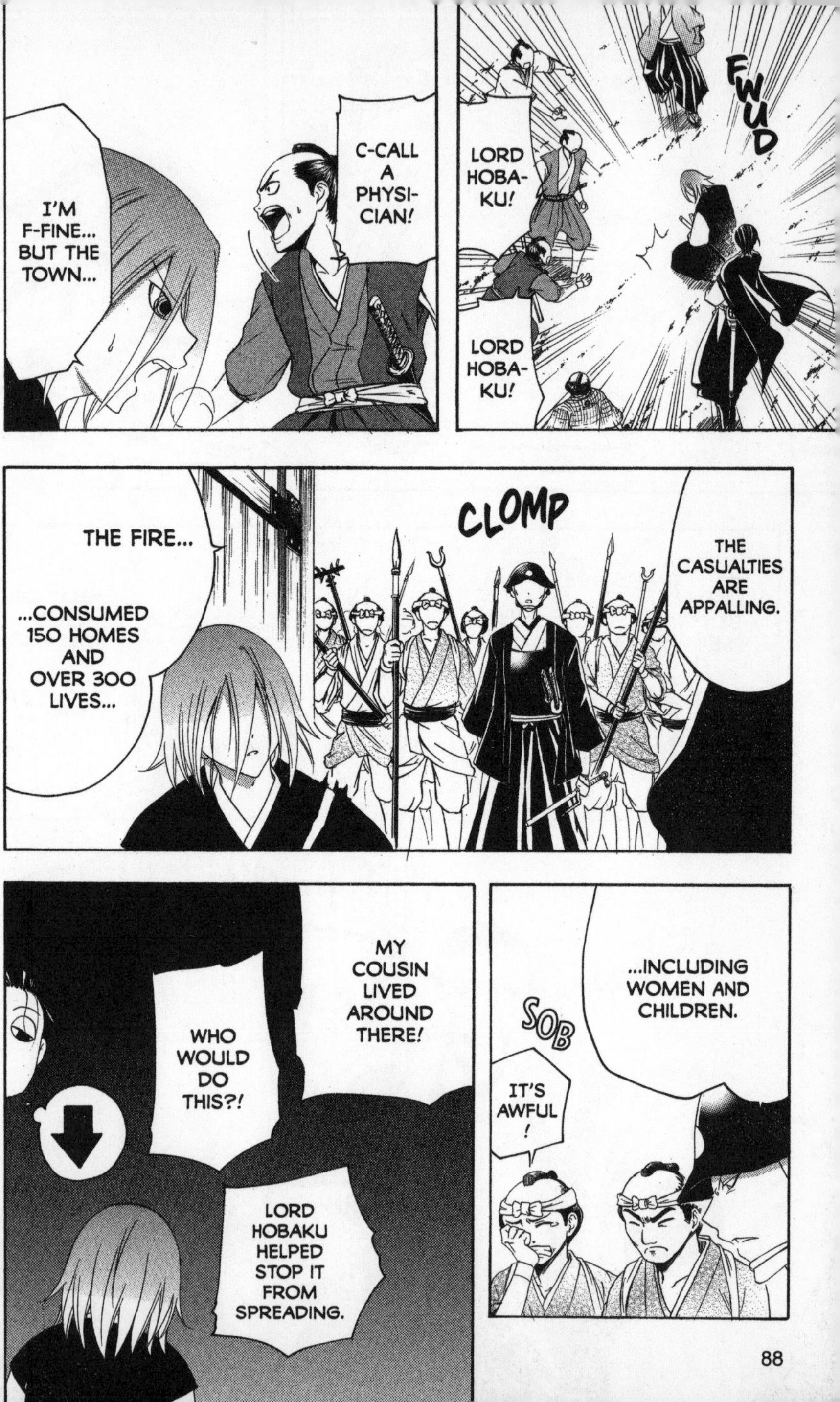
FWUD
LORD HOBAKU!
LORD HOBAKU!
C-CALL A PHYSICIAN!
I'M F-FINE... BUT THE TOWN...
THE CASUALTIES ARE APPALLING.
CLOMP
THE FIRE...
...CONSUMED 150 HOMES AND OVER 300 LIVES...
...INCLUDING WOMEN AND CHILDREN.
SOB
IT'S AWFUL!
MY COUSIN LIVED AROUND THERE!
WHO WOULD DO THIS?!
LORD HOBAKU HELPED STOP IT FROM SPREADING.

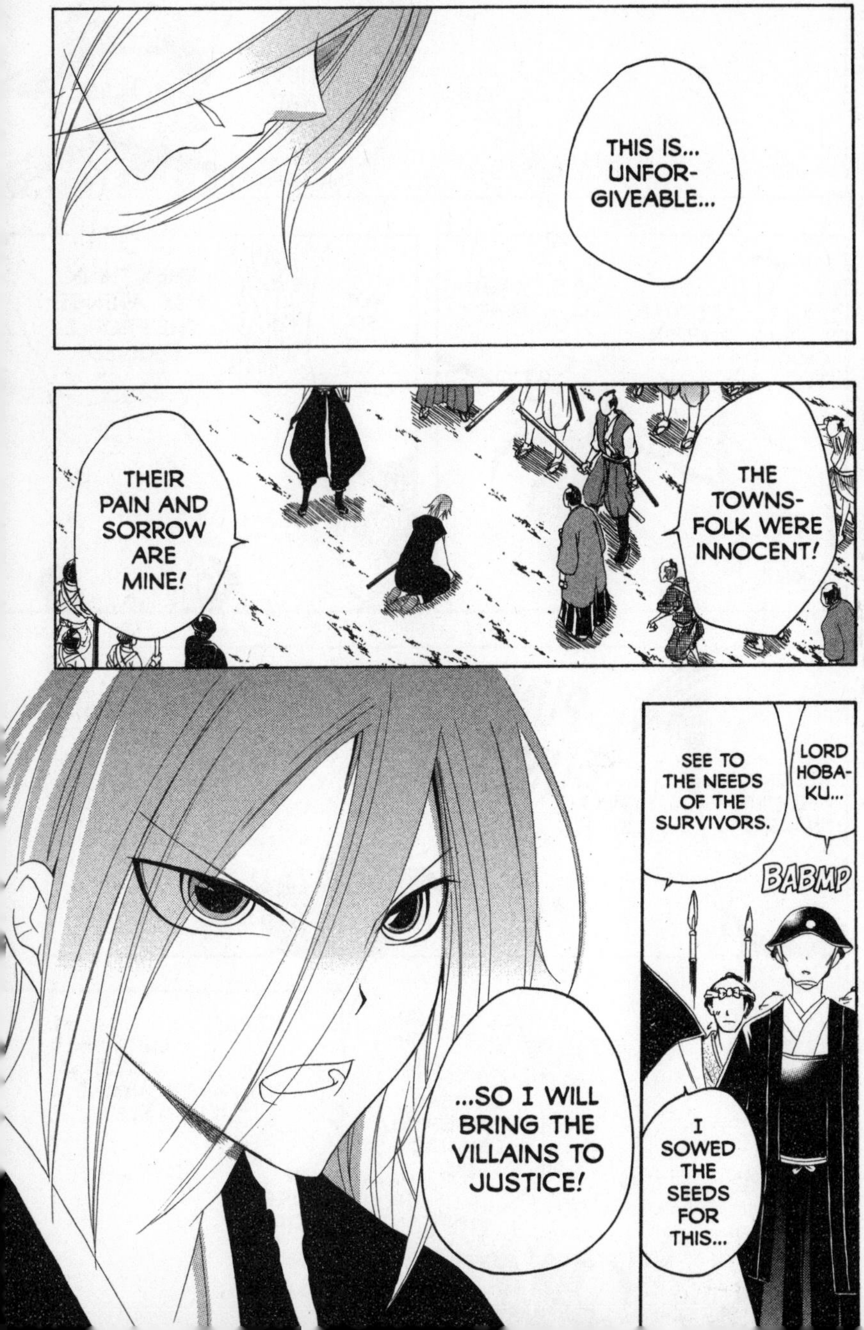
THIS IS... UNFOR-GIVEABLE...
THE TOWNS-FOLK WERE INNOCENT!
THEIR PAIN AND SORROW ARE MINE!
LORD HOBA-KU...
SEE TO THE NEEDS OF THE SURVIVORS.
BABMP
I SOWED THE SEEDS FOR THIS...
...SO I WILL BRING THE VILLAINS TO JUSTICE!

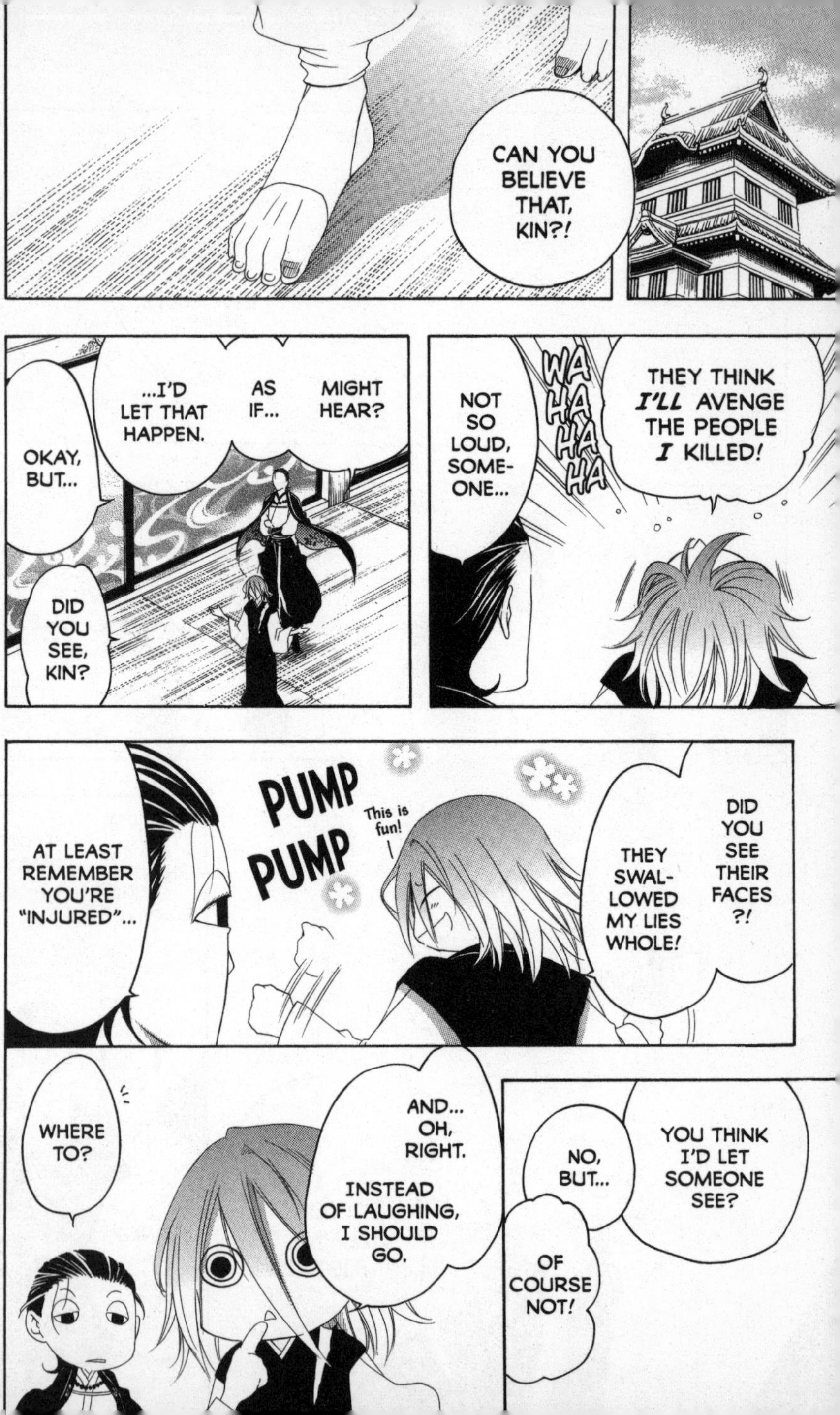
CAN YOU BELIEVE THAT, KIN?!
THEY THINK I'LL AVENGE THE PEOPLE I KILLED!
WAHAHAHAHA
NOT SO LOUD, SOMEONE...
MIGHT HEAR?
AS IF...
...I'D LET THAT HAPPEN.
OKAY, BUT...
DID YOU SEE, KIN?
DID YOU SEE THEIR FACES?!
THEY SWALLOWED MY LIES WHOLE!
This is fun!
PUMP PUMP
AT LEAST REMEMBER YOU'RE "INJURED"...
YOU THINK I'D LET SOMEONE SEE?
NO, BUT...
OF COURSE NOT!
AND... OH, RIGHT.
INSTEAD OF LAUGHING, I SHOULD GO.
WHERE TO?

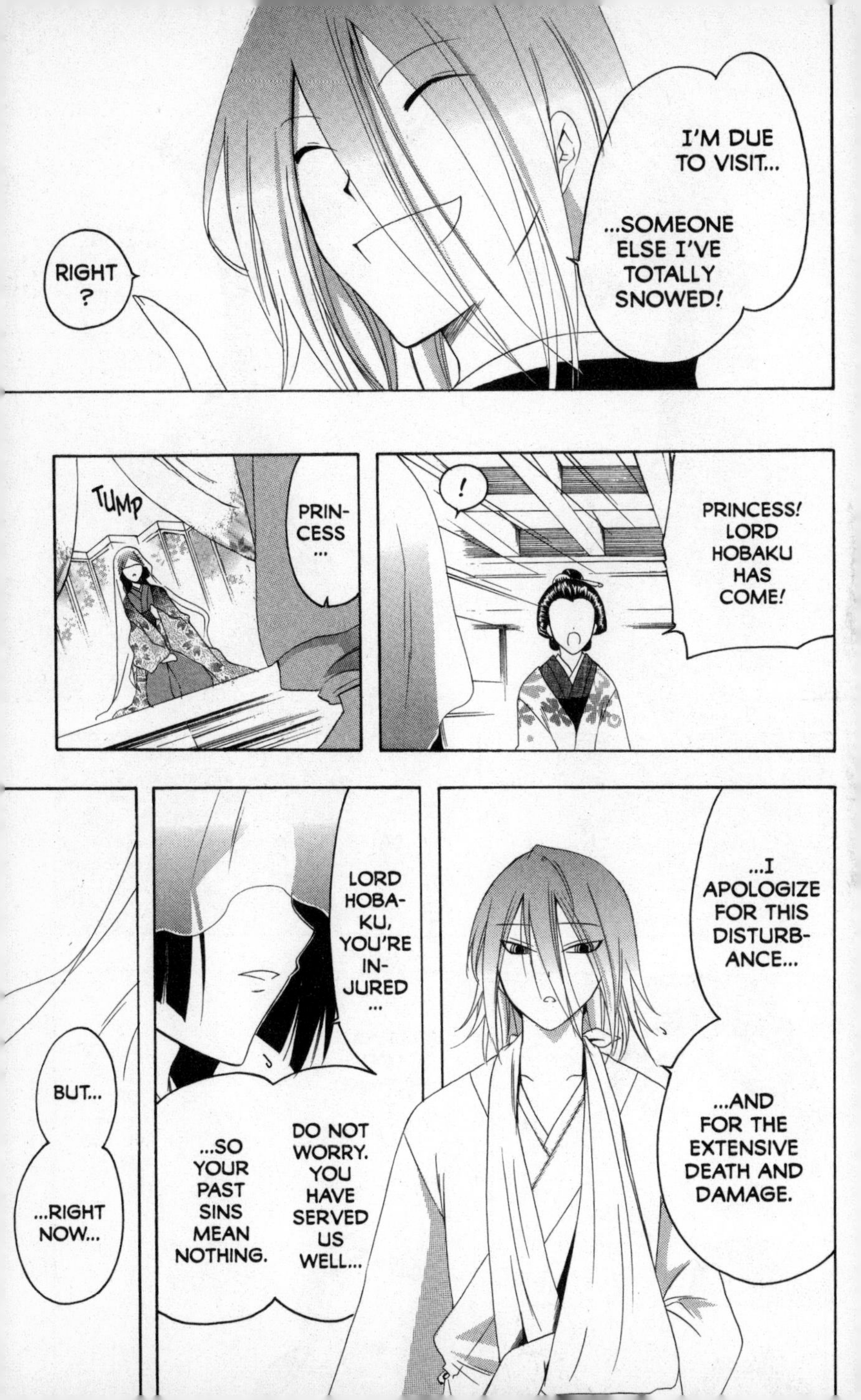
I'M DUE TO VISIT...
...SOMEONE ELSE I'VE TOTALLY SNOWED!
RIGHT?
!
PRINCESS! LORD HOBAKU HAS COME!
PRINCESS...
TUMP
...I APOLOGIZE FOR THIS DISTURBANCE...
...AND FOR THE EXTENSIVE DEATH AND DAMAGE.
LORD HOBAKU, YOU'RE INJURED...
DO NOT WORRY. YOU HAVE SERVED US WELL...
...SO YOUR PAST SINS MEAN NOTHING.
BUT...
...RIGHT NOW...

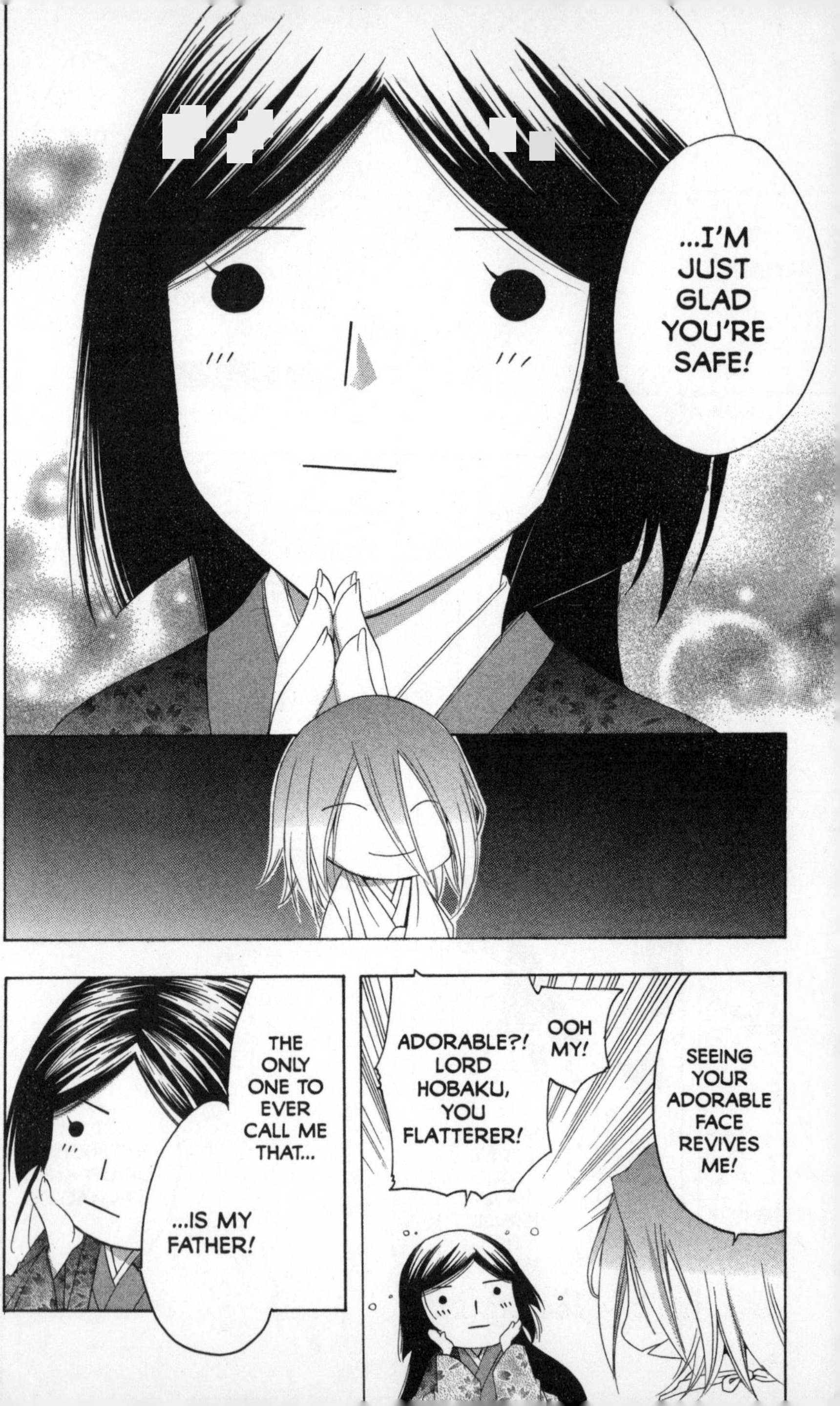
...I'M JUST GLAD YOU'RE SAFE!
SEEING YOUR ADORABLE FACE REVIVES ME!
OOH MY!
ADORABLE?! LORD HOBAKU, YOU FLATTERER!
THE ONLY ONE TO EVER CALL ME THAT...
...IS MY FATHER!

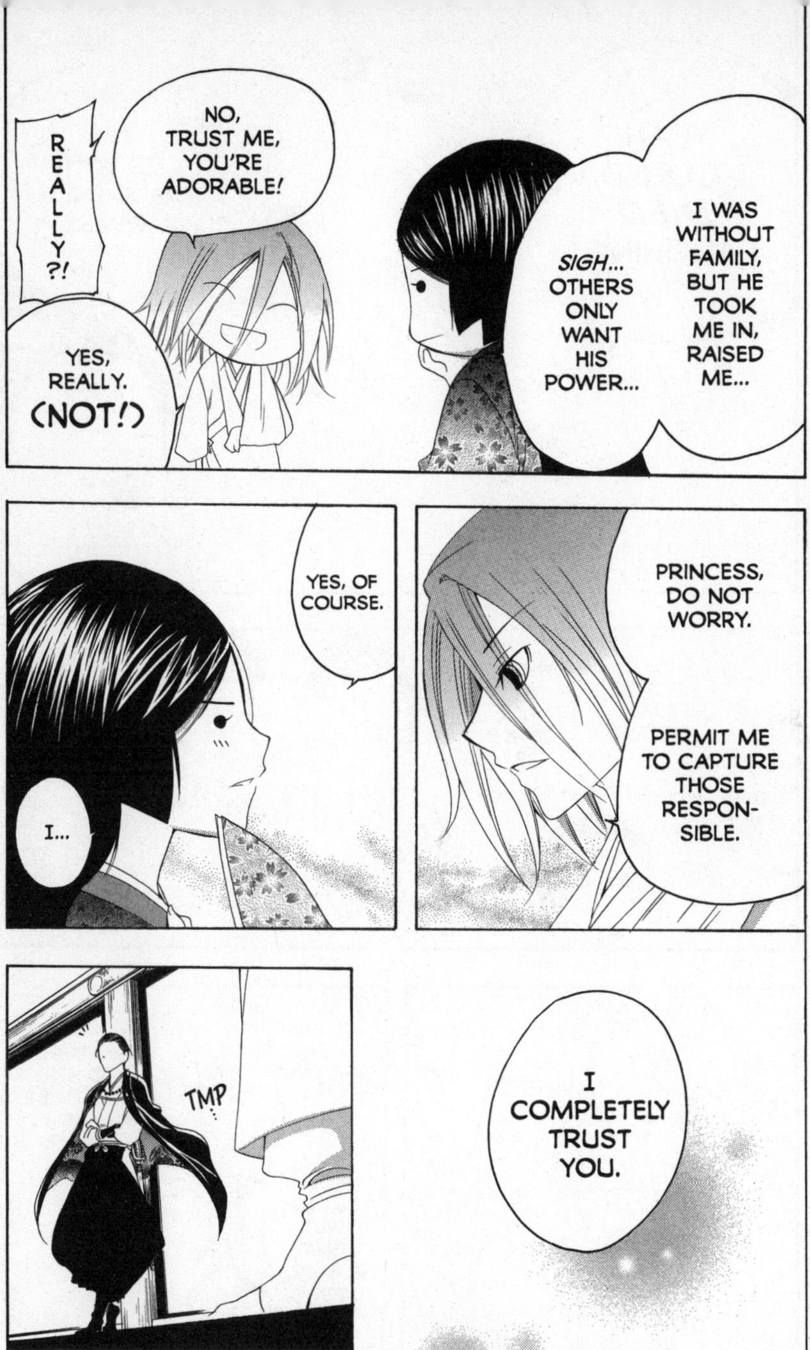
I WAS WITHOUT FAMILY, BUT HE TOOK ME IN, RAISED ME...
SIGH... OTHERS ONLY WANT HIS POWER...
NO, TRUST ME, YOU'RE ADORABLE!
REALLY?!
YES, REALLY. (NOT!)
PRINCESS, DO NOT WORRY.
PERMIT ME TO CAPTURE THOSE RESPONSIBLE.
YES, OF COURSE.
I...
I COMPLETELY TRUST YOU.
TMP

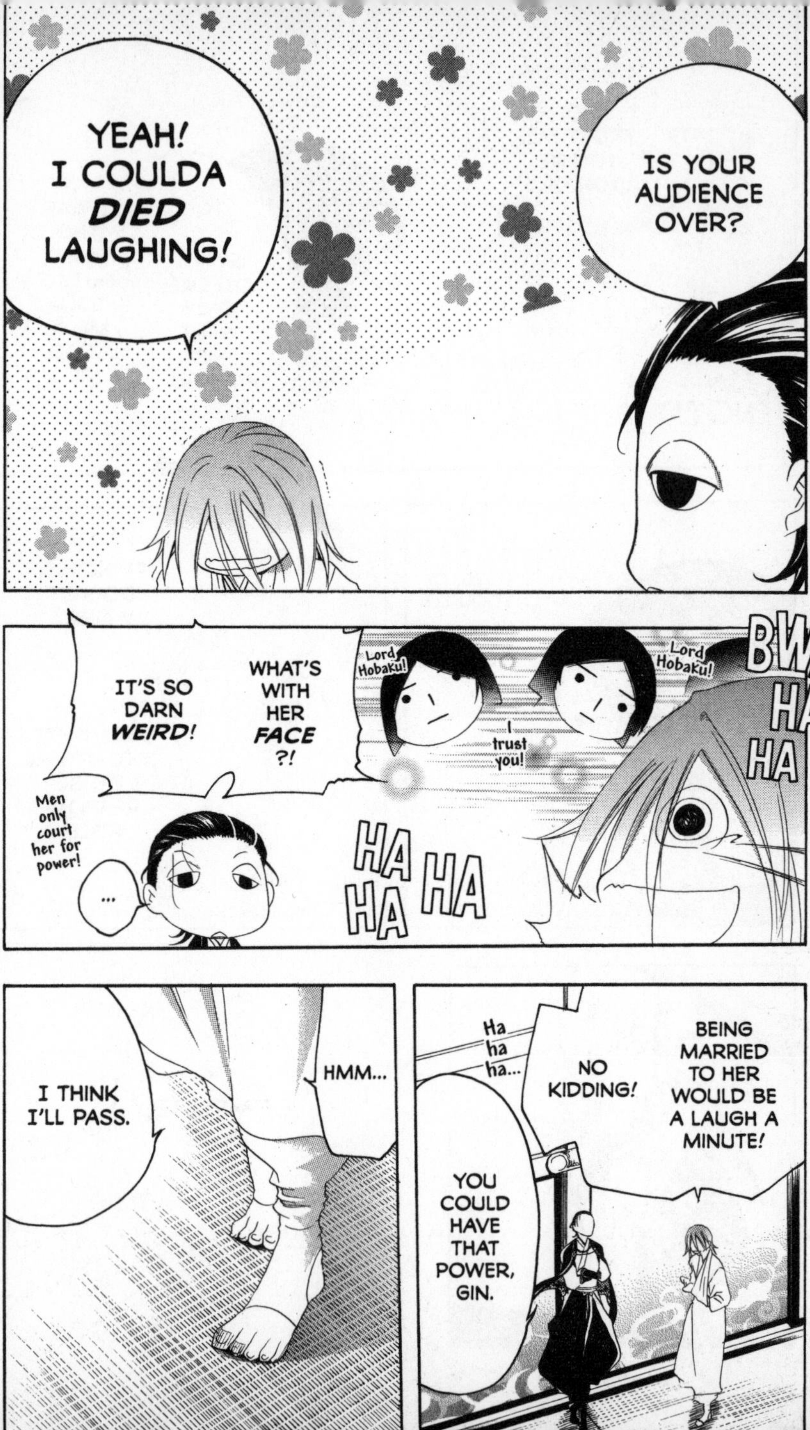
IS YOUR AUDIENCE OVER?
YEAH! I COULDA *DIED* LAUGHING!
BWA HA HA
Lord Hobaku!
Lord Hobaku!
I trust you!
WHAT'S WITH HER *FACE* ?!
IT'S SO DARN *WEIRD*!
HA HA HA HA
Men only court her for power!
...
BEING MARRIED TO HER WOULD BE A LAUGH A MINUTE!
NO KIDDING!
Ha ha ha...
YOU COULD HAVE THAT POWER, GIN.
HMM...
I THINK I'LL PASS.

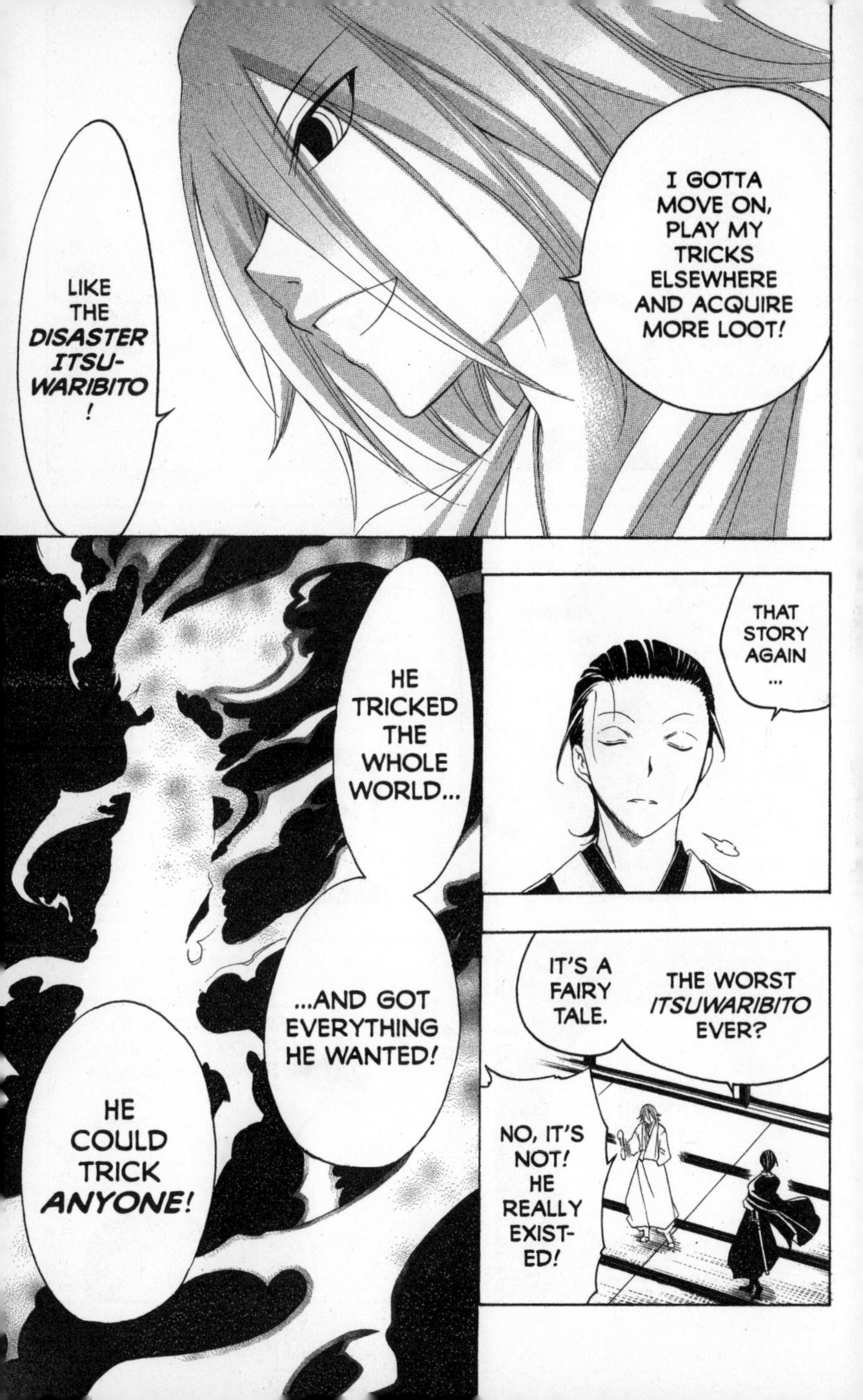
I GOTTA MOVE ON, PLAY MY TRICKS ELSEWHERE AND ACQUIRE MORE LOOT!
LIKE THE *DISASTER ITSU-WARIBITO*!
THAT STORY AGAIN...
THE WORST *ITSUWARIBITO* EVER?
IT'S A FAIRY TALE.
NO, IT'S NOT! HE REALLY EXIST-ED!
HE TRICKED THE WHOLE WORLD...
...AND GOT EVERYTHING HE WANTED!
HE COULD TRICK *ANYONE*!

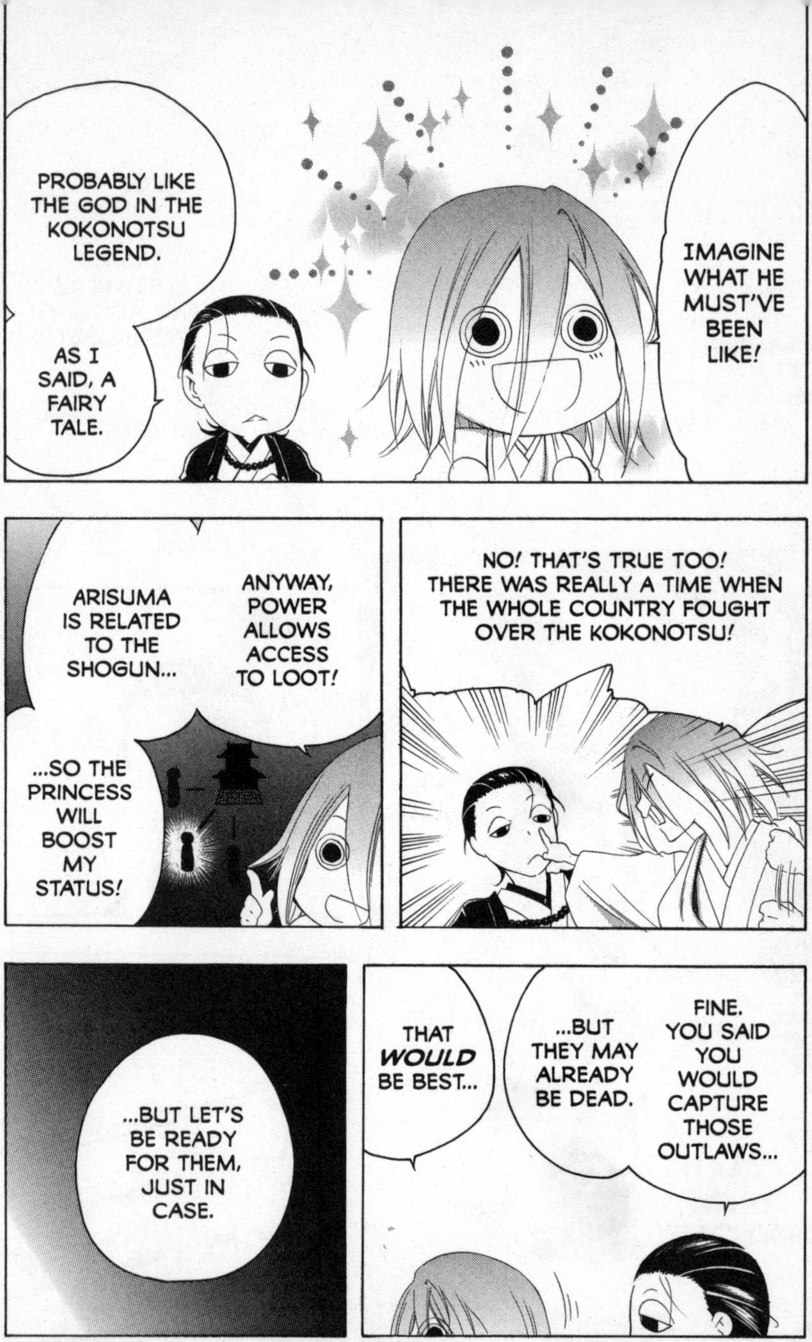
IMAGINE WHAT HE MUST'VE BEEN LIKE!
PROBABLY LIKE THE GOD IN THE KOKONOTSU LEGEND.
AS I SAID, A FAIRY TALE.
NO! THAT'S TRUE TOO! THERE WAS REALLY A TIME WHEN THE WHOLE COUNTRY FOUGHT OVER THE KOKONOTSU!
ANYWAY, POWER ALLOWS ACCESS TO LOOT!
ARISUMA IS RELATED TO THE SHOGUN...
...SO THE PRINCESS WILL BOOST MY STATUS!
FINE. YOU SAID YOU WOULD CAPTURE THOSE OUTLAWS...
...BUT THEY MAY ALREADY BE DEAD.
THAT *WOULD* BE BEST...
...BUT LET'S BE READY FOR THEM, JUST IN CASE.

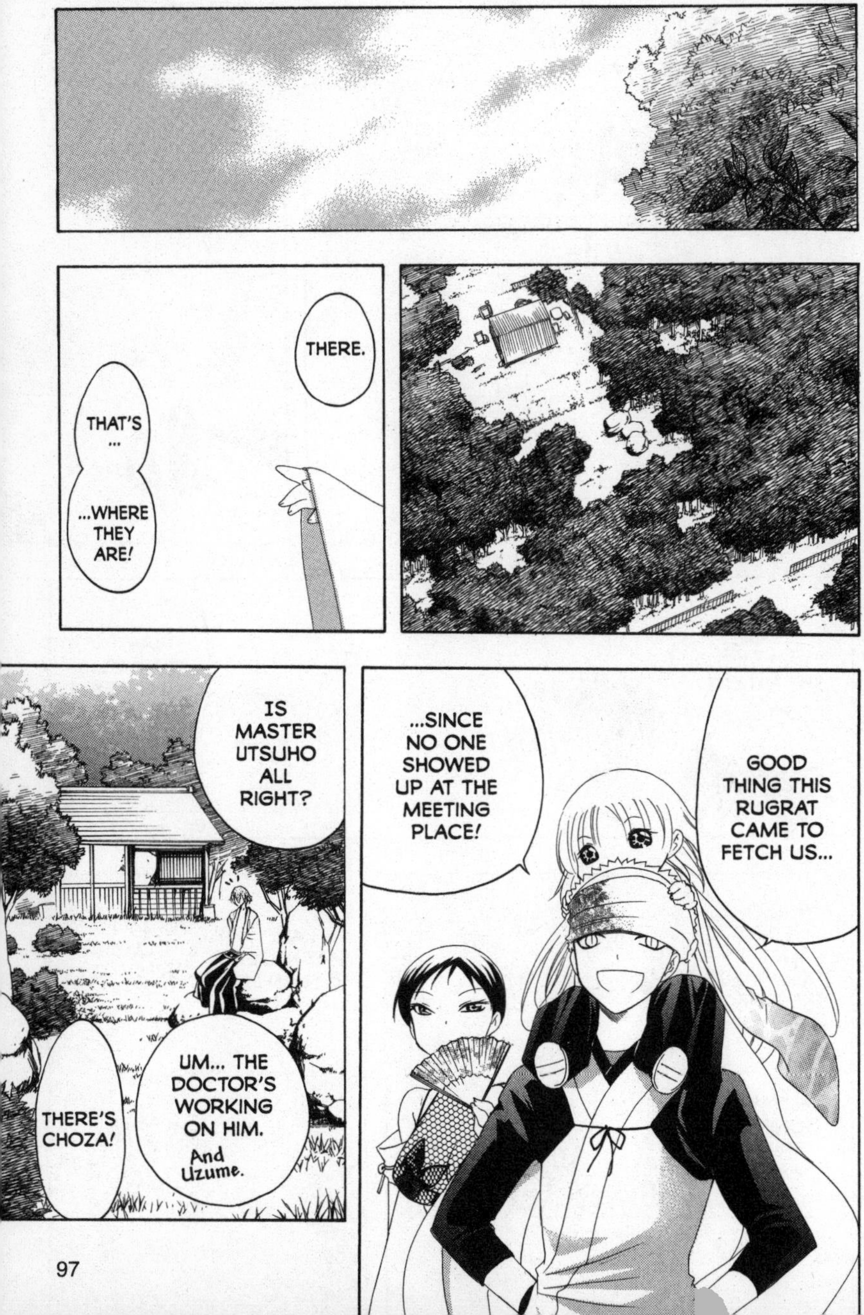
THERE.
THAT'S... ...WHERE THEY ARE!
GOOD THING THIS RUGRAT CAME TO FETCH US...
...SINCE NO ONE SHOWED UP AT THE MEETING PLACE!
IS MASTER UTSUHO ALL RIGHT?
UM... THE DOCTOR'S WORKING ON HIM.
And Uzume.
THERE'S CHOZA!

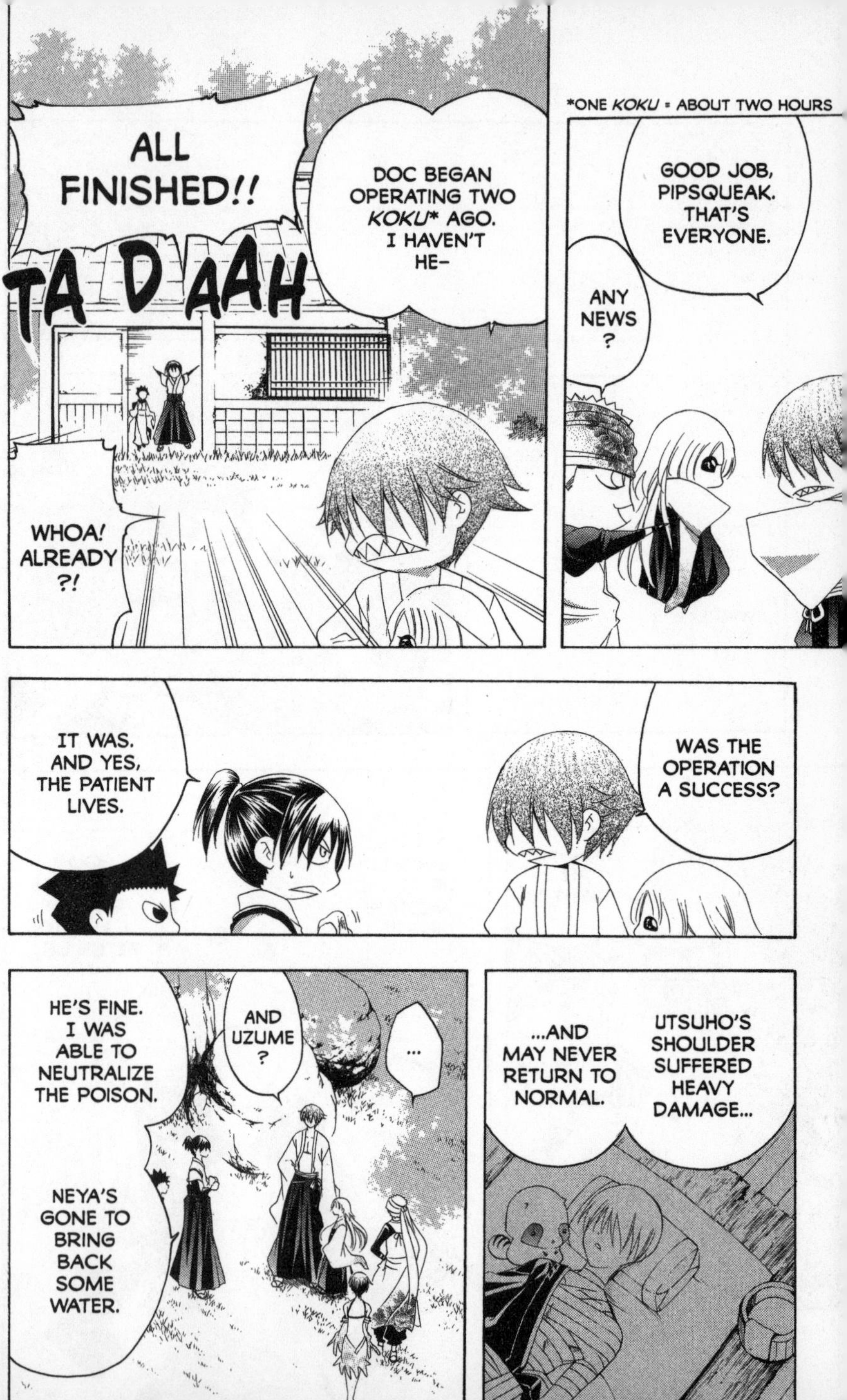
*ONE KOKU = ABOUT TWO HOURS
GOOD JOB, PIPSQUEAK. THAT'S EVERYONE.
ANY NEWS?
DOC BEGAN OPERATING TWO KOKU* AGO. I HAVEN'T HE–
ALL FINISHED!!
TA DAAH
WHOA! ALREADY?!
WAS THE OPERATION A SUCCESS?
IT WAS. AND YES, THE PATIENT LIVES.
UTSUHO'S SHOULDER SUFFERED HEAVY DAMAGE...
...AND MAY NEVER RETURN TO NORMAL.
...
AND UZUME?
HE'S FINE. I WAS ABLE TO NEUTRALIZE THE POISON.
NEYA'S GONE TO BRING BACK SOME WATER.

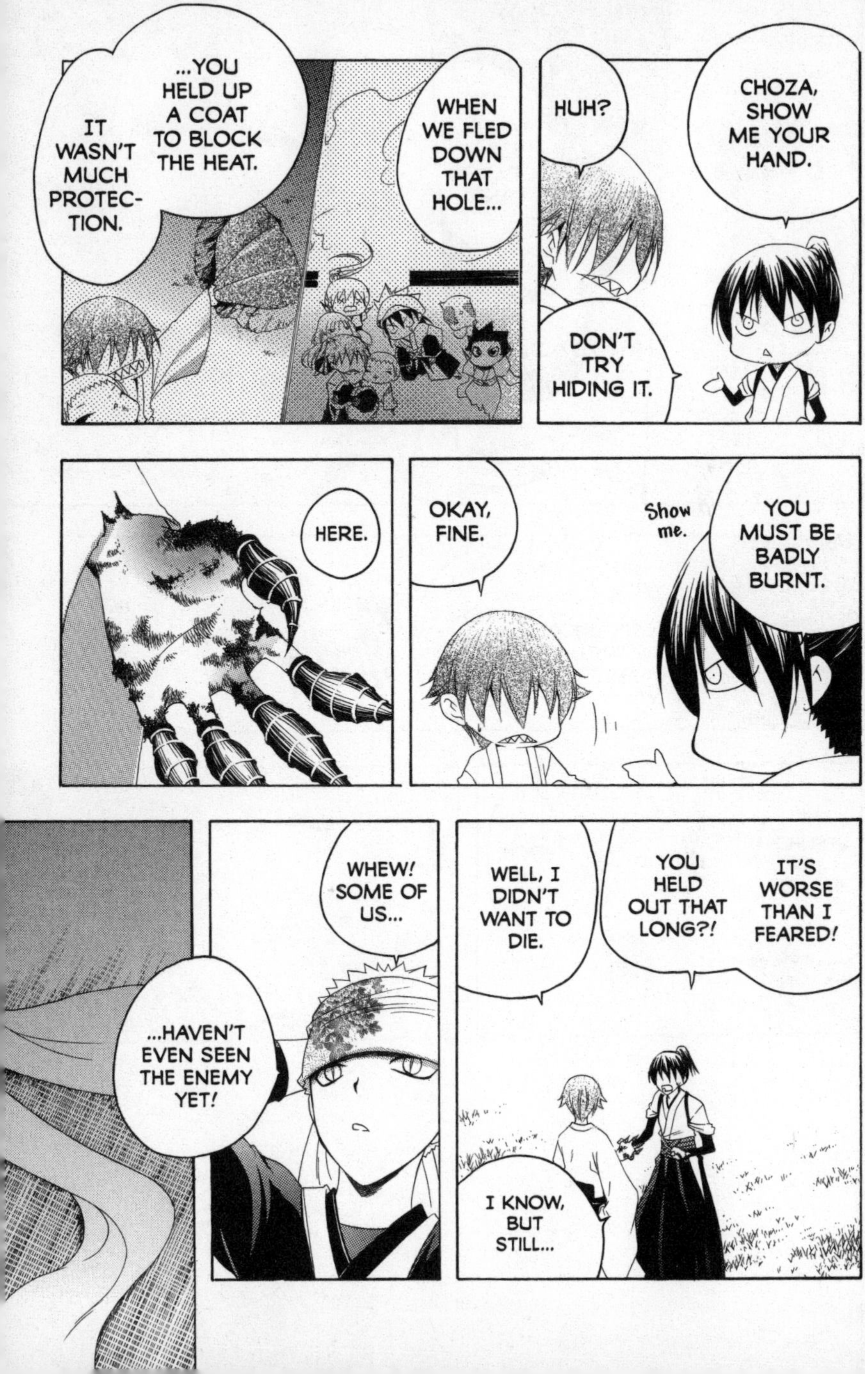
CHOZA, SHOW ME YOUR HAND.
HUH?
DON'T TRY HIDING IT.
WHEN WE FLED DOWN THAT HOLE...
...YOU HELD UP A COAT TO BLOCK THE HEAT.
IT WASN'T MUCH PROTECTION.
YOU MUST BE BADLY BURNT.
Show me.
OKAY, FINE.
HERE.
IT'S WORSE THAN I FEARED!
YOU HELD OUT THAT LONG?!
WELL, I DIDN'T WANT TO DIE.
I KNOW, BUT STILL...
WHEW! SOME OF US...
...HAVEN'T EVEN SEEN THE ENEMY YET!

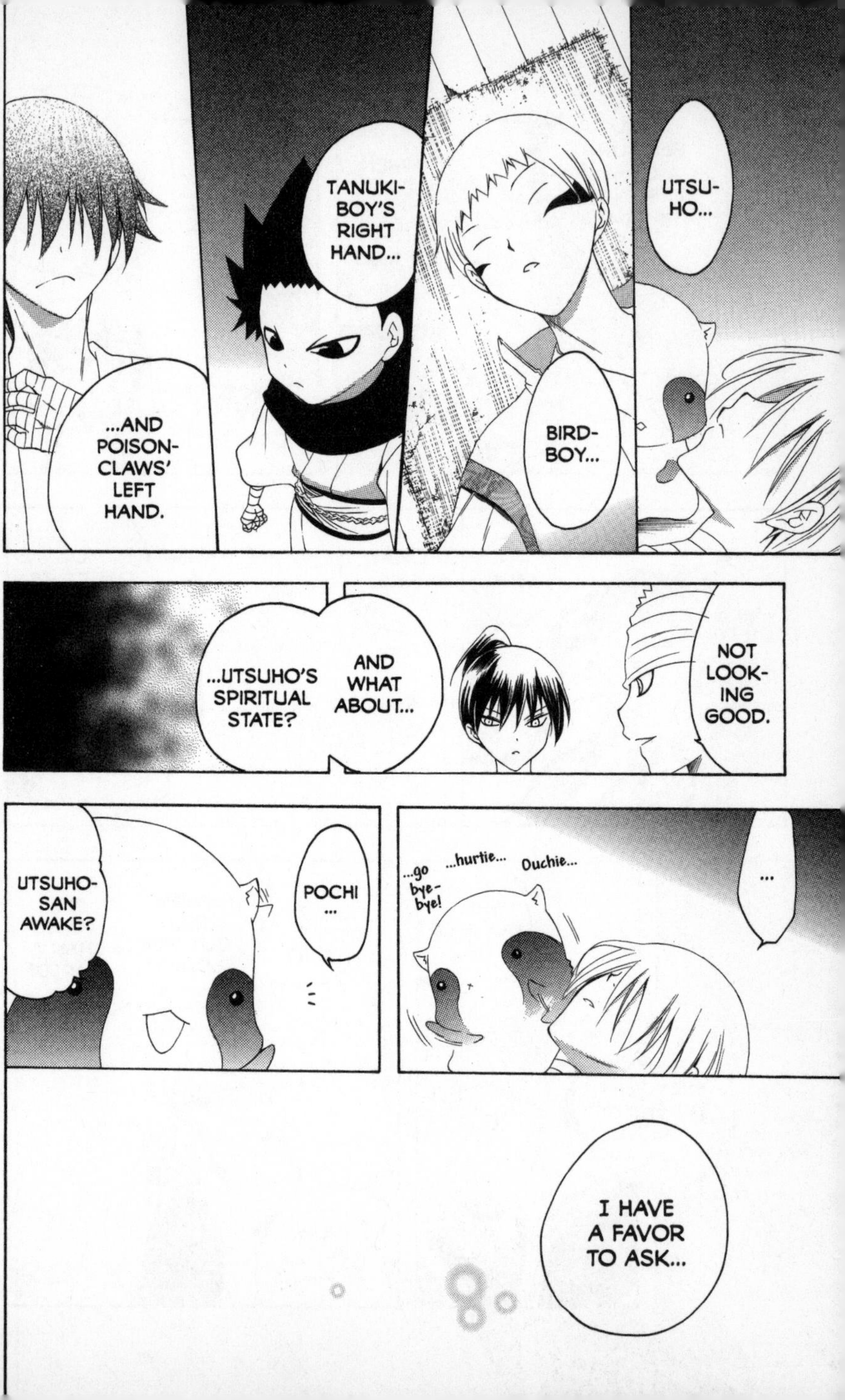
UTSU-HO...
BIRD-BOY...
TANUKI-BOY'S RIGHT HAND...
...AND POISON-CLAWS' LEFT HAND.
NOT LOOK-ING GOOD.
AND WHAT ABOUT...
...UTSUHO'S SPIRITUAL STATE?
...
Ouchie...
...hurtie...
...go bye-bye!
POCHI ...
UTSUHO-SAN AWAKE?
I HAVE A FAVOR TO ASK...

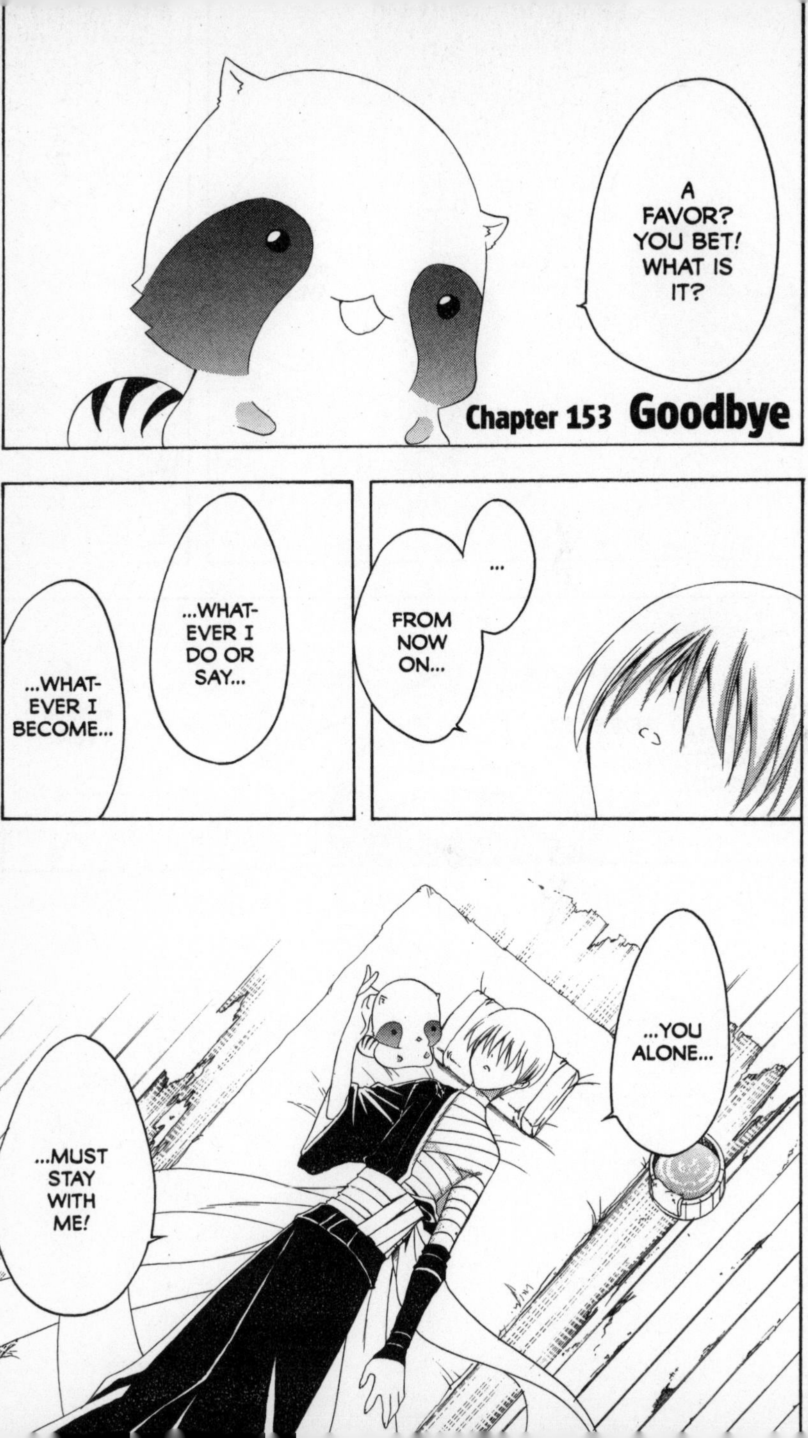
A FAVOR? YOU BET! WHAT IS IT?
Chapter 153 Goodbye
...
FROM NOW ON...
...WHAT-EVER I DO OR SAY...
...WHAT-EVER I BECOME...
...YOU ALONE...
...MUST STAY WITH ME!

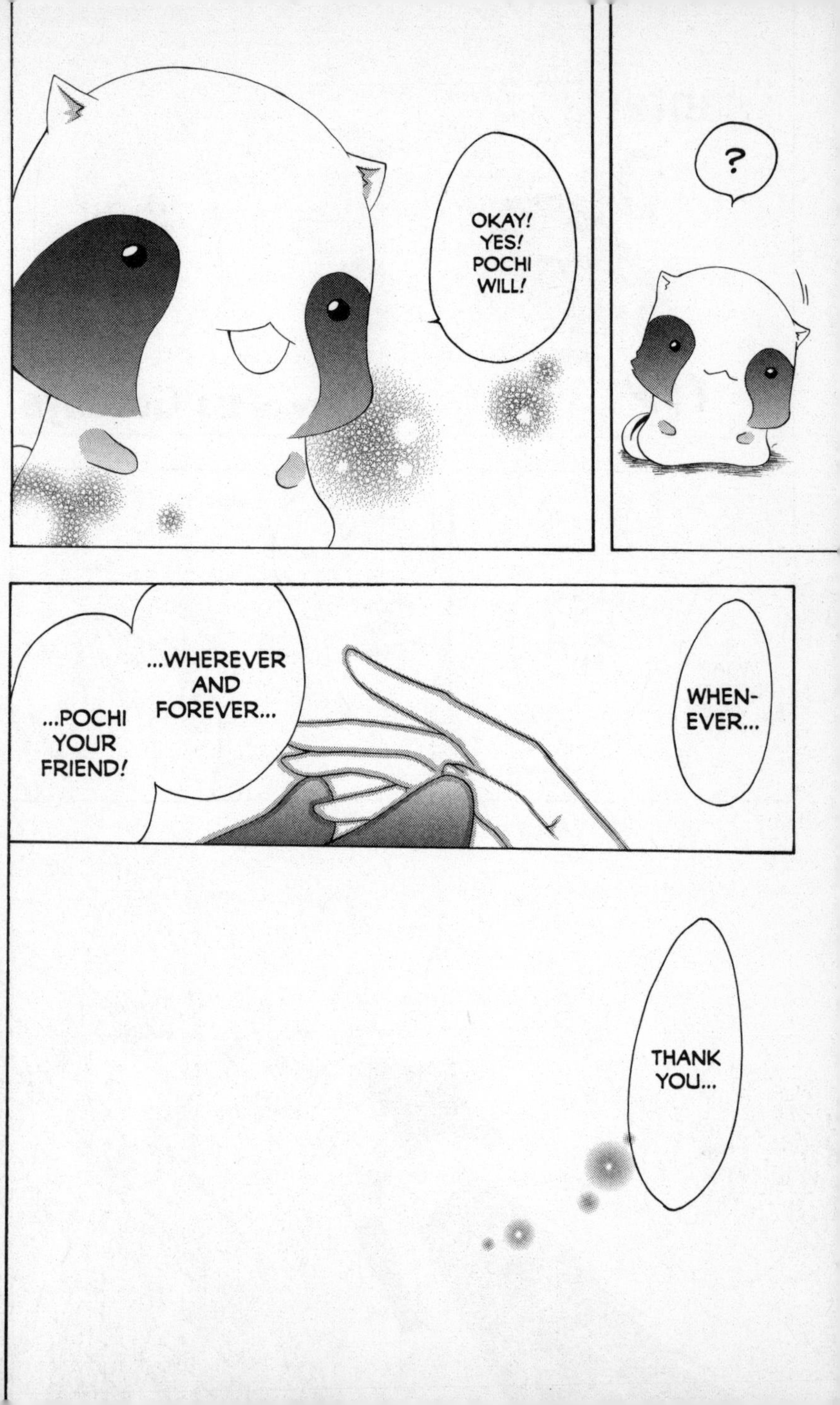
?
OKAY! YES! POCHI WILL!
WHEN-EVER...
...WHEREVER AND FOREVER...
...POCHI YOUR FRIEND!
THANK YOU...

Chapter 153
Goodbye

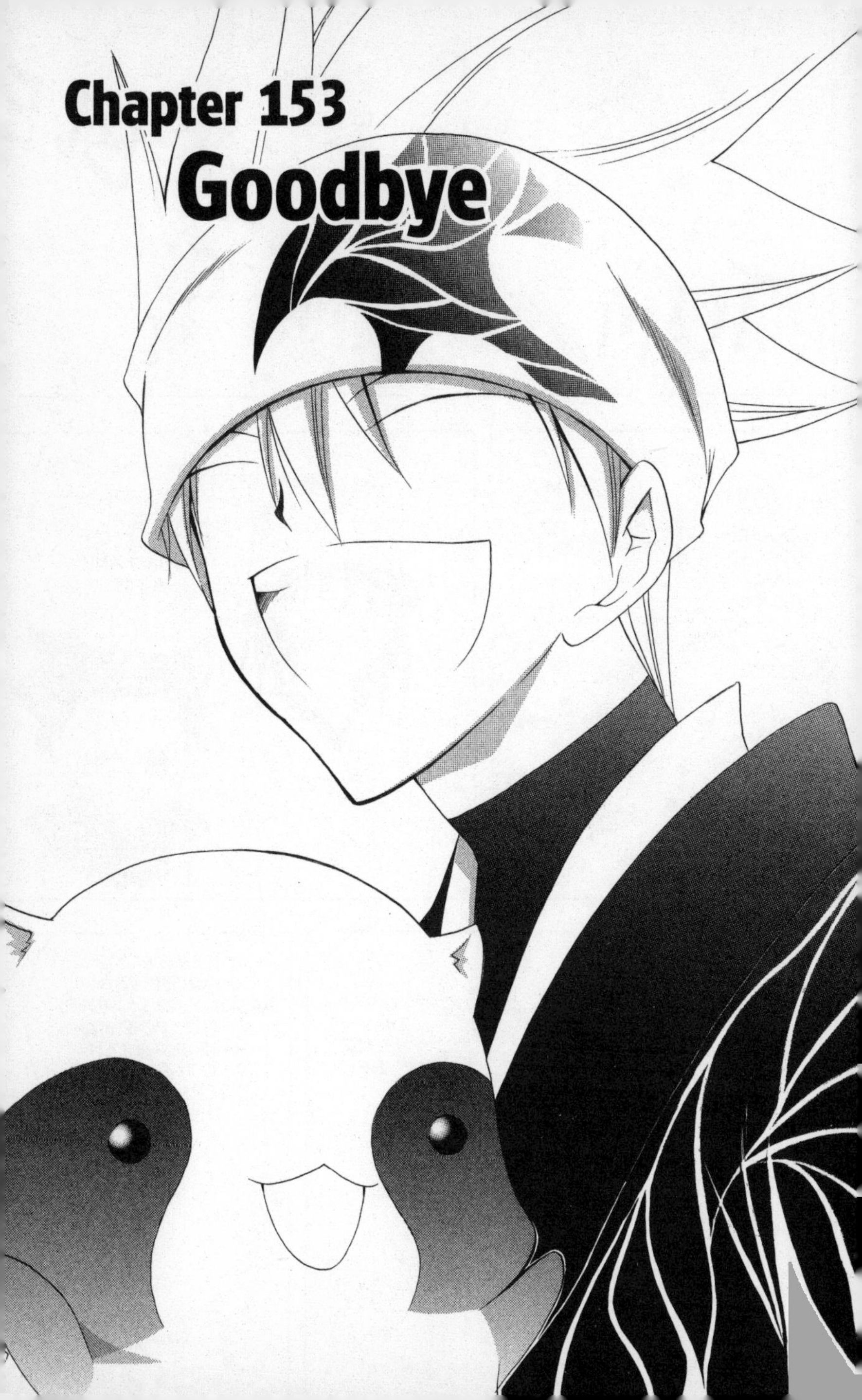

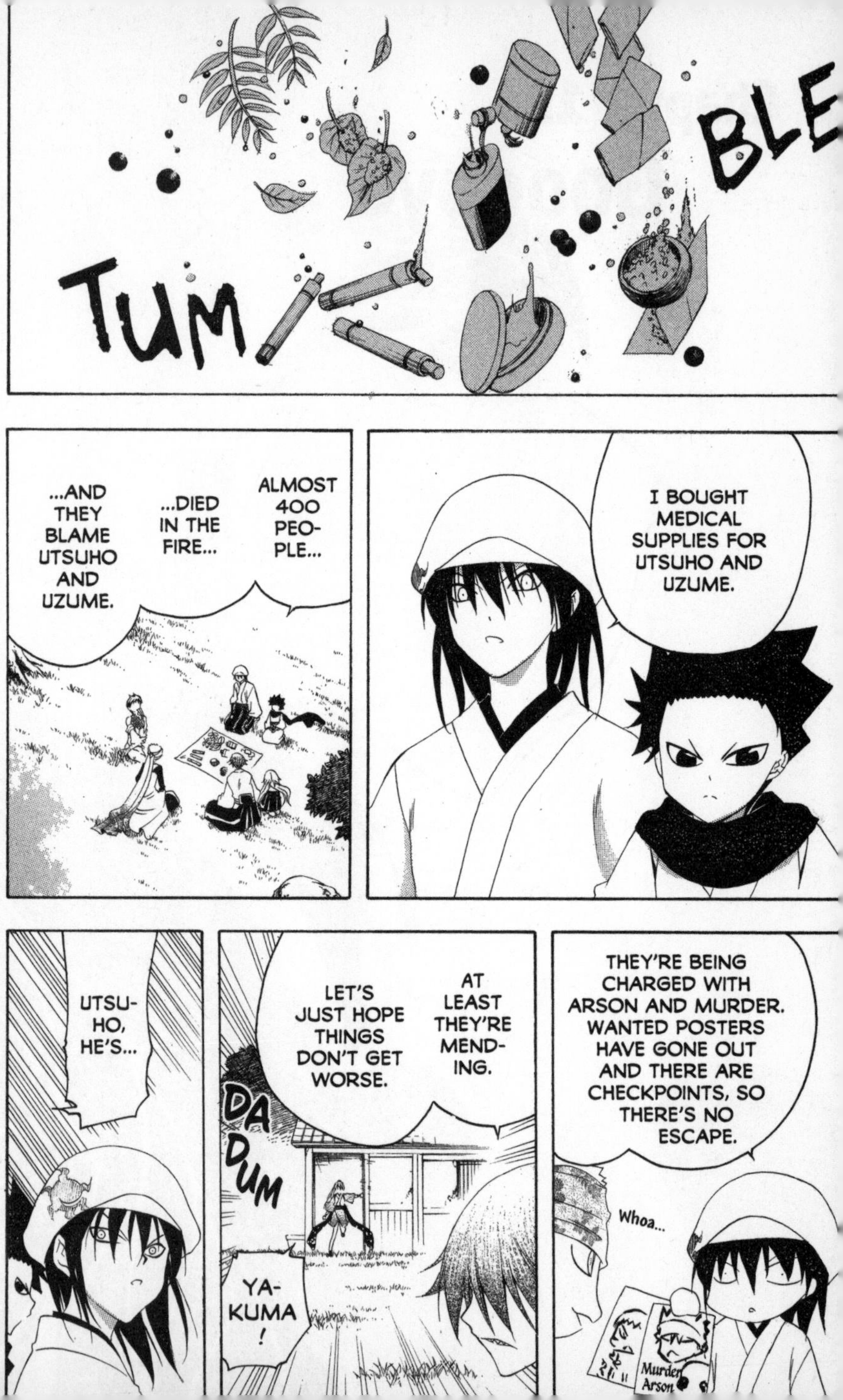
TUM
BLE
I BOUGHT MEDICAL SUPPLIES FOR UTSUHO AND UZUME.
ALMOST 400 PEO-PLE...
...DIED IN THE FIRE...
...AND THEY BLAME UTSUHO AND UZUME.
THEY'RE BEING CHARGED WITH ARSON AND MURDER. WANTED POSTERS HAVE GONE OUT AND THERE ARE CHECKPOINTS, SO THERE'S NO ESCAPE.
Whoa...
Murder
Arson
AT LEAST THEY'RE MEND-ING.
LET'S JUST HOPE THINGS DON'T GET WORSE.
DA DUM
YA-KUMA!
UTSU-HO, HE'S...

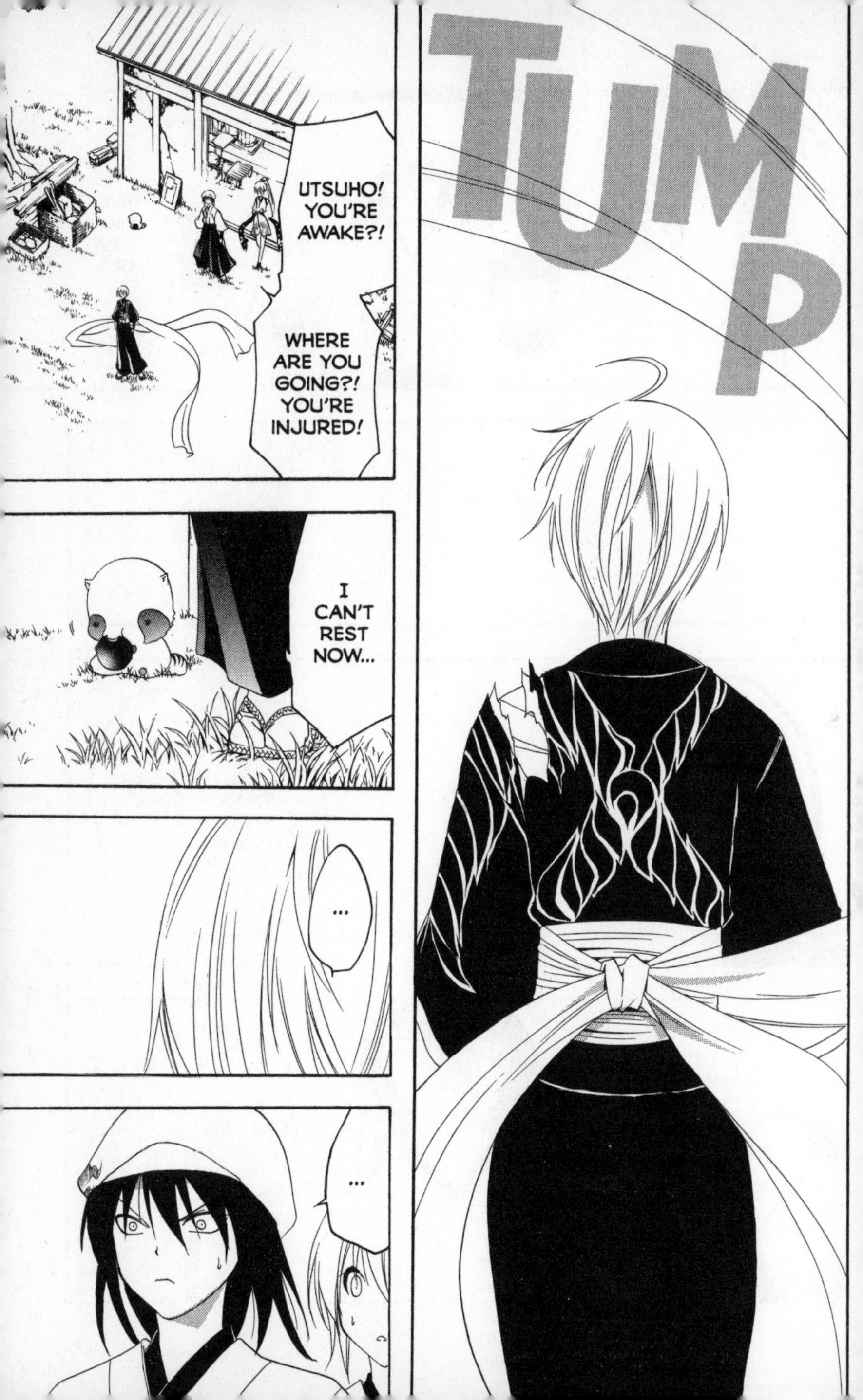
TUMP
UTSUHO! YOU'RE AWAKE?!
WHERE ARE YOU GOING?! YOU'RE INJURED!
I CAN'T REST NOW...
...
...

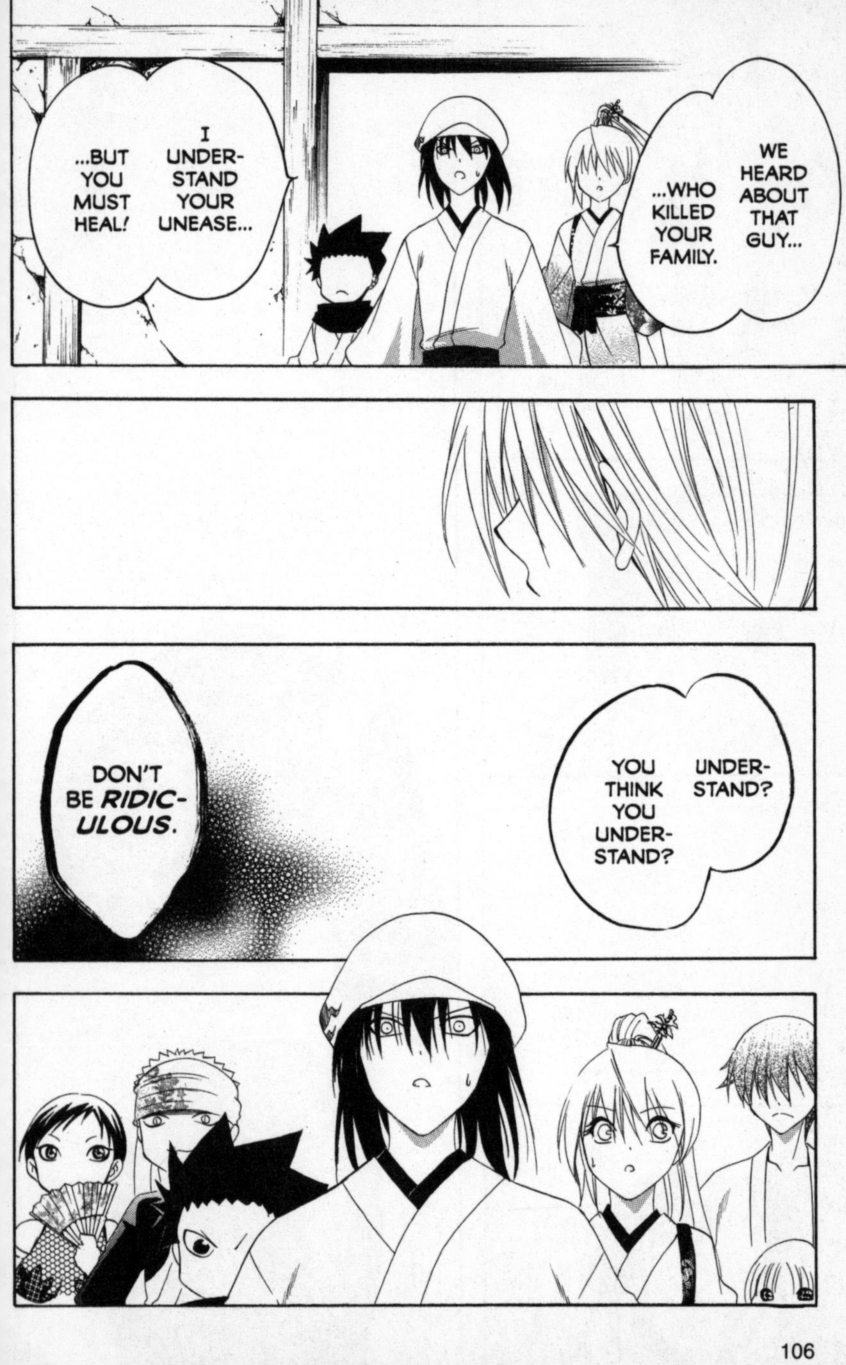
WE HEARD ABOUT THAT GUY... ...WHO KILLED YOUR FAMILY.
I UNDERSTAND YOUR UNEASE... ...BUT YOU MUST HEAL!
UNDERSTAND? YOU THINK YOU UNDERSTAND?
DON'T BE *RIDICULOUS*.

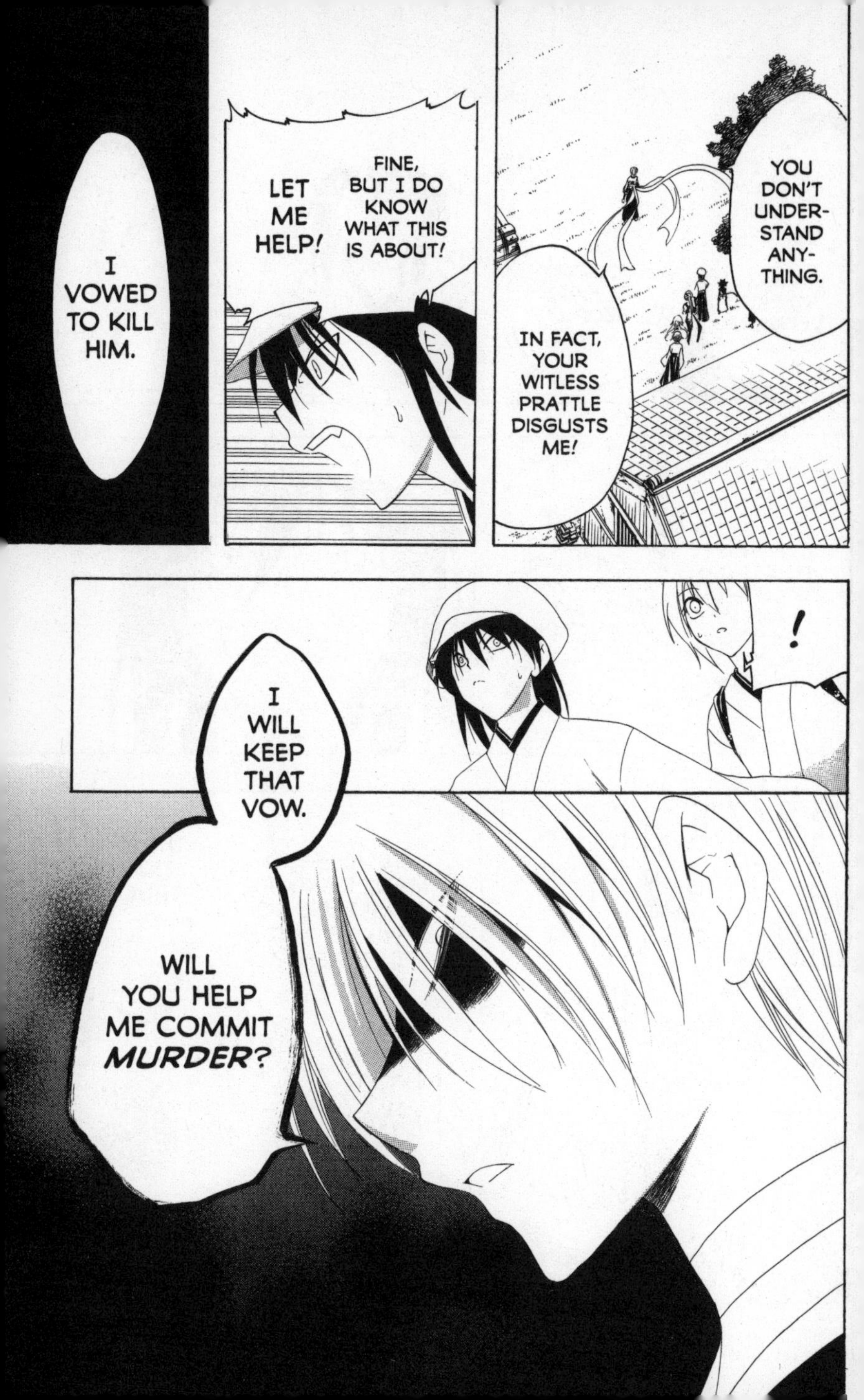
YOU DON'T UNDERSTAND ANYTHING.
IN FACT, YOUR WITLESS PRATTLE DISGUSTS ME!
FINE, BUT I DO KNOW WHAT THIS IS ABOUT!
LET ME HELP!
I VOWED TO KILL HIM.
!
I WILL KEEP THAT VOW.
WILL YOU HELP ME COMMIT *MURDER*?

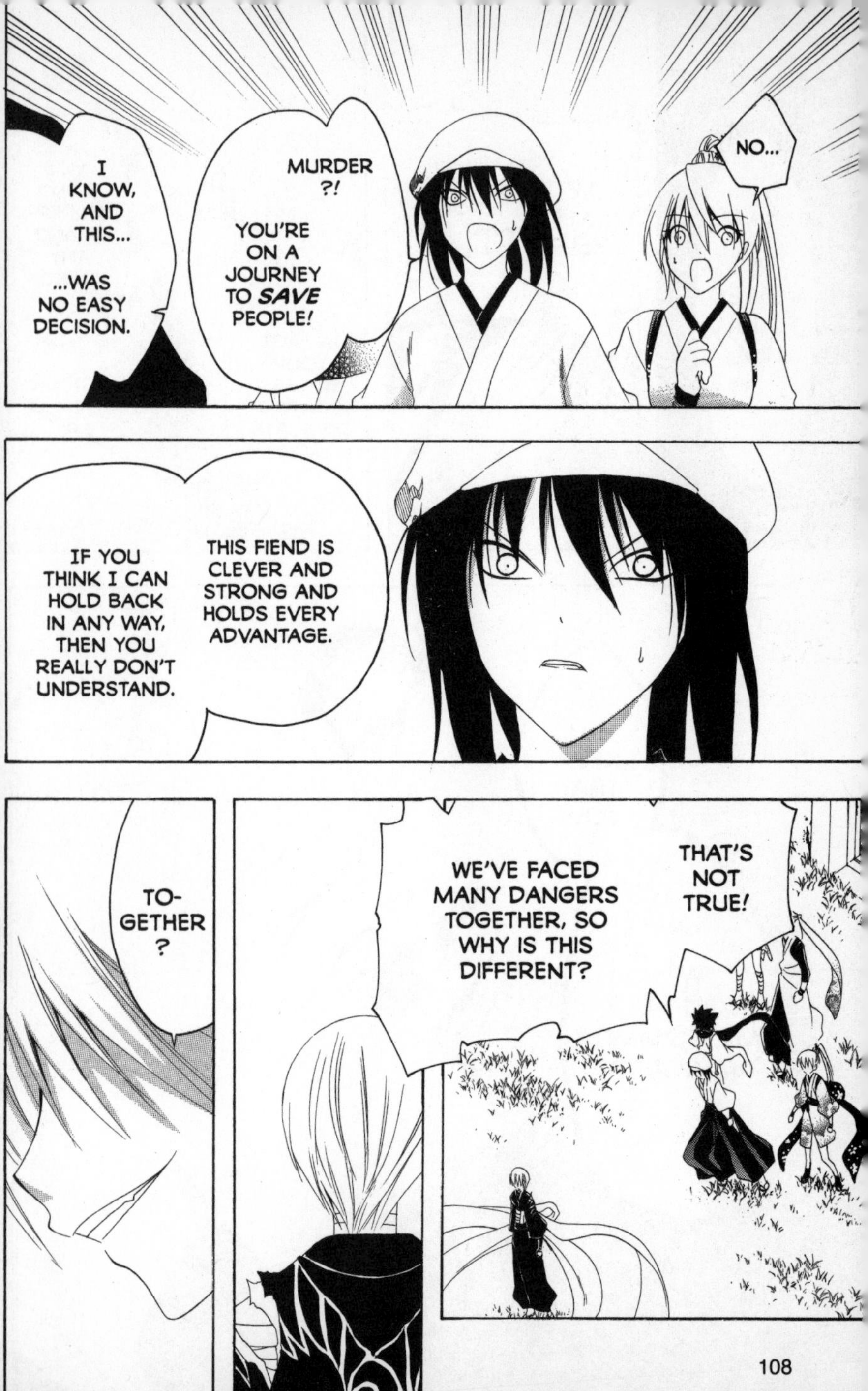
NO...
MURDER?!
YOU'RE ON A JOURNEY TO *SAVE* PEOPLE!
I KNOW, AND THIS...
...WAS NO EASY DECISION.
THIS FIEND IS CLEVER AND STRONG AND HOLDS EVERY ADVANTAGE.
IF YOU THINK I CAN HOLD BACK IN ANY WAY, THEN YOU REALLY DON'T UNDERSTAND.
THAT'S NOT TRUE!
WE'VE FACED MANY DANGERS TOGETHER, SO WHY IS THIS DIFFERENT?
TO-GETHER?

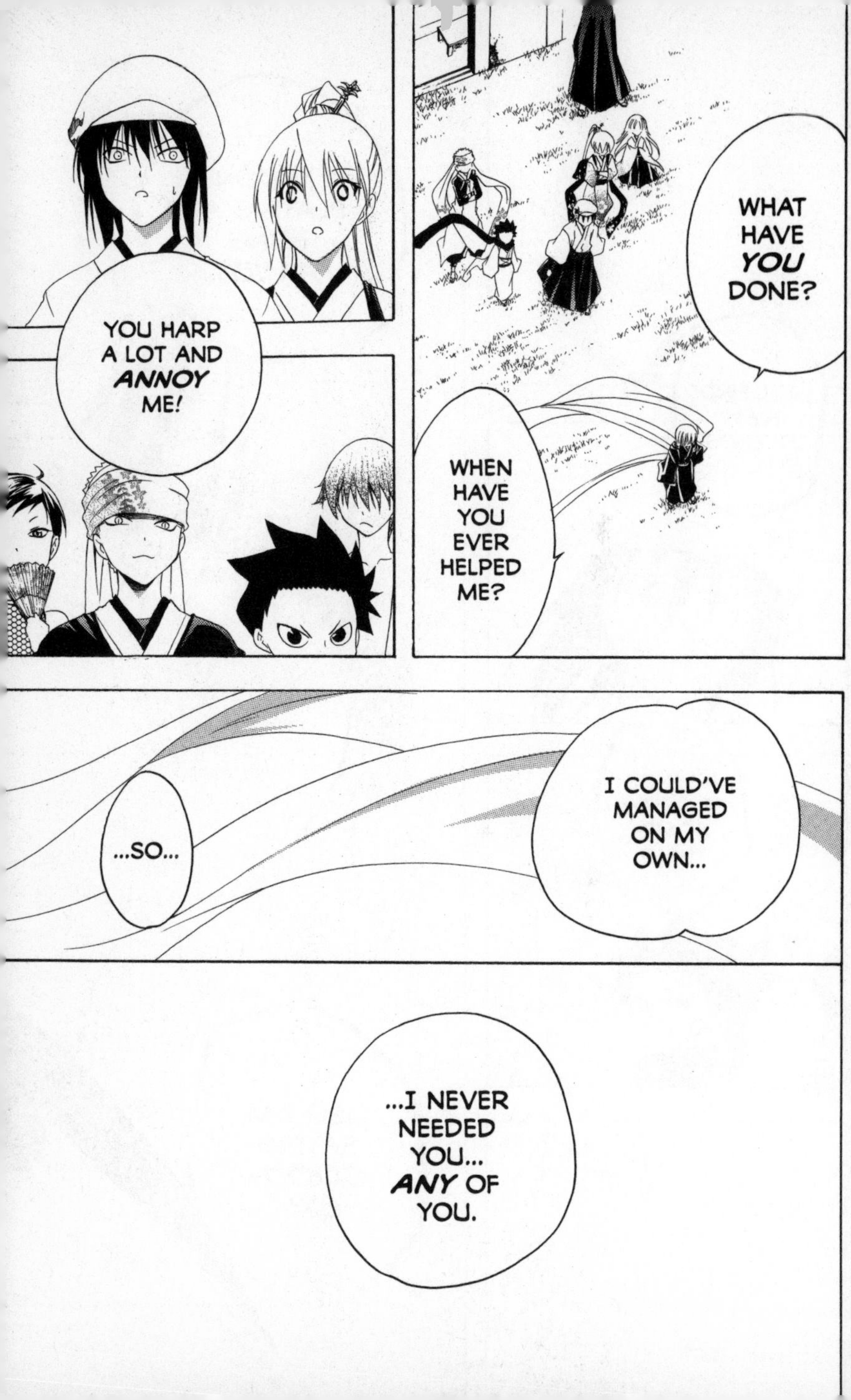
WHAT HAVE *YOU* DONE?
WHEN HAVE YOU EVER HELPED ME?
YOU HARP A LOT AND *ANNOY* ME!
I COULD'VE MANAGED ON MY OWN...
...SO...
...I NEVER NEEDED YOU... *ANY* OF YOU.

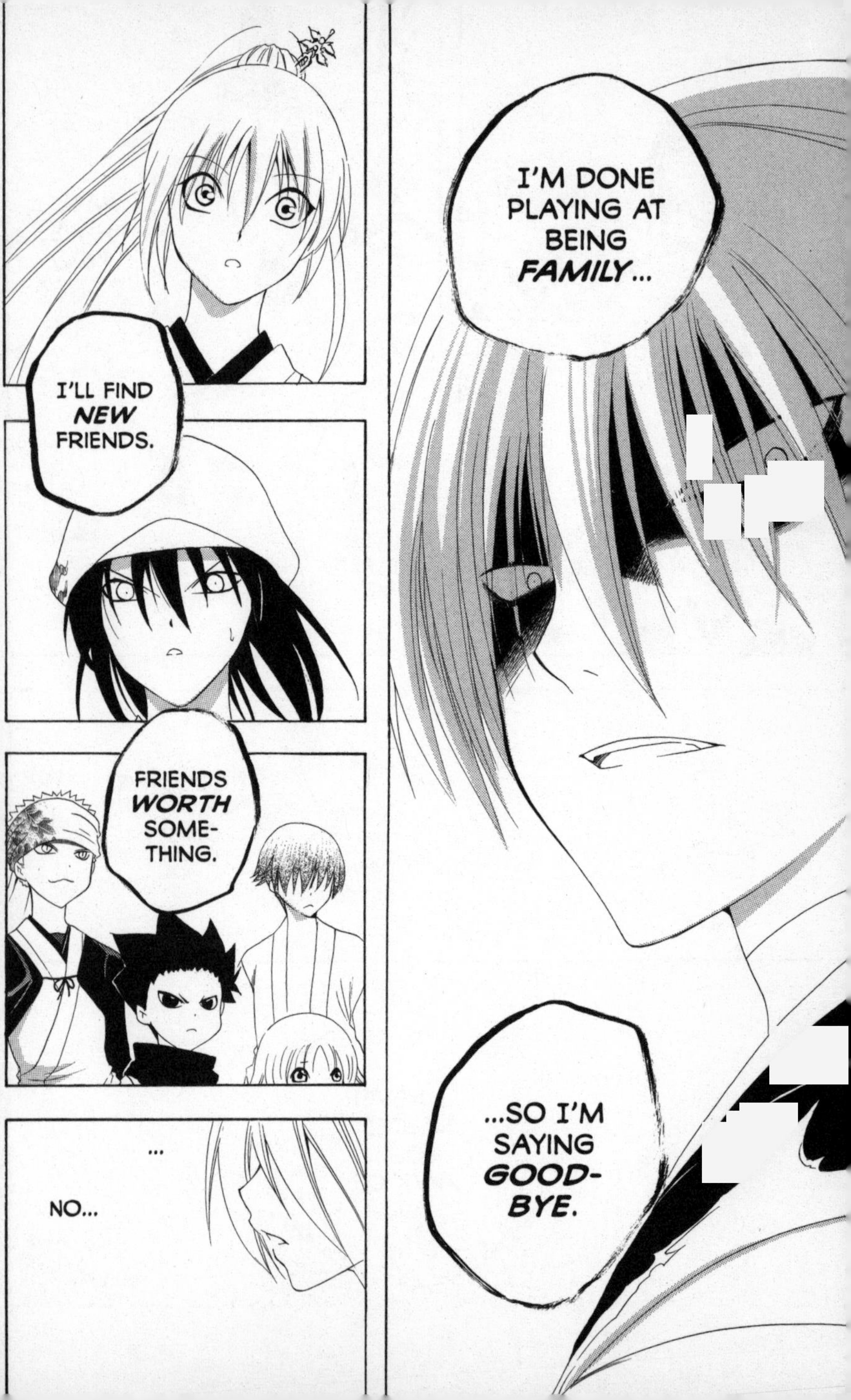
I'M DONE PLAYING AT BEING *FAMILY*...
...SO I'M SAYING *GOOD-BYE*.
I'LL FIND *NEW* FRIENDS.
FRIENDS *WORTH* SOME-THING.
...
NO...

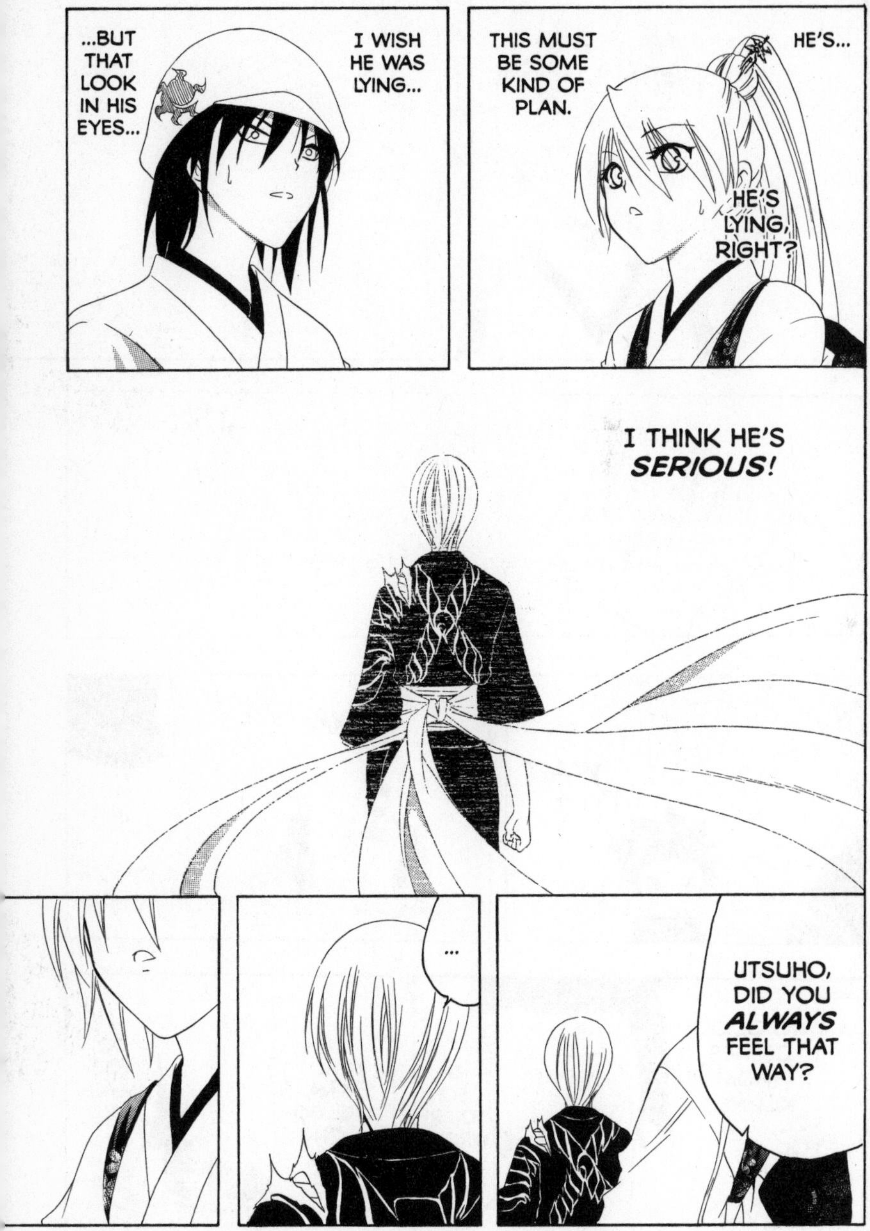
HE'S...
THIS MUST BE SOME KIND OF PLAN.
HE'S LYING, RIGHT?
I WISH HE WAS LYING...
...BUT THAT LOOK IN HIS EYES...
I THINK HE'S *SERIOUS*!
UTSUHO, DID YOU *ALWAYS* FEEL THAT WAY?
...

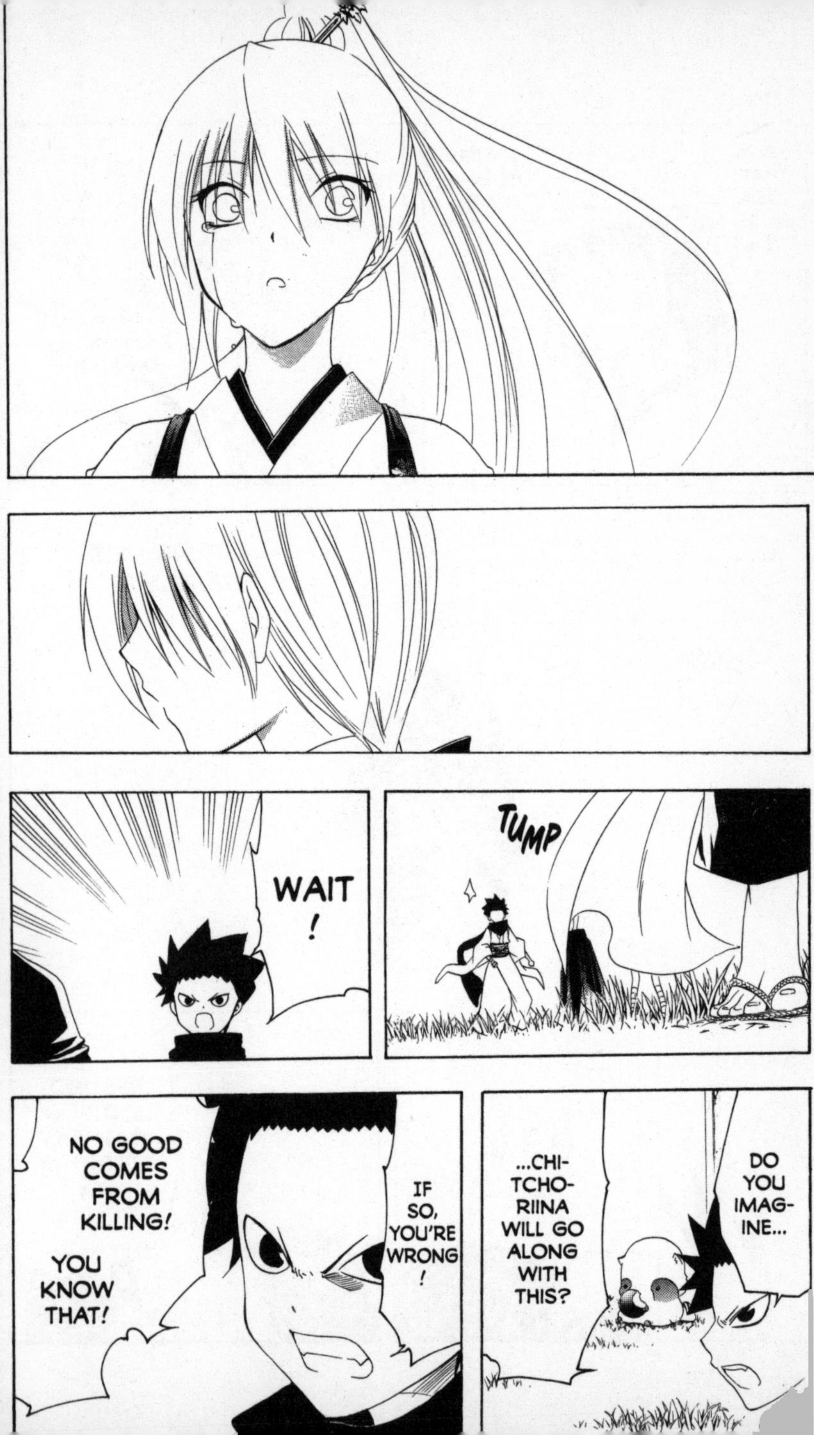
TUMP
WAIT!
DO YOU IMAGINE...
...CHITCHORIINA WILL GO ALONG WITH THIS?
IF SO, YOU'RE WRONG!
NO GOOD COMES FROM KILLING!
YOU KNOW THAT!

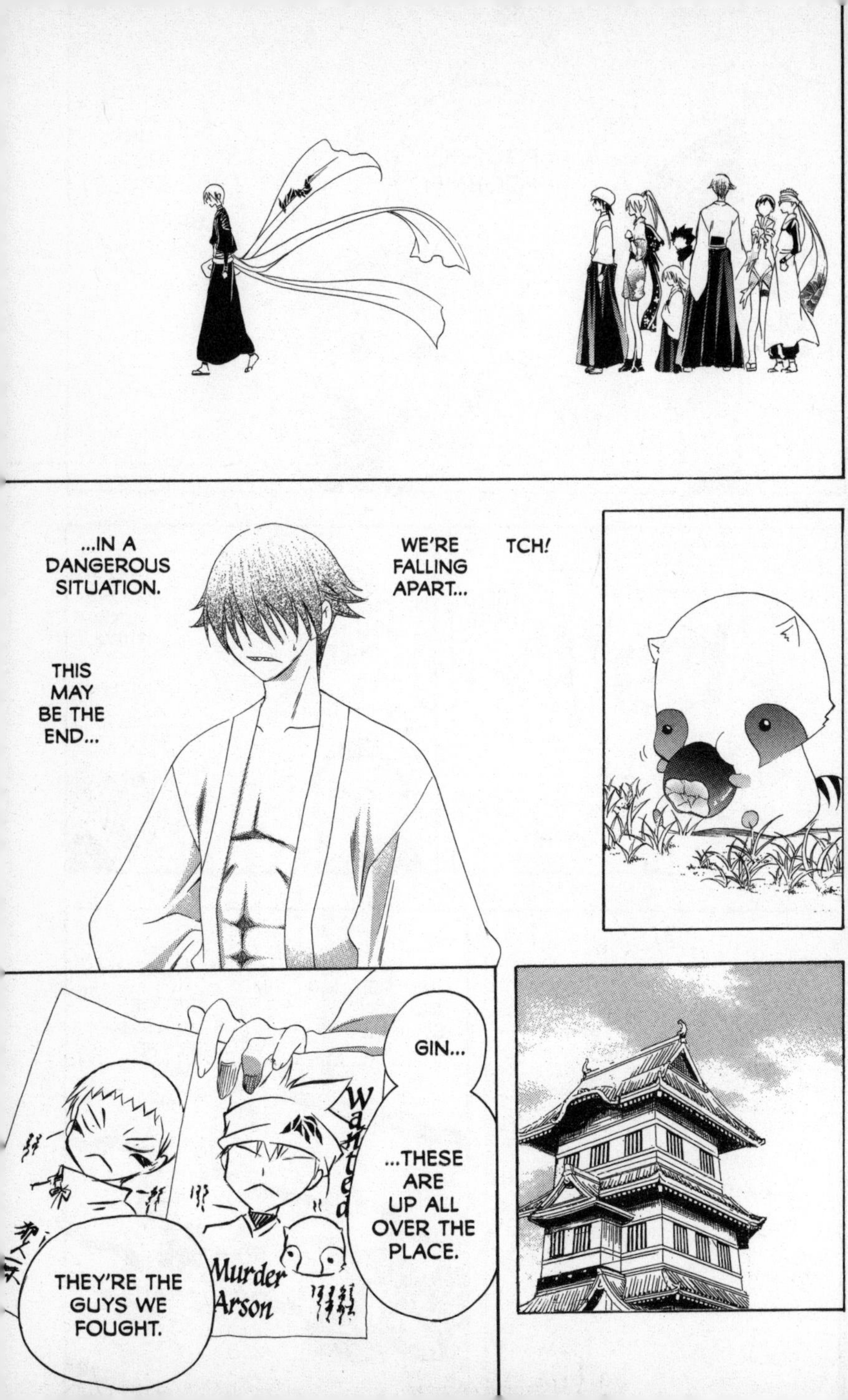
TCH!
WE'RE FALLING APART...
...IN A DANGEROUS SITUATION.
THIS MAY BE THE END...
GIN...
...THESE ARE UP ALL OVER THE PLACE.
Wanted
Murder
Arson
THEY'RE THE GUYS WE FOUGHT.

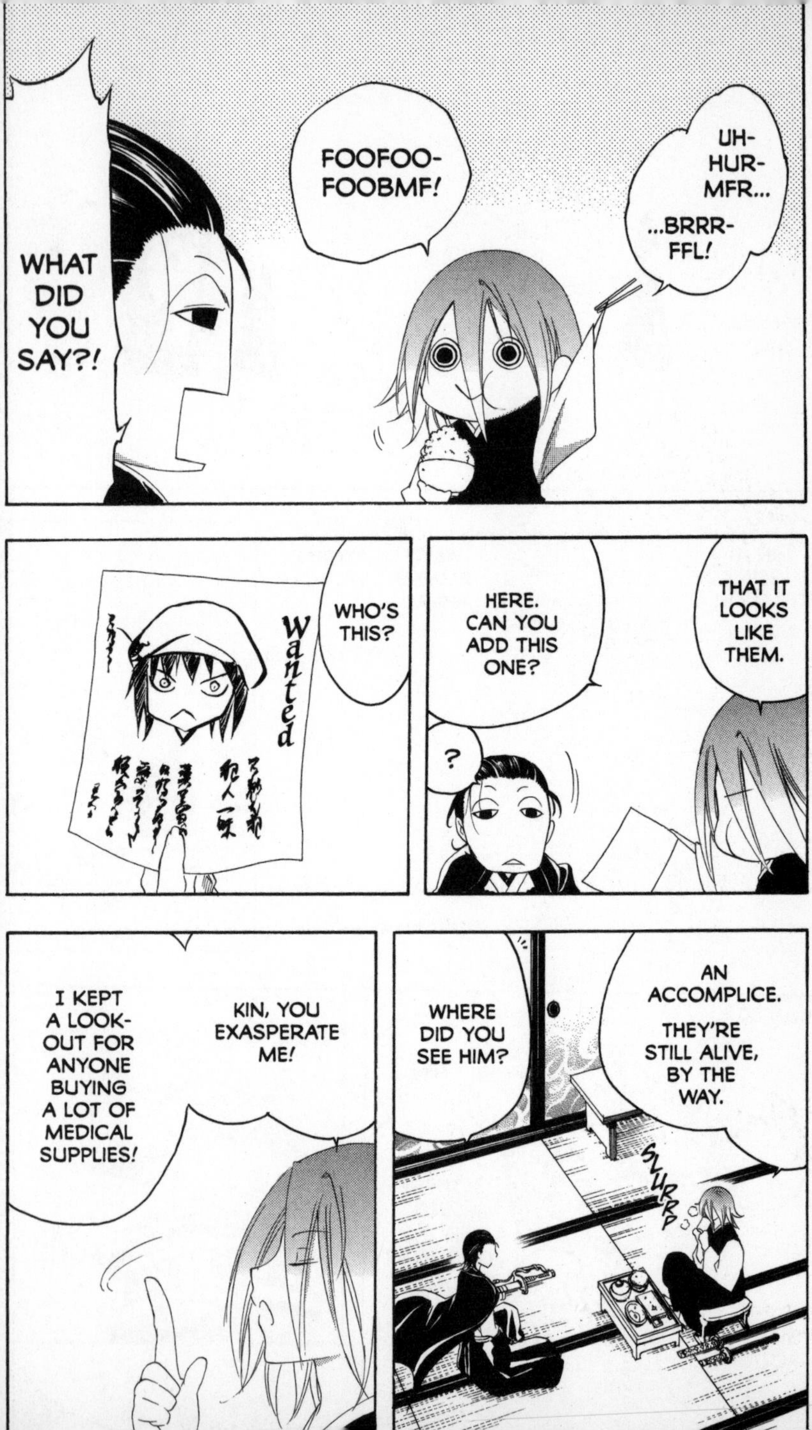
UH-HUR-MFR... ...BRRR-FFL!
FOOFOO-FOOBMF!
WHAT DID YOU SAY?!
THAT IT LOOKS LIKE THEM.
HERE. CAN YOU ADD THIS ONE?
?
WHO'S THIS?
Wanted
AN ACCOMPLICE.
THEY'RE STILL ALIVE, BY THE WAY.
WHERE DID YOU SEE HIM?
SLURRP
KIN, YOU EXASPERATE ME!
I KEPT A LOOK-OUT FOR ANYONE BUYING A LOT OF MEDICAL SUPPLIES!

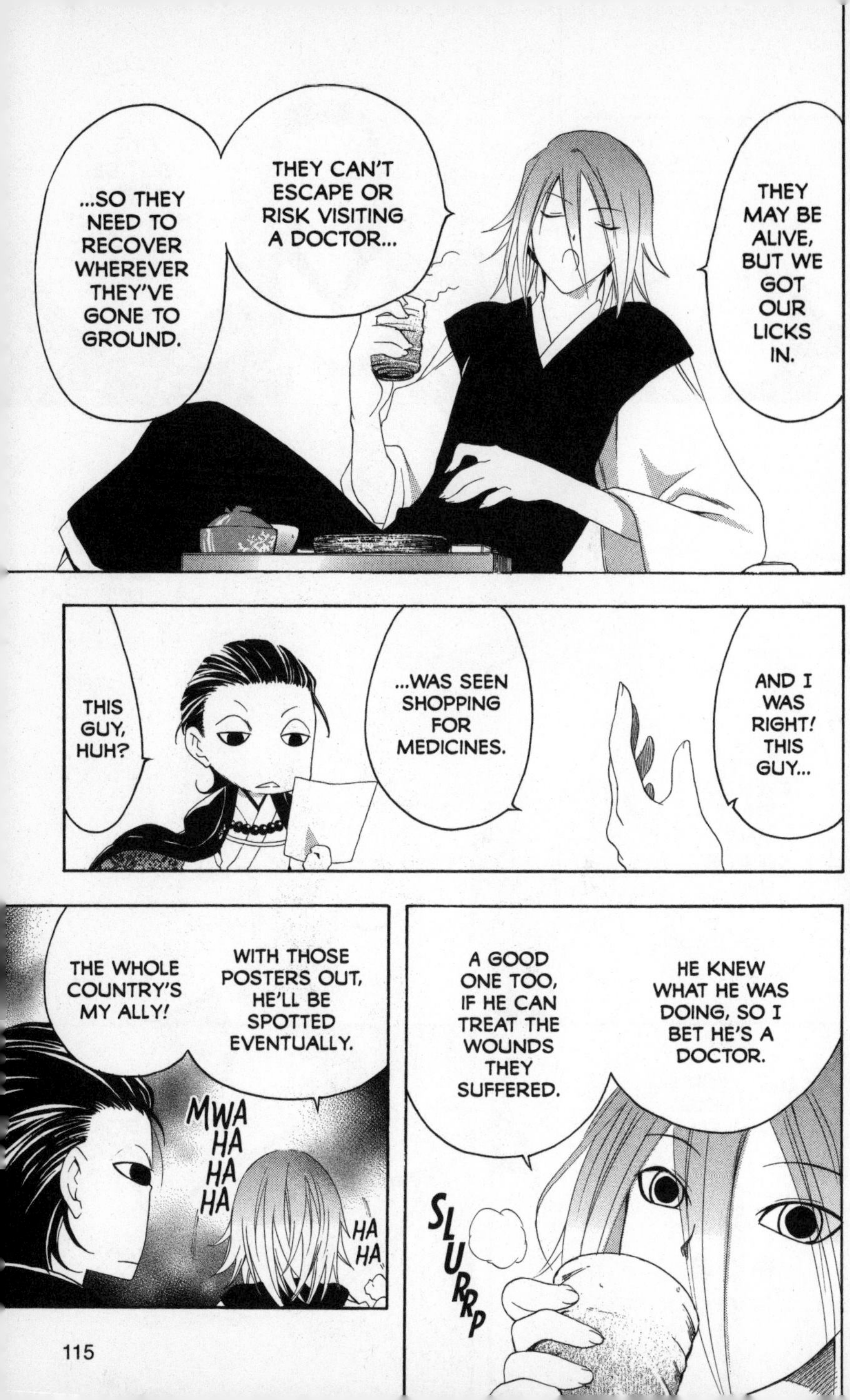
THEY MAY BE ALIVE, BUT WE GOT OUR LICKS IN.
THEY CAN'T ESCAPE OR RISK VISITING A DOCTOR...
...SO THEY NEED TO RECOVER WHEREVER THEY'VE GONE TO GROUND.
AND I WAS RIGHT! THIS GUY...
...WAS SEEN SHOPPING FOR MEDICINES.
THIS GUY, HUH?
HE KNEW WHAT HE WAS DOING, SO I BET HE'S A DOCTOR.
A GOOD ONE TOO, IF HE CAN TREAT THE WOUNDS THEY SUFFERED.
SLURRP
WITH THOSE POSTERS OUT, HE'LL BE SPOTTED EVENTUALLY.
THE WHOLE COUNTRY'S MY ALLY!
MWA HA HA HA
HA HA

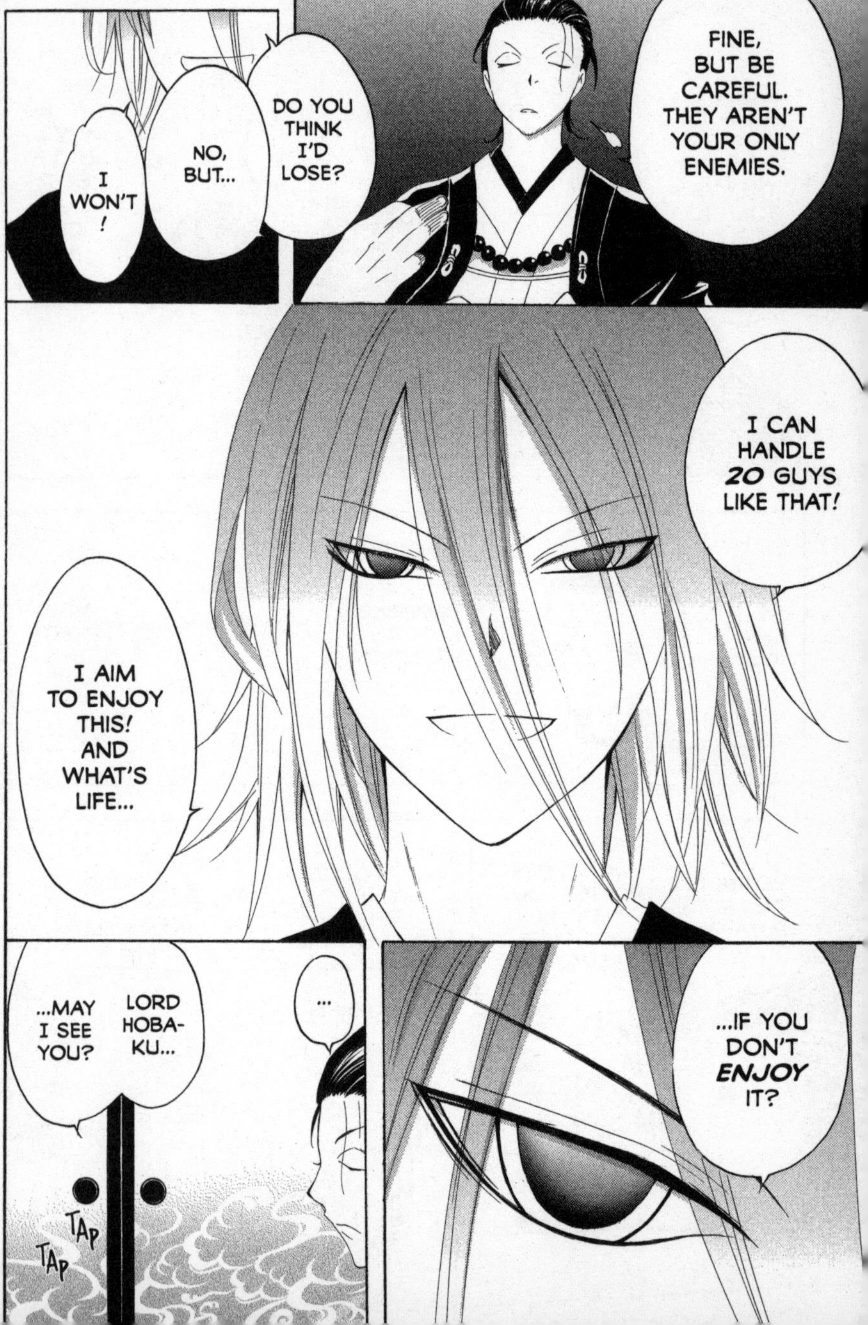
FINE, BUT BE CAREFUL. THEY AREN'T YOUR ONLY ENEMIES.
DO YOU THINK I'D LOSE?
NO, BUT...
I WON'T!
I CAN HANDLE 20 GUYS LIKE THAT!
I AIM TO ENJOY THIS! AND WHAT'S LIFE...
...IF YOU DON'T ENJOY IT?
...
LORD HOBA-KU...
...MAY I SEE YOU?
TAP
TAP

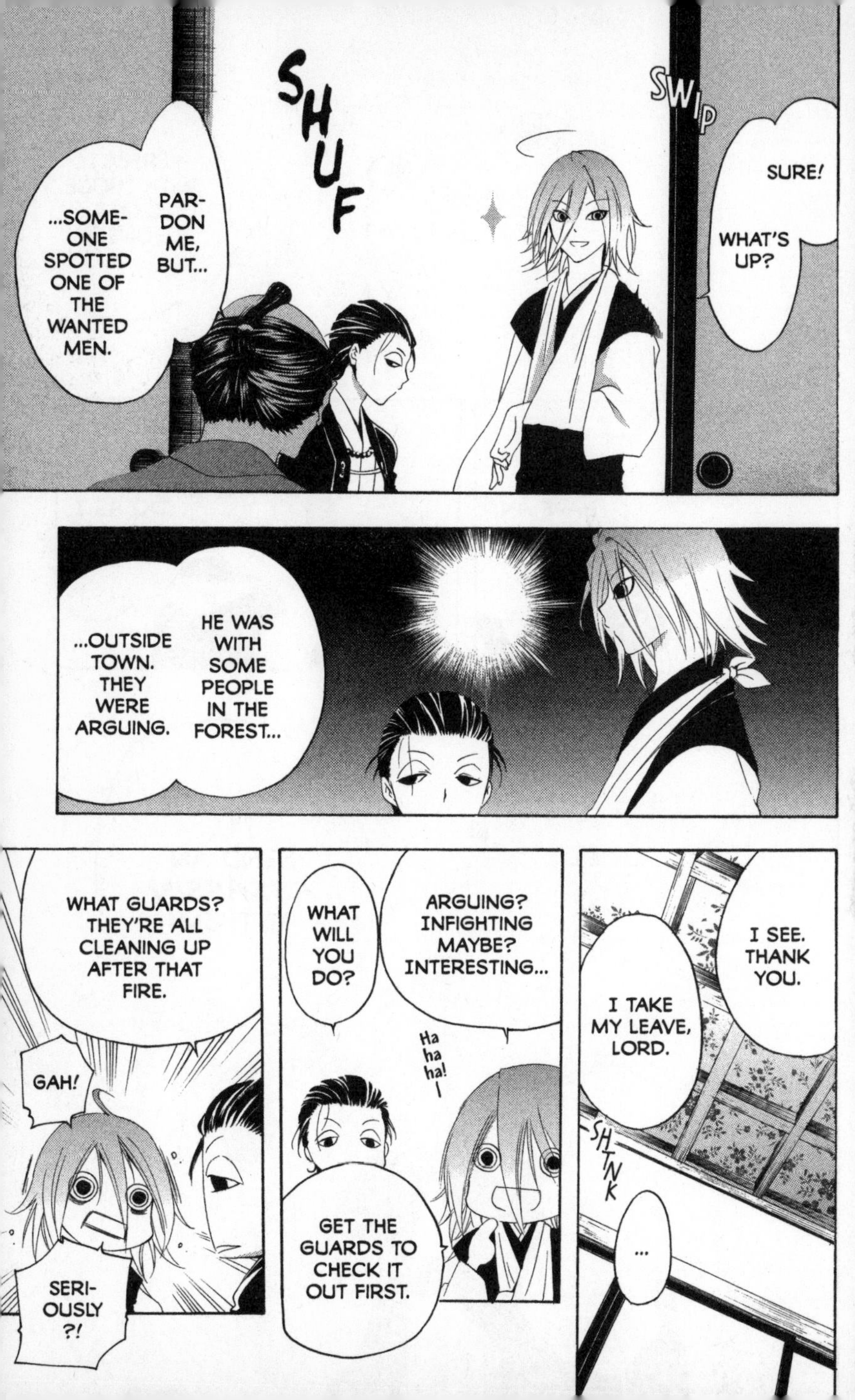
SWIP
SURE! WHAT'S UP?
SHUF
PAR-DON ME, BUT...
...SOME-ONE SPOTTED ONE OF THE WANTED MEN.
HE WAS WITH SOME PEOPLE IN THE FOREST...
...OUTSIDE TOWN. THEY WERE ARGUING.
I SEE. THANK YOU.
I TAKE MY LEAVE, LORD.
SHTNK
...
ARGUING? INFIGHTING MAYBE? INTERESTING...
WHAT WILL YOU DO?
Ha ha ha!
GET THE GUARDS TO CHECK IT OUT FIRST.
WHAT GUARDS? THEY'RE ALL CLEANING UP AFTER THAT FIRE.
GAH!
SERI-OUSLY ?!

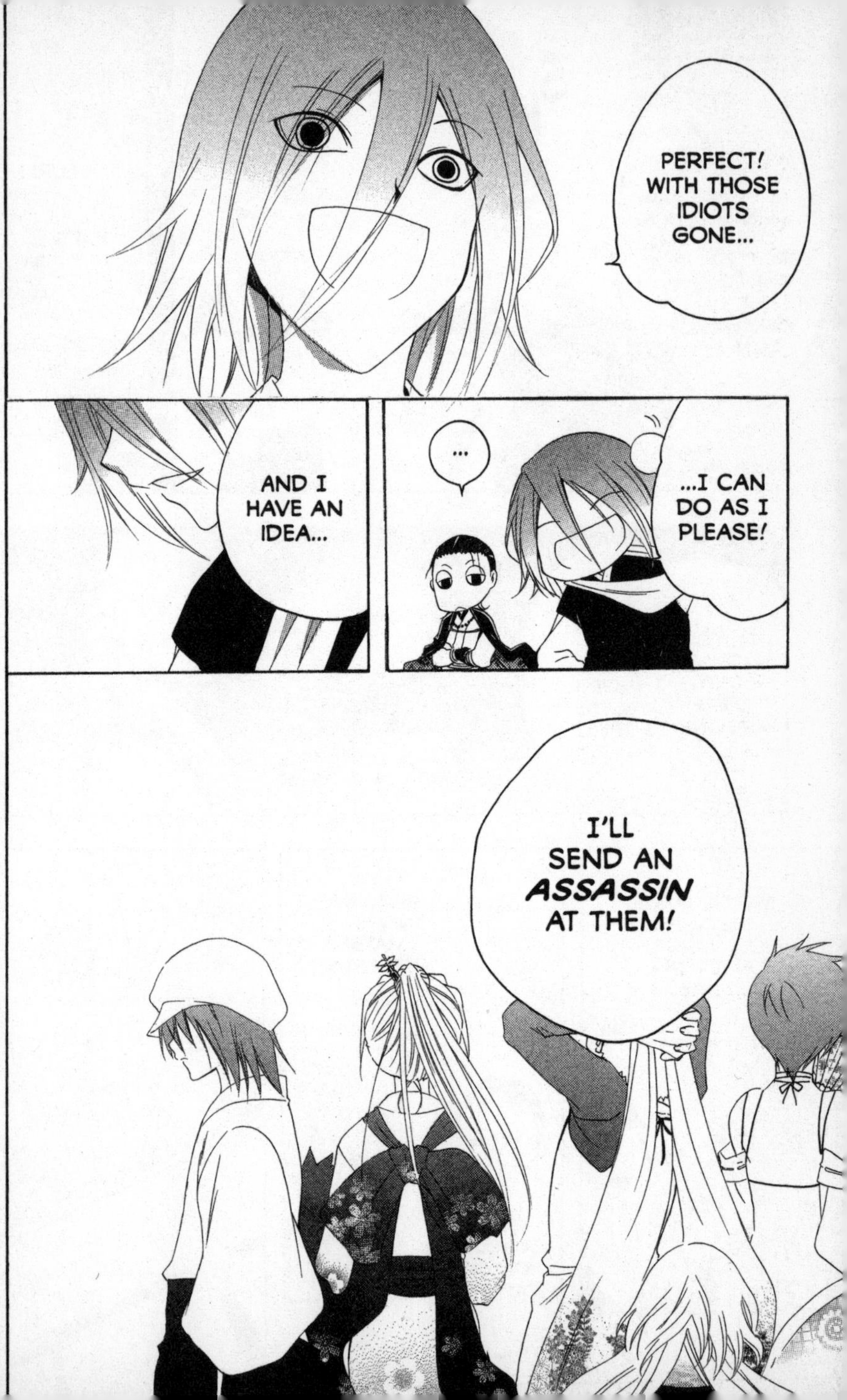
PERFECT! WITH THOSE IDIOTS GONE...
...I CAN DO AS I PLEASE!
...
AND I HAVE AN IDEA...
I'LL SEND AN *ASSASSIN* AT THEM!

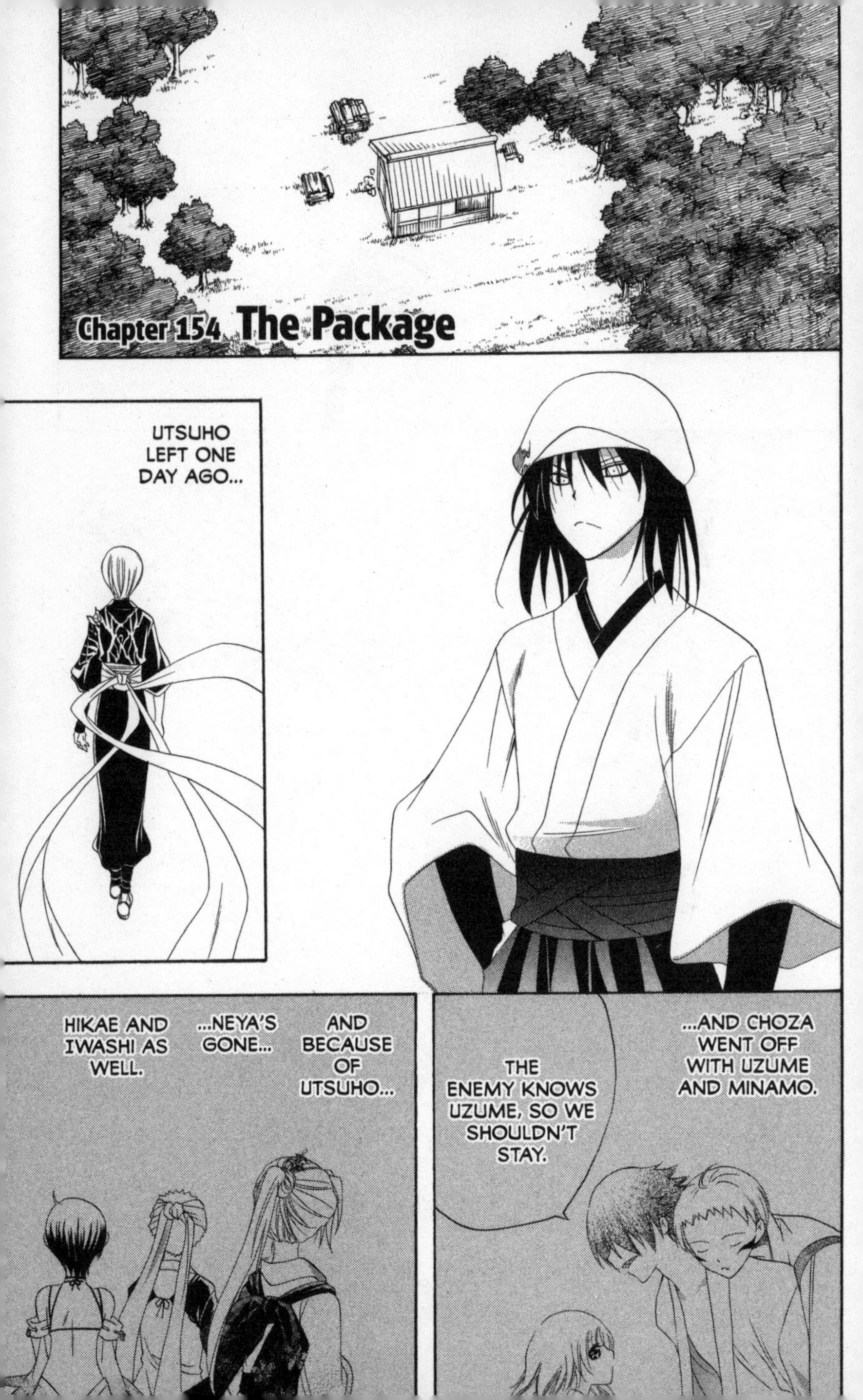
Chapter 154 The Package
UTSUHO LEFT ONE DAY AGO...
...AND CHOZA WENT OFF WITH UZUME AND MINAMO.
THE ENEMY KNOWS UZUME, SO WE SHOULDN'T STAY.
AND BECAUSE OF UTSUHO...
...NEYA'S GONE...
HIKAE AND IWASHI AS WELL.

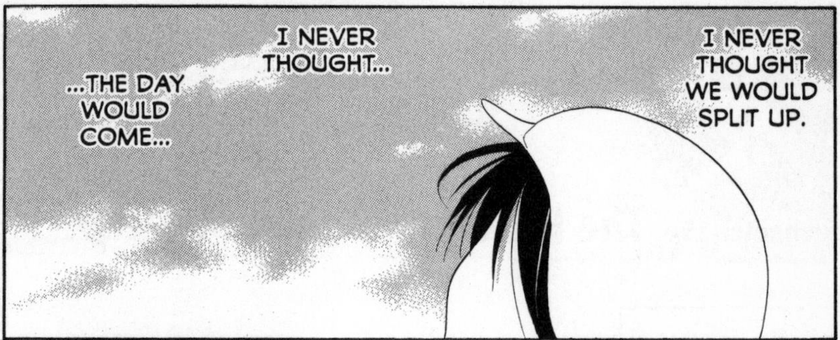
I NEVER THOUGHT WE WOULD SPLIT UP.
I NEVER THOUGHT...
...THE DAY WOULD COME...
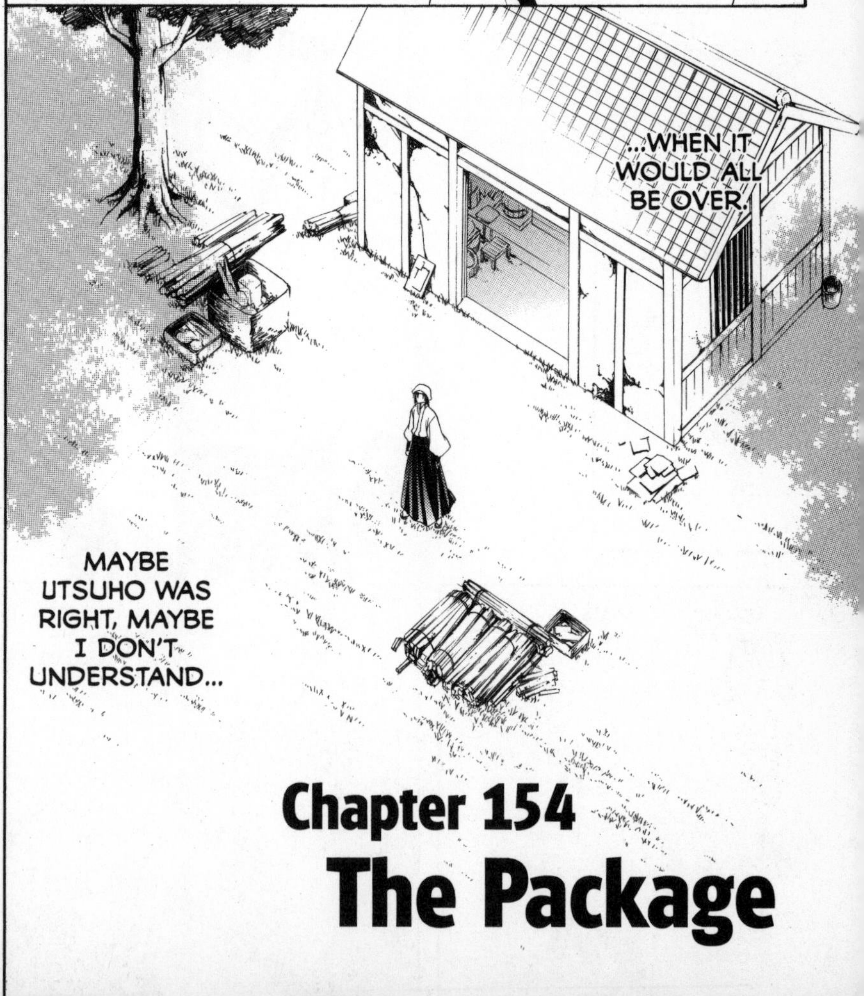
...WHEN IT WOULD ALL BE OVER.
MAYBE UTSUHO WAS RIGHT, MAYBE I DON'T UNDERSTAND...

Chapter 154
The Package

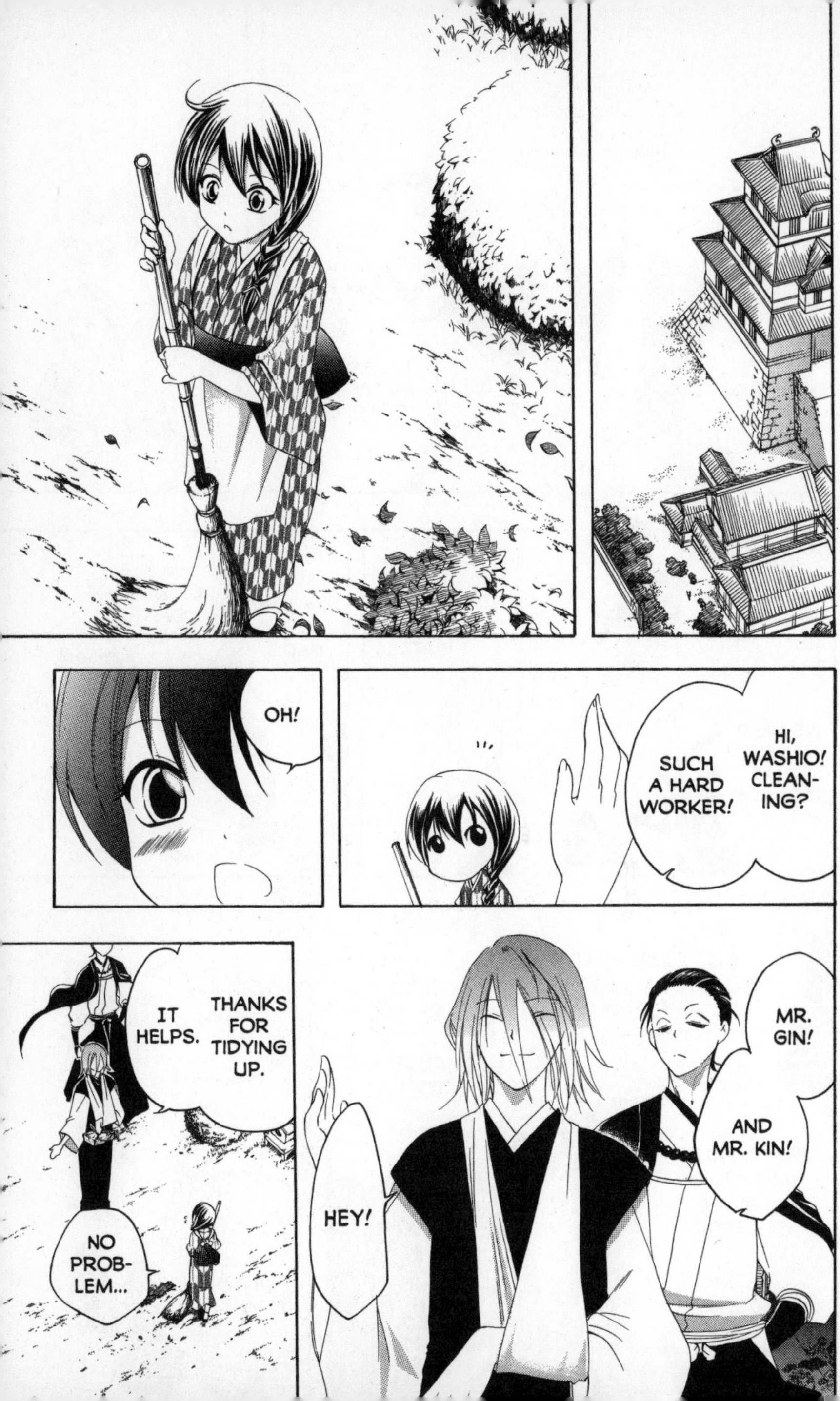

HI, WASHIO! CLEANING?
SUCH A HARD WORKER!
OH!
MR. GIN!
AND MR. KIN!
HEY!
THANKS FOR TIDYING UP.
IT HELPS.
NO PROBLEM...

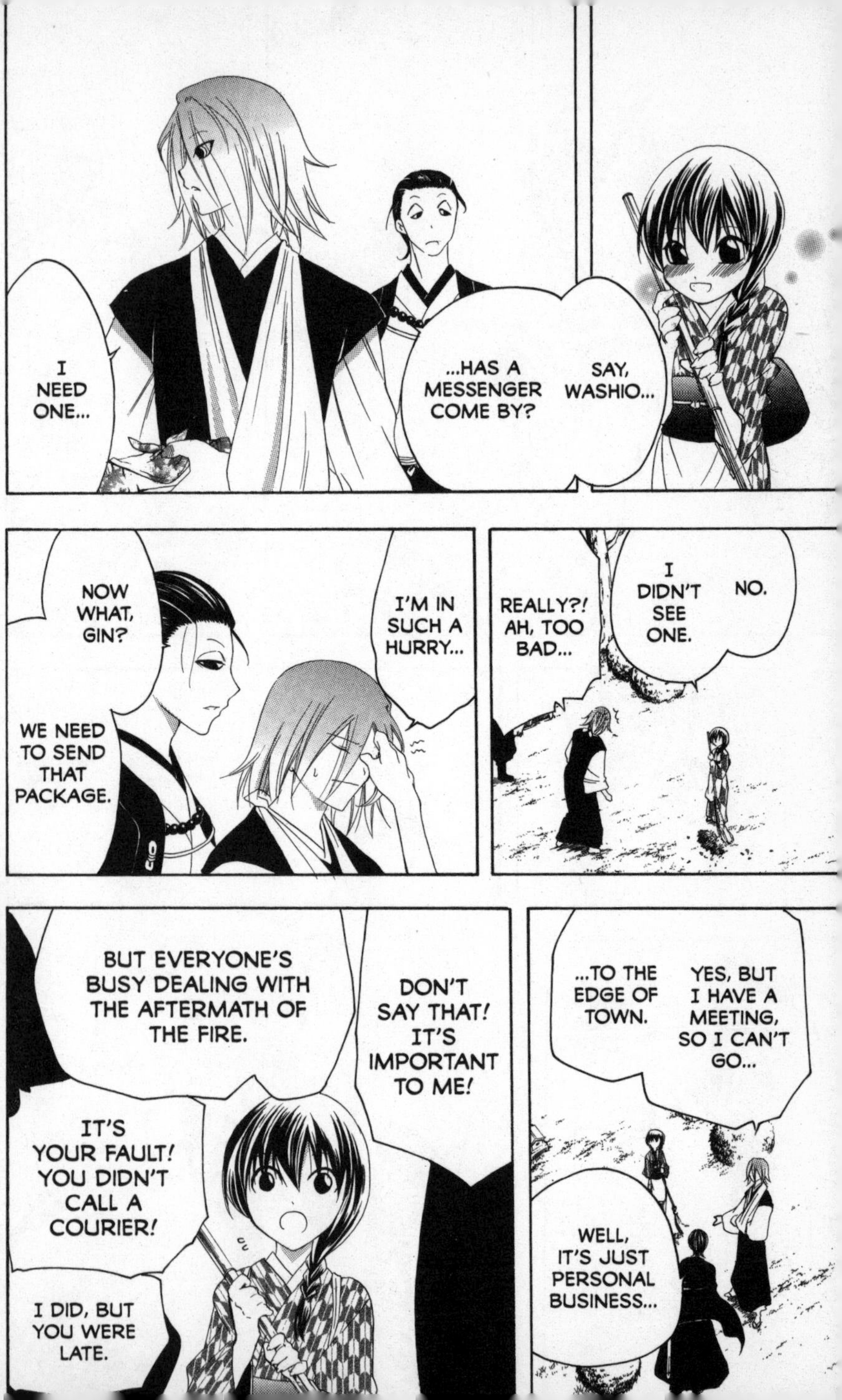
SAY, WASHIO...
...HAS A MESSENGER COME BY?
I NEED ONE...
NO.
I DIDN'T SEE ONE.
REALLY?! AH, TOO BAD...
I'M IN SUCH A HURRY...
NOW WHAT, GIN?
WE NEED TO SEND THAT PACKAGE.
YES, BUT I HAVE A MEETING, SO I CAN'T GO...
...TO THE EDGE OF TOWN.
WELL, IT'S JUST PERSONAL BUSINESS...
DON'T SAY THAT! IT'S IMPORTANT TO ME!
BUT EVERYONE'S BUSY DEALING WITH THE AFTERMATH OF THE FIRE.
IT'S YOUR FAULT! YOU DIDN'T CALL A COURIER!
I DID, BUT YOU WERE LATE.

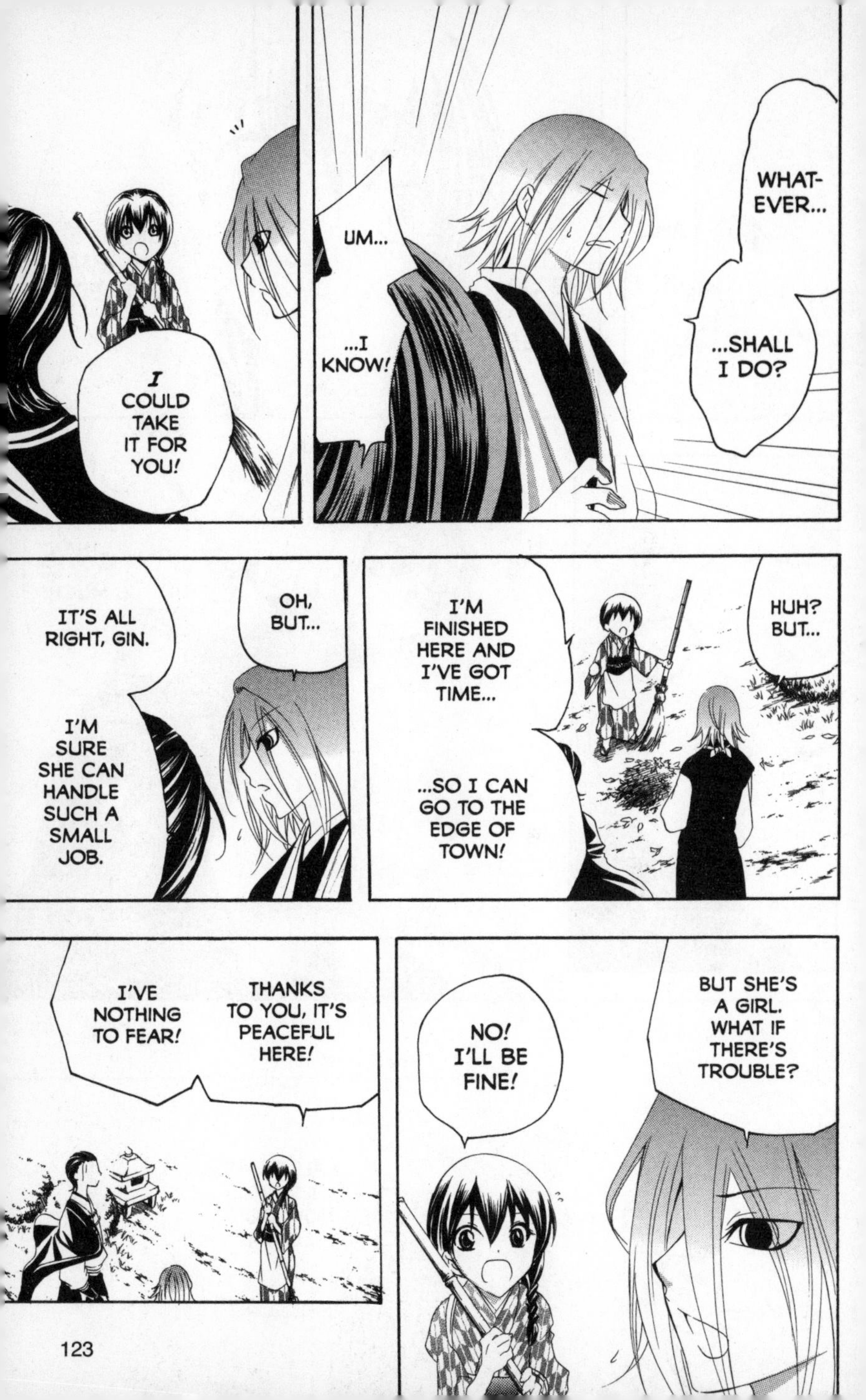
WHAT-EVER...
...SHALL I DO?
UM...
...I KNOW!
I COULD TAKE IT FOR YOU!
HUH? BUT...
I'M FINISHED HERE AND I'VE GOT TIME...
...SO I CAN GO TO THE EDGE OF TOWN!
OH, BUT...
IT'S ALL RIGHT, GIN.
I'M SURE SHE CAN HANDLE SUCH A SMALL JOB.
BUT SHE'S A GIRL. WHAT IF THERE'S TROUBLE?
NO! I'LL BE FINE!
THANKS TO YOU, IT'S PEACEFUL HERE!
I'VE NOTHING TO FEAR!

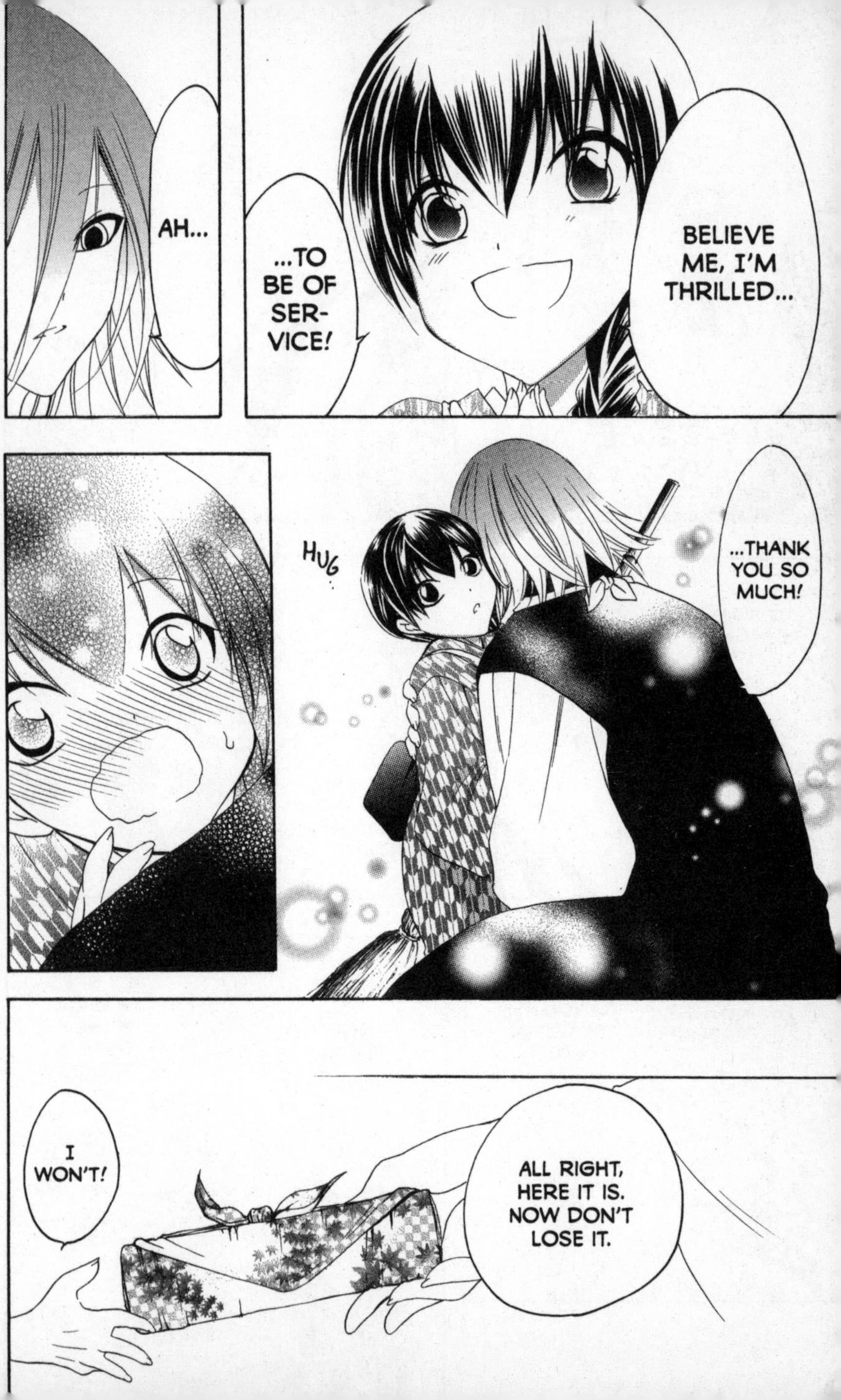
BELIEVE ME, I'M THRILLED...
...TO BE OF SER-VICE!
AH...
...THANK YOU SO MUCH!
HUG
ALL RIGHT, HERE IT IS. NOW DON'T LOSE IT.
I WON'T!

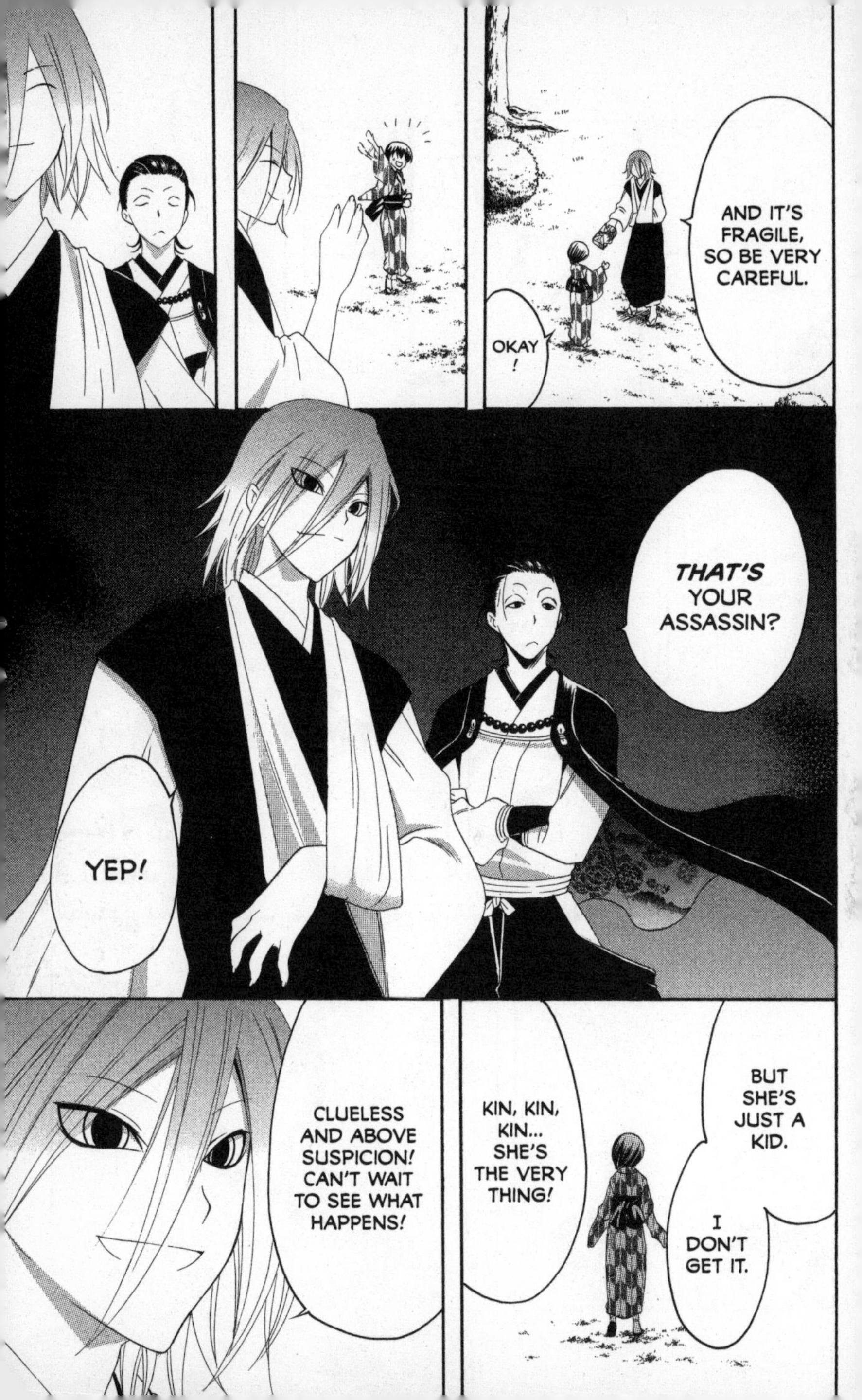
AND IT'S FRAGILE, SO BE VERY CAREFUL.
OKAY!
THAT'S YOUR ASSASSIN?
YEP!
BUT SHE'S JUST A KID.
I DON'T GET IT.
KIN, KIN, KIN... SHE'S THE VERY THING!
CLUELESS AND ABOVE SUSPICION! CAN'T WAIT TO SEE WHAT HAPPENS!

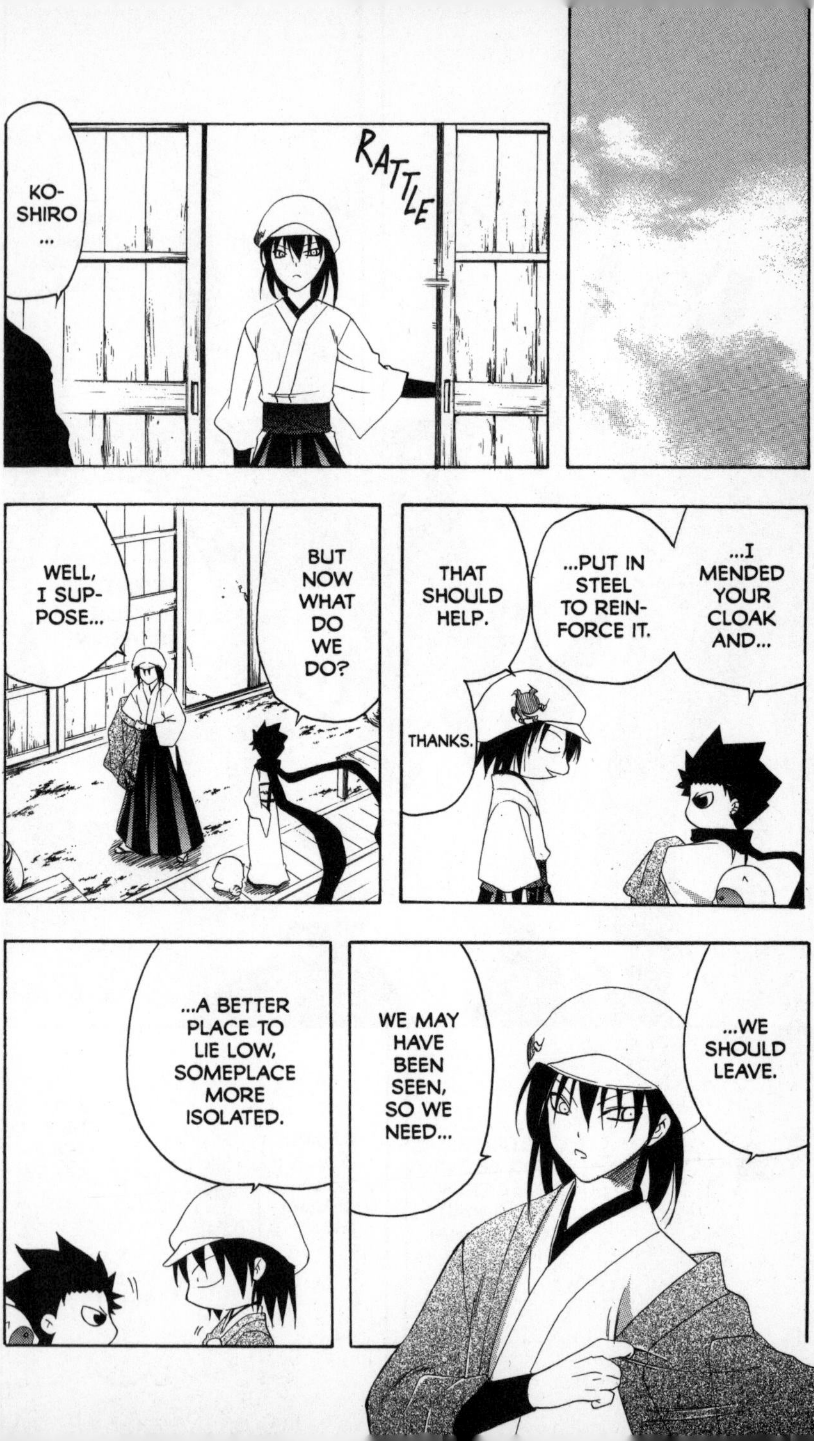
RATTLE
KO-SHIRO ...
...I MENDED YOUR CLOAK AND...
...PUT IN STEEL TO REIN-FORCE IT.
THAT SHOULD HELP.
THANKS.
BUT NOW WHAT DO WE DO?
WELL, I SUP-POSE...
...WE SHOULD LEAVE.
WE MAY HAVE BEEN SEEN, SO WE NEED...
...A BETTER PLACE TO LIE LOW, SOMEPLACE MORE ISOLATED.

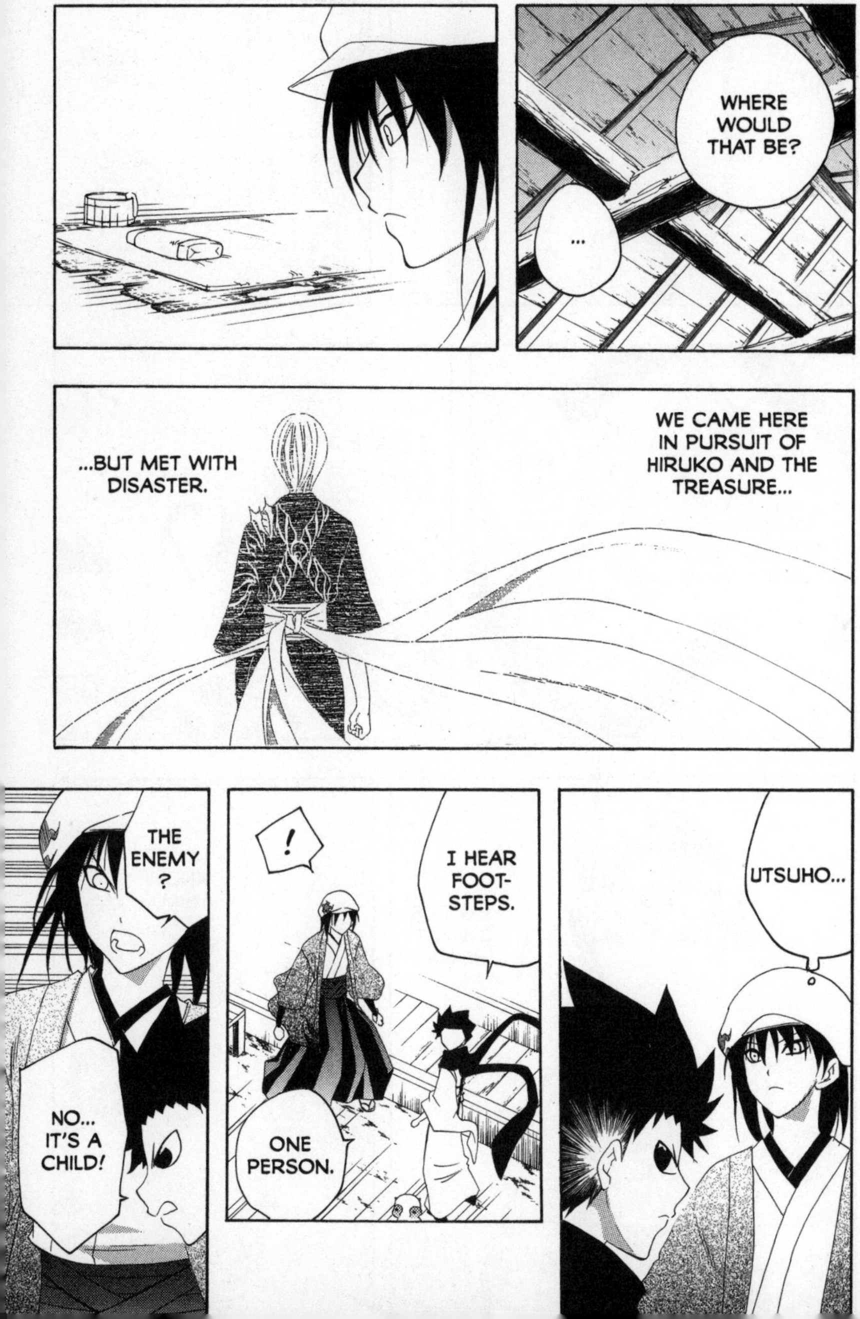
WHERE WOULD THAT BE?
...
WE CAME HERE IN PURSUIT OF HIRUKO AND THE TREASURE...
...BUT MET WITH DISASTER.
UTSUHO...
I HEAR FOOT-STEPS.
!
ONE PERSON.
THE ENEMY?
NO... IT'S A CHILD!

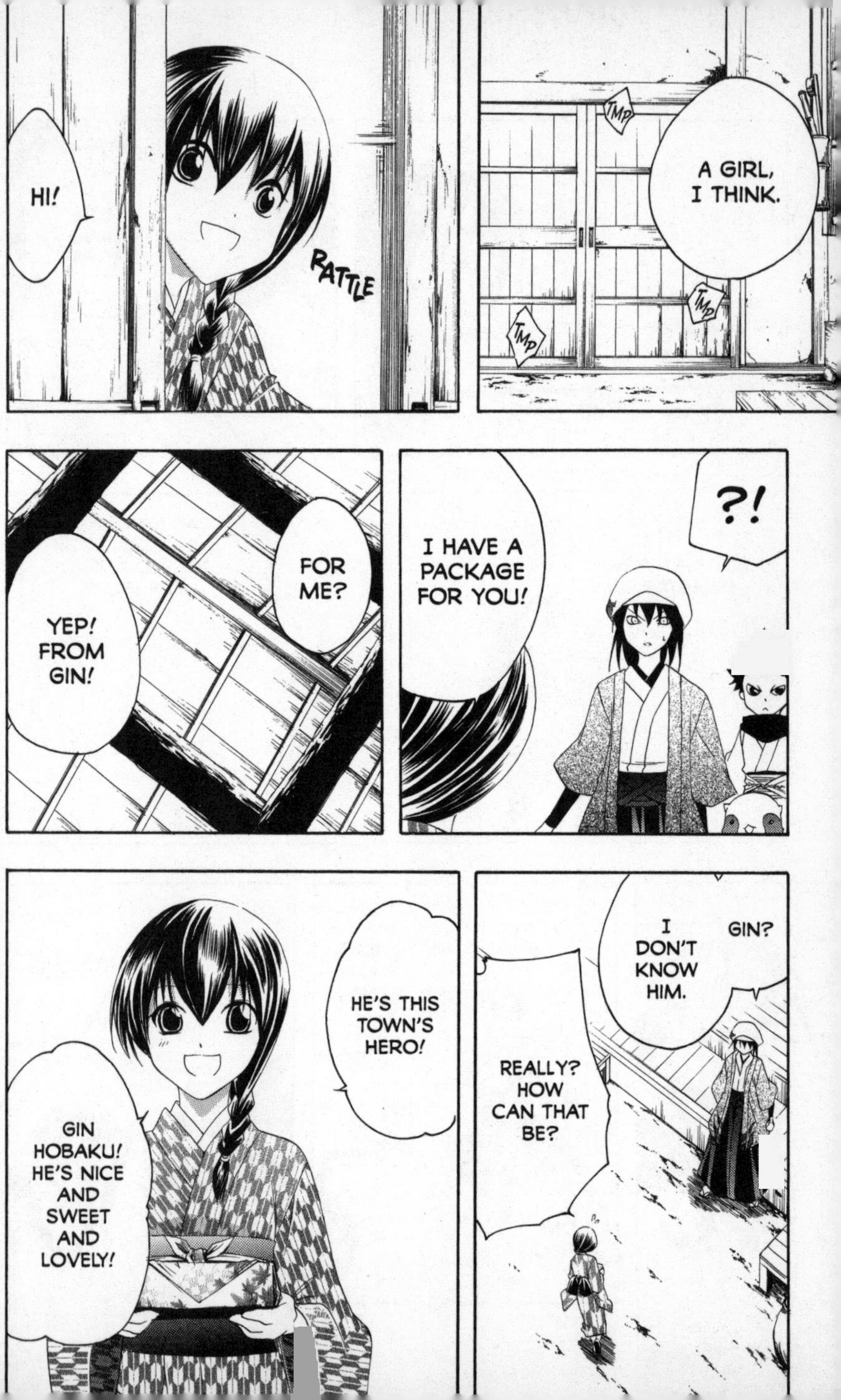

TMP
TMP
TMP
A GIRL, I THINK.
RATTLE
HI!
?!
I HAVE A PACKAGE FOR YOU!
FOR ME?
YEP! FROM GIN!
GIN?
I DON'T KNOW HIM.
REALLY? HOW CAN THAT BE?
HE'S THIS TOWN'S HERO!
GIN HOBAKU! HE'S NICE AND SWEET AND LOVELY!

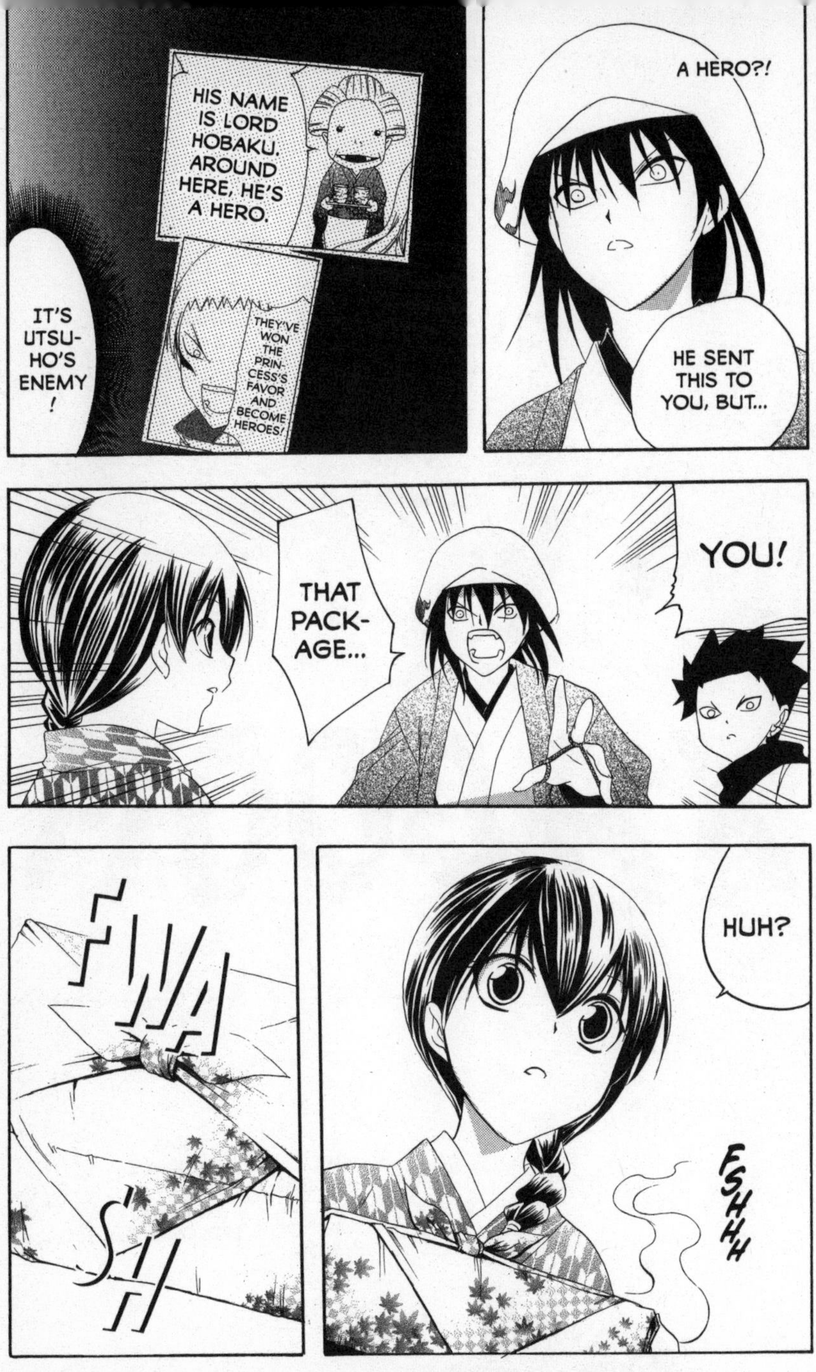
A HERO?!
HE SENT THIS TO YOU, BUT...
HIS NAME IS LORD HOBAKU. AROUND HERE, HE'S A HERO.
THEY'VE WON THE PRINCESS'S FAVOR AND BECOME HEROES!
IT'S UTSUHO'S ENEMY!
YOU!
THAT PACKAGE...
HUH?
FSHHH
FWA
SH

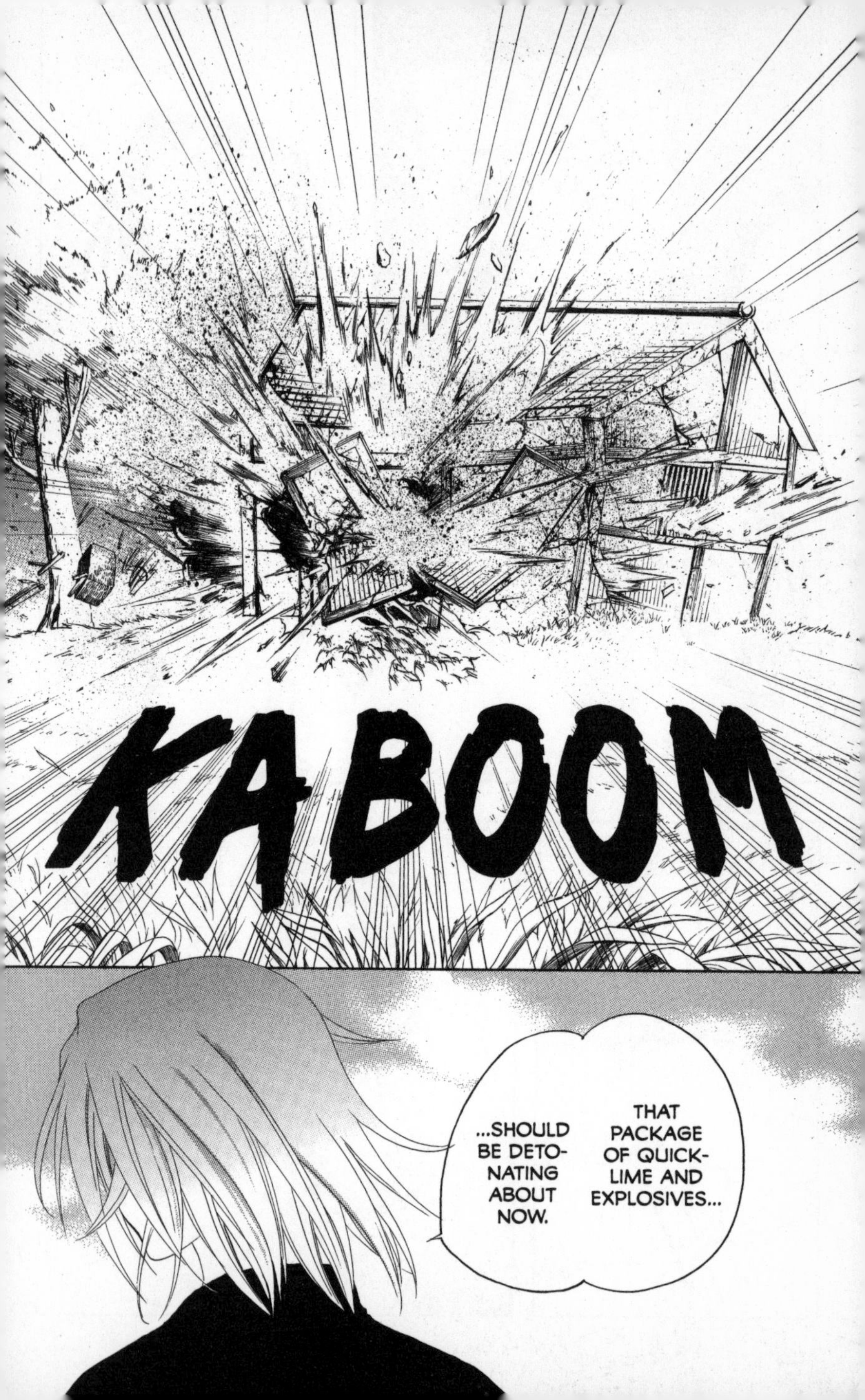
KABOOM
THAT PACKAGE OF QUICK-LIME AND EXPLOSIVES...
...SHOULD BE DETO-NATING ABOUT NOW.

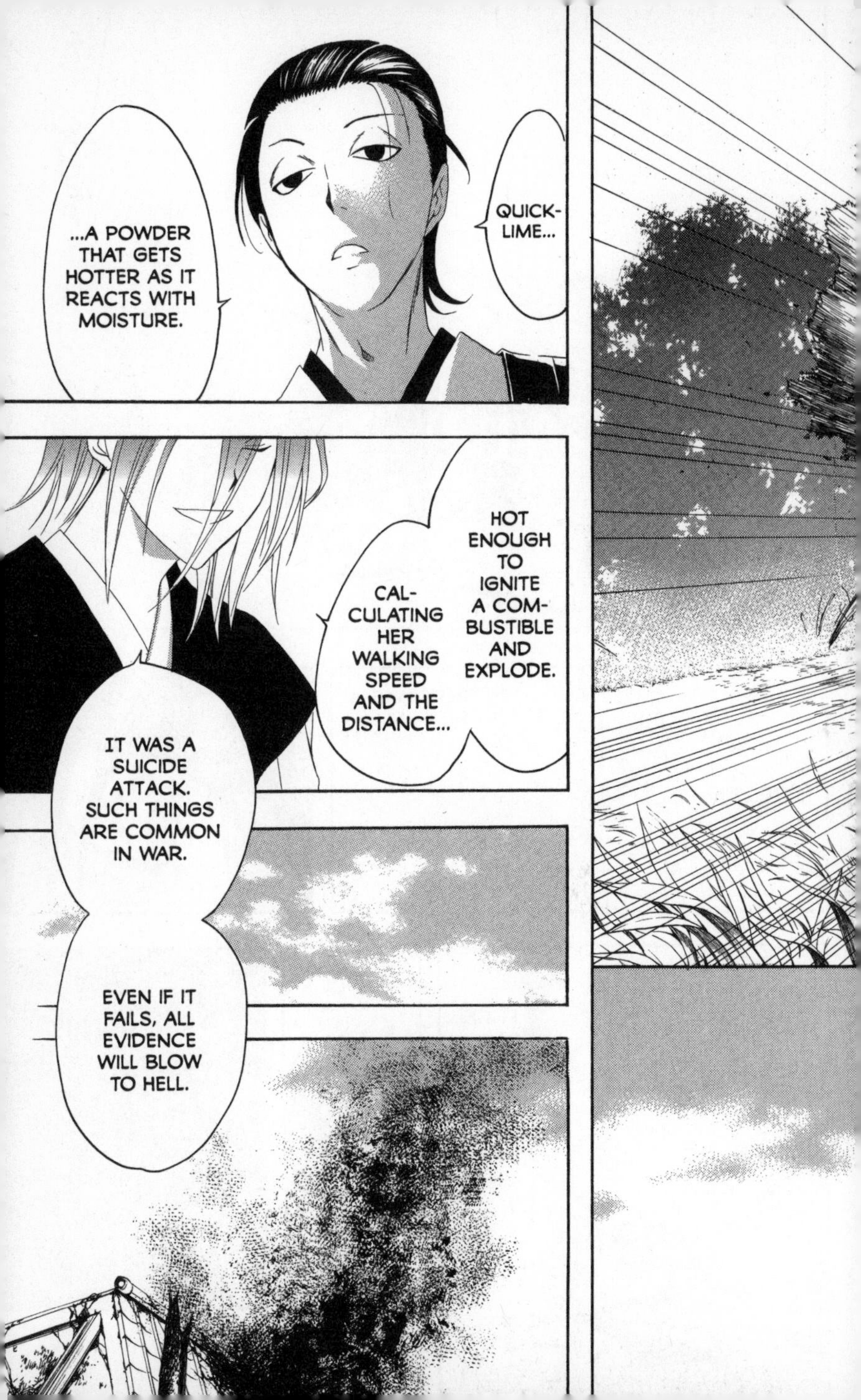
QUICK-LIME...
...A POWDER THAT GETS HOTTER AS IT REACTS WITH MOISTURE.
HOT ENOUGH TO IGNITE A COM-BUSTIBLE AND EXPLODE.
CAL-CULATING HER WALKING SPEED AND THE DISTANCE...
IT WAS A SUICIDE ATTACK. SUCH THINGS ARE COMMON IN WAR.
EVEN IF IT FAILS, ALL EVIDENCE WILL BLOW TO HELL.

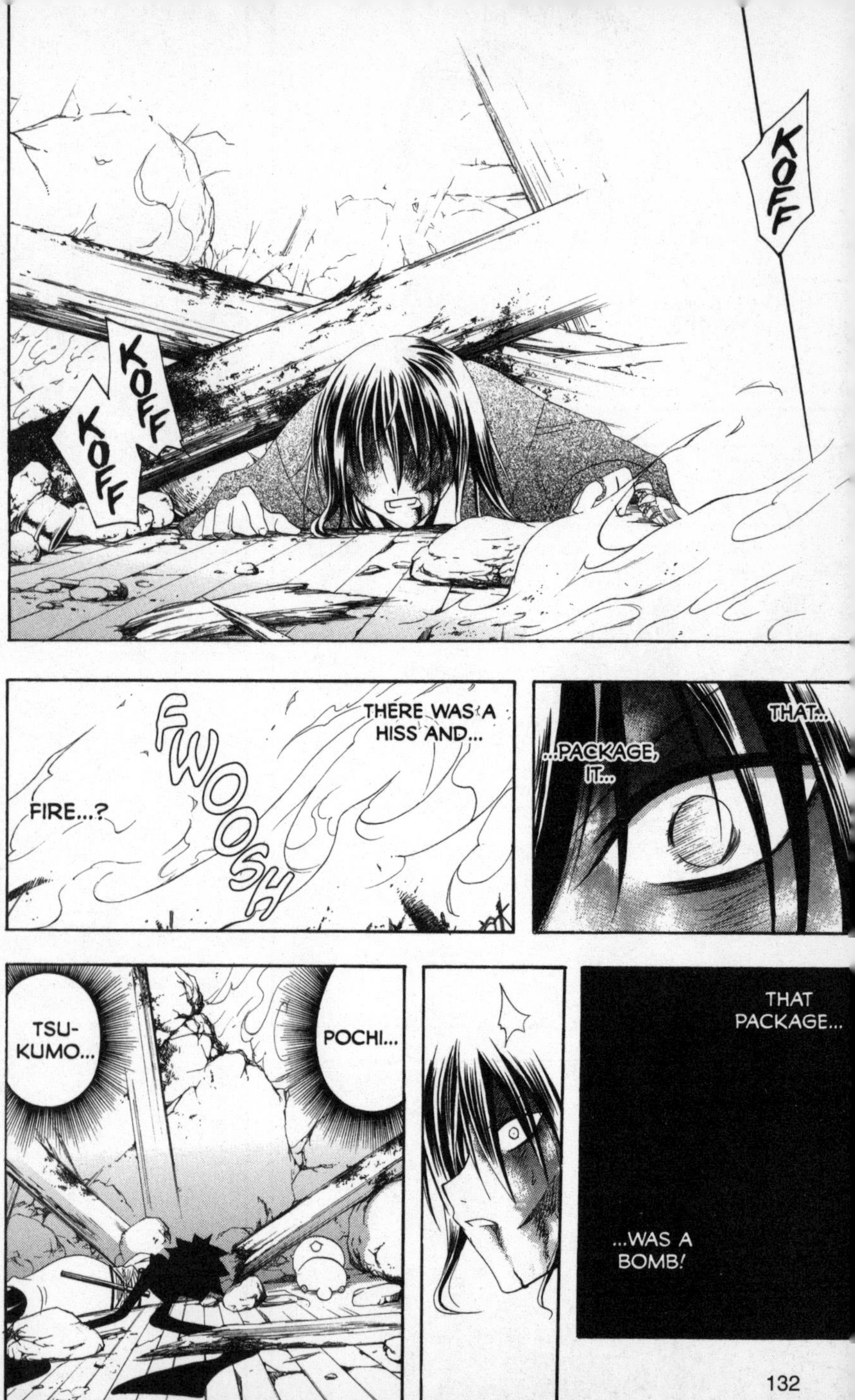
KOFF
KOFF
KOFF
THAT...
...PACKAGE, IT...
THERE WAS A HISS AND...
FWOOSH
FIRE...?
THAT PACKAGE...
...WAS A BOMB!
POCHI...
TSU-KUMO...

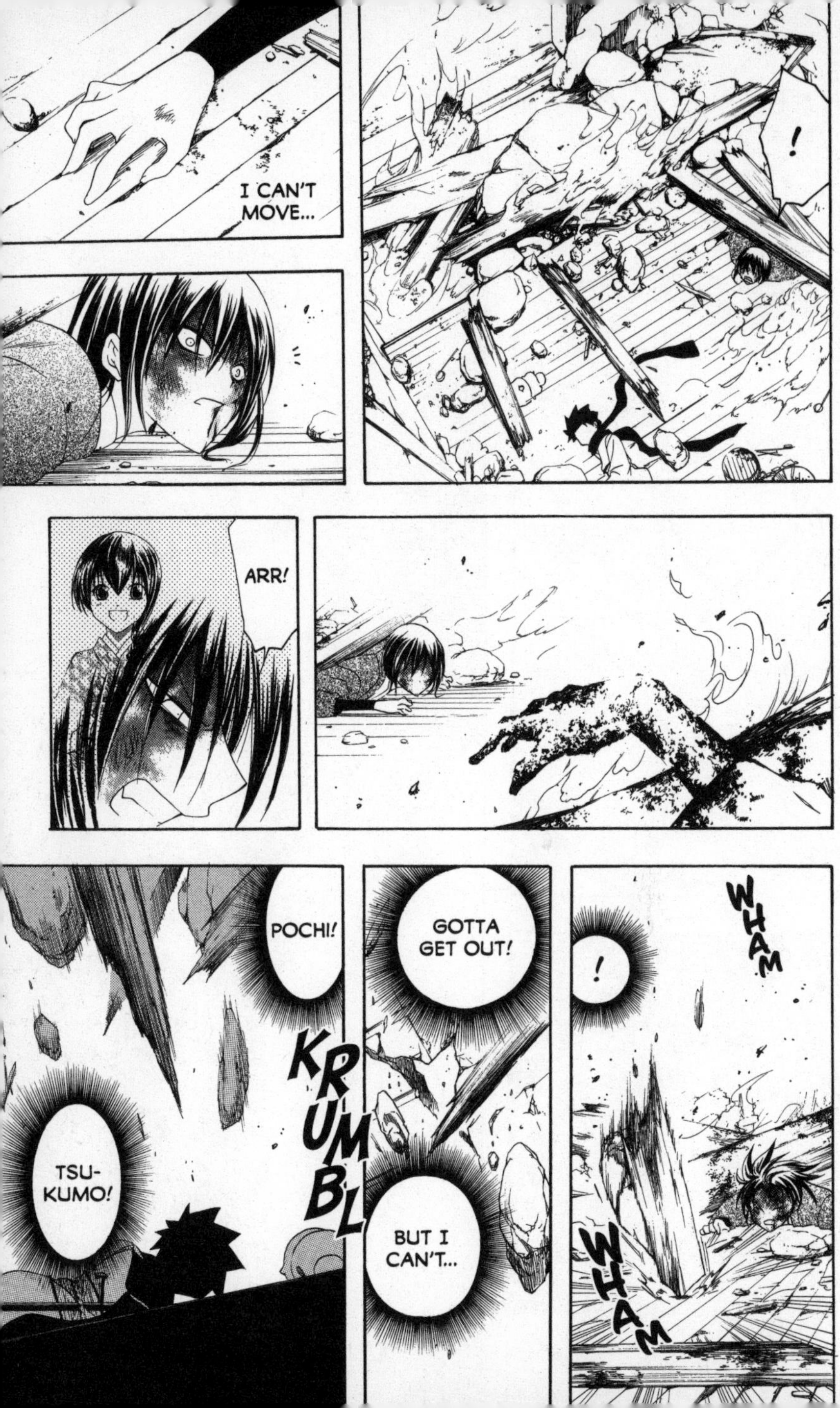
!
I CAN'T MOVE...
ARR!
!
WHAM
WHAM
GOTTA GET OUT!
BUT I CAN'T...
POCHI!
KRUMBL
TSU-KUMO!

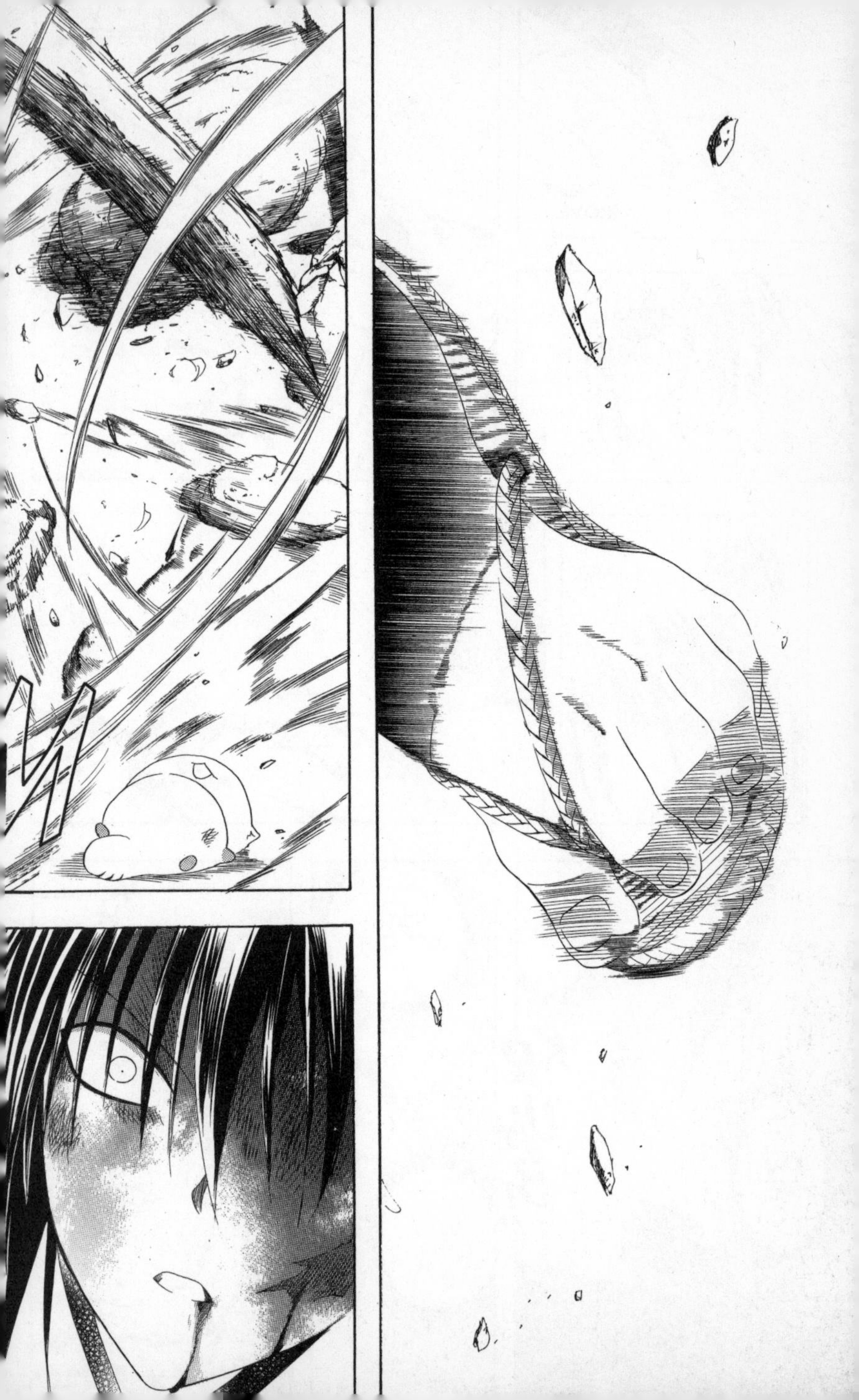

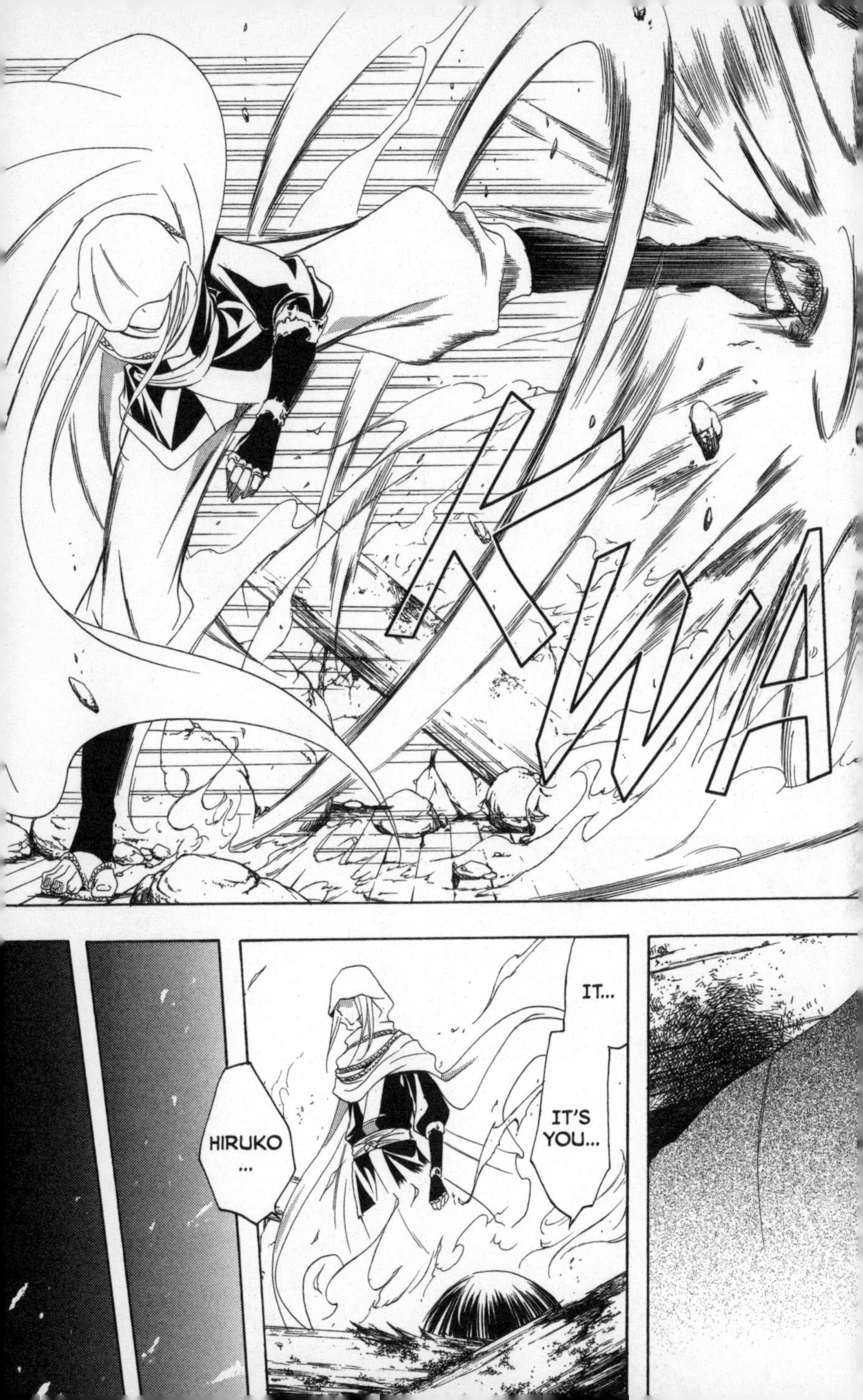
KWA
IT...
IT'S YOU...
HIRUKO ...

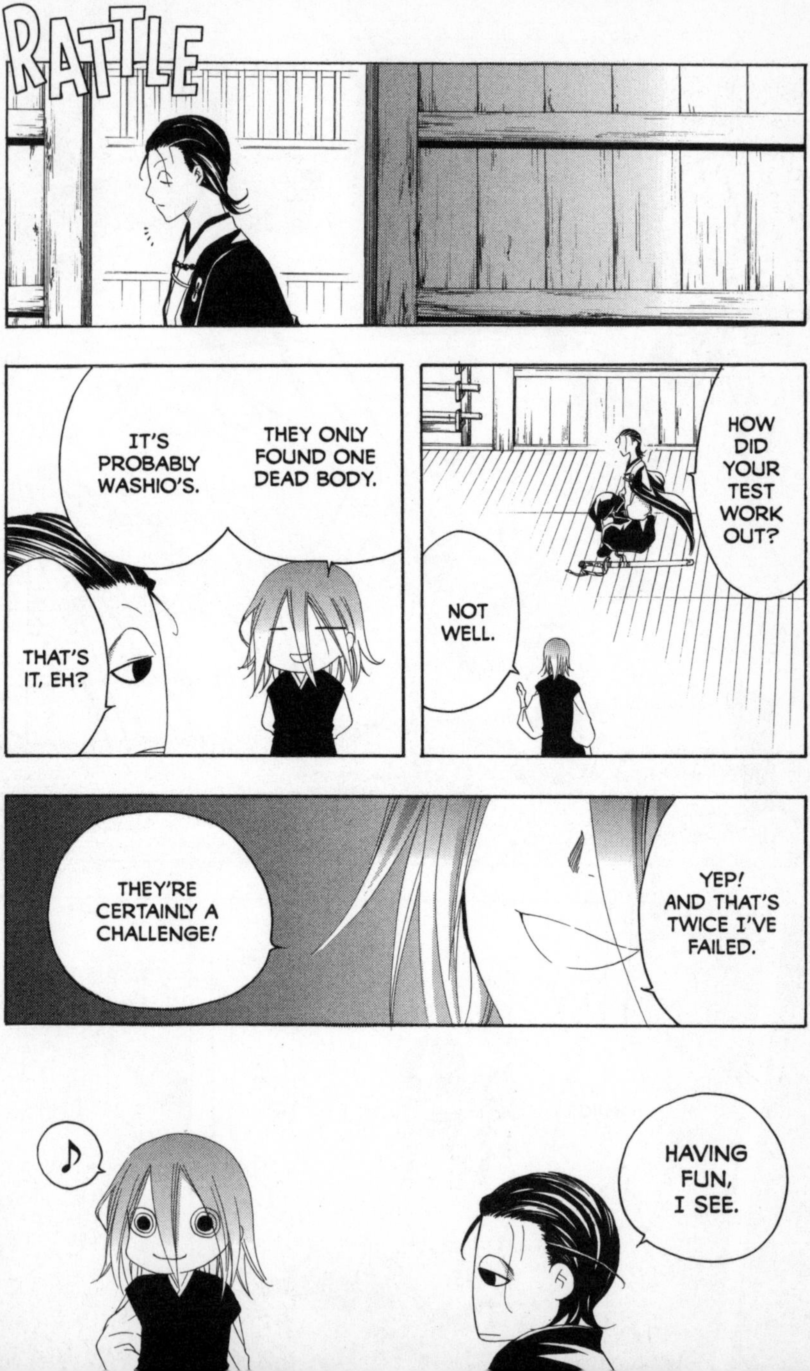
RATTLE
HOW DID YOUR TEST WORK OUT?
NOT WELL.
THEY ONLY FOUND ONE DEAD BODY.
IT'S PROBABLY WASHIO'S.
THAT'S IT, EH?
YEP! AND THAT'S TWICE I'VE FAILED.
THEY'RE CERTAINLY A CHALLENGE!
HAVING FUN, I SEE.
♪

Chapter 155 Gin's Past

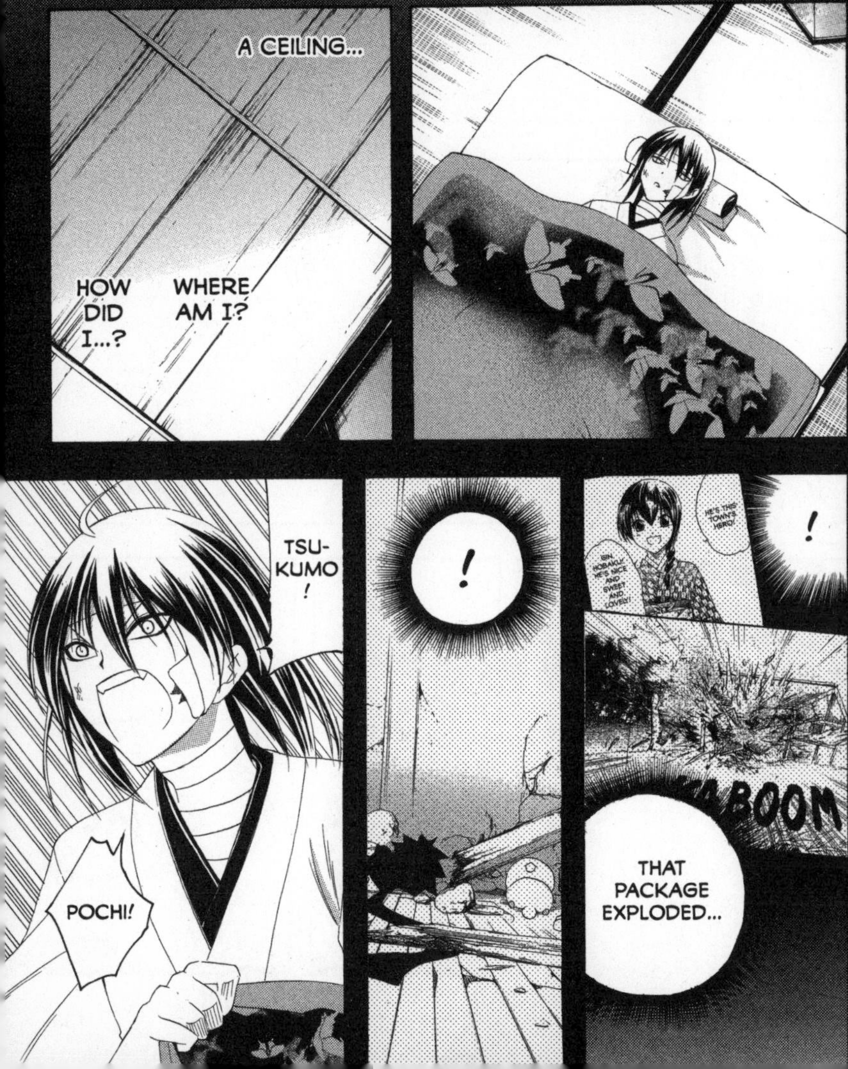
A CEILING...
WHERE AM I?
HOW DID I...?
!
HE'S THIS TOWN'S HERO!
GIN HOBAKU! HE'S NICE AND SWEET AND LOVELY!
BOOM
THAT PACKAGE EXPLODED...
!
TSU-KUMO!
POCHI!

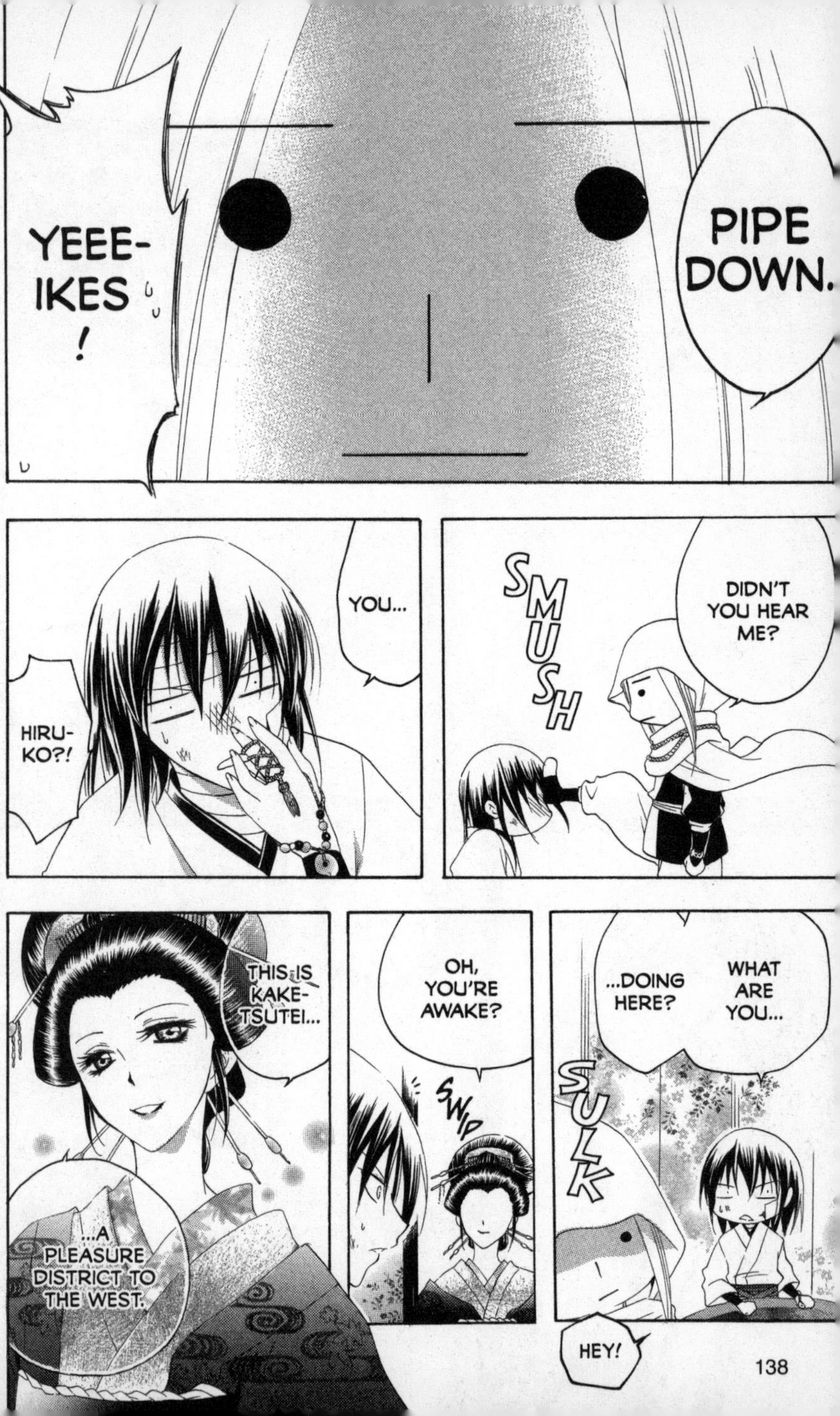
PIPE DOWN.
YEEE-IKES!
SMUSH
DIDN'T YOU HEAR ME?
YOU...
HIRU-KO?!
WHAT ARE YOU...
...DOING HERE?
SULK
HEY!
OH, YOU'RE AWAKE?
SNIP
THIS IS KAKE-TSUTEI...
...A PLEASURE DISTRICT TO THE WEST.

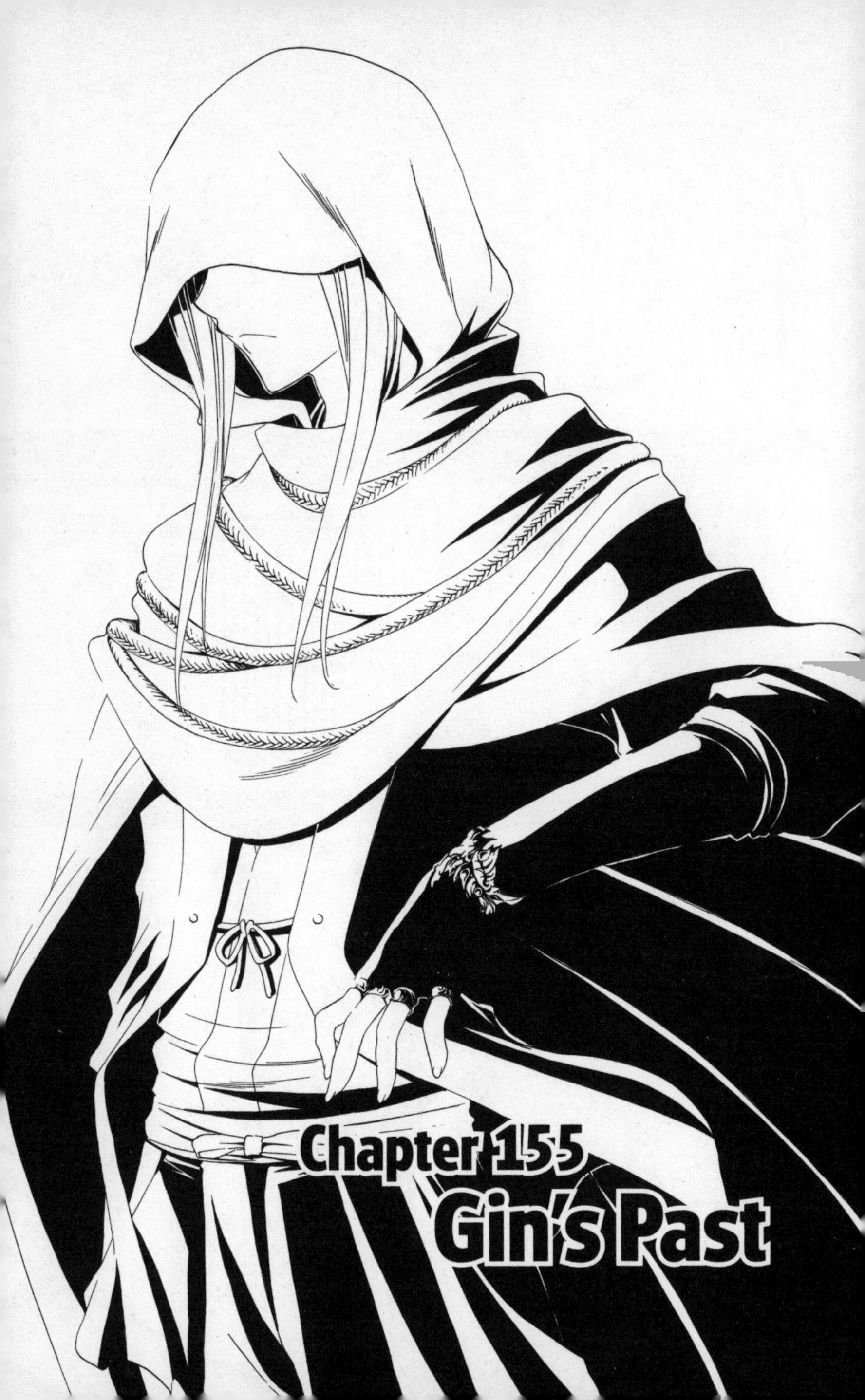
Chapter 155
Gin's Past

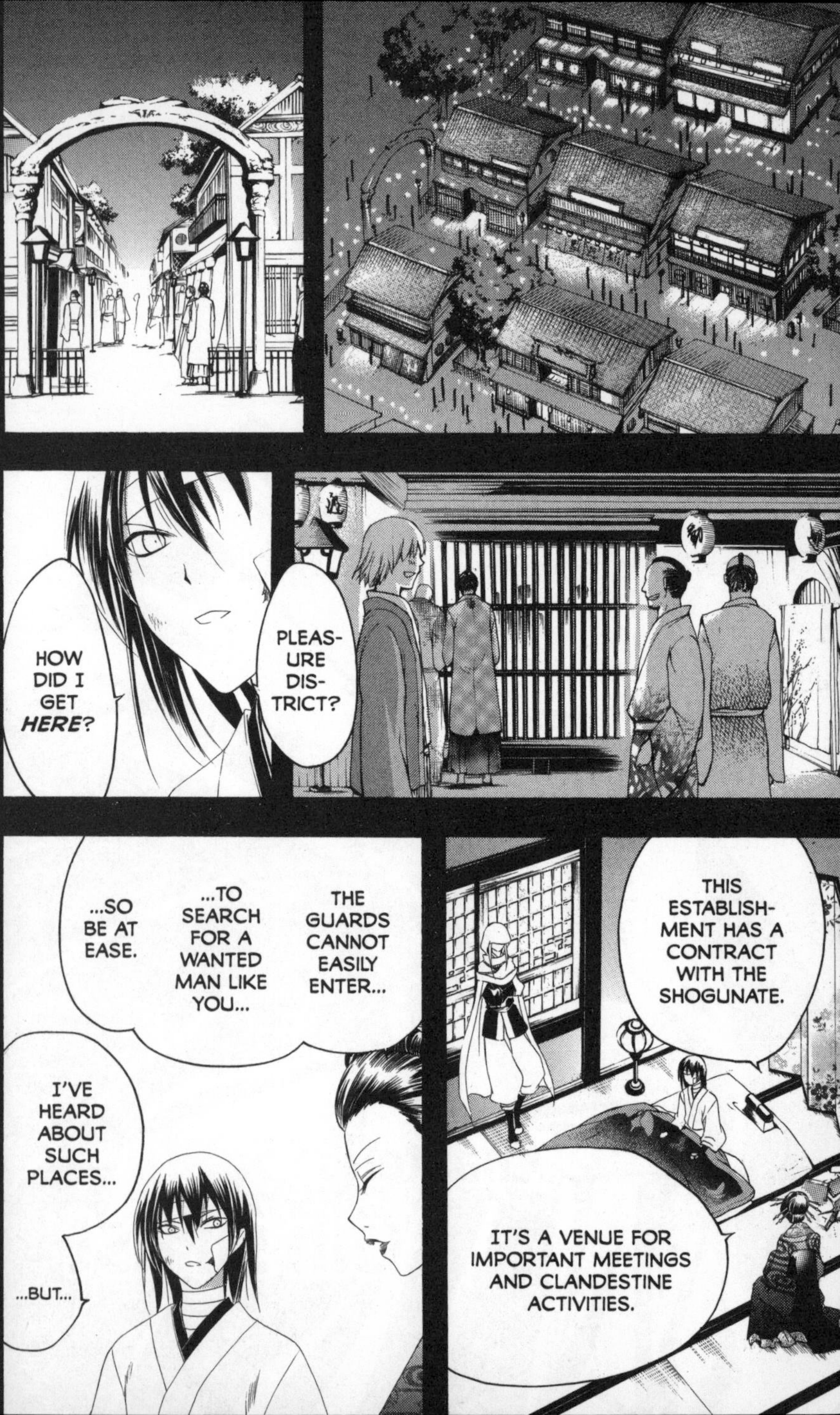
PLEAS-URE DIS-TRICT?
HOW DID I GET *HERE*?
THIS ESTABLISH-MENT HAS A CONTRACT WITH THE SHOGUNATE.
IT'S A VENUE FOR IMPORTANT MEETINGS AND CLANDESTINE ACTIVITIES.
THE GUARDS CANNOT EASILY ENTER...
...TO SEARCH FOR A WANTED MAN LIKE YOU...
...SO BE AT EASE.
I'VE HEARD ABOUT SUCH PLACES...
...BUT...

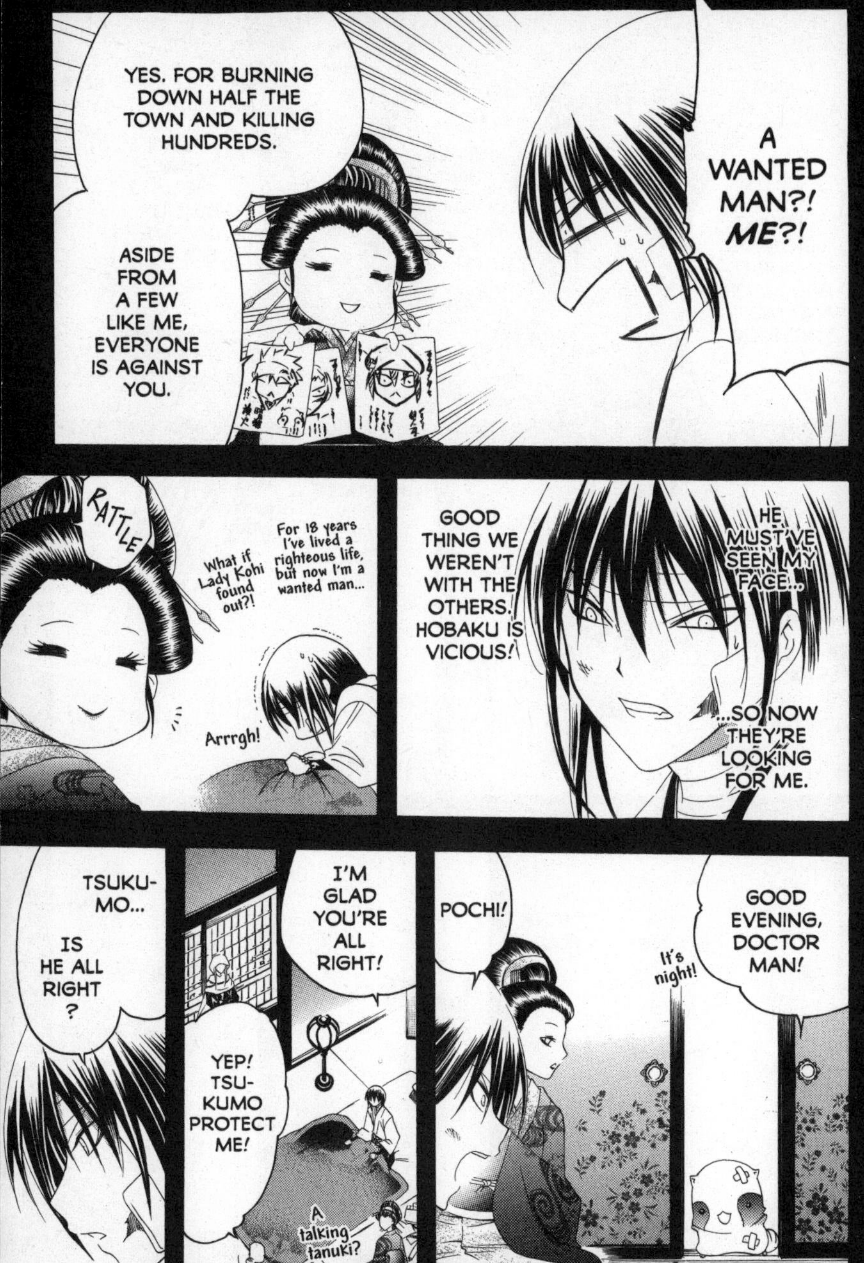
A WANTED MAN?! ***ME***?!
YES. FOR BURNING DOWN HALF THE TOWN AND KILLING HUNDREDS.
ASIDE FROM A FEW LIKE ME, EVERYONE IS AGAINST YOU.
HE MUST'VE SEEN MY FACE...
GOOD THING WE WEREN'T WITH THE OTHERS. HOBAKU IS VICIOUS!
...SO NOW THEY'RE LOOKING FOR ME.
RATTLE
For 18 years I've lived a righteous life, but now I'm a wanted man...
What if Lady Kohi found out?!
Arrrgh!
GOOD EVENING, DOCTOR MAN!
It's night!
POCHI!
I'M GLAD YOU'RE ALL RIGHT!
YEP! TSUKUMO PROTECT ME!
A talking tanuki?
TSUKUMO...
IS HE ALL RIGHT?

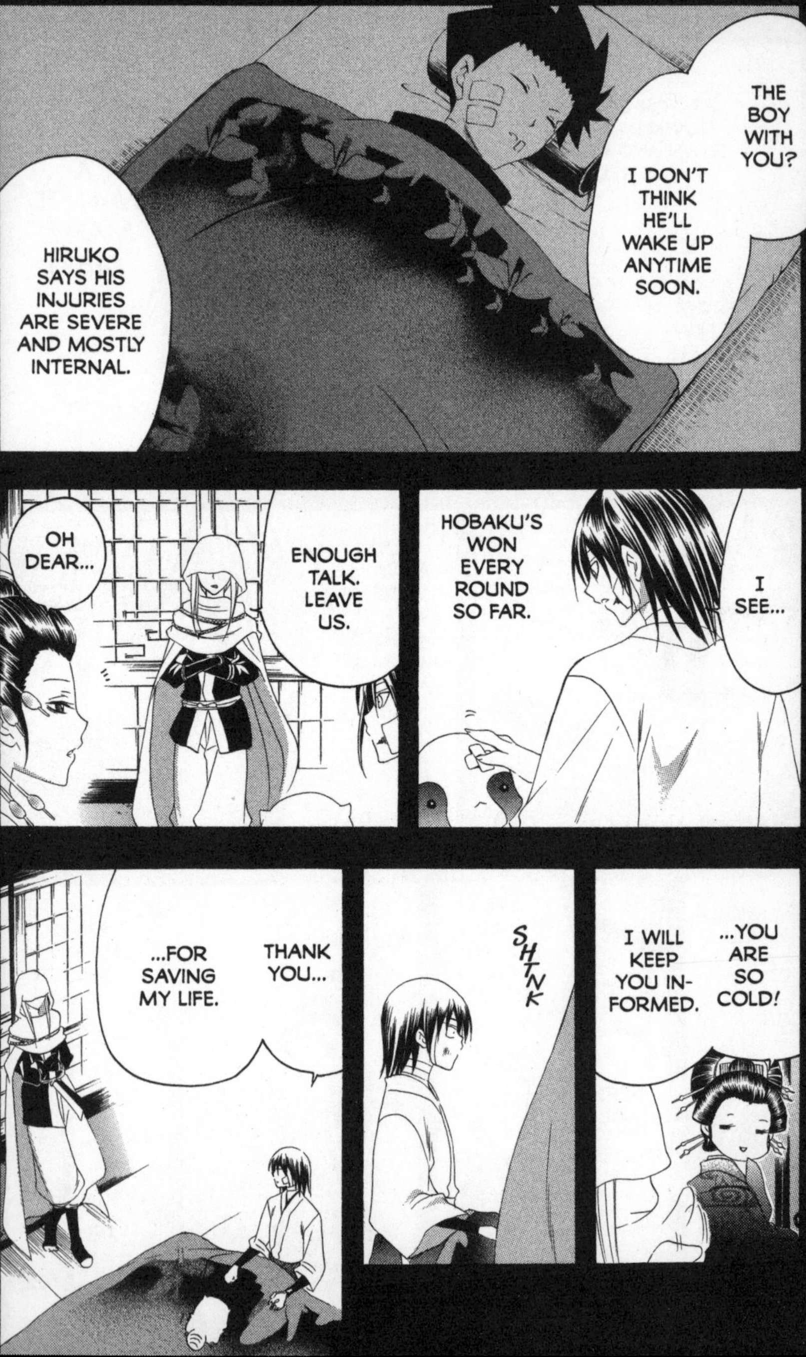
THE BOY WITH YOU?
I DON'T THINK HE'LL WAKE UP ANYTIME SOON.
HIRUKO SAYS HIS INJURIES ARE SEVERE AND MOSTLY INTERNAL.
I SEE...
HOBAKU'S WON EVERY ROUND SO FAR.
ENOUGH TALK. LEAVE US.
OH DEAR...
...YOU ARE SO COLD!
I WILL KEEP YOU IN-FORMED.
SHTNK
THANK YOU...
...FOR SAVING MY LIFE.

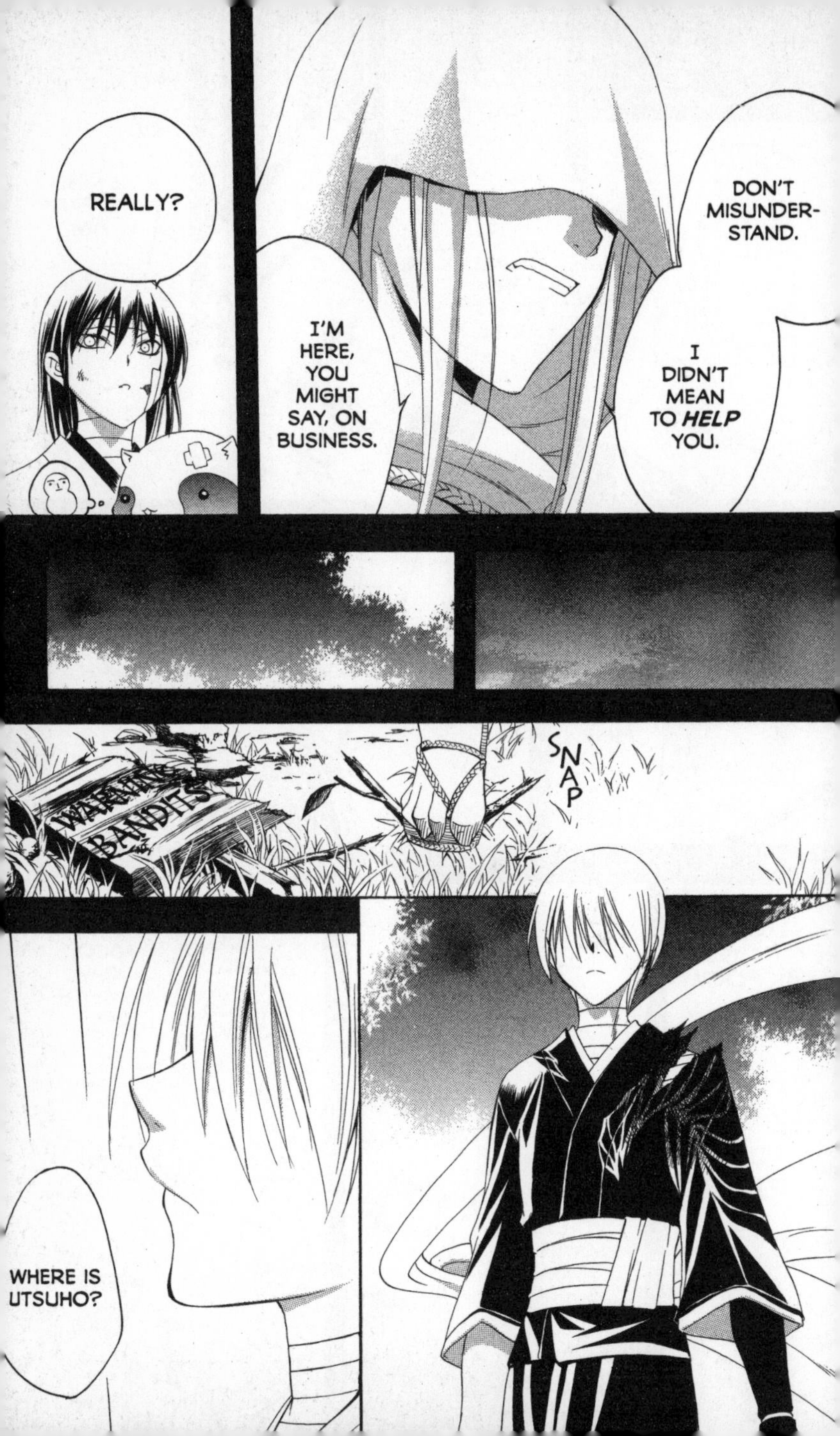
DON'T MISUNDERSTAND.
I DIDN'T MEAN TO *HELP* YOU.
I'M HERE, YOU MIGHT SAY, ON BUSINESS.
REALLY?
BANDITS
SNAP
WHERE IS UTSUHO?

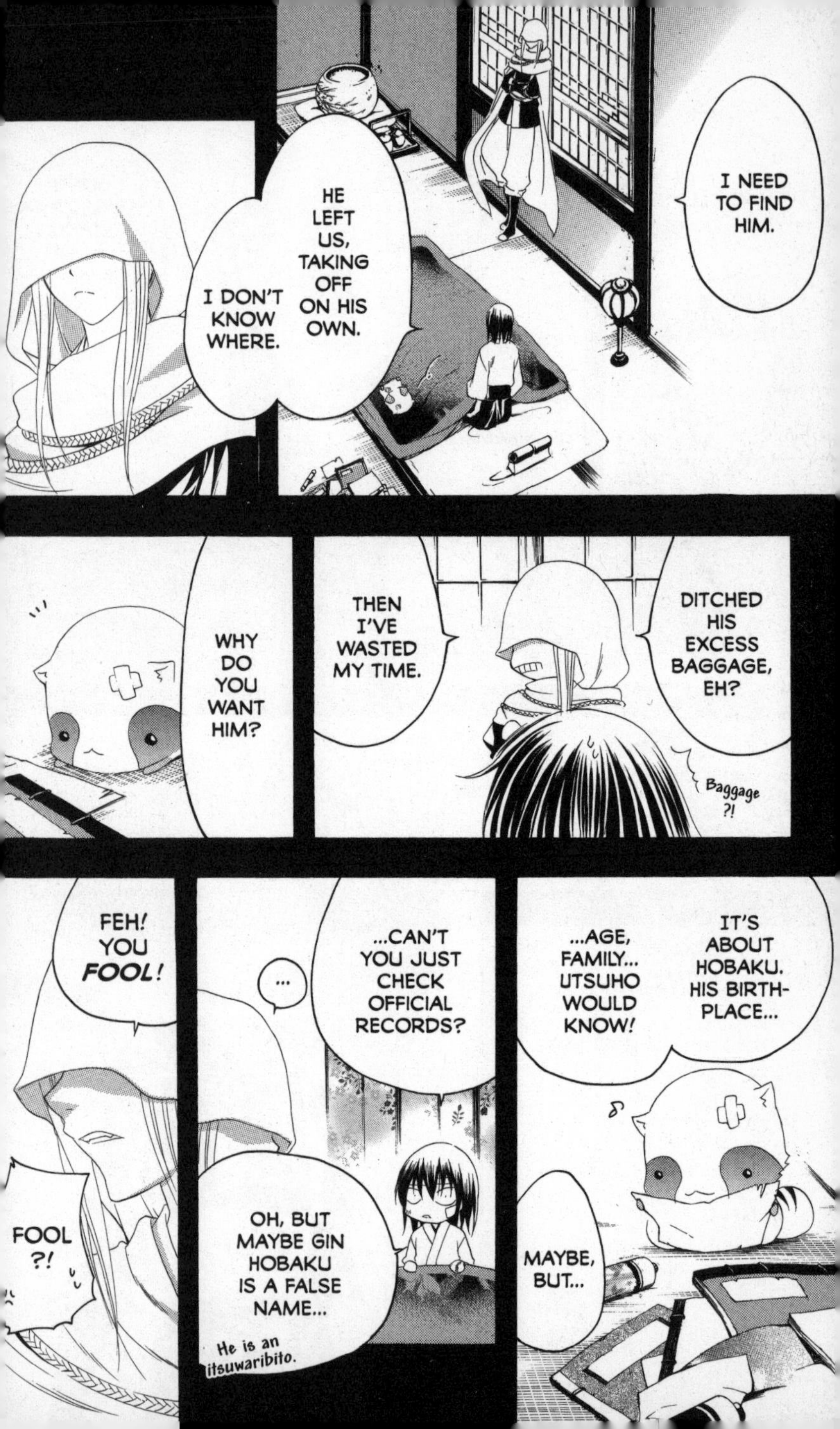
I NEED TO FIND HIM.
HE LEFT US, TAKING OFF ON HIS OWN.
I DON'T KNOW WHERE.
DITCHED HIS EXCESS BAGGAGE, EH?
Baggage ?!
THEN I'VE WASTED MY TIME.
WHY DO YOU WANT HIM?
IT'S ABOUT HOBAKU. HIS BIRTH-PLACE...
...AGE, FAMILY... UTSUHO WOULD KNOW!
MAYBE, BUT...
...CAN'T YOU JUST CHECK OFFICIAL RECORDS?
...
OH, BUT MAYBE GIN HOBAKU IS A FALSE NAME...
He is an itsuwaribito.
FEH! YOU *FOOL*!
FOOL ?!

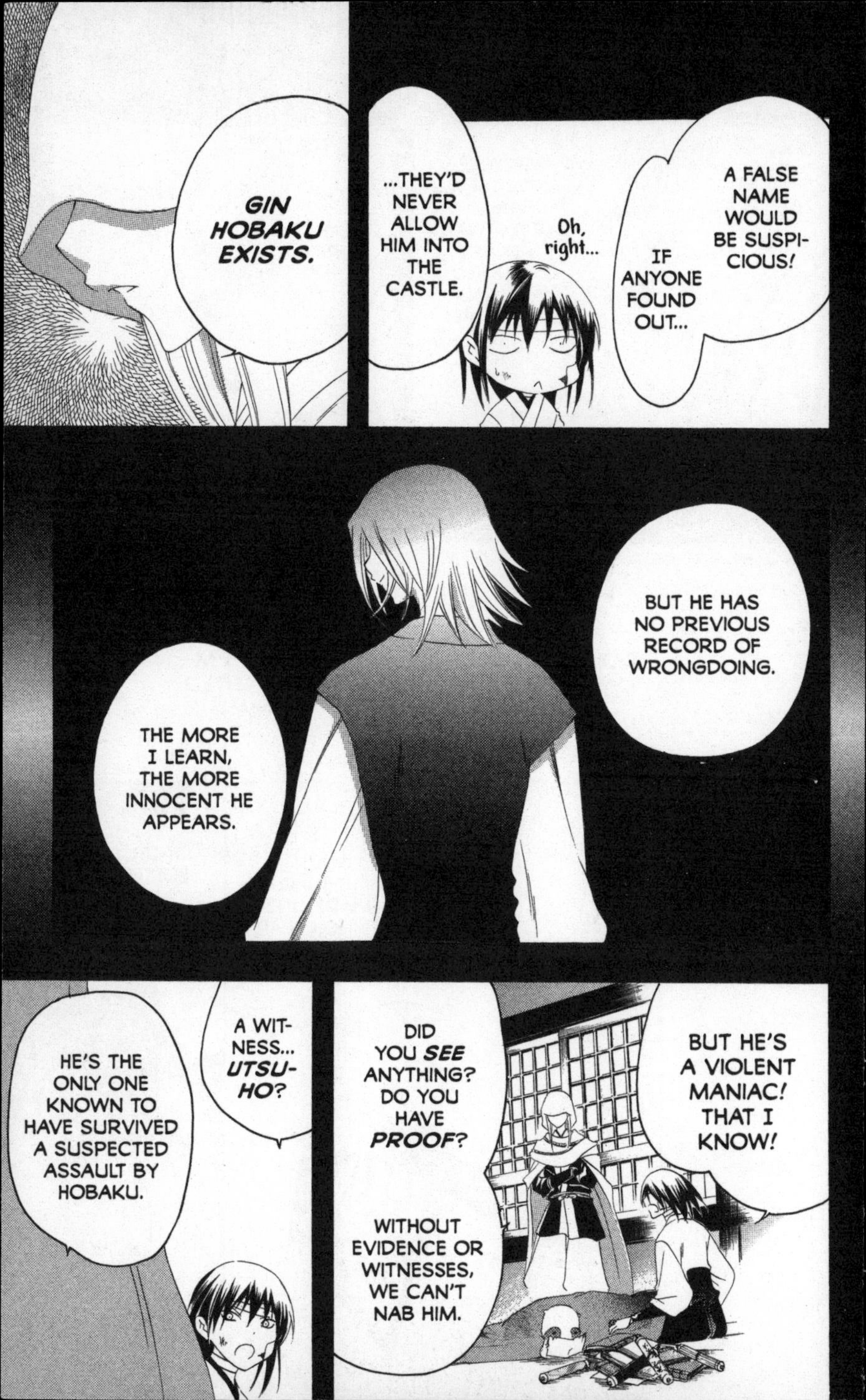
A FALSE NAME WOULD BE SUSPICIOUS!
IF ANYONE FOUND OUT...
Oh, right...
...THEY'D NEVER ALLOW HIM INTO THE CASTLE.
GIN HOBAKU EXISTS.
BUT HE HAS NO PREVIOUS RECORD OF WRONGDOING.
THE MORE I LEARN, THE MORE INNOCENT HE APPEARS.
BUT HE'S A VIOLENT MANIAC! THAT I KNOW!
DID YOU *SEE* ANYTHING? DO YOU HAVE *PROOF*?
WITHOUT EVIDENCE OR WITNESSES, WE CAN'T NAB HIM.
A WITNESS... *UTSUHO*?
HE'S THE ONLY ONE KNOWN TO HAVE SURVIVED A SUSPECTED ASSAULT BY HOBAKU.

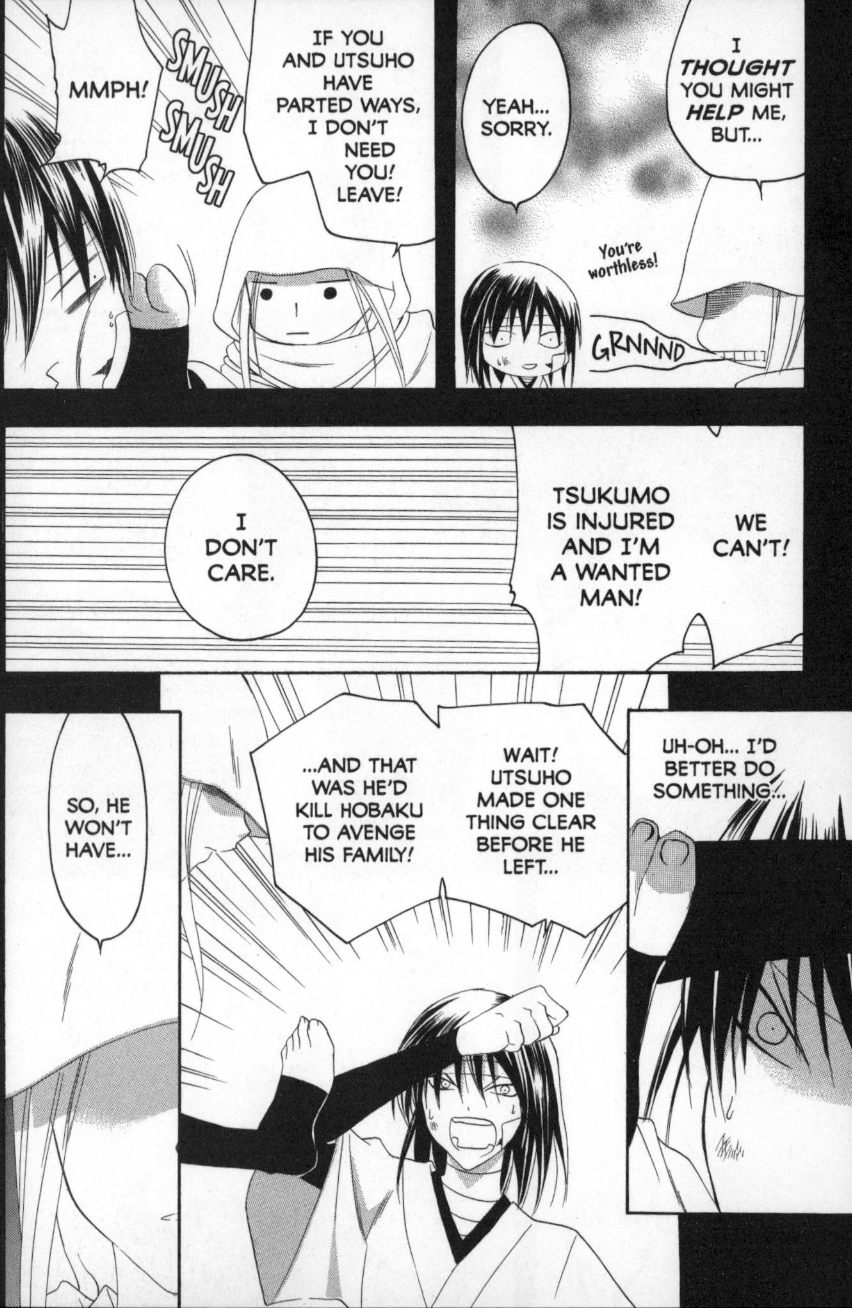
I *THOUGHT* YOU MIGHT *HELP* ME, BUT...
YEAH... SORRY.
You're worthless!
GRNNND
IF YOU AND UTSUHO HAVE PARTED WAYS, I DON'T NEED YOU! LEAVE!
MMPH!
SMUSH SMUSH
WE CAN'T!
TSUKUMO IS INJURED AND I'M A WANTED MAN!
I DON'T CARE.
UH-OH... I'D BETTER DO SOMETHING...
WAIT! UTSUHO MADE ONE THING CLEAR BEFORE HE LEFT...
...AND THAT WAS HE'D KILL HOBAKU TO AVENGE HIS FAMILY!
SO, HE WON'T HAVE...

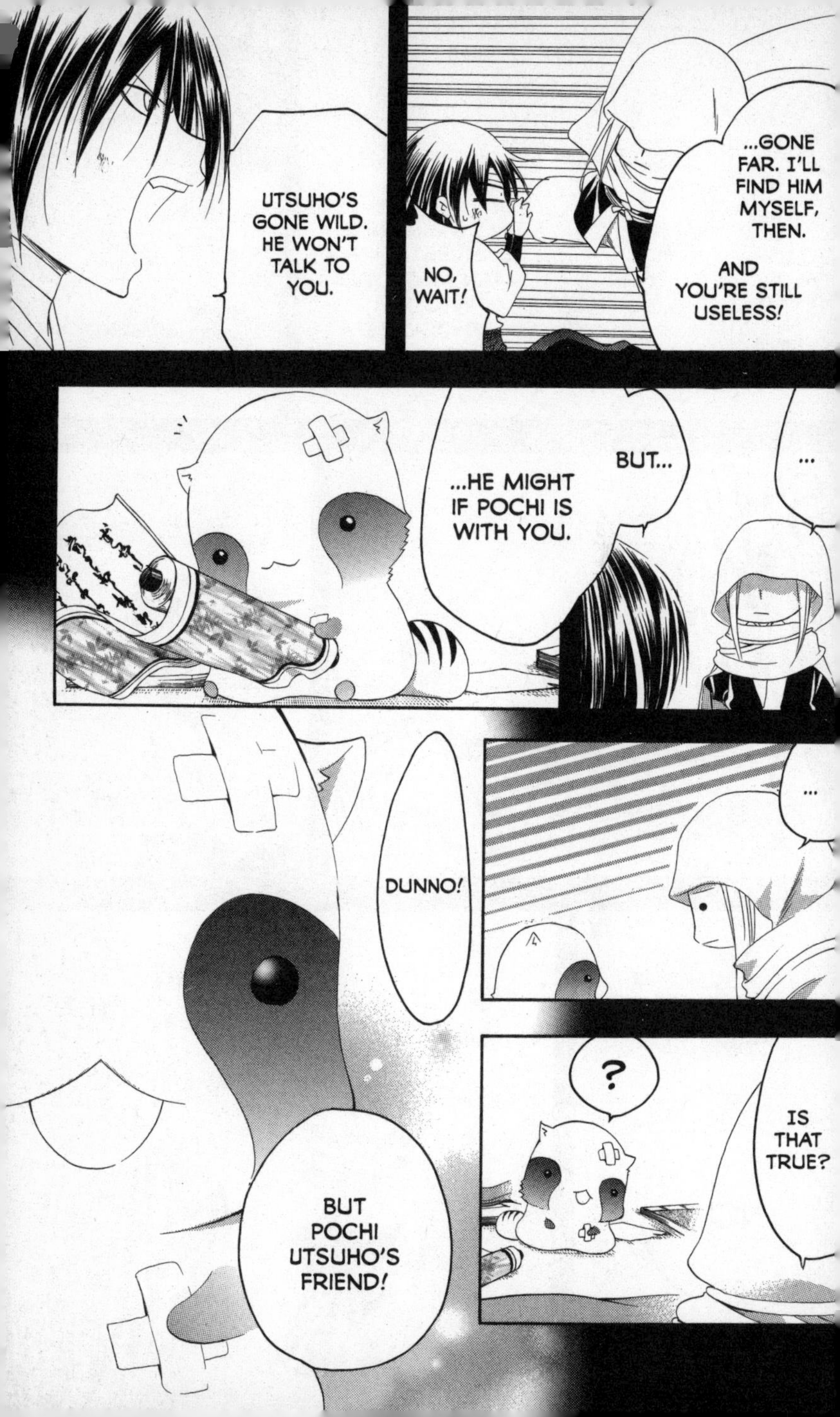
...GONE FAR. I'LL FIND HIM MYSELF, THEN.
AND YOU'RE STILL USELESS!
NO, WAIT!
UTSUHO'S GONE WILD. HE WON'T TALK TO YOU.
...
BUT...
...HE MIGHT IF POCHI IS WITH YOU.
...
IS THAT TRUE?
?
DUNNO!
BUT POCHI UTSUHO'S FRIEND!

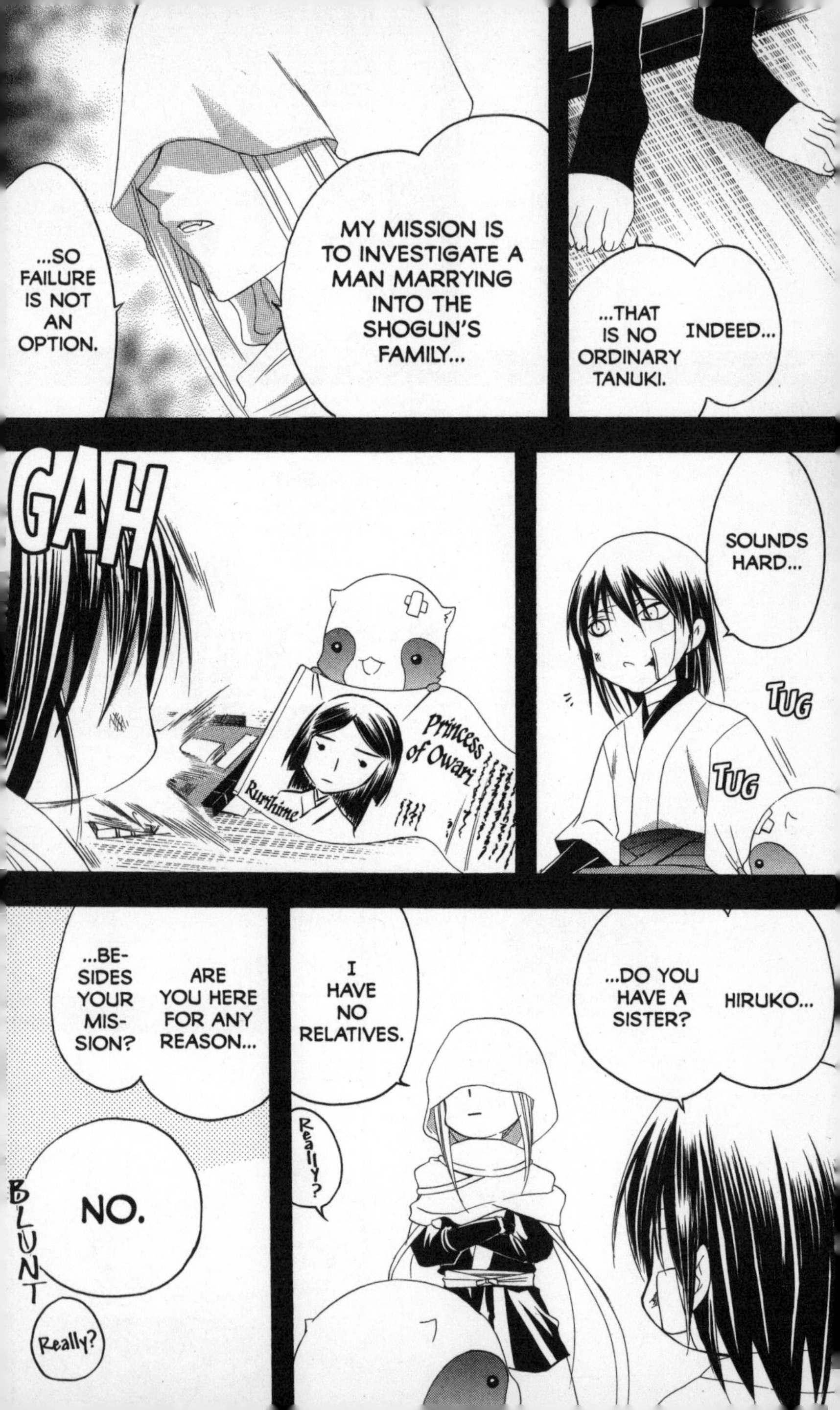
INDEED...
...THAT IS NO ORDINARY TANUKI.
MY MISSION IS TO INVESTIGATE A MAN MARRYING INTO THE SHOGUN'S FAMILY...
...SO FAILURE IS NOT AN OPTION.
SOUNDS HARD...
TUG
TUG
GAH
Princess of Owari
Rurihime
HIRUKO...
...DO YOU HAVE A SISTER?
I HAVE NO RELATIVES.
Really?
ARE YOU HERE FOR ANY REASON...
...BESIDES YOUR MISSION?
NO.
BLUNT
Really?

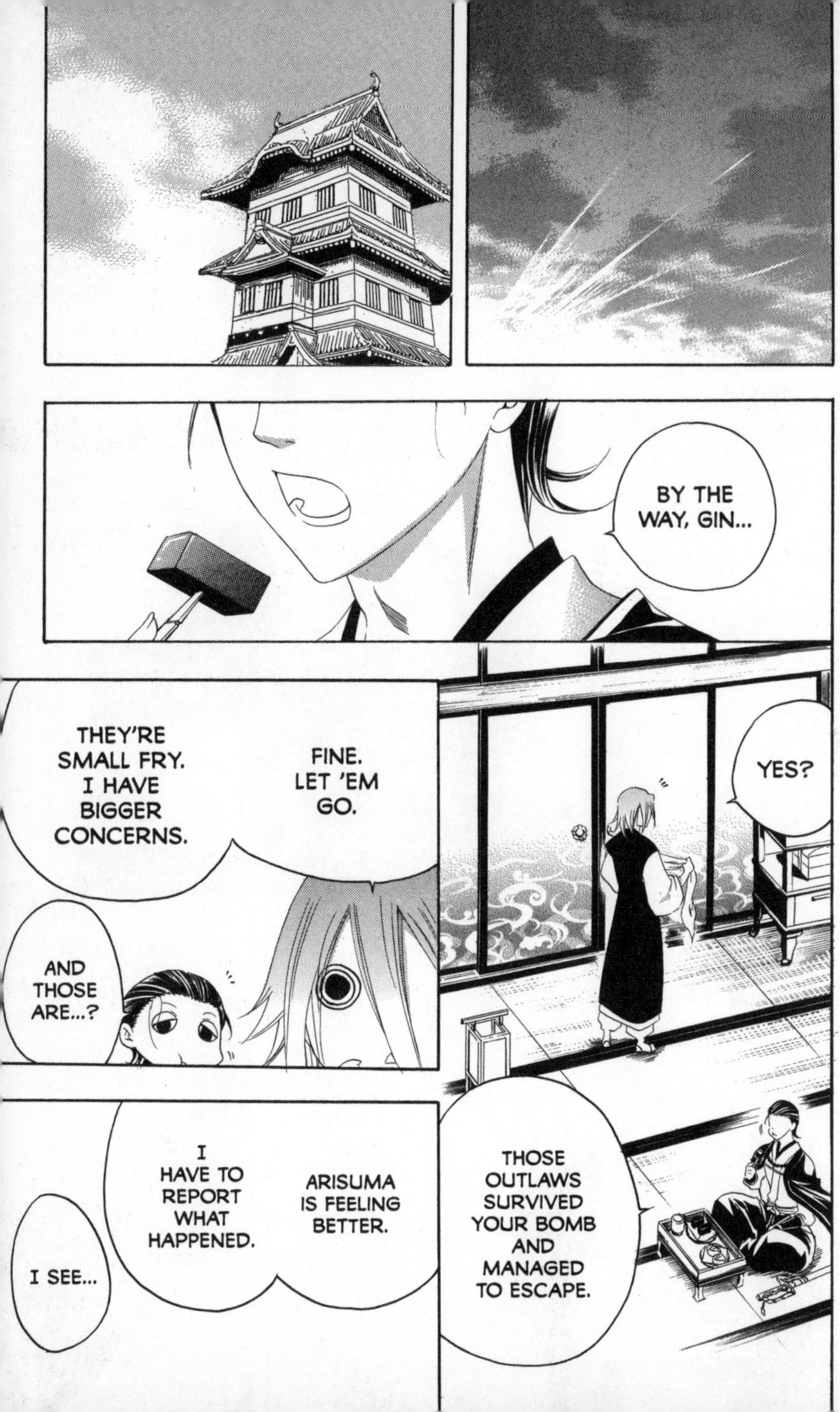
BY THE WAY, GIN...
YES?
THOSE OUTLAWS SURVIVED YOUR BOMB AND MANAGED TO ESCAPE.
FINE. LET 'EM GO.
THEY'RE SMALL FRY. I HAVE BIGGER CONCERNS.
AND THOSE ARE...?
ARISUMA IS FEELING BETTER.
I HAVE TO REPORT WHAT HAPPENED.
I SEE...

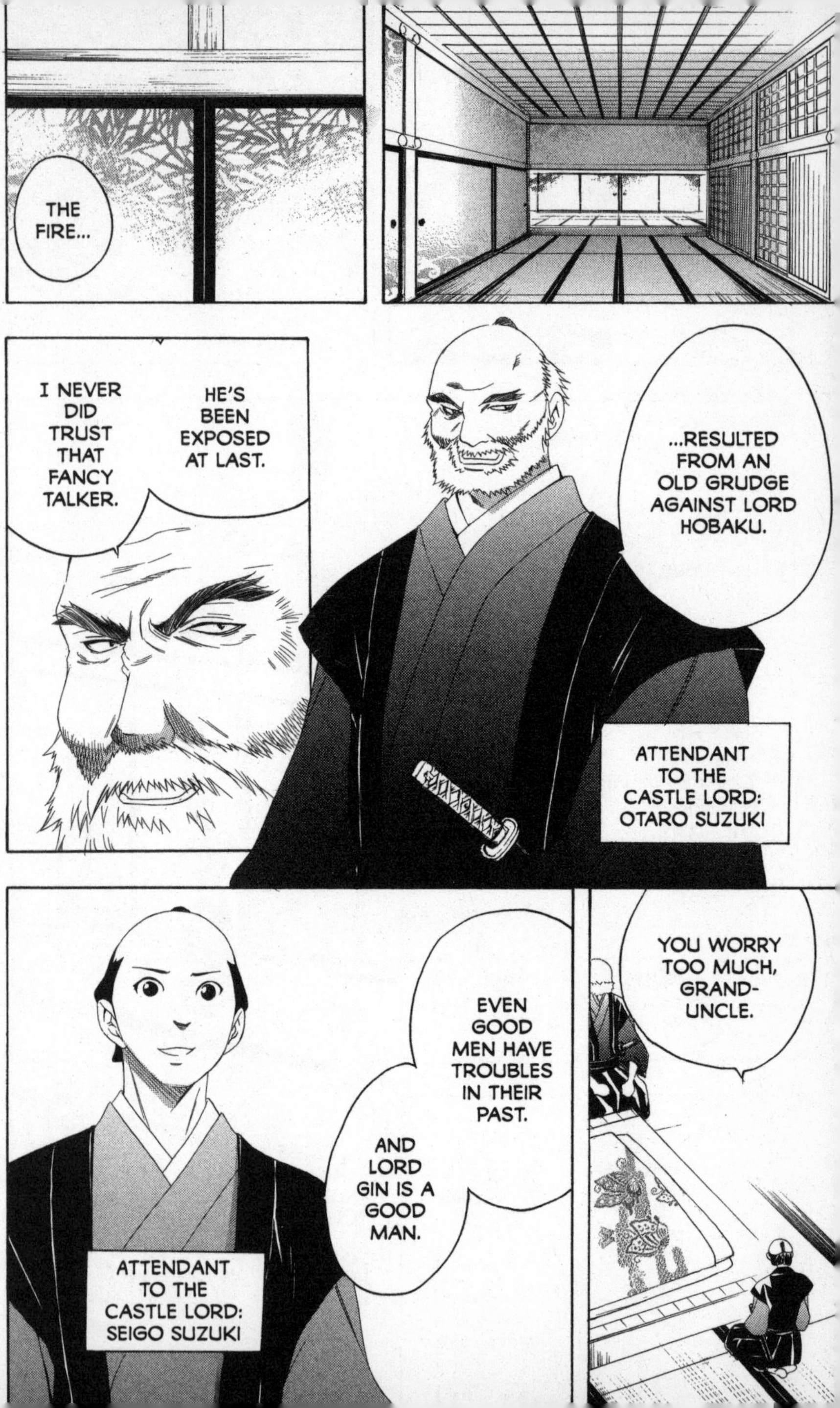
THE FIRE...
...RESULTED FROM AN OLD GRUDGE AGAINST LORD HOBAKU.
ATTENDANT TO THE CASTLE LORD: OTARO SUZUKI
HE'S BEEN EXPOSED AT LAST.
I NEVER DID TRUST THAT FANCY TALKER.
YOU WORRY TOO MUCH, GRAND-UNCLE.
EVEN GOOD MEN HAVE TROUBLES IN THEIR PAST.
AND LORD GIN IS A GOOD MAN.
ATTENDANT TO THE CASTLE LORD: SEIGO SUZUKI

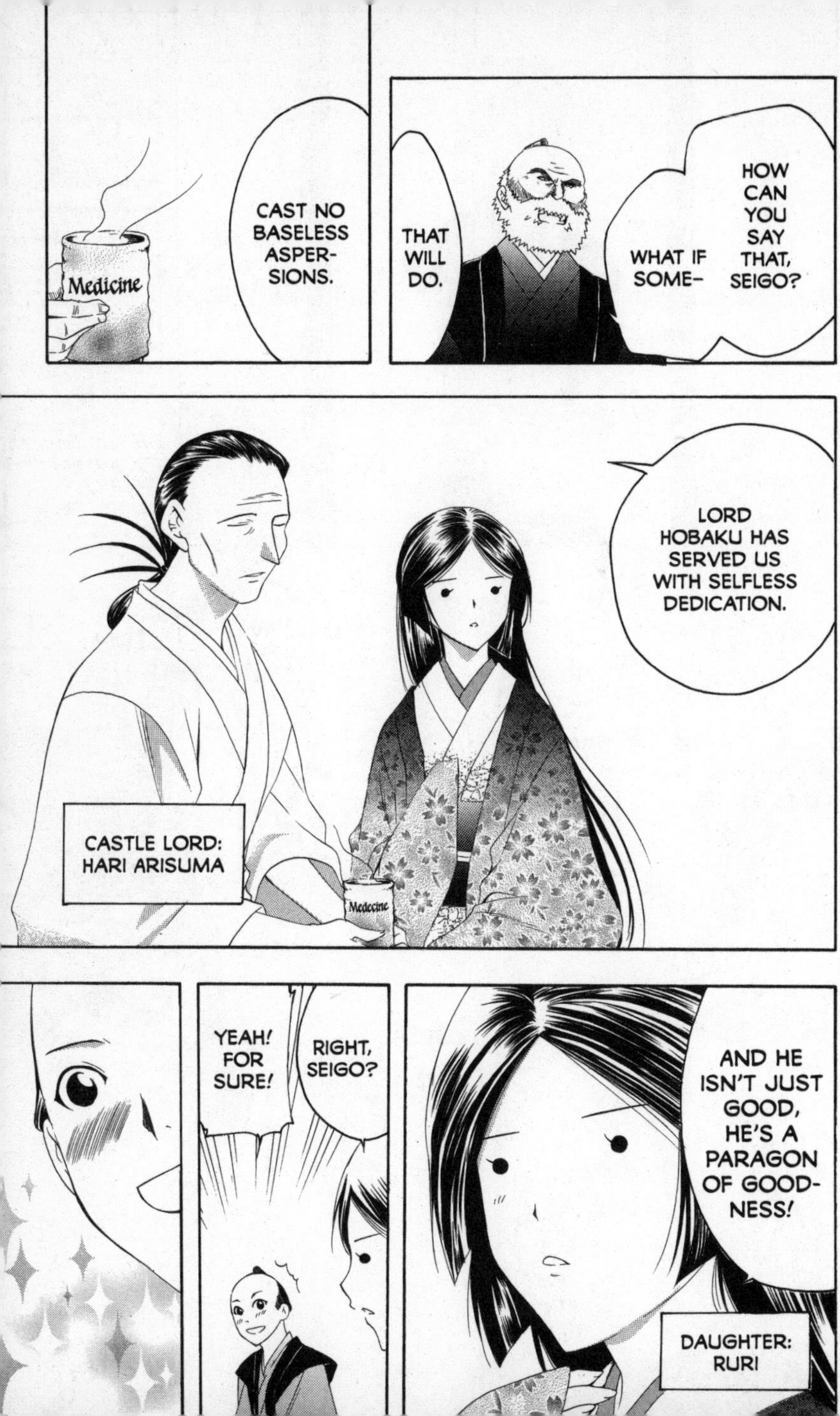
HOW CAN YOU SAY THAT, SEIGO?
WHAT IF SOME–
THAT WILL DO.
CAST NO BASELESS ASPER-SIONS.
Medicine
LORD HOBAKU HAS SERVED US WITH SELFLESS DEDICATION.
CASTLE LORD: HARI ARISUMA
Medecine
AND HE ISN'T JUST GOOD, HE'S A PARAGON OF GOOD-NESS!
DAUGHTER: RURI
RIGHT, SEIGO?
YEAH! FOR SURE!

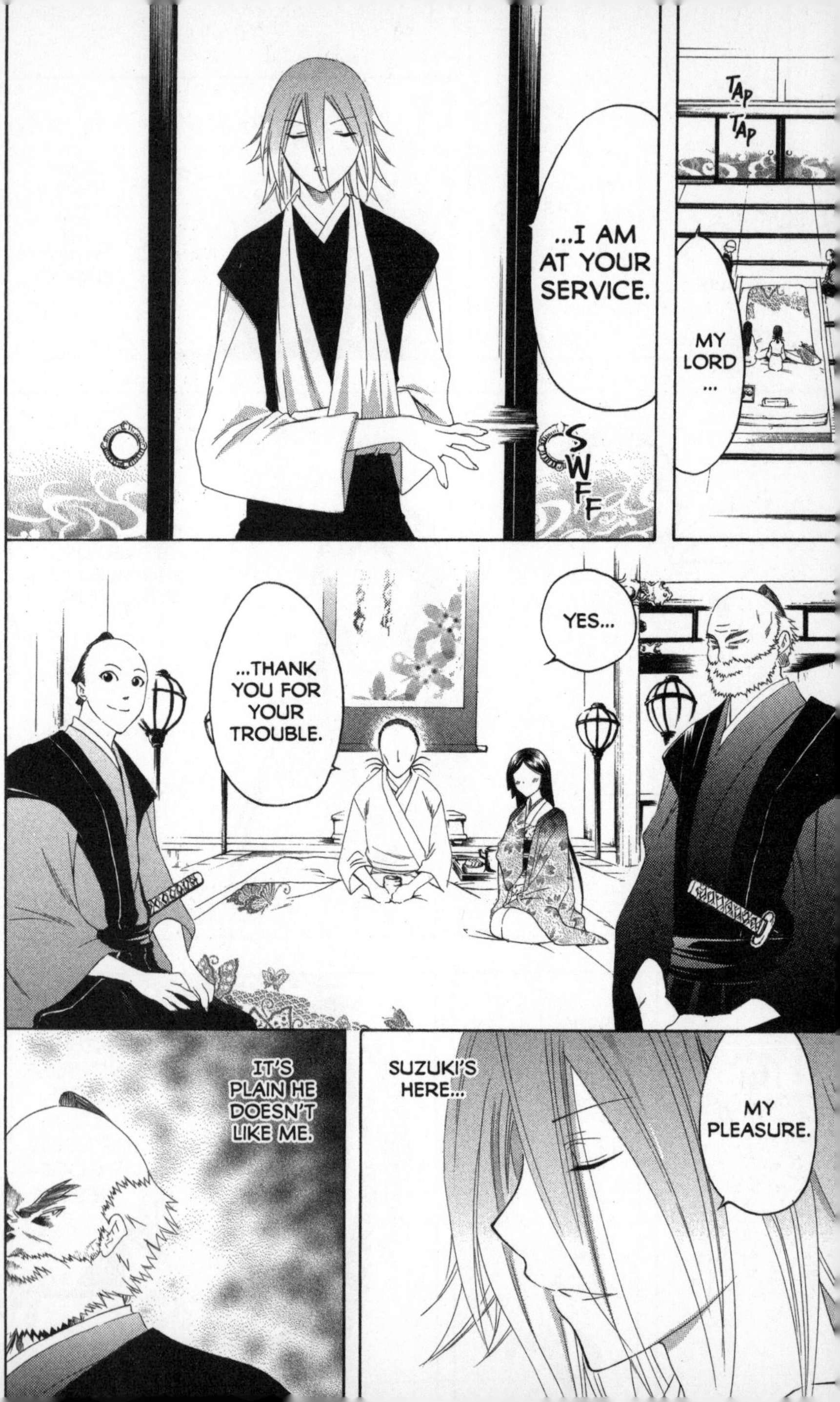
TAP
TAP
MY LORD ...
...I AM AT YOUR SERVICE.
SWFF
YES...
...THANK YOU FOR YOUR TROUBLE.
MY PLEASURE.
SUZUKI'S HERE...
IT'S PLAIN HE DOESN'T LIKE ME.

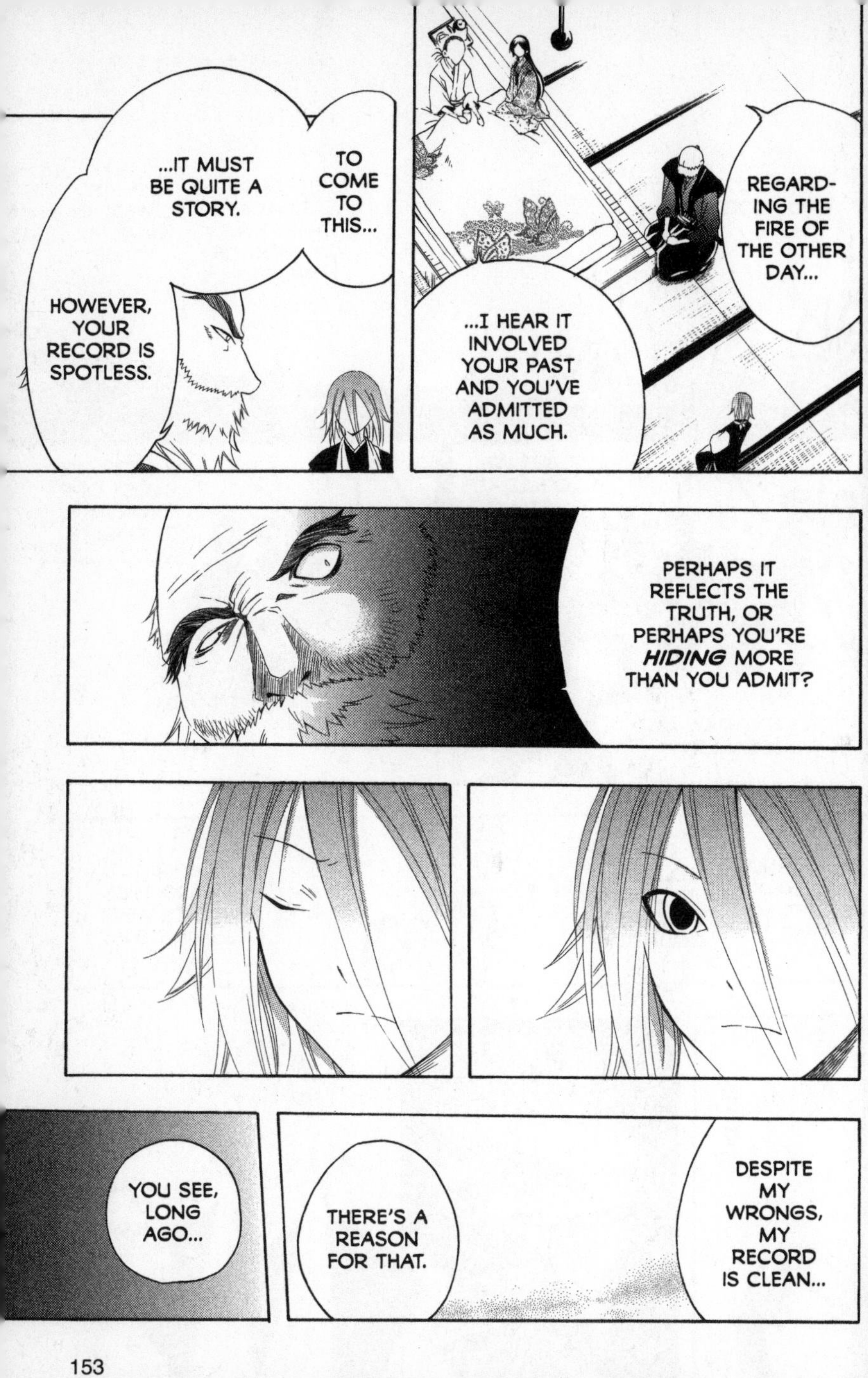
REGARDING THE FIRE OF THE OTHER DAY...
...I HEAR IT INVOLVED YOUR PAST AND YOU'VE ADMITTED AS MUCH.
TO COME TO THIS...
...IT MUST BE QUITE A STORY.
HOWEVER, YOUR RECORD IS SPOTLESS.
PERHAPS IT REFLECTS THE TRUTH, OR PERHAPS YOU'RE *HIDING* MORE THAN YOU ADMIT?
DESPITE MY WRONGS, MY RECORD IS CLEAN...
THERE'S A REASON FOR THAT.
YOU SEE, LONG AGO...

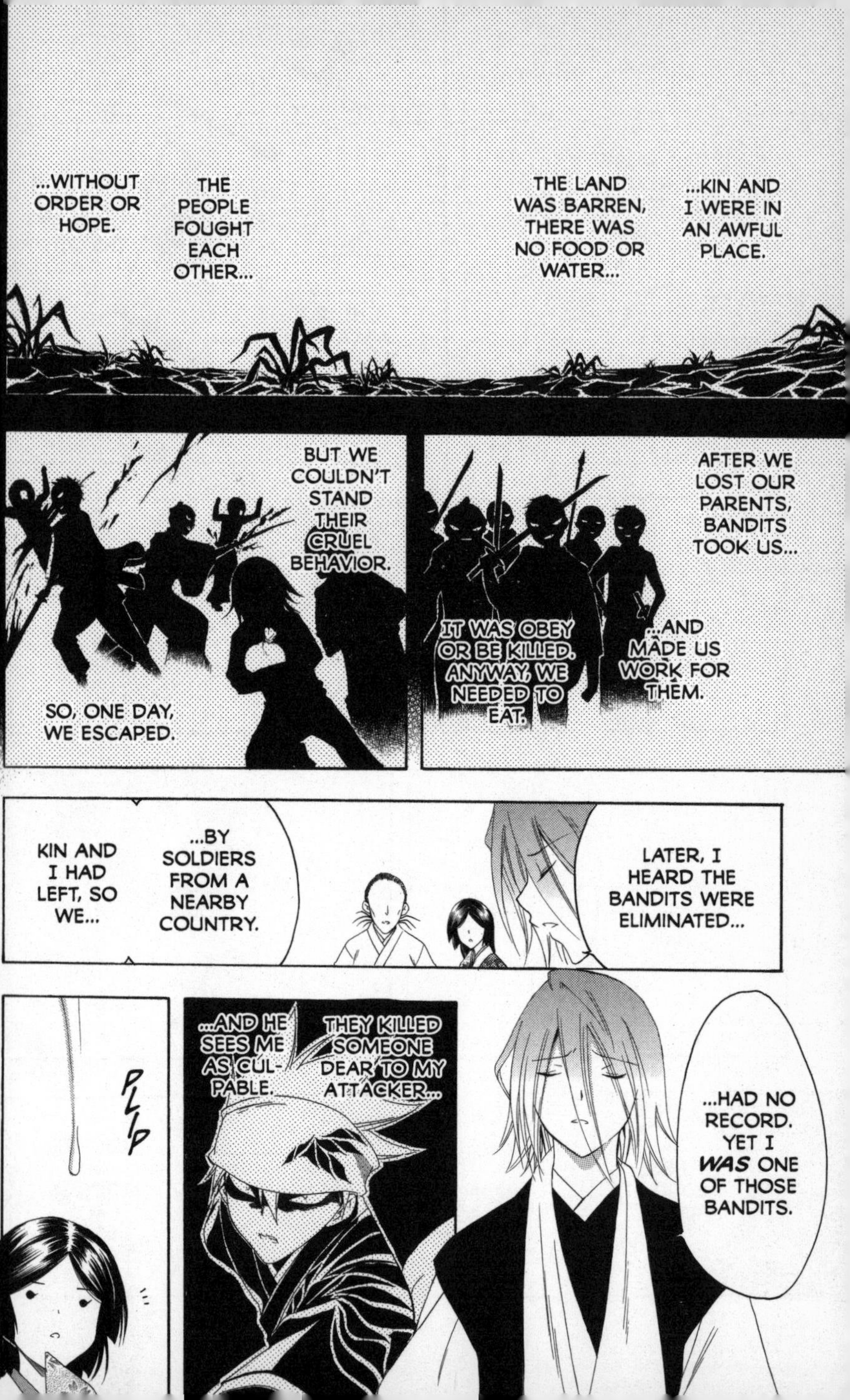
...KIN AND I WERE IN AN AWFUL PLACE.
THE LAND WAS BARREN, THERE WAS NO FOOD OR WATER...
THE PEOPLE FOUGHT EACH OTHER...
...WITHOUT ORDER OR HOPE.
AFTER WE LOST OUR PARENTS, BANDITS TOOK US...
...AND MADE US WORK FOR THEM.
IT WAS OBEY OR BE KILLED. ANYWAY, WE NEEDED TO EAT.
BUT WE COULDN'T STAND THEIR CRUEL BEHAVIOR.
SO, ONE DAY, WE ESCAPED.
LATER, I HEARD THE BANDITS WERE ELIMINATED...
...BY SOLDIERS FROM A NEARBY COUNTRY.
KIN AND I HAD LEFT, SO WE...
...HAD NO RECORD. YET I *WAS* ONE OF THOSE BANDITS.
THEY KILLED SOMEONE DEAR TO MY ATTACKER...
...AND HE SEES ME AS CUL-PABLE.
PLIP

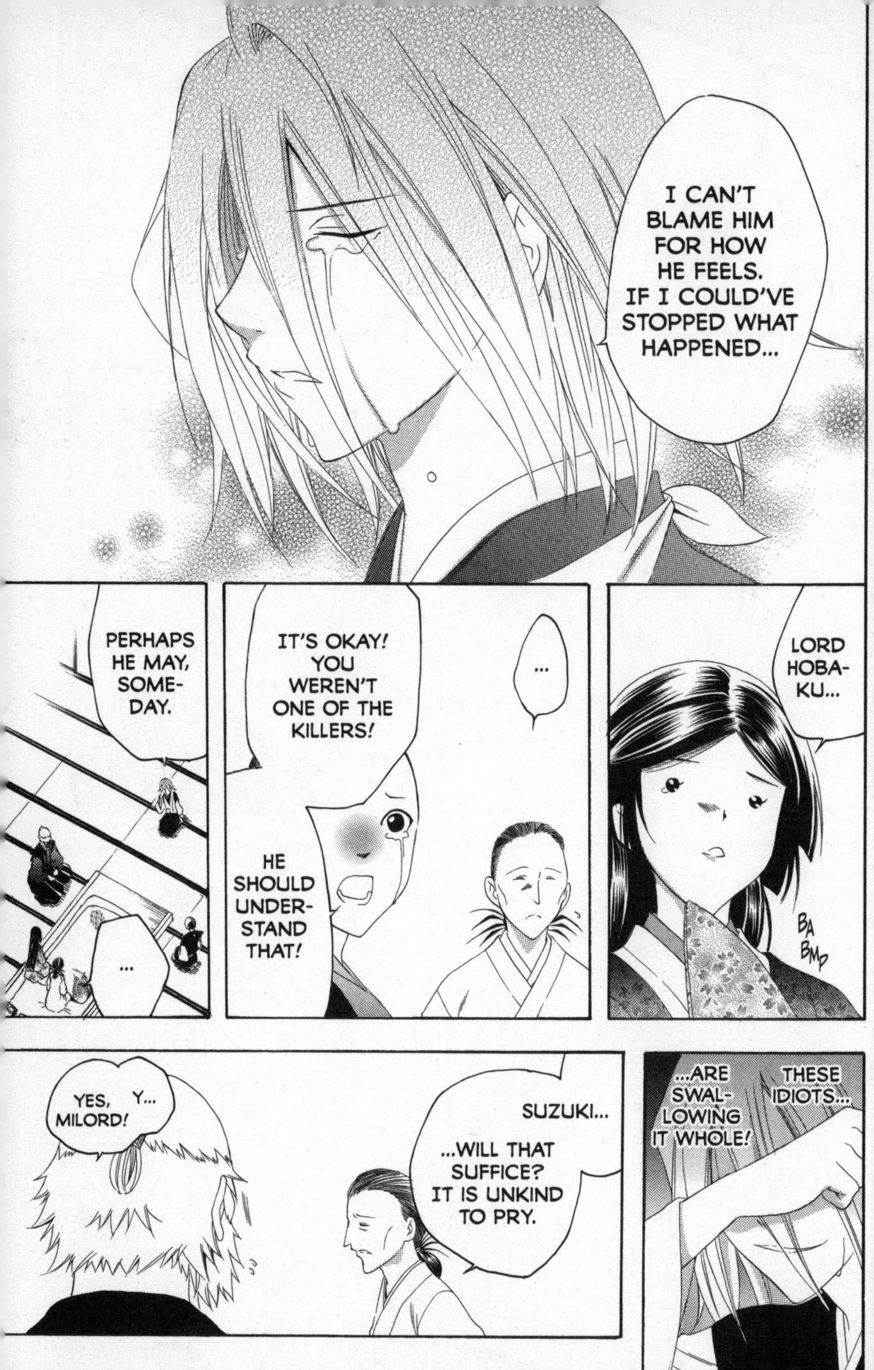
I CAN'T BLAME HIM FOR HOW HE FEELS. IF I COULD'VE STOPPED WHAT HAPPENED...
LORD HOBA-KU...
BA BMP
...
IT'S OKAY! YOU WEREN'T ONE OF THE KILLERS!
HE SHOULD UNDER-STAND THAT!
PERHAPS HE MAY, SOME-DAY.
...
THESE IDIOTS...
...ARE SWAL-LOWING IT WHOLE!
SUZUKI...
...WILL THAT SUFFICE? IT IS UNKIND TO PRY.
Y... YES, MILORD!

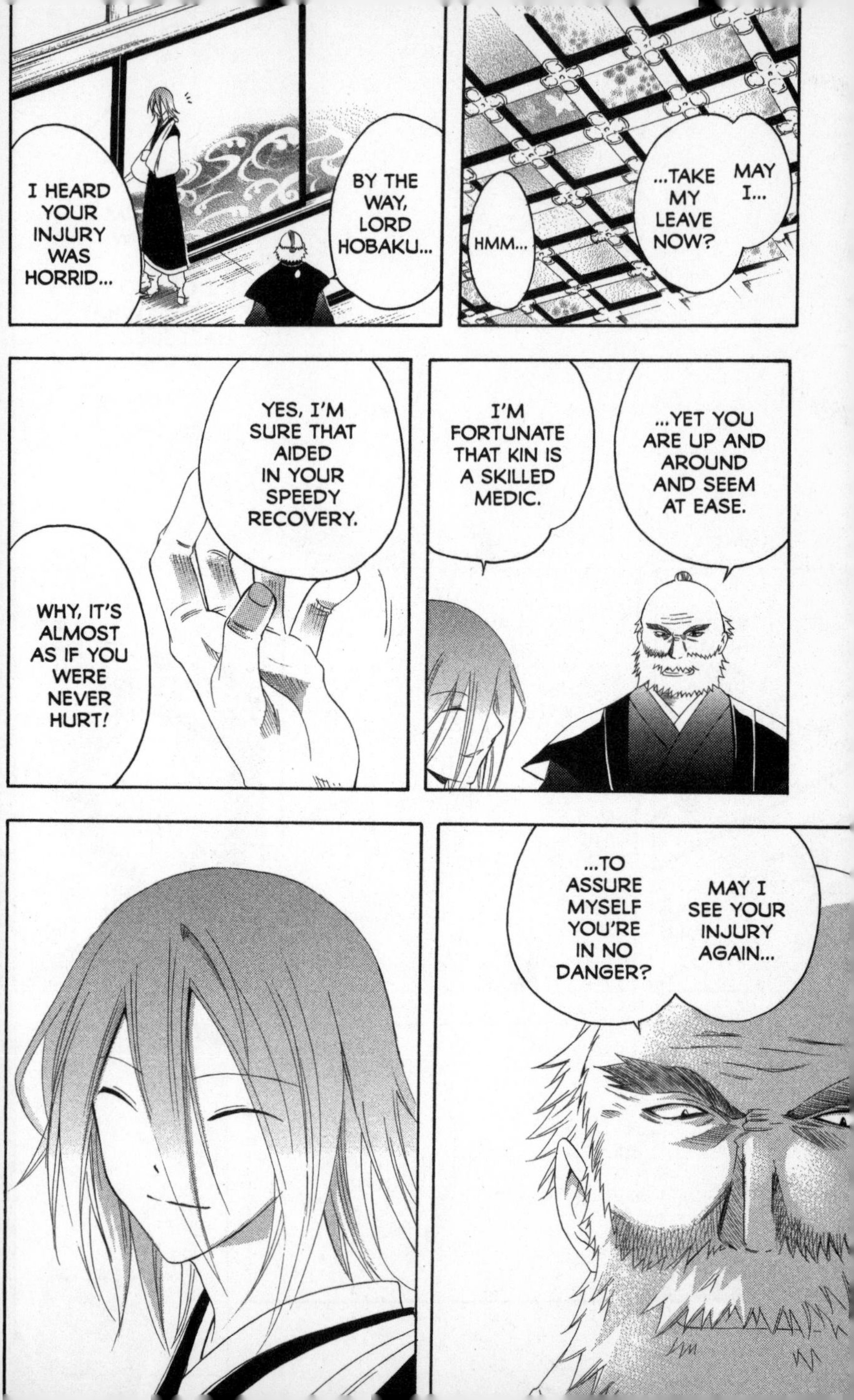
MAY I...
...TAKE MY LEAVE NOW?
HMM...
BY THE WAY, LORD HOBAKU...
I HEARD YOUR INJURY WAS HORRID...
...YET YOU ARE UP AND AROUND AND SEEM AT EASE.
I'M FORTUNATE THAT KIN IS A SKILLED MEDIC.
YES, I'M SURE THAT AIDED IN YOUR SPEEDY RECOVERY.
WHY, IT'S ALMOST AS IF YOU WERE NEVER HURT!
MAY I SEE YOUR INJURY AGAIN...
...TO ASSURE MYSELF YOU'RE IN NO DANGER?

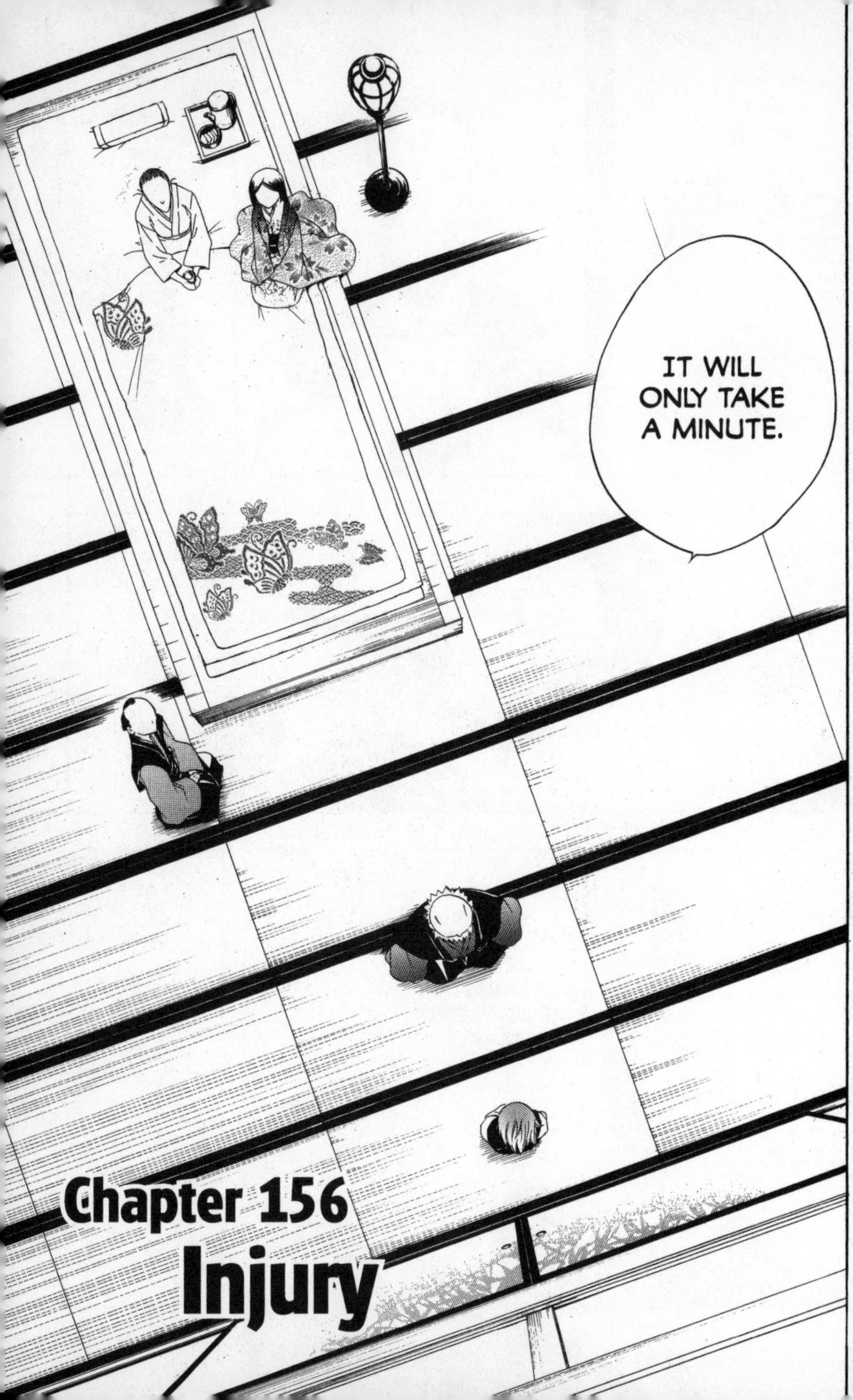
IT WILL ONLY TAKE A MINUTE.
Chapter 156
Injury

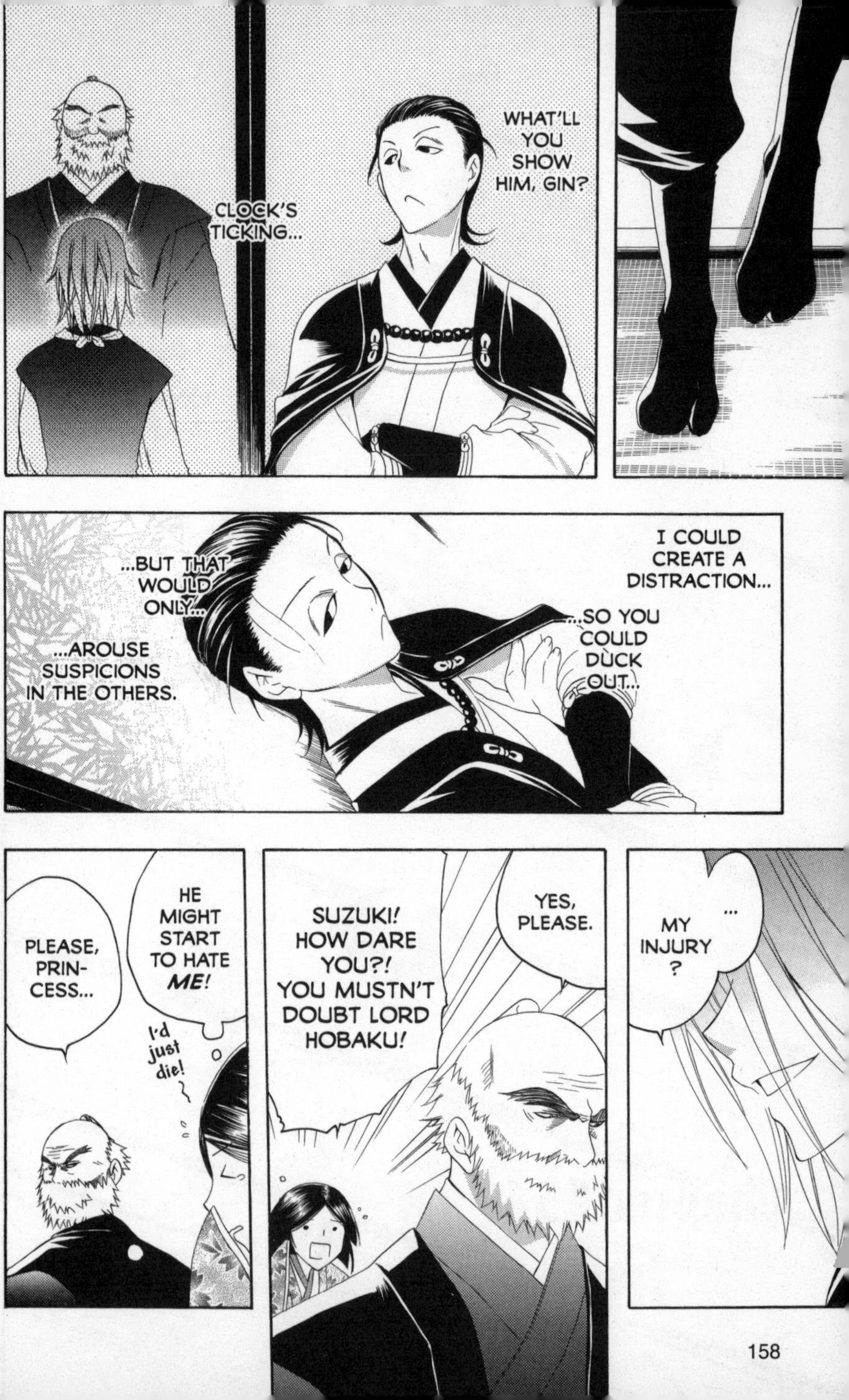
WHAT'LL YOU SHOW HIM, GIN?
CLOCK'S TICKING...
I COULD CREATE A DISTRACTION...
...SO YOU COULD DUCK OUT...
...BUT THAT WOULD ONLY...
...AROUSE SUSPICIONS IN THE OTHERS.
... MY INJURY?
YES, PLEASE.
SUZUKI! HOW DARE YOU?! YOU MUSTN'T DOUBT LORD HOBAKU!
HE MIGHT START TO HATE *ME*!
I'd just die!
PLEASE, PRINCESS...

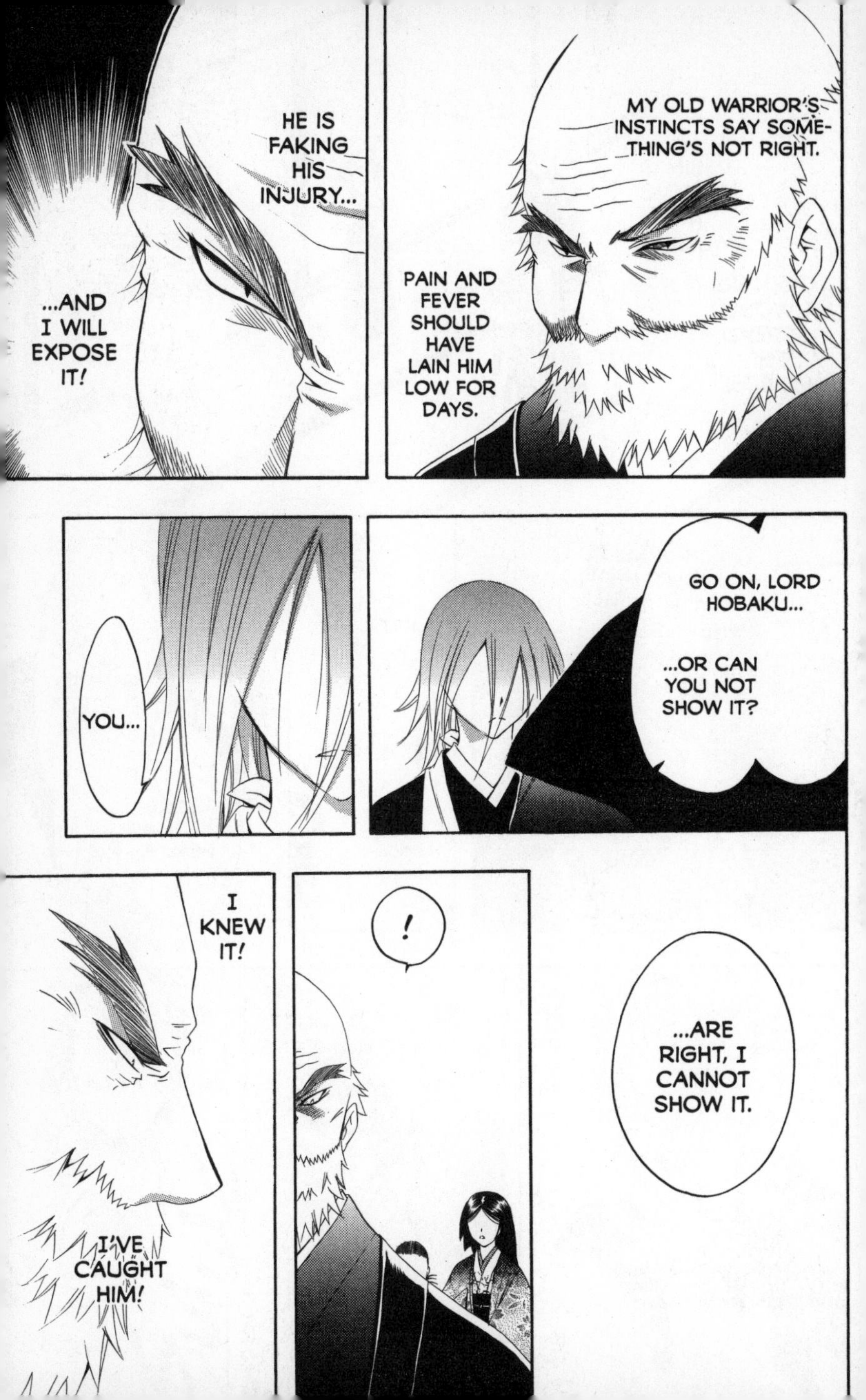
MY OLD WARRIOR'S INSTINCTS SAY SOME-THING'S NOT RIGHT.
PAIN AND FEVER SHOULD HAVE LAIN HIM LOW FOR DAYS.
HE IS FAKING HIS INJURY...
...AND I WILL EXPOSE IT!
GO ON, LORD HOBAKU...
...OR CAN YOU NOT SHOW IT?
YOU...
...ARE RIGHT, I CANNOT SHOW IT.
!
I KNEW IT!
I'VE CAUGHT HIM!

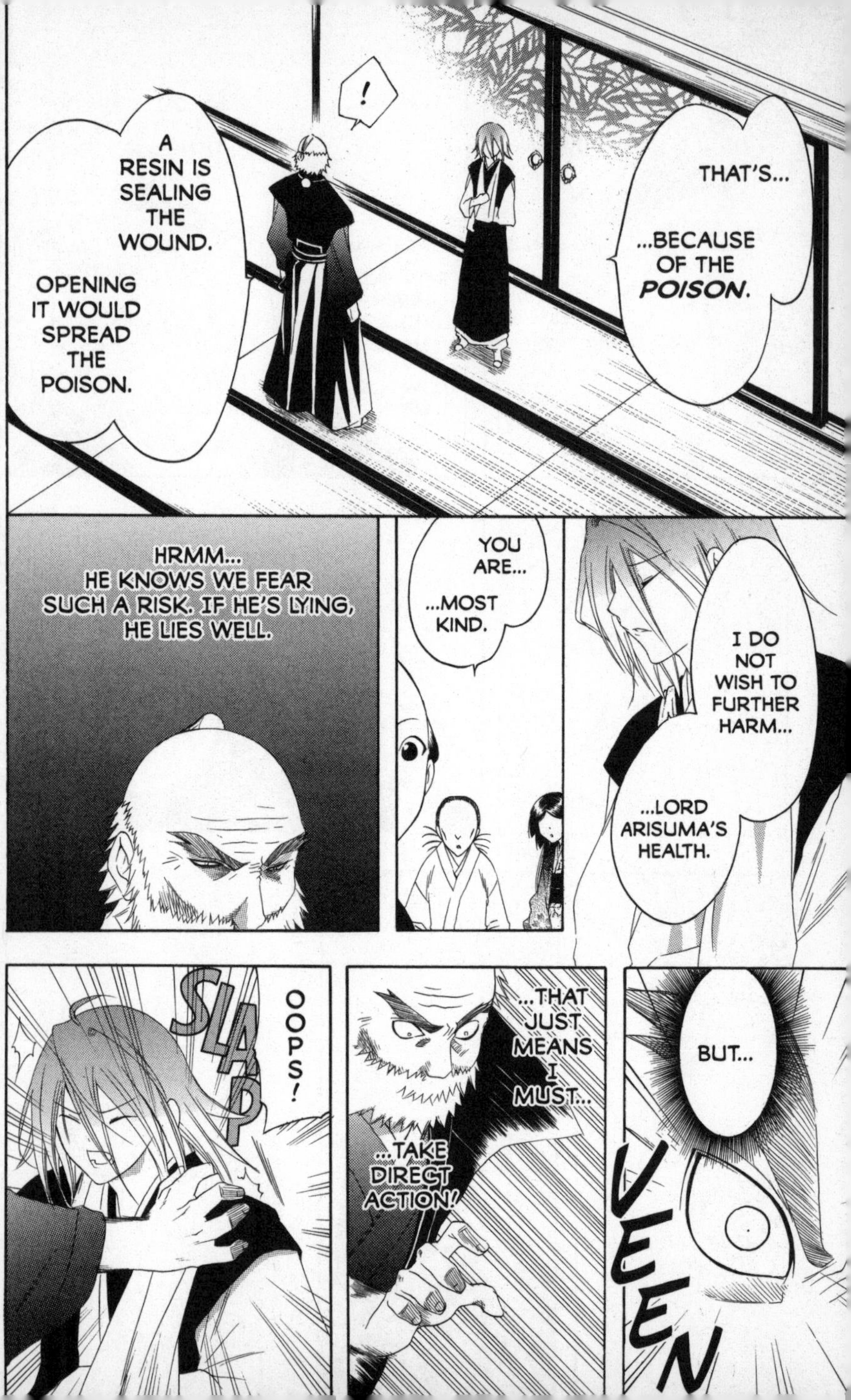
THAT'S...
...BECAUSE OF THE *POISON*.
!
A RESIN IS SEALING THE WOUND.
OPENING IT WOULD SPREAD THE POISON.
I DO NOT WISH TO FURTHER HARM...
...LORD ARISUMA'S HEALTH.
YOU ARE...
...MOST KIND.
HRMM... HE KNOWS WE FEAR SUCH A RISK. IF HE'S LYING, HE LIES WELL.
BUT...
VEEN
...THAT JUST MEANS I MUST...
...TAKE DIRECT ACTION!
OOPS!
SLAP

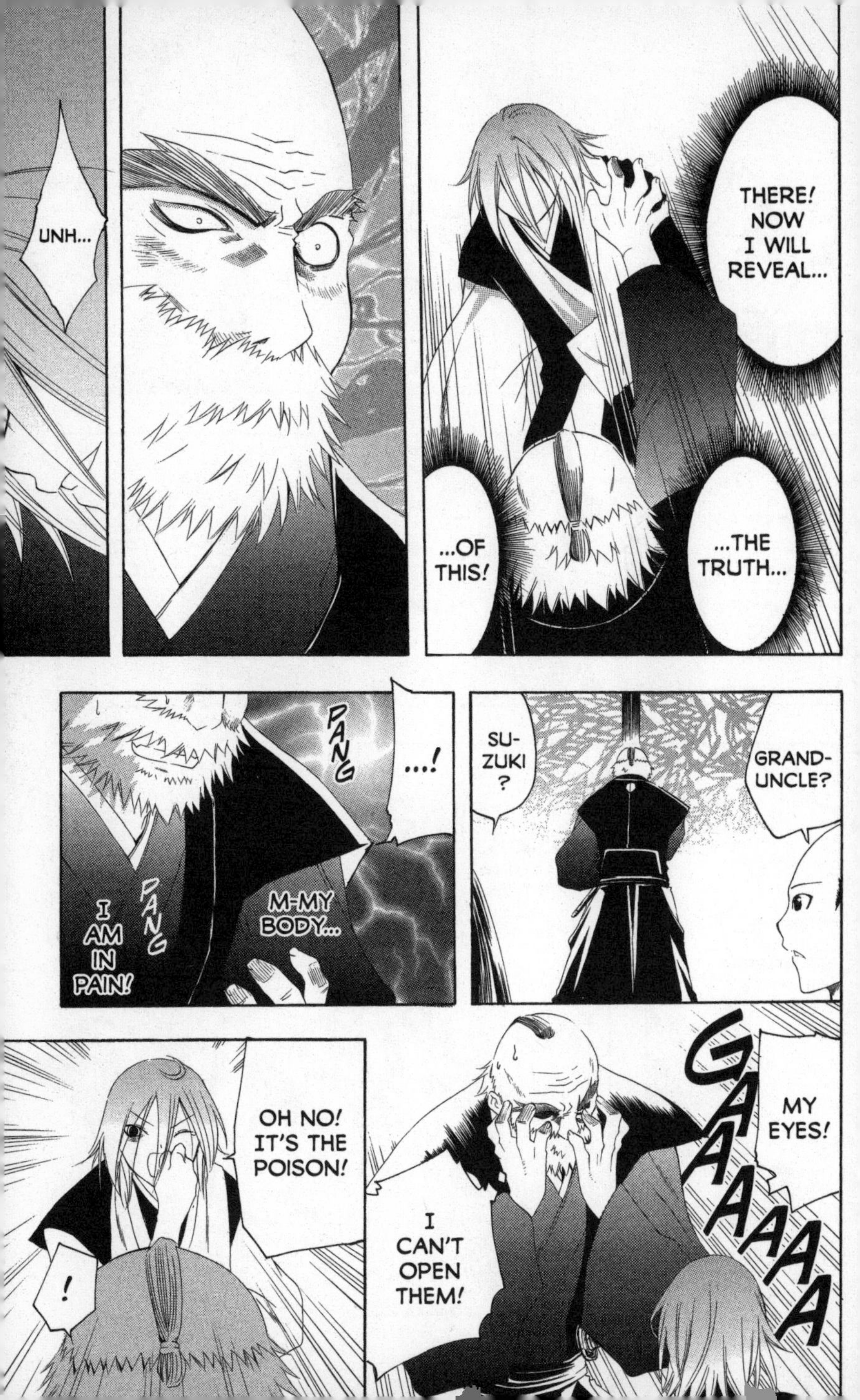
THERE! NOW I WILL REVEAL...
...THE TRUTH...
...OF THIS!
UNH...
GRAND-UNCLE?
SU-ZUKI?
...!
PANG
M-MY BODY...
PANG
I AM IN PAIN!
GAAAAAAA
MY EYES!
I CAN'T OPEN THEM!
OH NO! IT'S THE POISON!
!

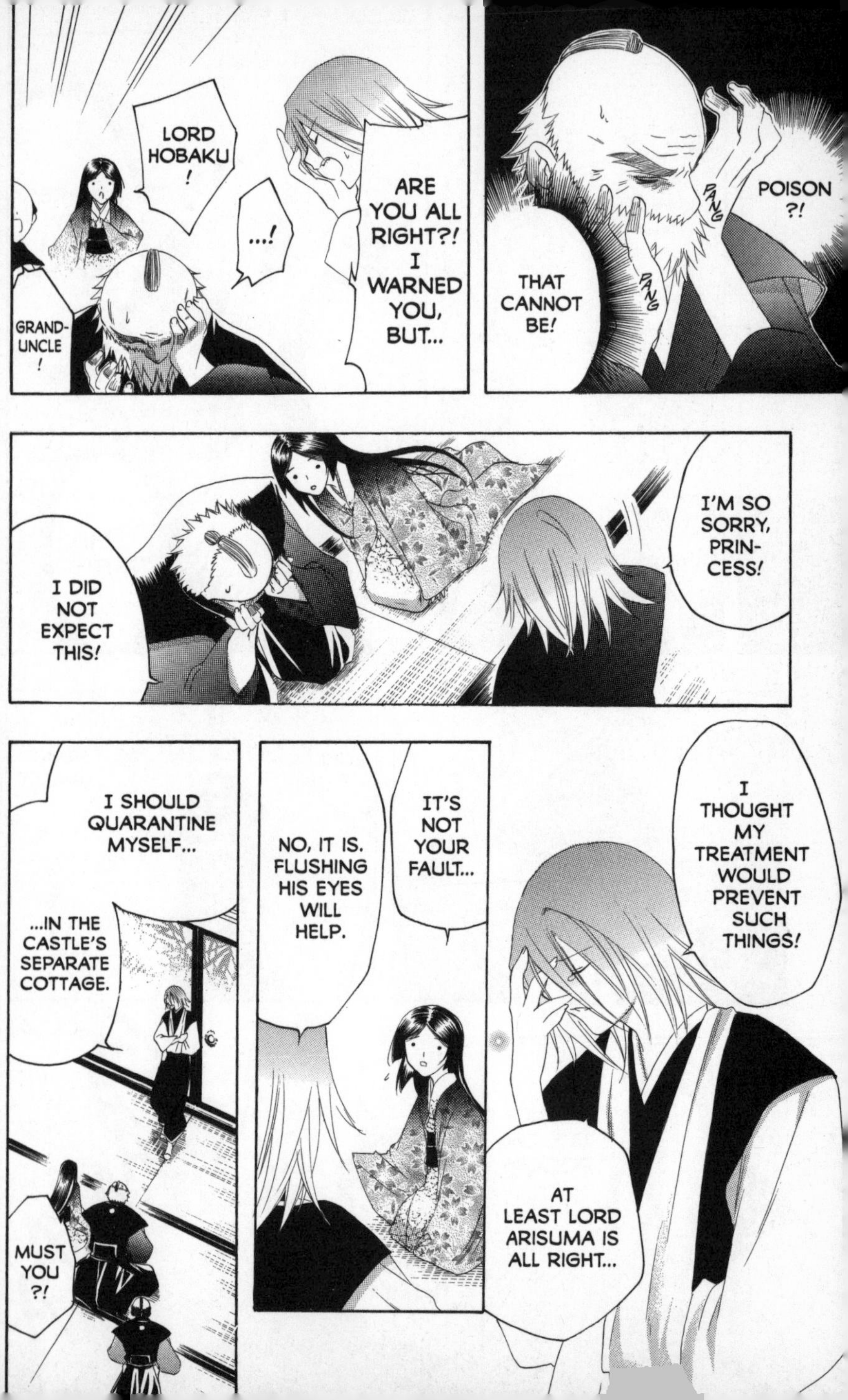
POISON ?!
PANG
PANG
THAT CANNOT BE!
ARE YOU ALL RIGHT?! I WARNED YOU, BUT...
...!
LORD HOBAKU!
GRAND-UNCLE!
I'M SO SORRY, PRIN-CESS!
I DID NOT EXPECT THIS!
I THOUGHT MY TREATMENT WOULD PREVENT SUCH THINGS!
AT LEAST LORD ARISUMA IS ALL RIGHT...
IT'S NOT YOUR FAULT...
NO, IT IS. FLUSHING HIS EYES WILL HELP.
I SHOULD QUARANTINE MYSELF...
...IN THE CASTLE'S SEPARATE COTTAGE.
MUST YOU ?!

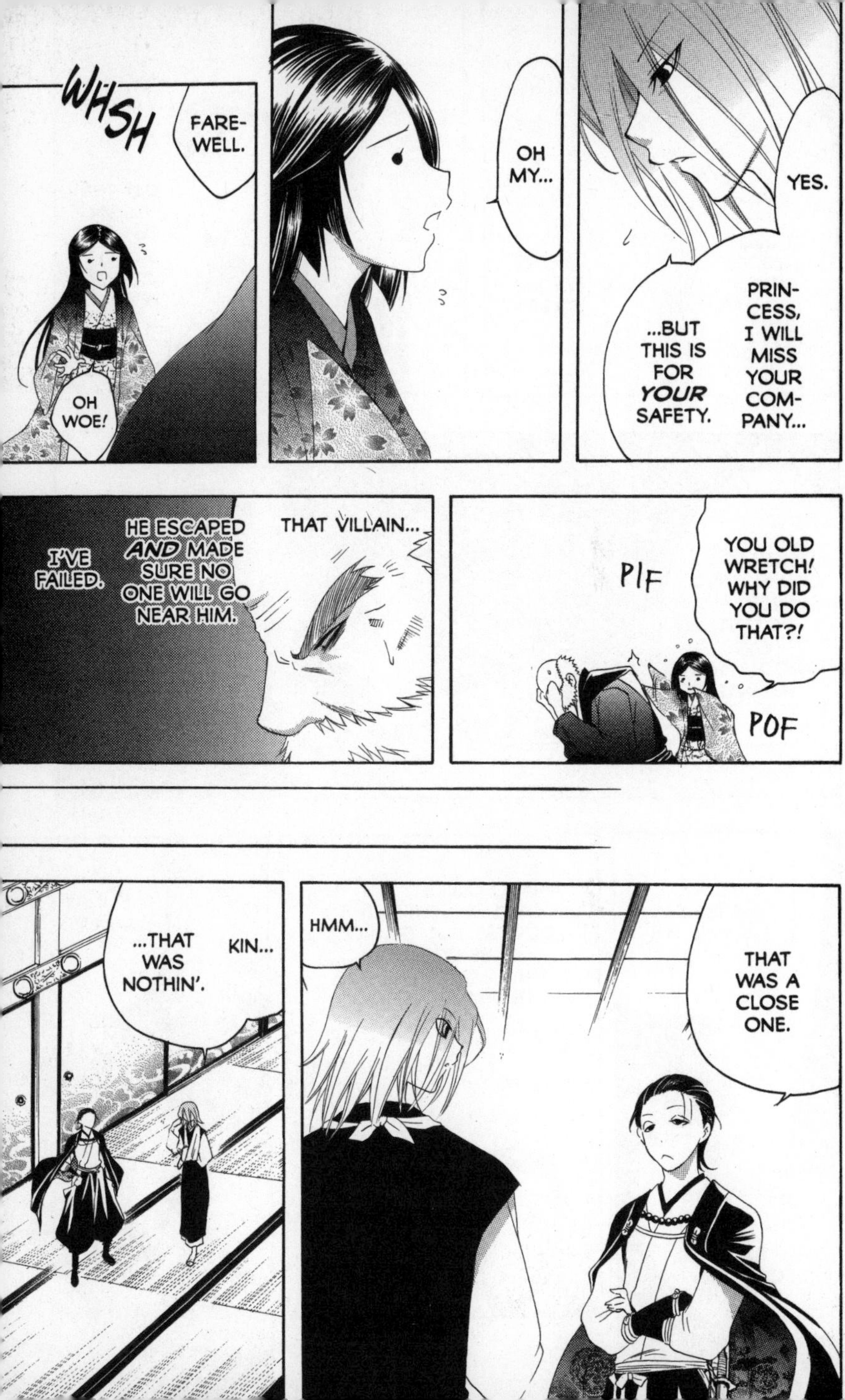
YES.
PRINCESS, I WILL MISS YOUR COMPANY...
...BUT THIS IS FOR *YOUR* SAFETY.
OH MY...
WHSH
FAREWELL.
OH WOE!
YOU OLD WRETCH! WHY DID YOU DO THAT?!
PIF
POF
THAT VILLAIN...
HE ESCAPED *AND* MADE SURE NO ONE WILL GO NEAR HIM.
I'VE FAILED.
THAT WAS A CLOSE ONE.
HMM...
KIN...
...THAT WAS NOTHIN'.

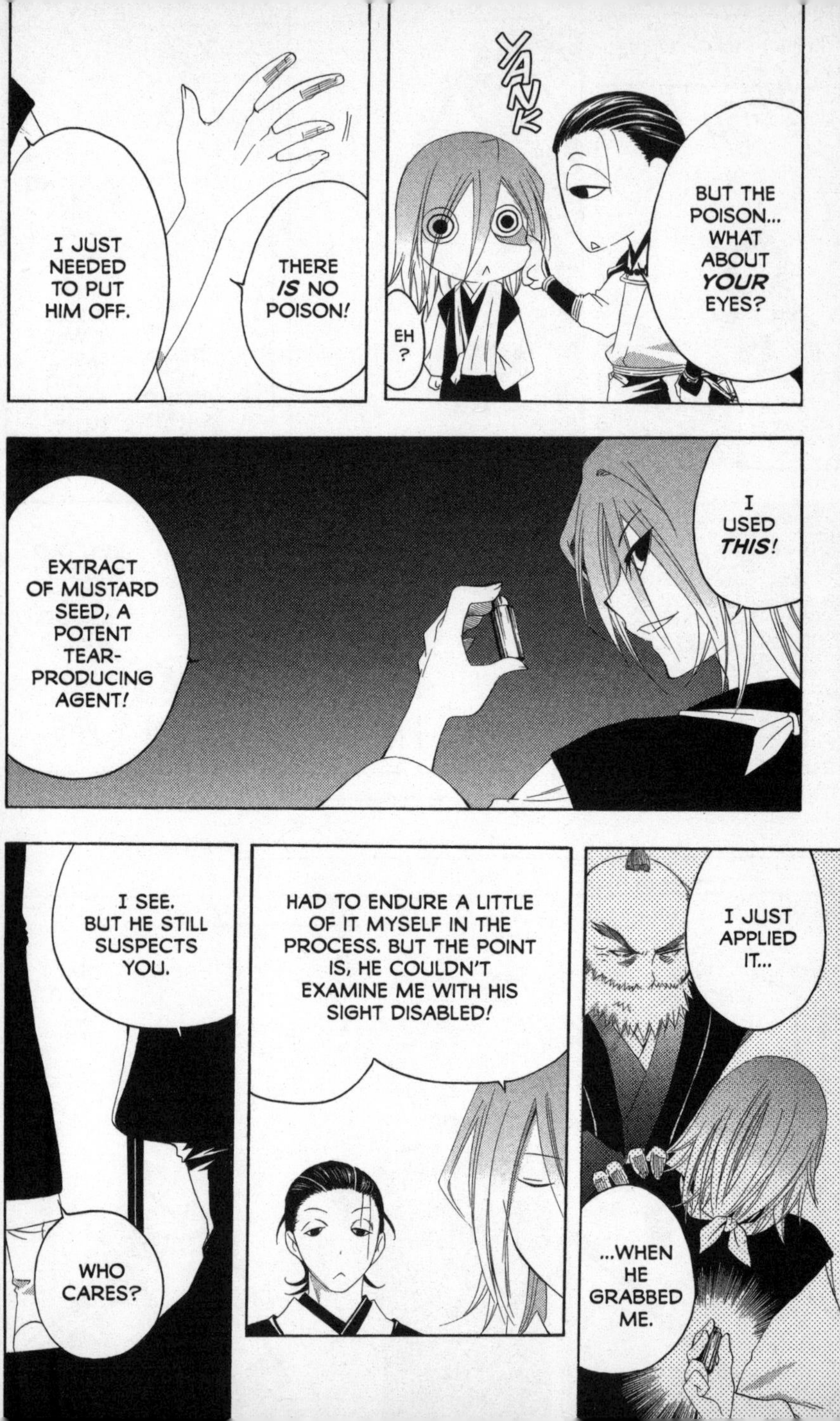
YANK
BUT THE POISON... WHAT ABOUT YOUR EYES?
EH?
THERE IS NO POISON!
I JUST NEEDED TO PUT HIM OFF.
I USED THIS!
EXTRACT OF MUSTARD SEED, A POTENT TEAR-PRODUCING AGENT!
I JUST APPLIED IT...
...WHEN HE GRABBED ME.
HAD TO ENDURE A LITTLE OF IT MYSELF IN THE PROCESS. BUT THE POINT IS, HE COULDN'T EXAMINE ME WITH HIS SIGHT DISABLED!
I SEE. BUT HE STILL SUSPECTS YOU.
WHO CARES?

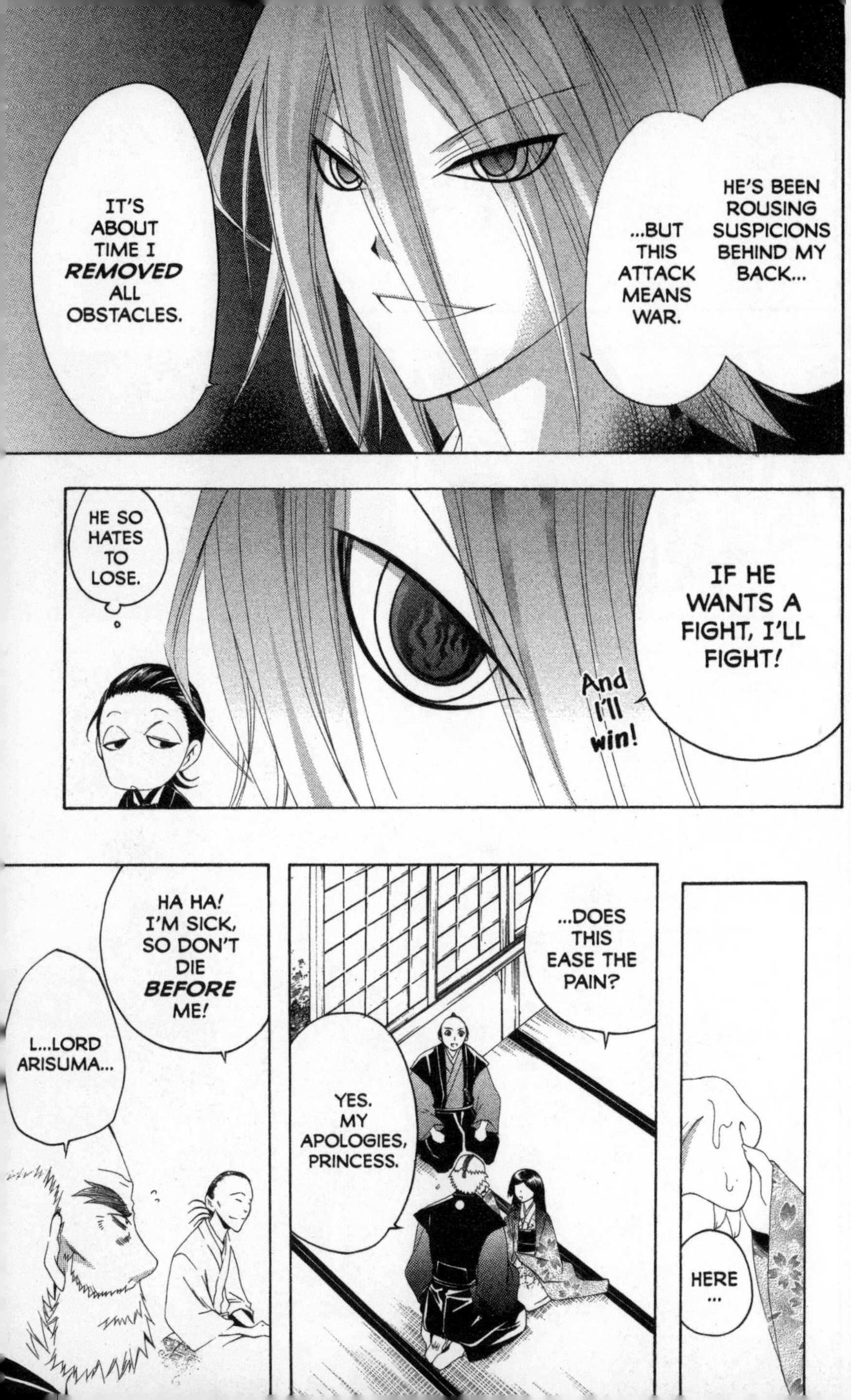
HE'S BEEN ROUSING SUSPICIONS BEHIND MY BACK...
...BUT THIS ATTACK MEANS WAR.
IT'S ABOUT TIME I *REMOVED* ALL OBSTACLES.
IF HE WANTS A FIGHT, I'LL FIGHT!
And I'll win!
HE SO HATES TO LOSE.
HERE ...
...DOES THIS EASE THE PAIN?
YES. MY APOLOGIES, PRINCESS.
HA HA! I'M SICK, SO DON'T DIE *BEFORE* ME!
L...LORD ARISUMA...

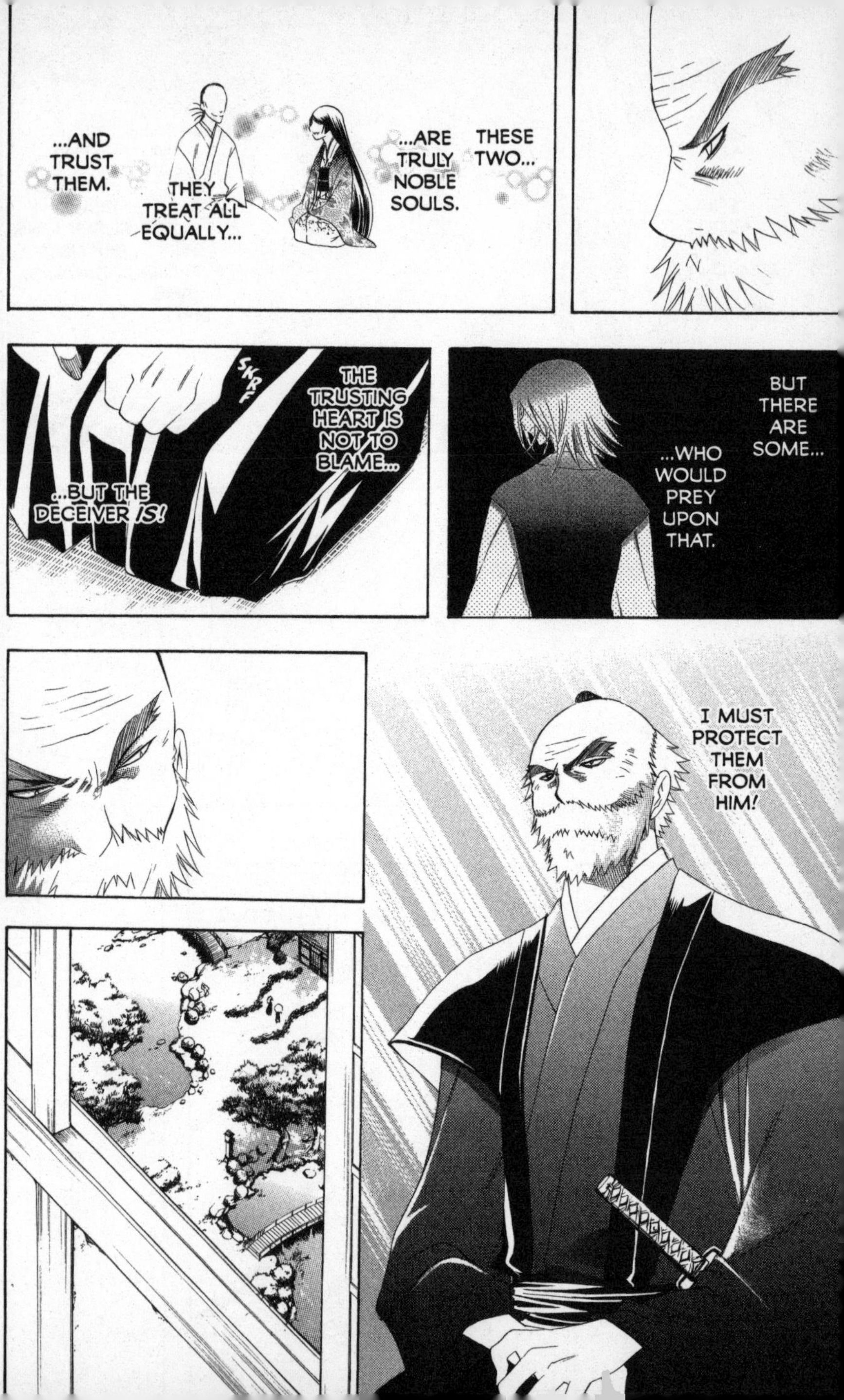
THESE TWO...
...ARE TRULY NOBLE SOULS.
THEY TREAT ALL EQUALLY...
...AND TRUST THEM.
BUT THERE ARE SOME...
...WHO WOULD PREY UPON THAT.
SKRF
THE TRUSTING HEART IS NOT TO BLAME...
...BUT THE DECEIVER *IS!*
I MUST PROTECT THEM FROM HIM!

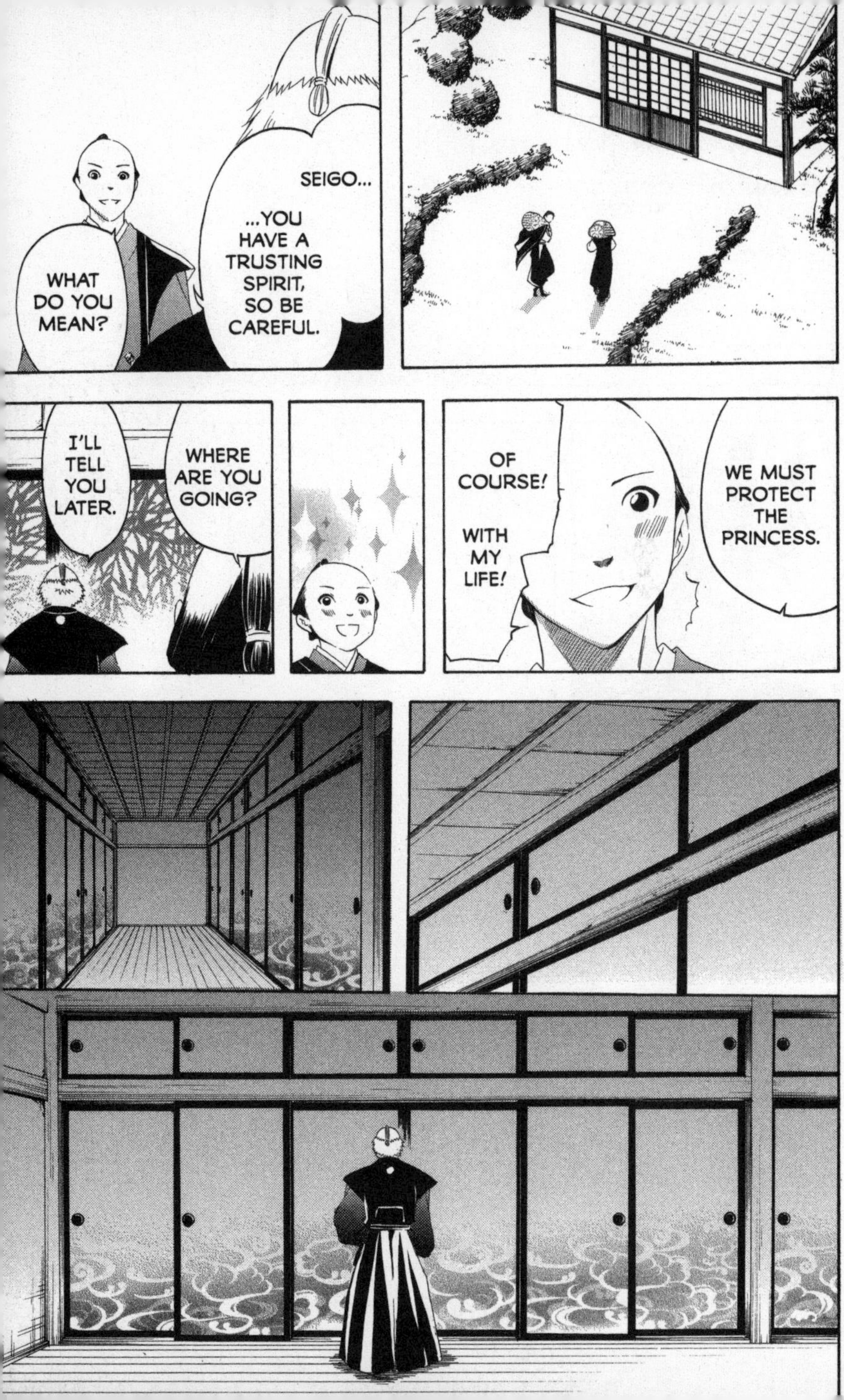
SEIGO...
...YOU HAVE A TRUSTING SPIRIT, SO BE CAREFUL.
WHAT DO YOU MEAN?
WE MUST PROTECT THE PRINCESS.
OF COURSE!
WITH MY LIFE!
WHERE ARE YOU GOING?
I'LL TELL YOU LATER.

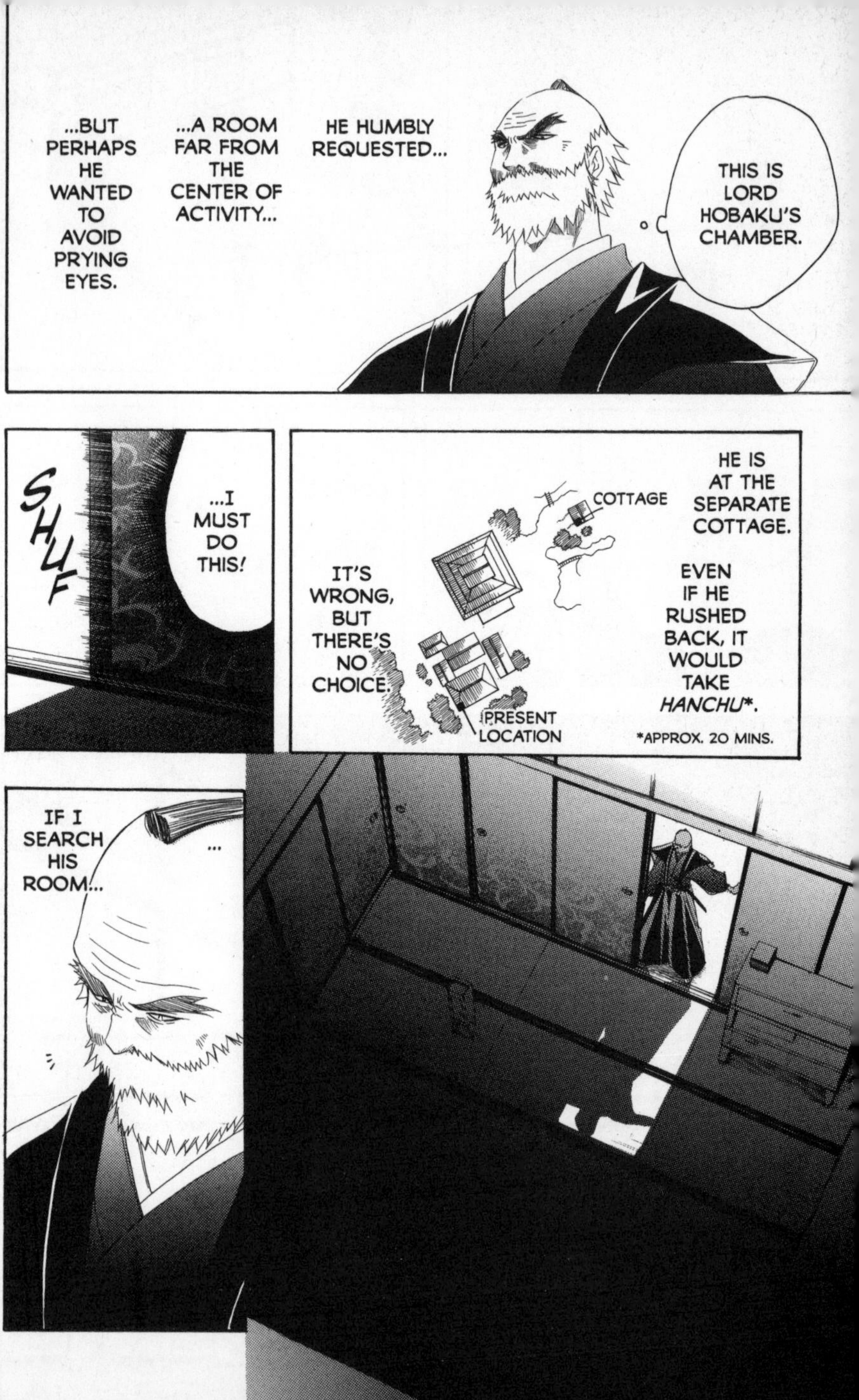
THIS IS LORD HOBAKU'S CHAMBER.
HE HUMBLY REQUESTED...
...A ROOM FAR FROM THE CENTER OF ACTIVITY...
...BUT PERHAPS HE WANTED TO AVOID PRYING EYES.
HE IS AT THE SEPARATE COTTAGE.
COTTAGE
EVEN IF HE RUSHED BACK, IT WOULD TAKE *HANCHU**.
IT'S WRONG, BUT THERE'S NO CHOICE.
PRESENT LOCATION
*APPROX. 20 MINS.
...I MUST DO THIS!
SHUF
...
IF I SEARCH HIS ROOM...

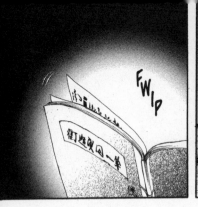

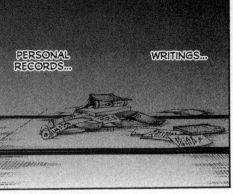

WRITINGS...
PERSONAL RECORDS...
FWIP
!
THIS IS IT!
THIS DETAILS HIS TRICKERY ALL OVER TOWN!
HE HAS EVEN ALTERED THE CASTLE...
...AND PREPARED AN UNDERGROUND ESCAPE ROUTE!
THIS IS SOLID PROOF!
I MUST SHOW IT TO LORD ARISUMA!
みし…
BUT...
...WHY IS THIS LYING OUT IN THE OPEN?
IT IS ALMOST AS IF...

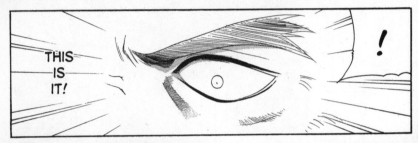

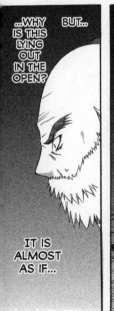

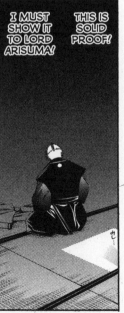

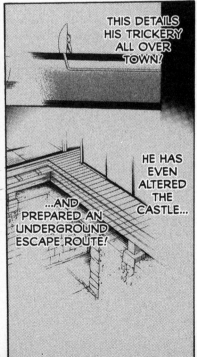

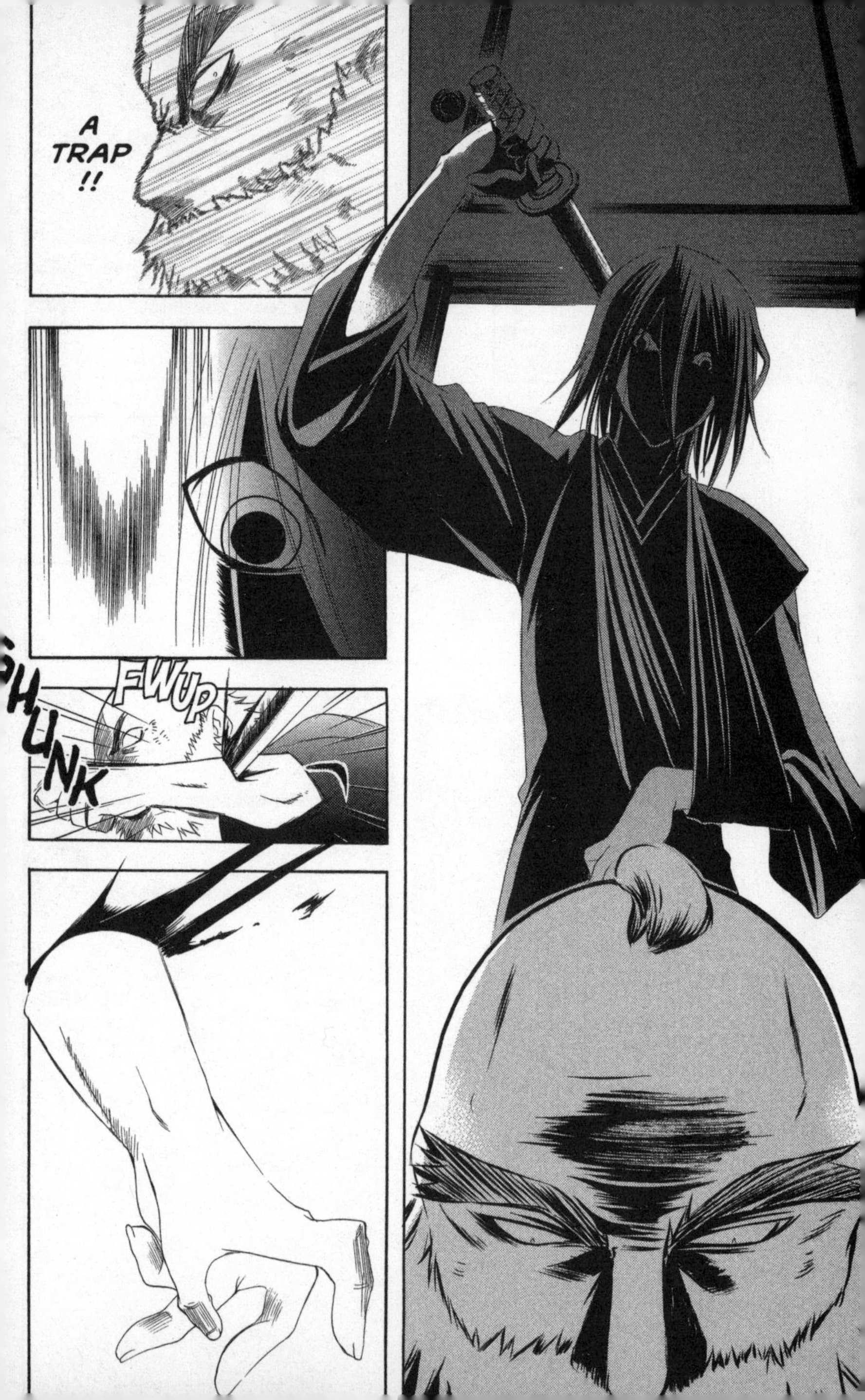
A TRAP !!
FWUP
SHUNK

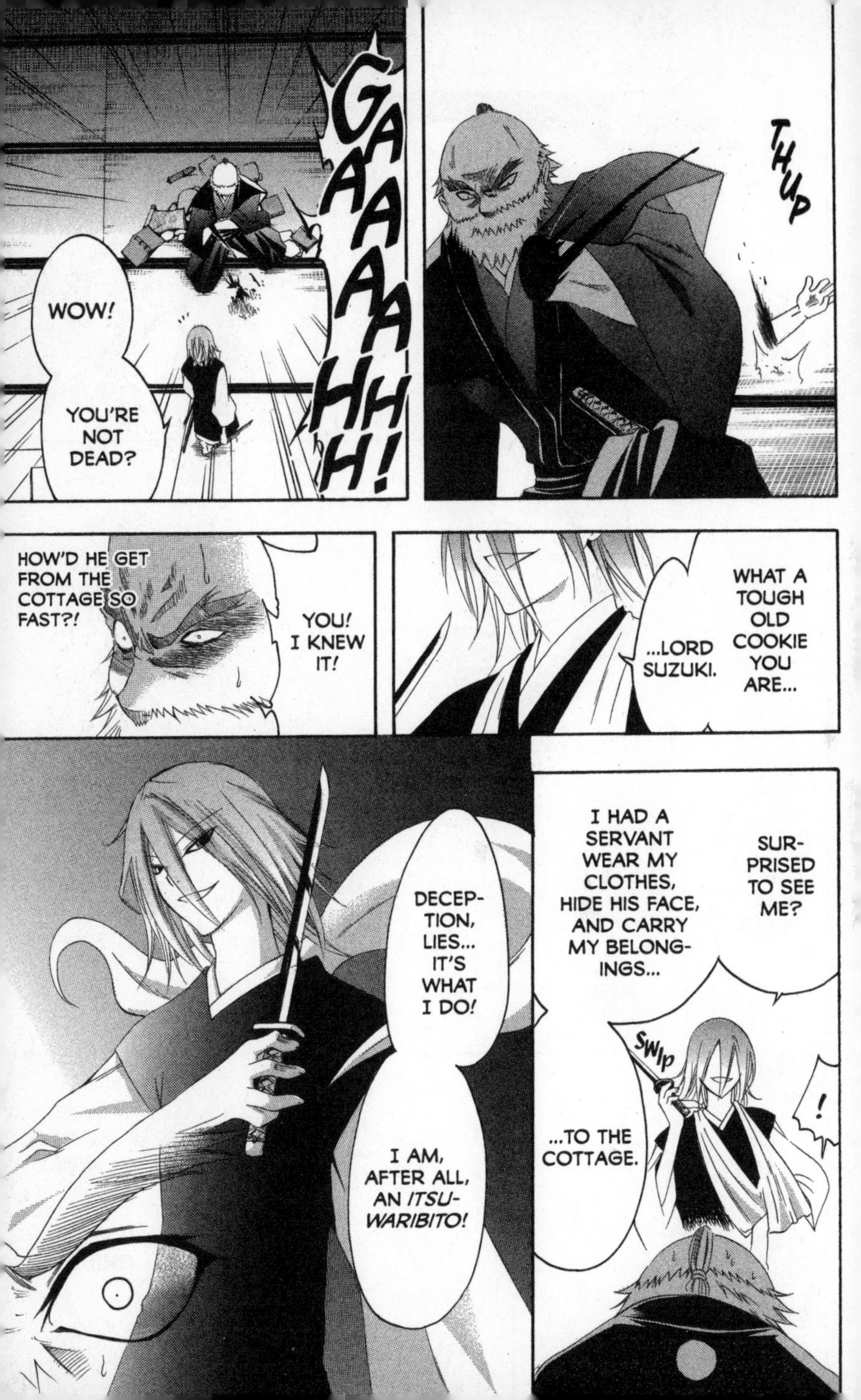
THUP
GAAAAAHHHH!
WOW!
YOU'RE NOT DEAD?
WHAT A TOUGH OLD COOKIE YOU ARE...
...LORD SUZUKI.
YOU! I KNEW IT!
HOW'D HE GET FROM THE COTTAGE SO FAST?!
SURPRISED TO SEE ME?
I HAD A SERVANT WEAR MY CLOTHES, HIDE HIS FACE, AND CARRY MY BELONGINGS...
!
SWIP
...TO THE COTTAGE.
DECEPTION, LIES... IT'S WHAT I DO!
I AM, AFTER ALL, AN *ITSUWARIBITO*!

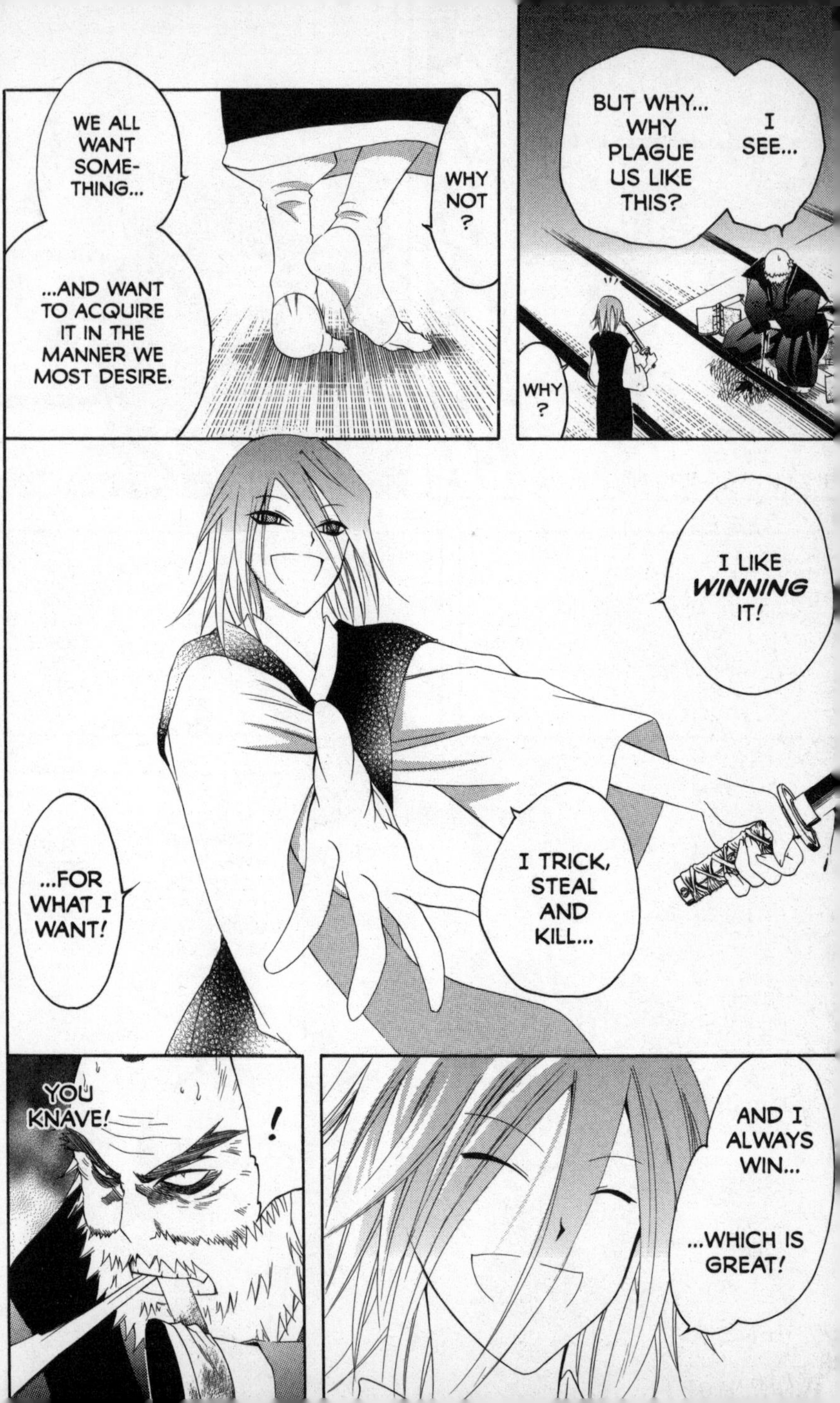
I SEE...
BUT WHY... WHY PLAGUE US LIKE THIS?
WHY?
WHY NOT?
WE ALL WANT SOME-THING...
...AND WANT TO ACQUIRE IT IN THE MANNER WE MOST DESIRE.
I LIKE *WINNING* IT!
I TRICK, STEAL AND KILL...
...FOR WHAT I WANT!
AND I ALWAYS WIN...
...WHICH IS GREAT!
!
YOU KNAVE!

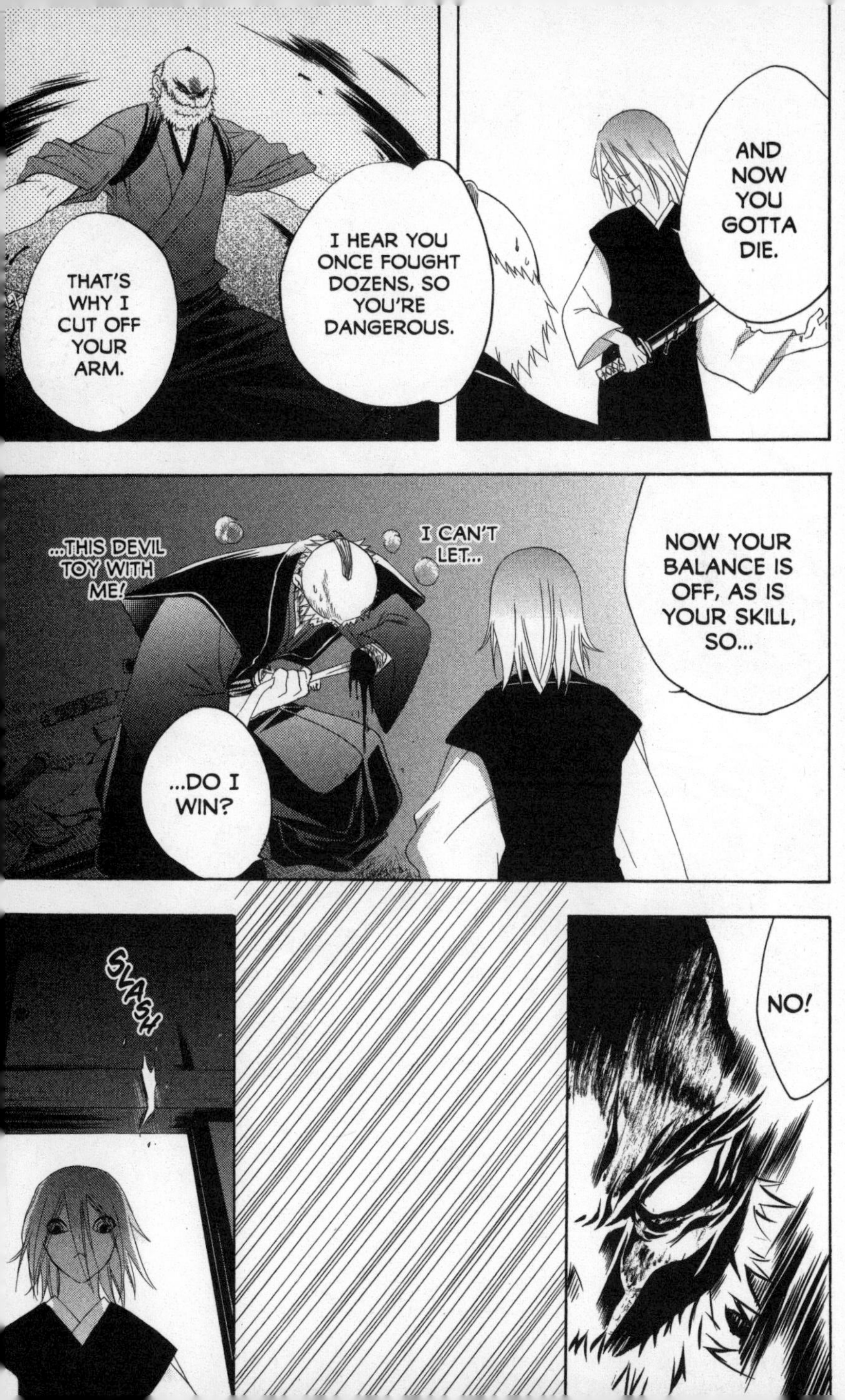
AND NOW YOU GOTTA DIE.
I HEAR YOU ONCE FOUGHT DOZENS, SO YOU'RE DANGEROUS.
THAT'S WHY I CUT OFF YOUR ARM.
NOW YOUR BALANCE IS OFF, AS IS YOUR SKILL, SO...
I CAN'T LET...
...THIS DEVIL TOY WITH ME!
...DO I WIN?
NO!
SLASH

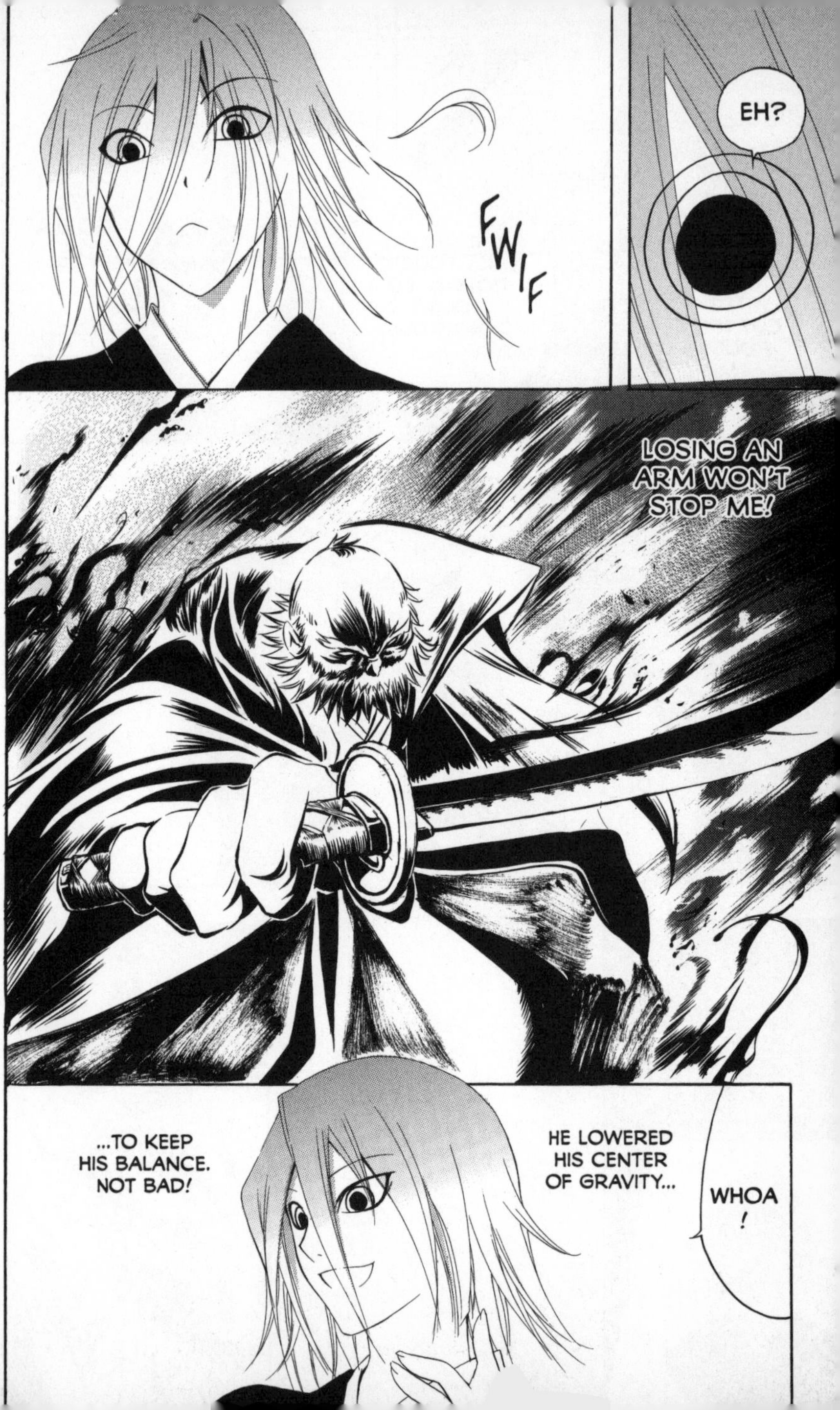
EH?
FWIF
LOSING AN ARM WON'T STOP ME!
WHOA!
HE LOWERED HIS CENTER OF GRAVITY...
...TO KEEP HIS BALANCE. NOT BAD!

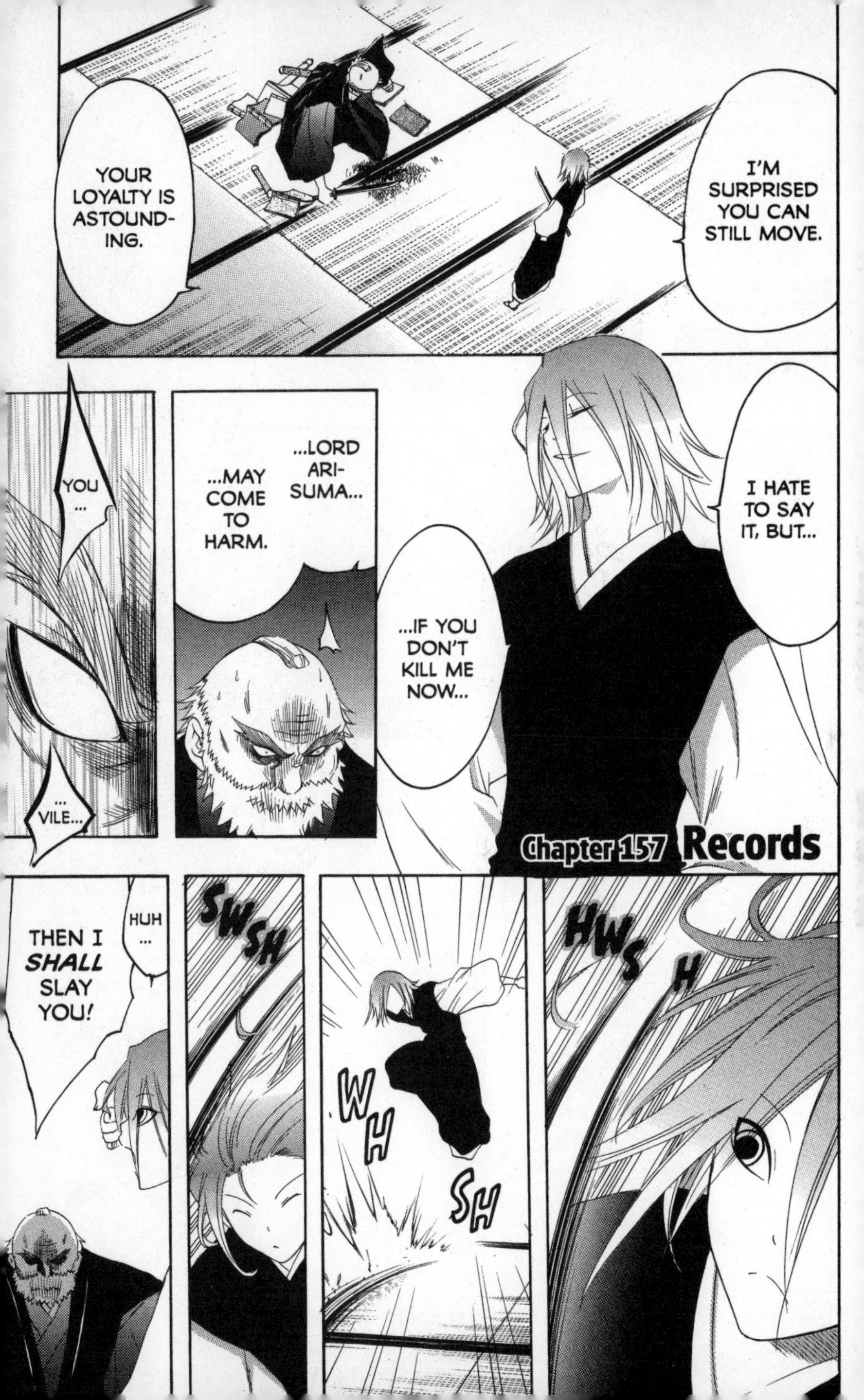
I'M SURPRISED YOU CAN STILL MOVE.
YOUR LOYALTY IS ASTOUND-ING.
I HATE TO SAY IT, BUT...
...IF YOU DON'T KILL ME NOW...
Chapter 157 Records
...LORD ARI-SUMA...
...MAY COME TO HARM.
YOU ...
... VILE...
HWSH
WHSH
SWSH
HUH ...
THEN I *SHALL* SLAY YOU!

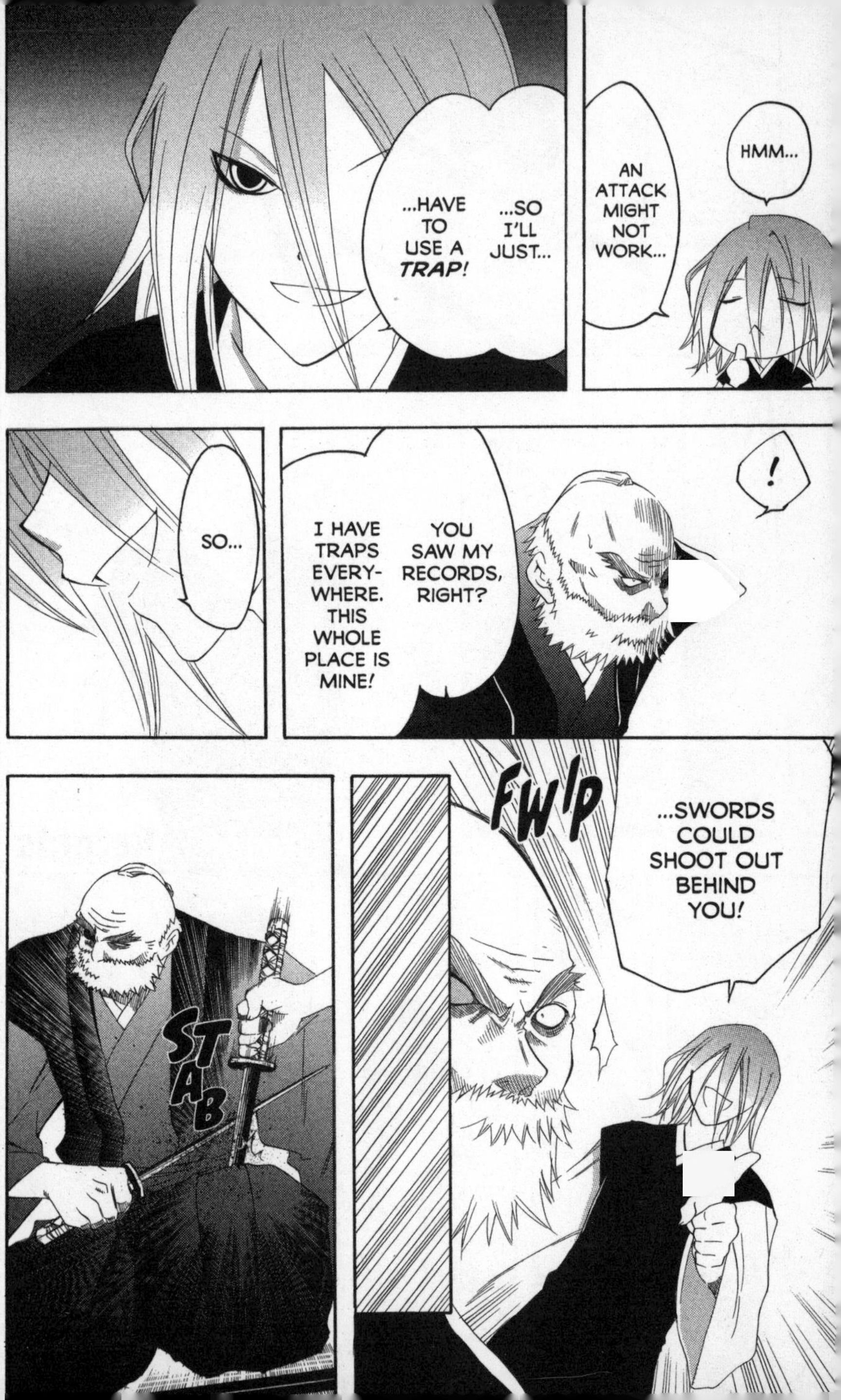
HMM...
AN ATTACK MIGHT NOT WORK...
...SO I'LL JUST...
...HAVE TO USE A *TRAP*!
!
YOU SAW MY RECORDS, RIGHT?
I HAVE TRAPS EVERY-WHERE. THIS WHOLE PLACE IS MINE!
SO...
FWIP
...SWORDS COULD SHOOT OUT BEHIND YOU!
STAB

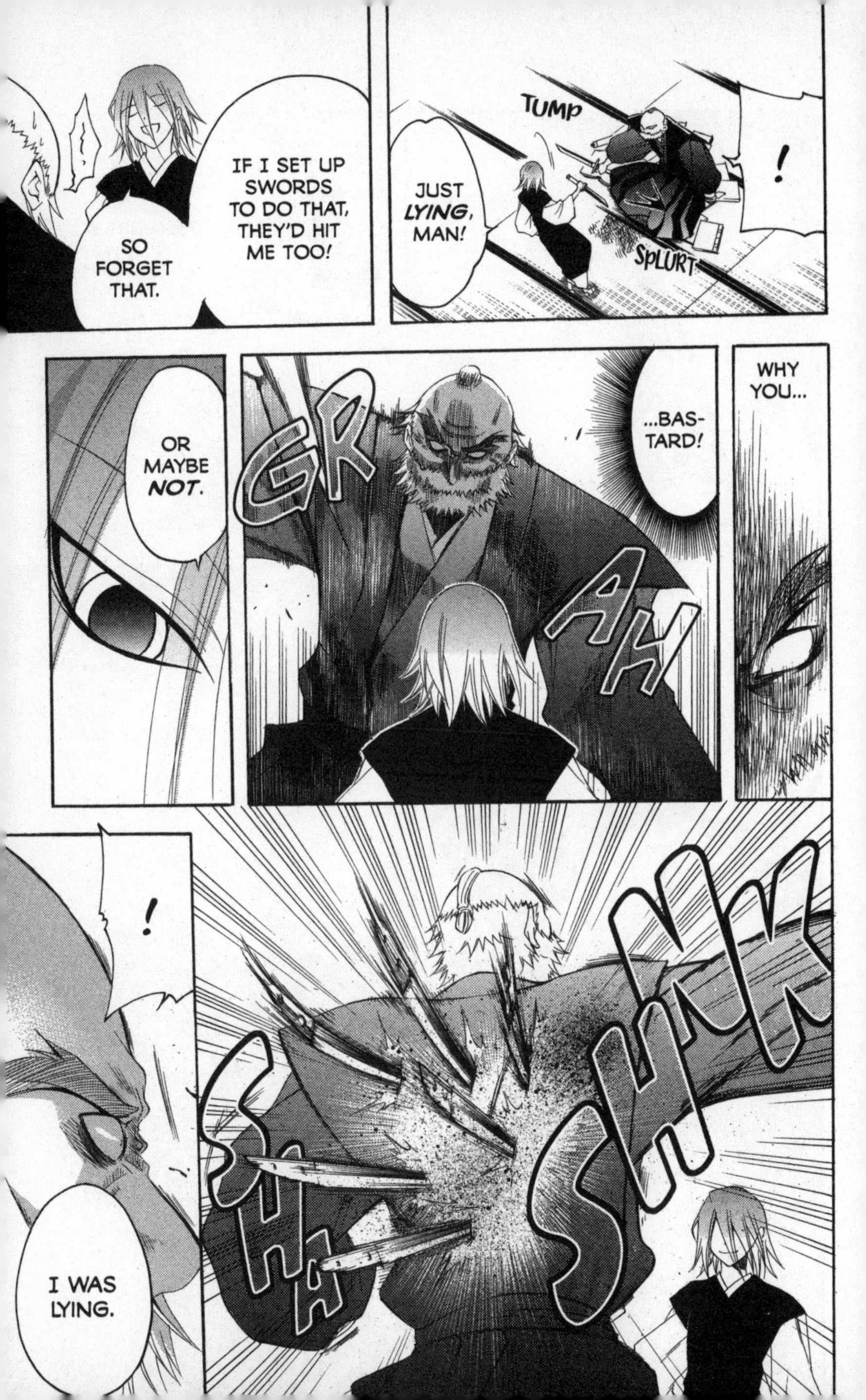
!
TUMP
JUST LYING, MAN!
SPLURT
!
IF I SET UP SWORDS TO DO THAT, THEY'D HIT ME TOO!
SO FORGET THAT.
WHY YOU...
...BAS-TARD!
GRAAH
OR MAYBE NOT.
SHUNK
SHHA
!
I WAS LYING.

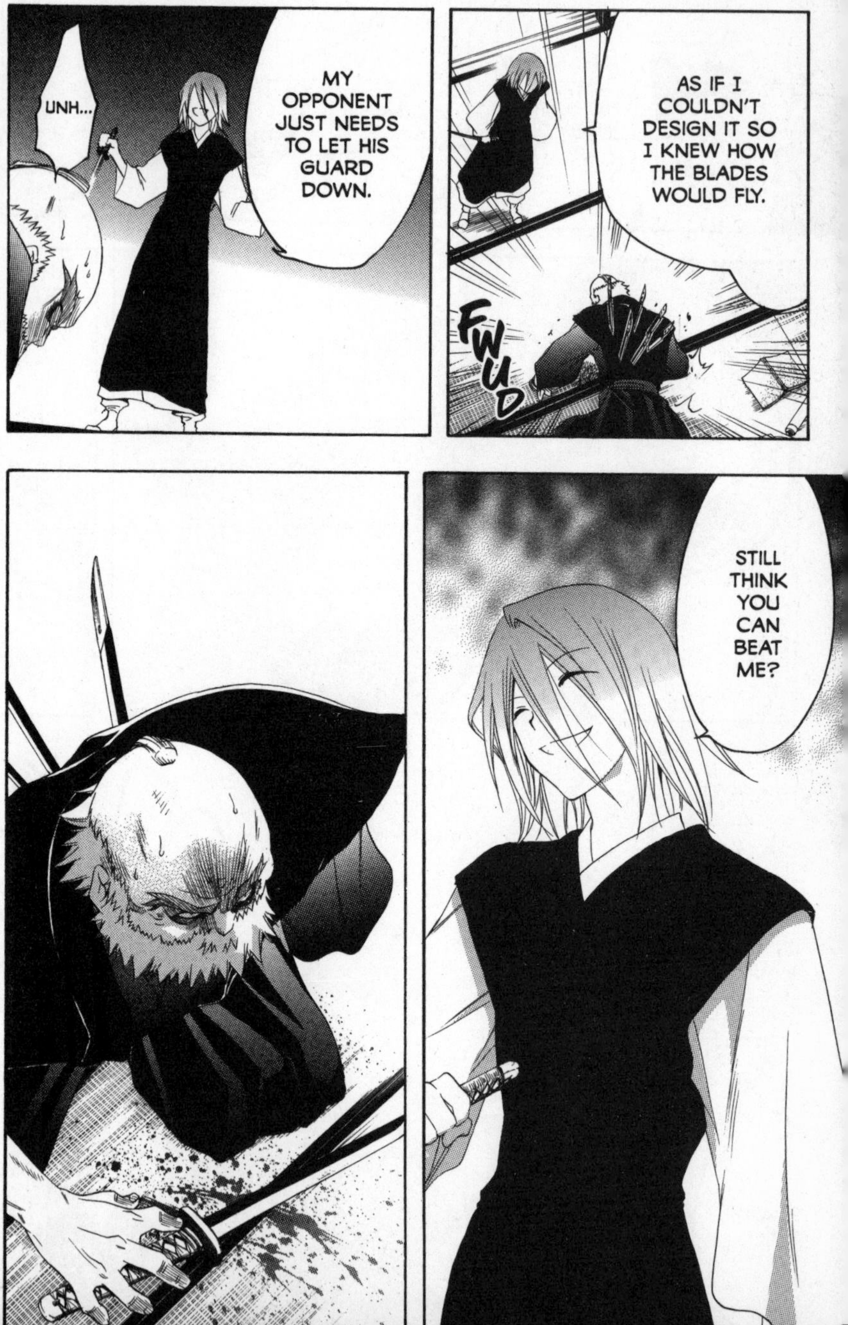
AS IF I COULDN'T DESIGN IT SO I KNEW HOW THE BLADES WOULD FLY.
FWUD
MY OPPONENT JUST NEEDS TO LET HIS GUARD DOWN.
UNH...
STILL THINK YOU CAN BEAT ME?

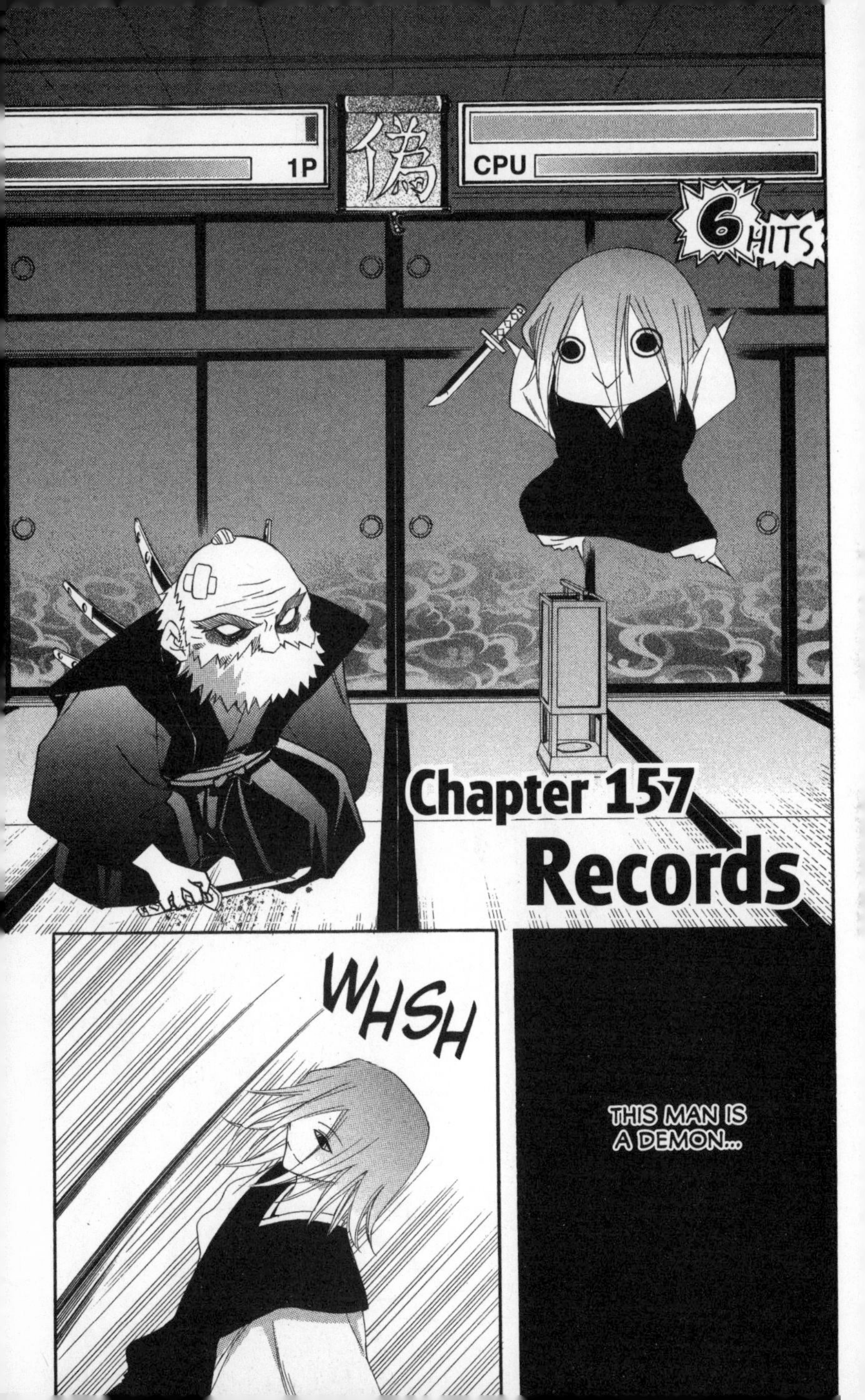
1P
偽
CPU
6 HITS
Chapter 157
Records
THIS MAN IS A DEMON...
WHSH

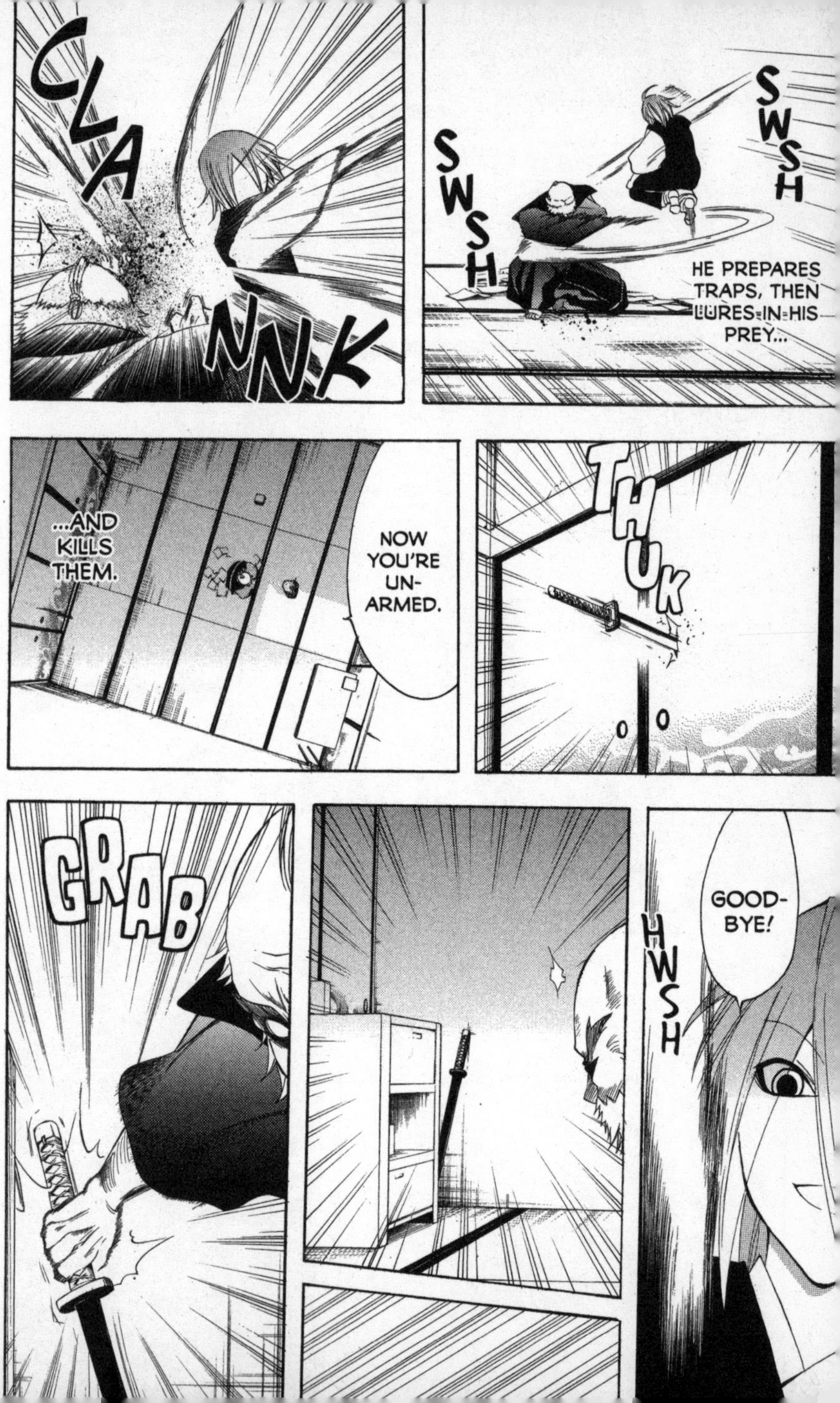
SWSH
SWSH
HE PREPARES TRAPS, THEN LURES IN HIS PREY...
CLANNNK
THUK
NOW YOU'RE UN-ARMED.
...AND KILLS THEM.
GOOD-BYE!
HWSH
GRAB

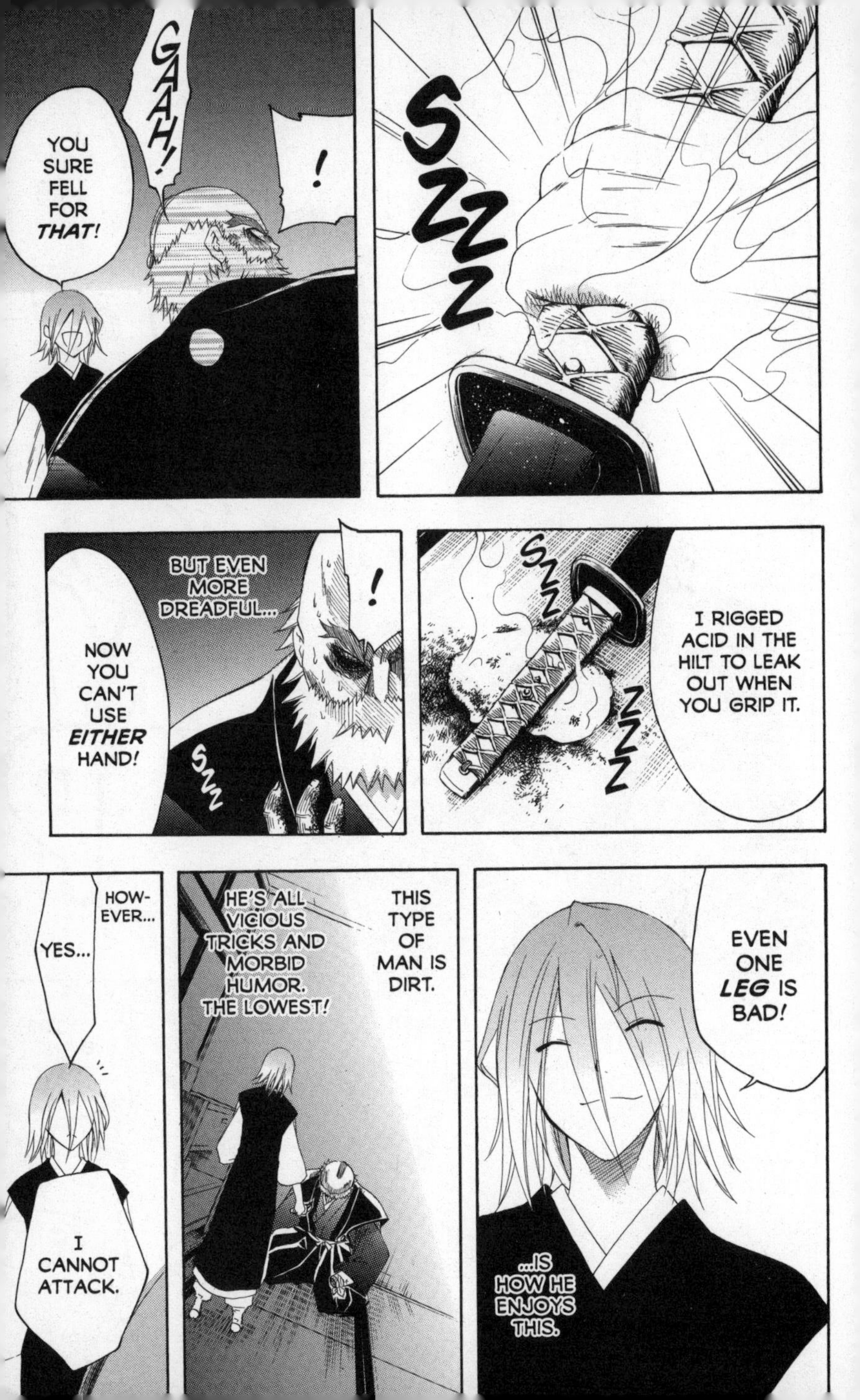
SZZZ
GAAH!
!
YOU SURE FELL FOR THAT!
SZZ
I RIGGED ACID IN THE HILT TO LEAK OUT WHEN YOU GRIP IT.
ZZZ
!
BUT EVEN MORE DREADFUL...
NOW YOU CAN'T USE EITHER HAND!
SZZ
EVEN ONE LEG IS BAD!
...IS HOW HE ENJOYS THIS.
THIS TYPE OF MAN IS DIRT.
HE'S ALL VICIOUS TRICKS AND MORBID HUMOR. THE LOWEST!
HOW-EVER...
YES...
I CANNOT ATTACK.

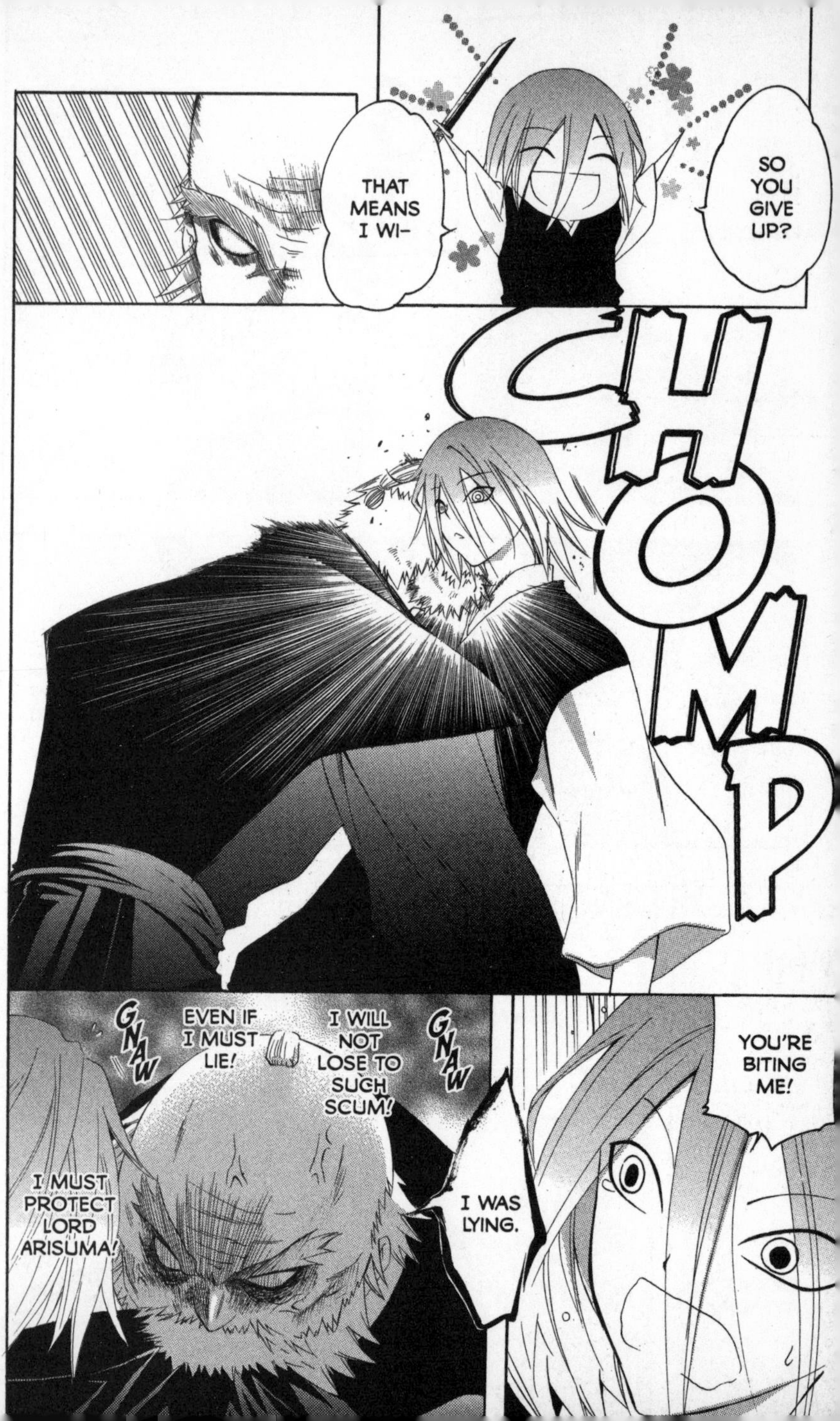
SO YOU GIVE UP?
THAT MEANS I WI-
CHOMP
YOU'RE BITING ME!
I WAS LYING.
I WILL NOT LOSE TO SUCH SCUM!
GNAW
EVEN IF I MUST LIE!
GNAW
I MUST PROTECT LORD ARISUMA!

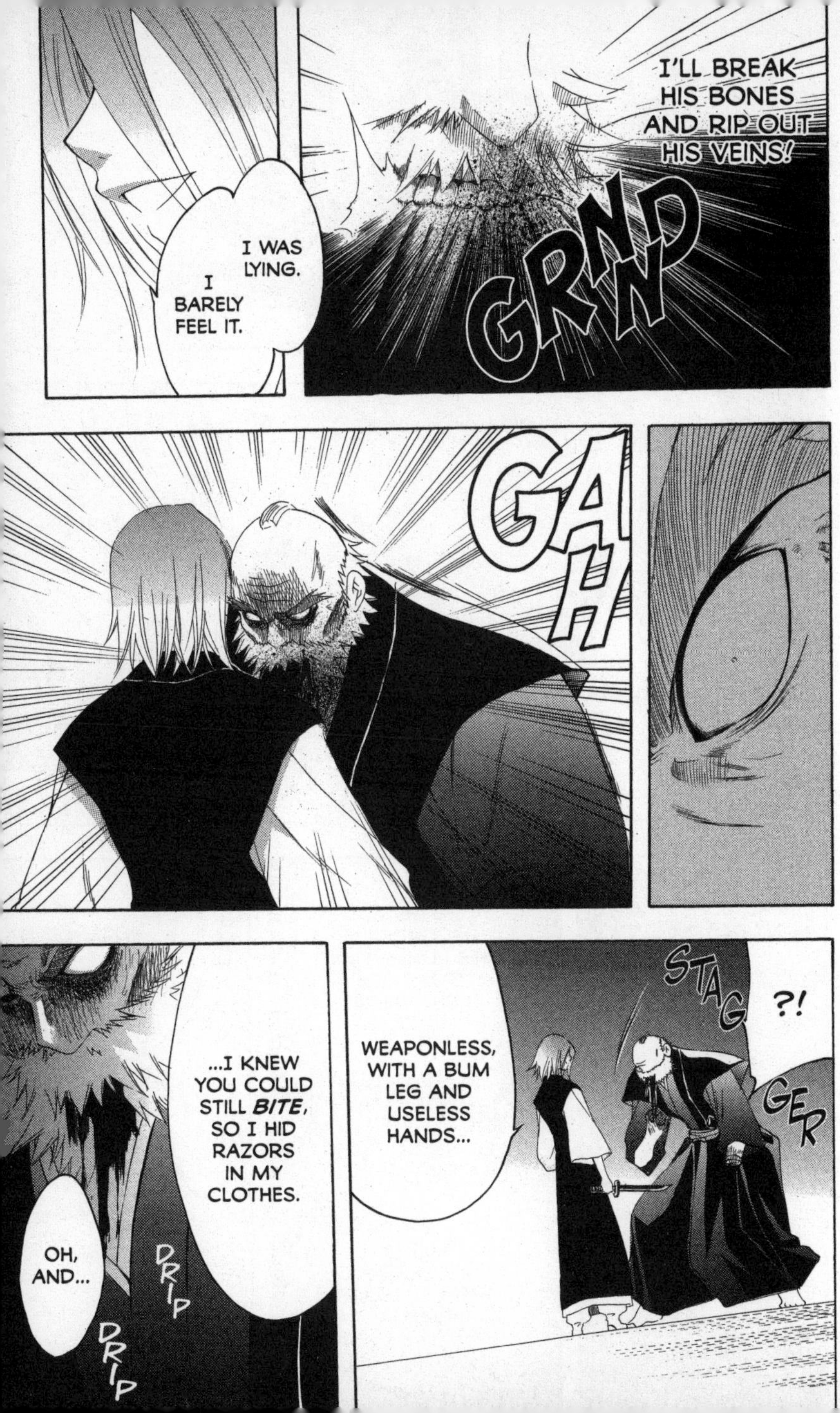
I'LL BREAK HIS BONES AND RIP OUT HIS VEINS!
GRND
I WAS LYING. I BARELY FEEL IT.
GAH
STAGGER
?!
WEAPONLESS, WITH A BUM LEG AND USELESS HANDS...
...I KNEW YOU COULD STILL *BITE*, SO I HID RAZORS IN MY CLOTHES.
OH, AND...
DRIP
DRIP

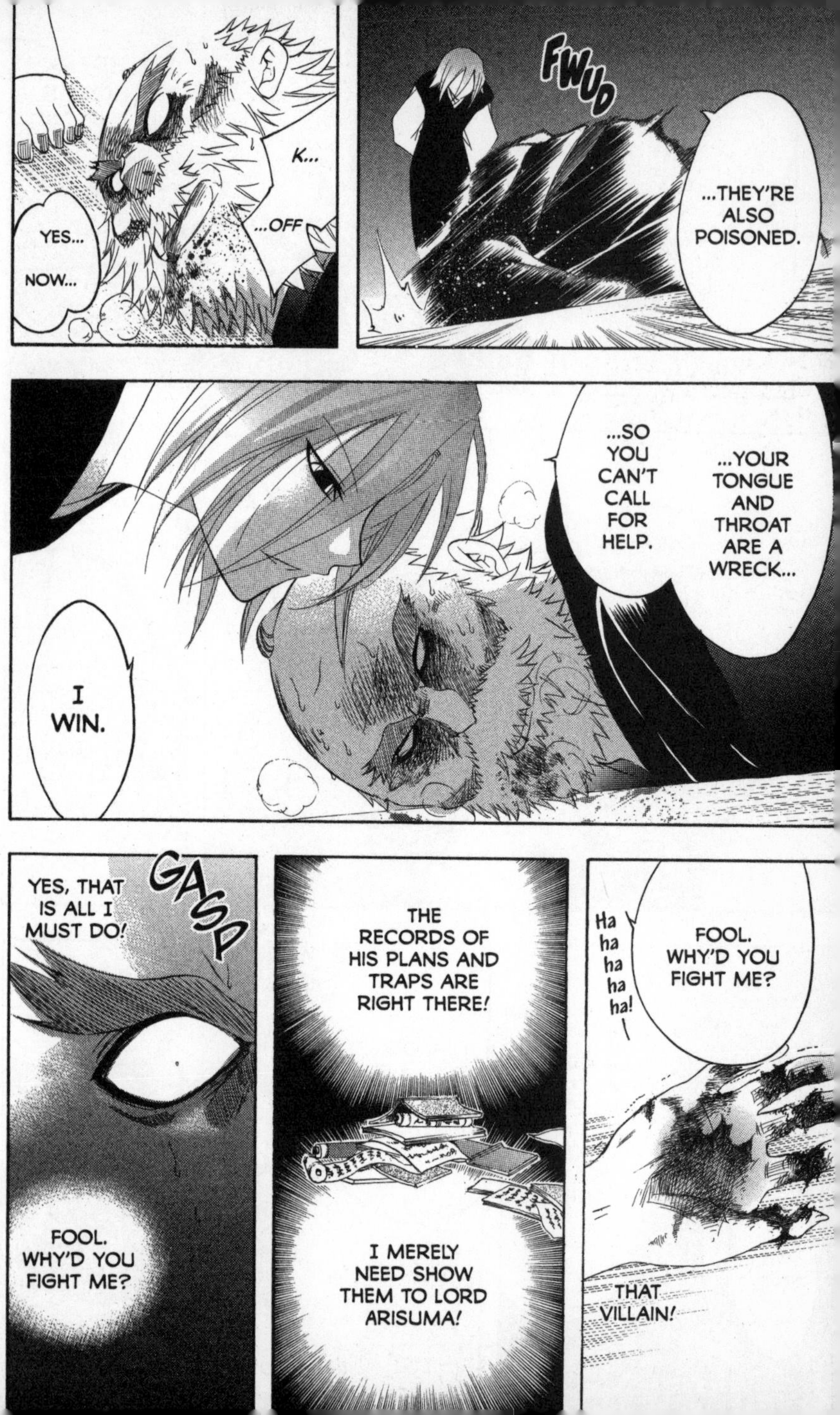
FWUD
...THEY'RE ALSO POISONED.
K...
...OFF
YES... NOW...
...YOUR TONGUE AND THROAT ARE A WRECK...
...SO YOU CAN'T CALL FOR HELP.
I WIN.
FOOL. WHY'D YOU FIGHT ME?
Ha ha ha ha ha!
THAT VILLAIN!
THE RECORDS OF HIS PLANS AND TRAPS ARE RIGHT THERE!
I MERELY NEED SHOW THEM TO LORD ARISUMA!
GASP
YES, THAT IS ALL I MUST DO!
FOOL. WHY'D YOU FIGHT ME?

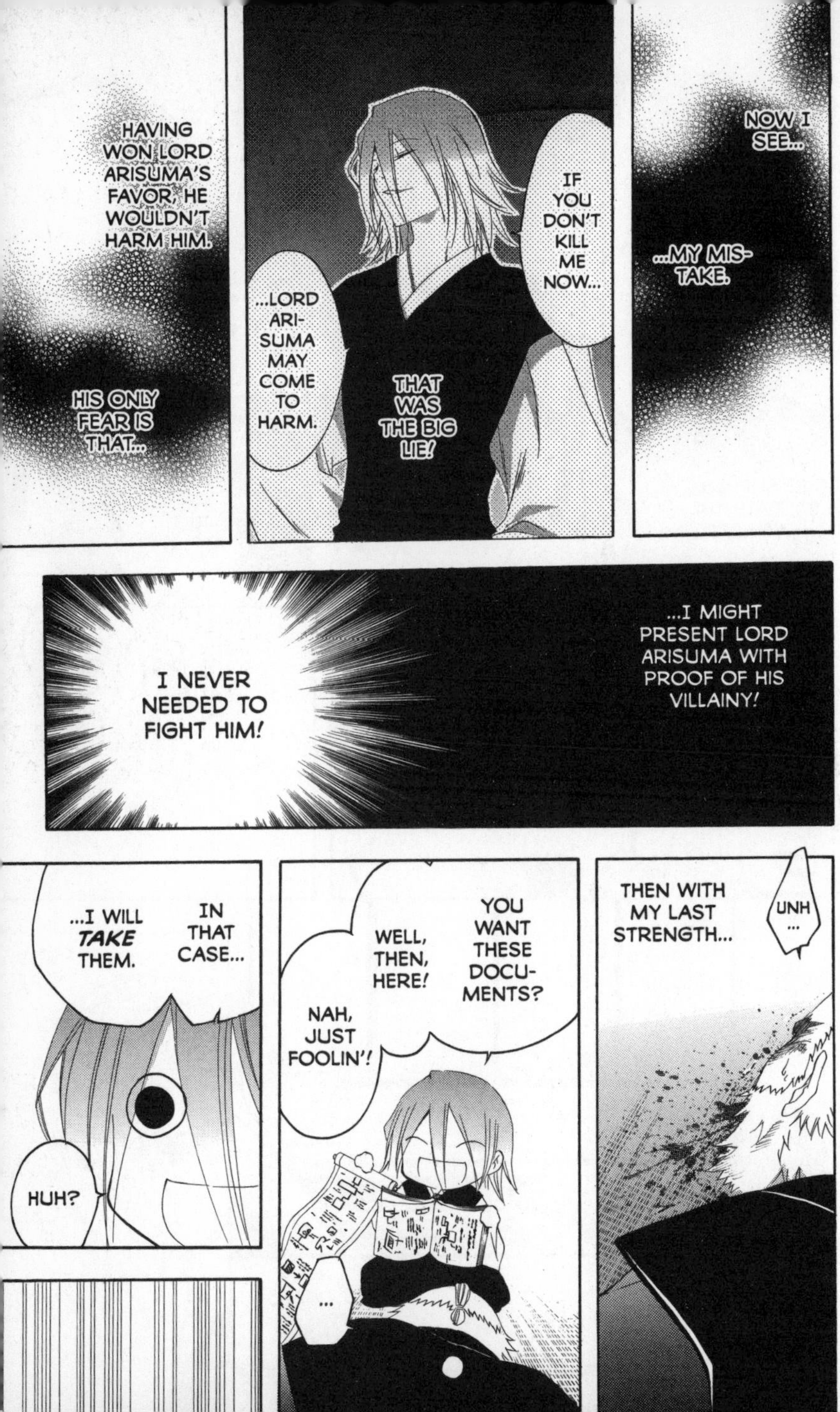
NOW I SEE...
...MY MIS-TAKE.
IF YOU DON'T KILL ME NOW...
...LORD ARI-SUMA MAY COME TO HARM.
THAT WAS THE BIG LIE!
HAVING WON LORD ARISUMA'S FAVOR, HE WOULDN'T HARM HIM.
HIS ONLY FEAR IS THAT...
...I MIGHT PRESENT LORD ARISUMA WITH PROOF OF HIS VILLAINY!
I NEVER NEEDED TO FIGHT HIM!
UNH...
THEN WITH MY LAST STRENGTH...
YOU WANT THESE DOCU-MENTS?
WELL, THEN, HERE!
NAH, JUST FOOLIN'!
...
IN THAT CASE...
...I WILL *TAKE* THEM.
HUH?

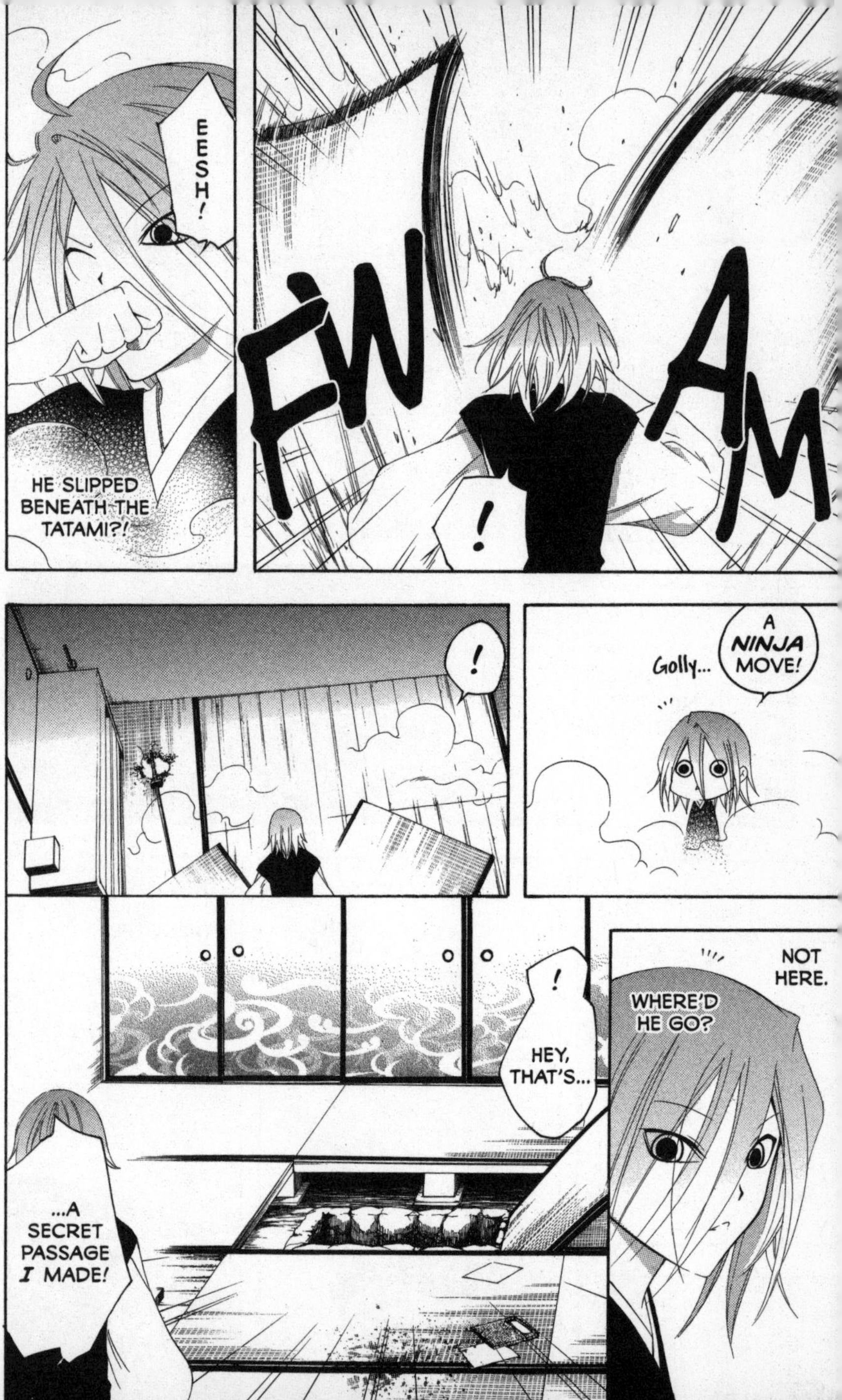
FWAM
!
EESH!
HE SLIPPED BENEATH THE TATAMI?!
A NINJA MOVE!
Golly...
!
NOT HERE.
WHERE'D HE GO?
!
HEY, THAT'S...
...A SECRET PASSAGE I MADE!

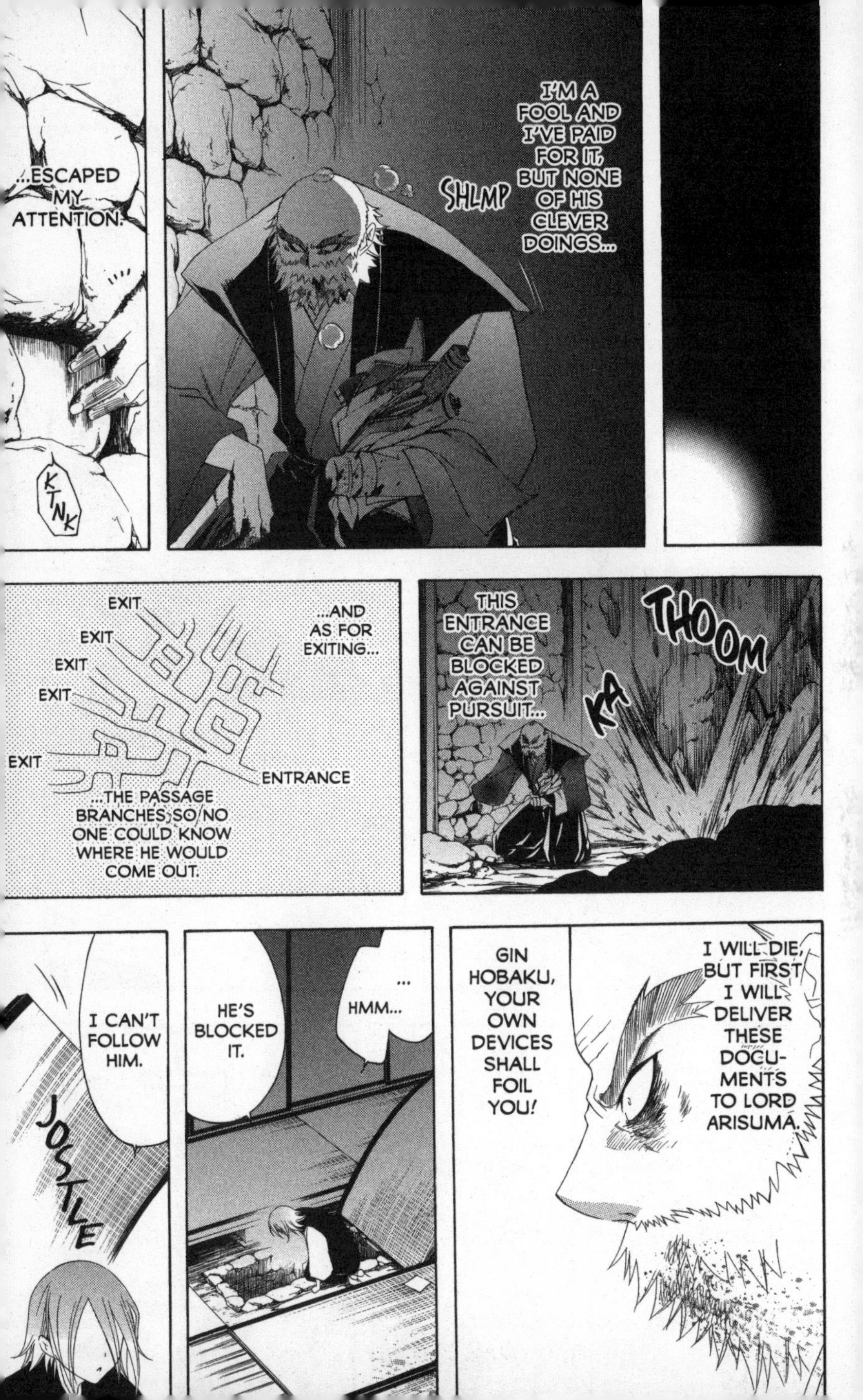
I'M A FOOL AND I'VE PAID FOR IT, BUT NONE OF HIS CLEVER DOINGS...
SHLMP
...ESCAPED MY ATTENTION.
KTNK
THIS ENTRANCE CAN BE BLOCKED AGAINST PURSUIT...
THOOM
KA
...AND AS FOR EXITING...
EXIT
EXIT
EXIT
EXIT
EXIT
ENTRANCE
...THE PASSAGE BRANCHES, SO NO ONE COULD KNOW WHERE HE WOULD COME OUT.
I WILL DIE, BUT FIRST I WILL DELIVER THESE DOCU-MENTS TO LORD ARISUMA.
GIN HOBAKU, YOUR OWN DEVICES SHALL FOIL YOU!
... HMM...
HE'S BLOCKED IT.
I CAN'T FOLLOW HIM.
JOSTLE

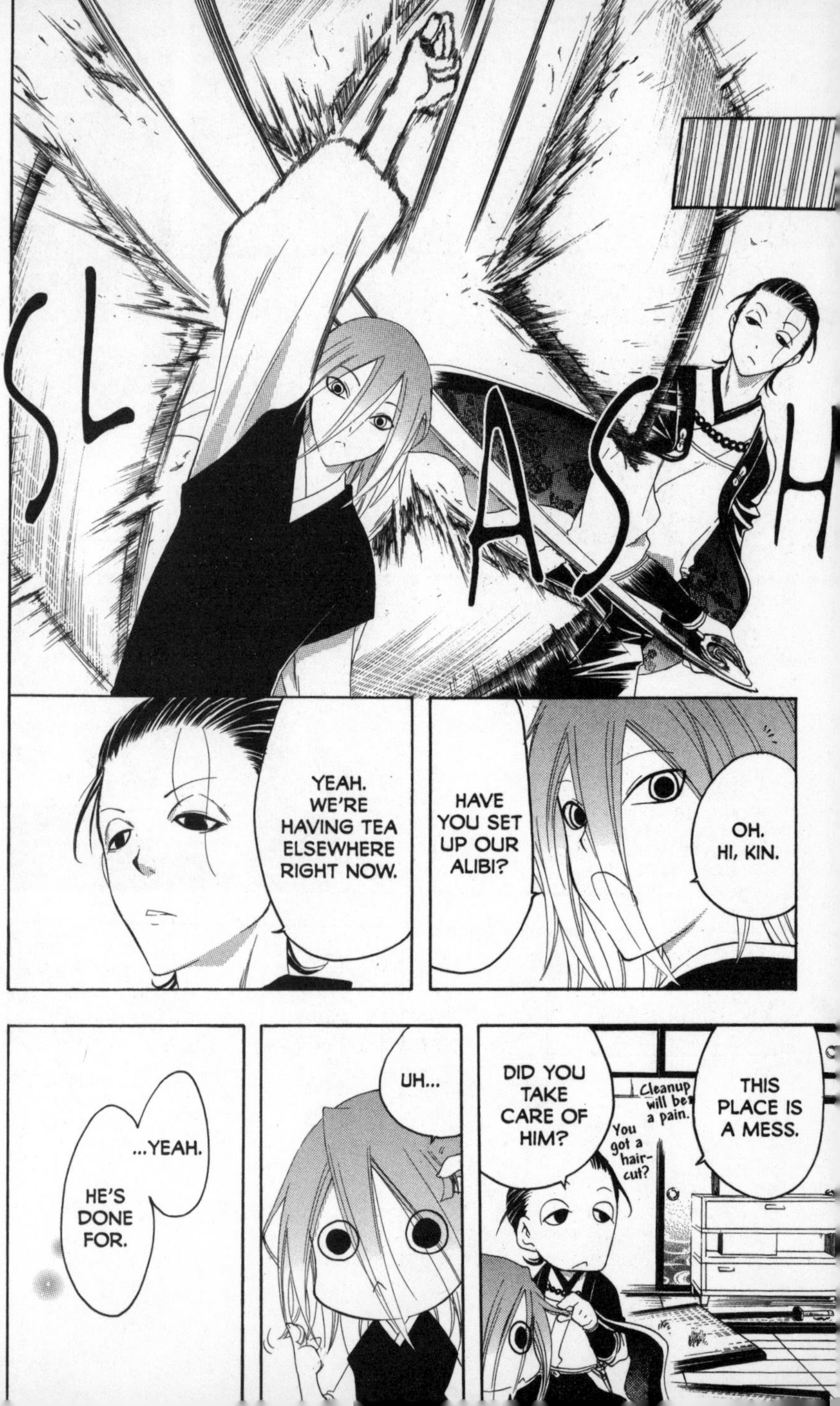
SLASH
OH. HI, KIN.
HAVE YOU SET UP OUR ALIBI?
YEAH. WE'RE HAVING TEA ELSEWHERE RIGHT NOW.
THIS PLACE IS A MESS.
Cleanup will be a pain.
DID YOU TAKE CARE OF HIM?
You got a hair-cut?
UH...
...YEAH.
HE'S DONE FOR.

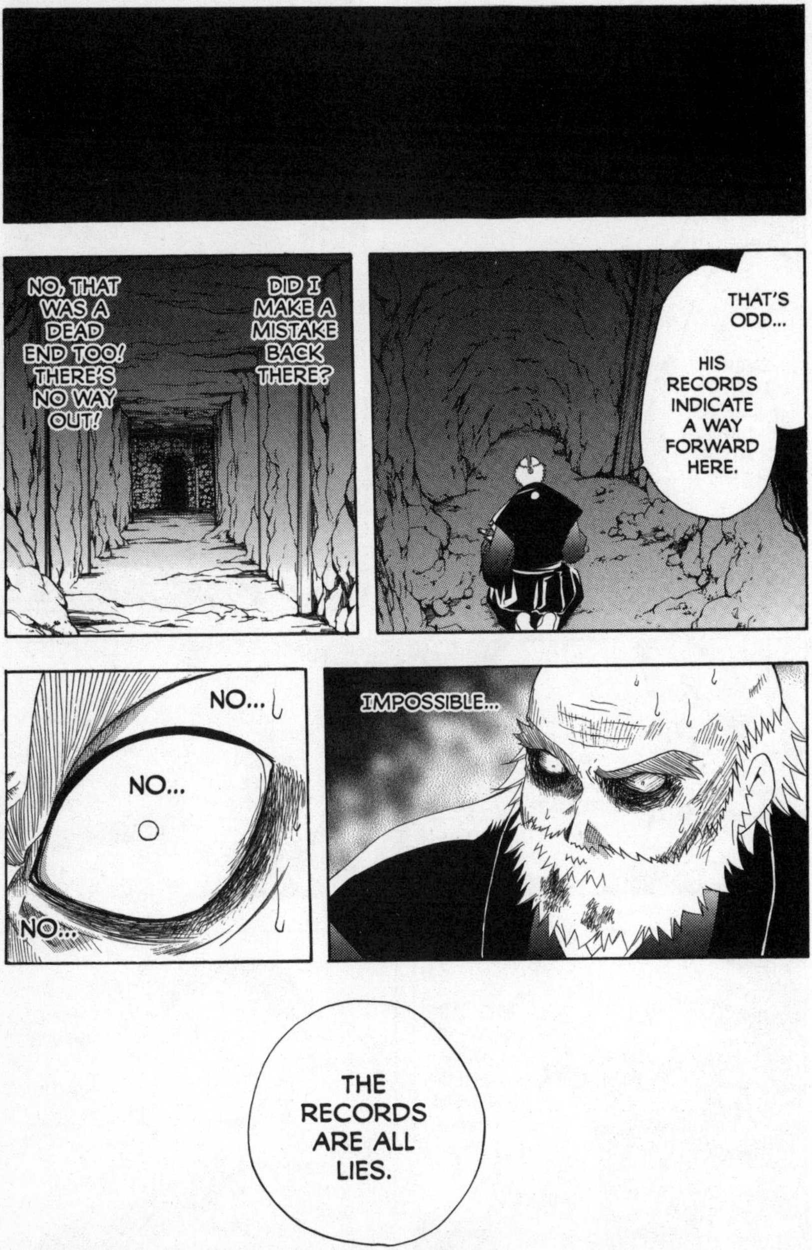
THAT'S ODD...
HIS RECORDS INDICATE A WAY FORWARD HERE.
DID I MAKE A MISTAKE BACK THERE?
NO, THAT WAS A DEAD END TOO! THERE'S NO WAY OUT!
IMPOSSIBLE...
NO...
NO...
NO...
THE RECORDS ARE ALL LIES.

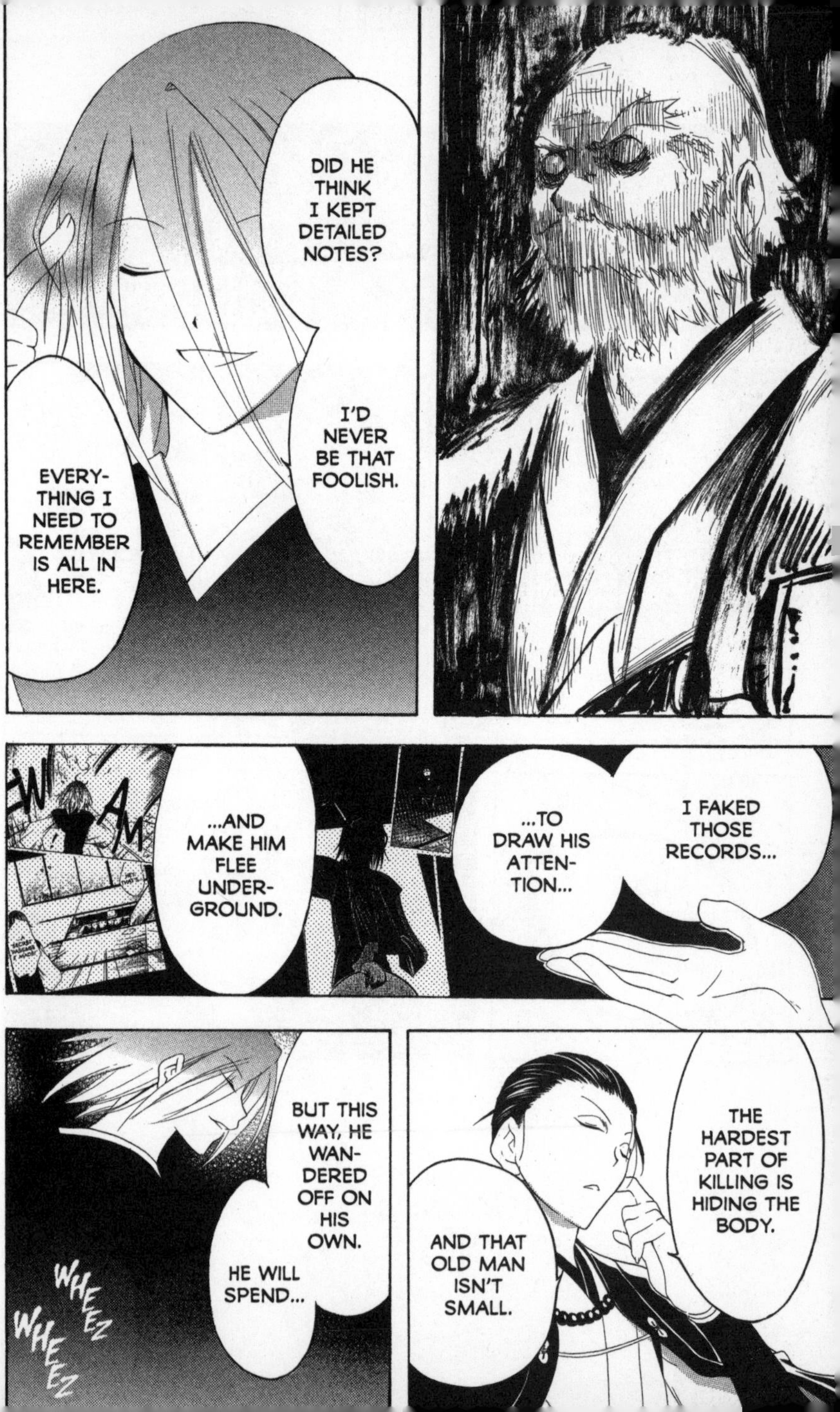
DID HE THINK I KEPT DETAILED NOTES?
I'D NEVER BE THAT FOOLISH.
EVERYTHING I NEED TO REMEMBER IS ALL IN HERE.
I FAKED THOSE RECORDS...
...TO DRAW HIS ATTENTION...
...AND MAKE HIM FLEE UNDERGROUND.
WHAM
THE HARDEST PART OF KILLING IS HIDING THE BODY.
AND THAT OLD MAN ISN'T SMALL.
BUT THIS WAY, HE WANDERED OFF ON HIS OWN.
HE WILL SPEND...
WHEEZ
WHEEZ

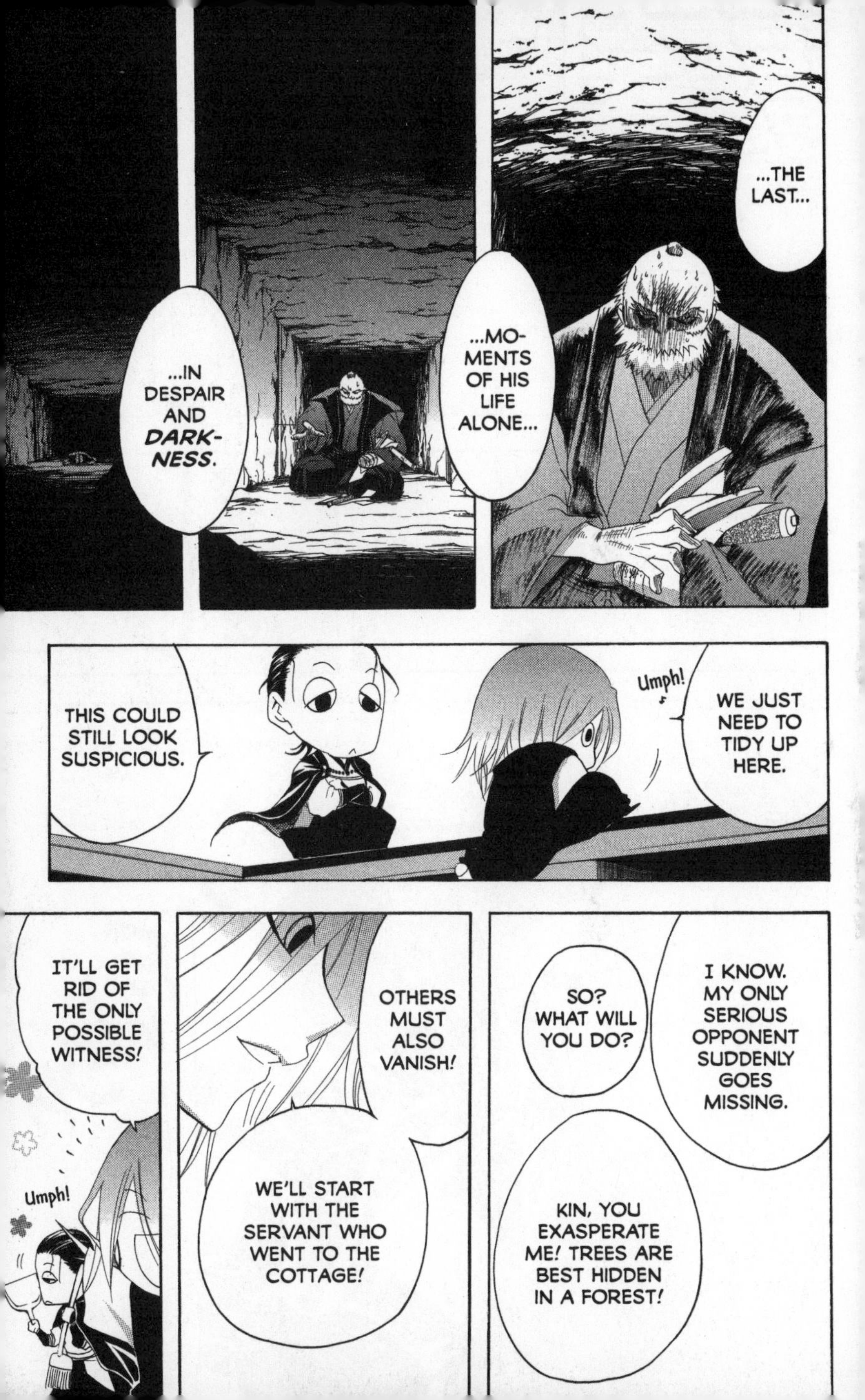
...THE LAST...
...MO-MENTS OF HIS LIFE ALONE...
...IN DESPAIR AND *DARK-NESS*.
Umph!
WE JUST NEED TO TIDY UP HERE.
THIS COULD STILL LOOK SUSPICIOUS.
I KNOW. MY ONLY SERIOUS OPPONENT SUDDENLY GOES MISSING.
SO? WHAT WILL YOU DO?
KIN, YOU EXASPERATE ME! TREES ARE BEST HIDDEN IN A FOREST!
OTHERS MUST ALSO VANISH!
WE'LL START WITH THE SERVANT WHO WENT TO THE COTTAGE!
IT'LL GET RID OF THE ONLY POSSIBLE WITNESS!
Umph!

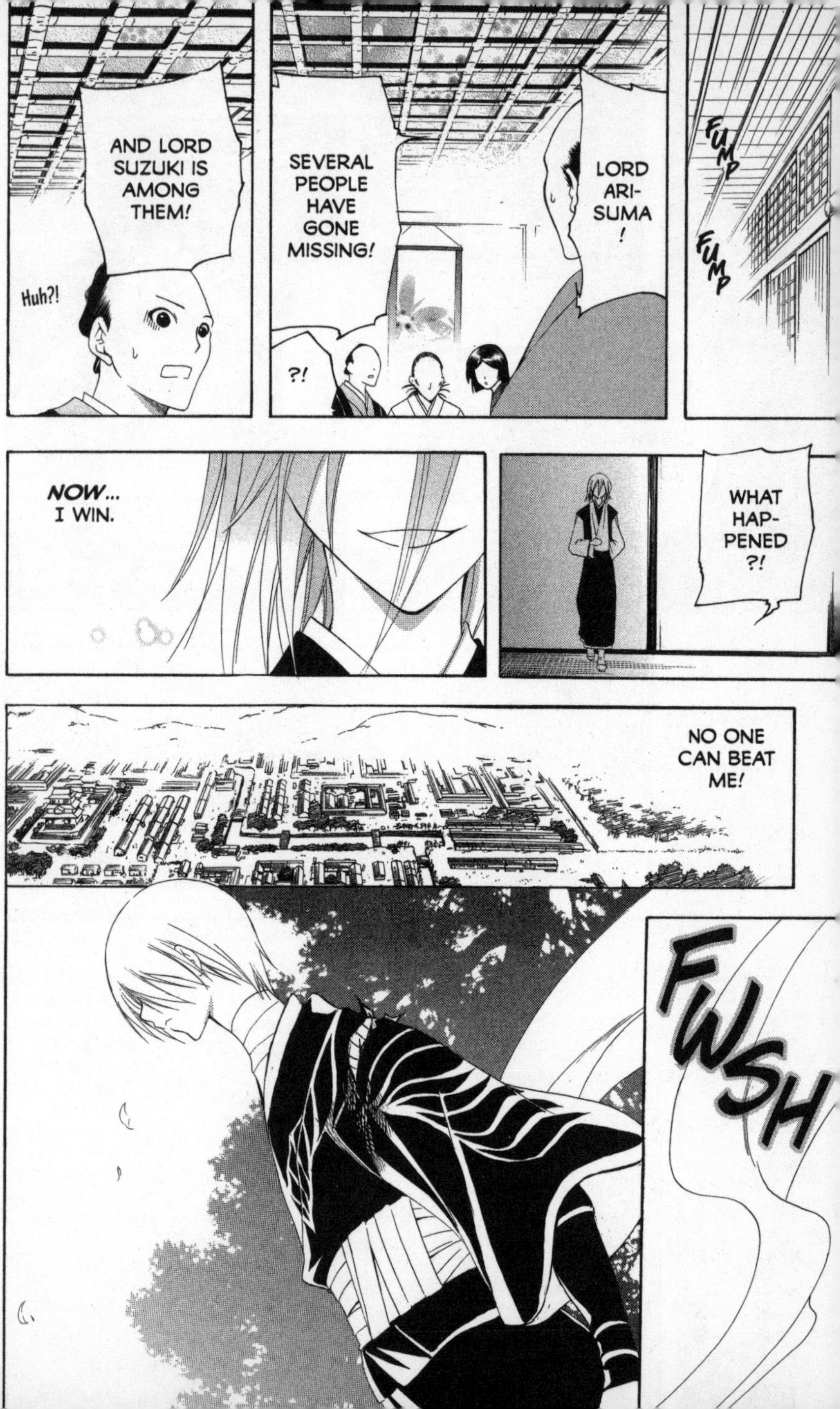
FUMP
FUMP
LORD ARISUMA!
SEVERAL PEOPLE HAVE GONE MISSING!
?!
AND LORD SUZUKI IS AMONG THEM!
Huh?!
WHAT HAPPENED?!
NOW... I WIN.
NO ONE CAN BEAT ME!
FWSH

Bonus Manga

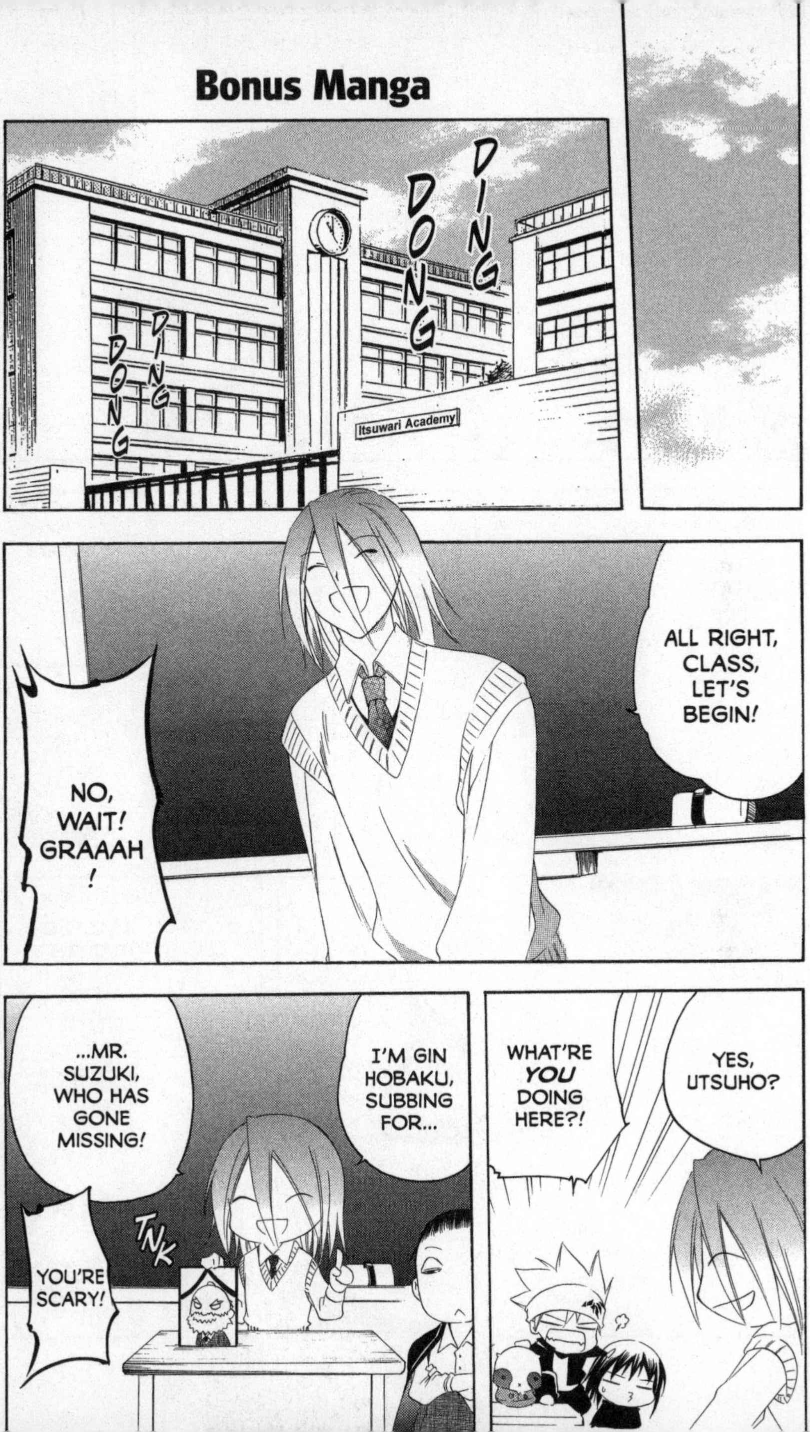
DING
DONG
DING
DONG
Itsuwari Academy
ALL RIGHT, CLASS, LET'S BEGIN!
NO, WAIT! GRAAAH!
YES, UTSUHO?
WHAT'RE *YOU* DOING HERE?!
I'M GIN HOBAKU, SUBBING FOR...
...MR. SUZUKI, WHO HAS GONE MISSING!
TNK
YOU'RE SCARY!

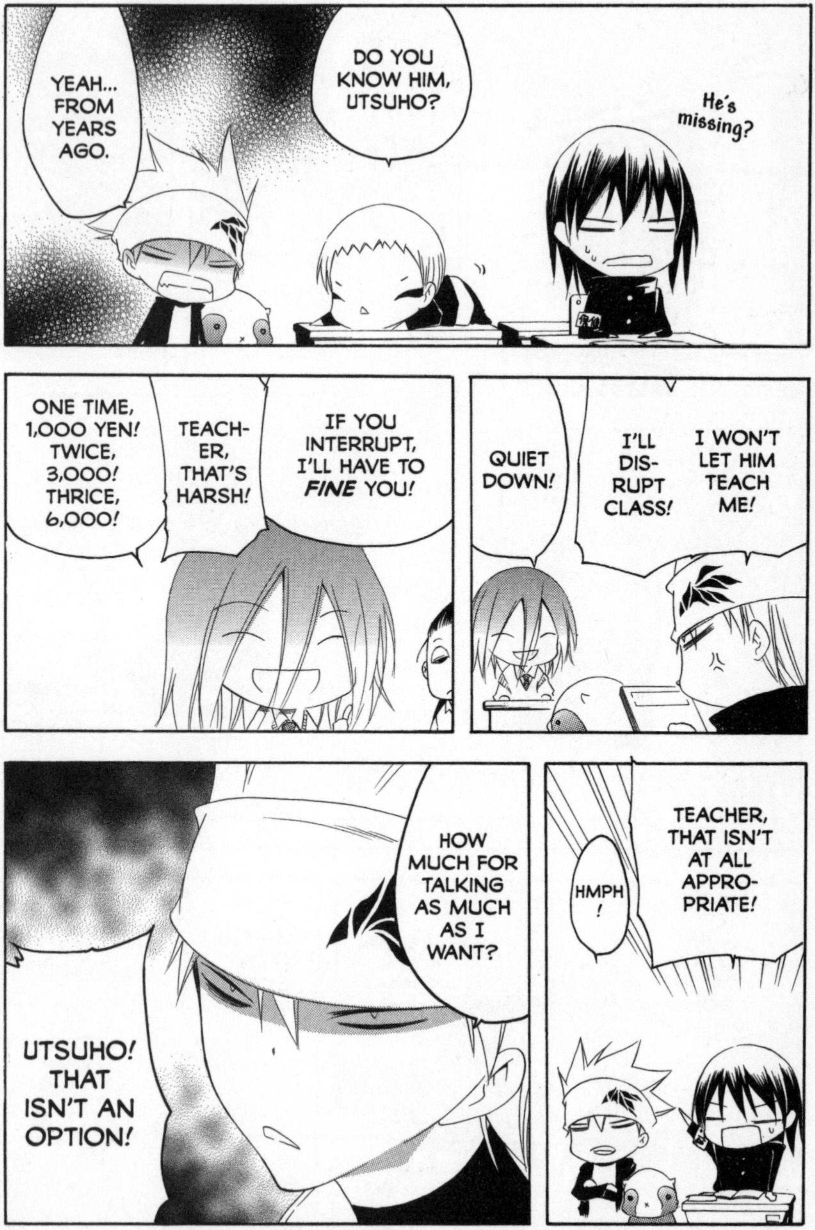
He's missing?
DO YOU KNOW HIM, UTSUHO?
YEAH... FROM YEARS AGO.
I WON'T LET HIM TEACH ME!
I'LL DIS-RUPT CLASS!
QUIET DOWN!
IF YOU INTERRUPT, I'LL HAVE TO *FINE* YOU!
TEACH-ER, THAT'S HARSH!
ONE TIME, 1,000 YEN! TWICE, 3,000! THRICE, 6,000!
TEACHER, THAT ISN'T AT ALL APPRO-PRIATE!
HMPH!
HOW MUCH FOR TALKING AS MUCH AS I WANT?
UTSUHO! THAT ISN'T AN OPTION!

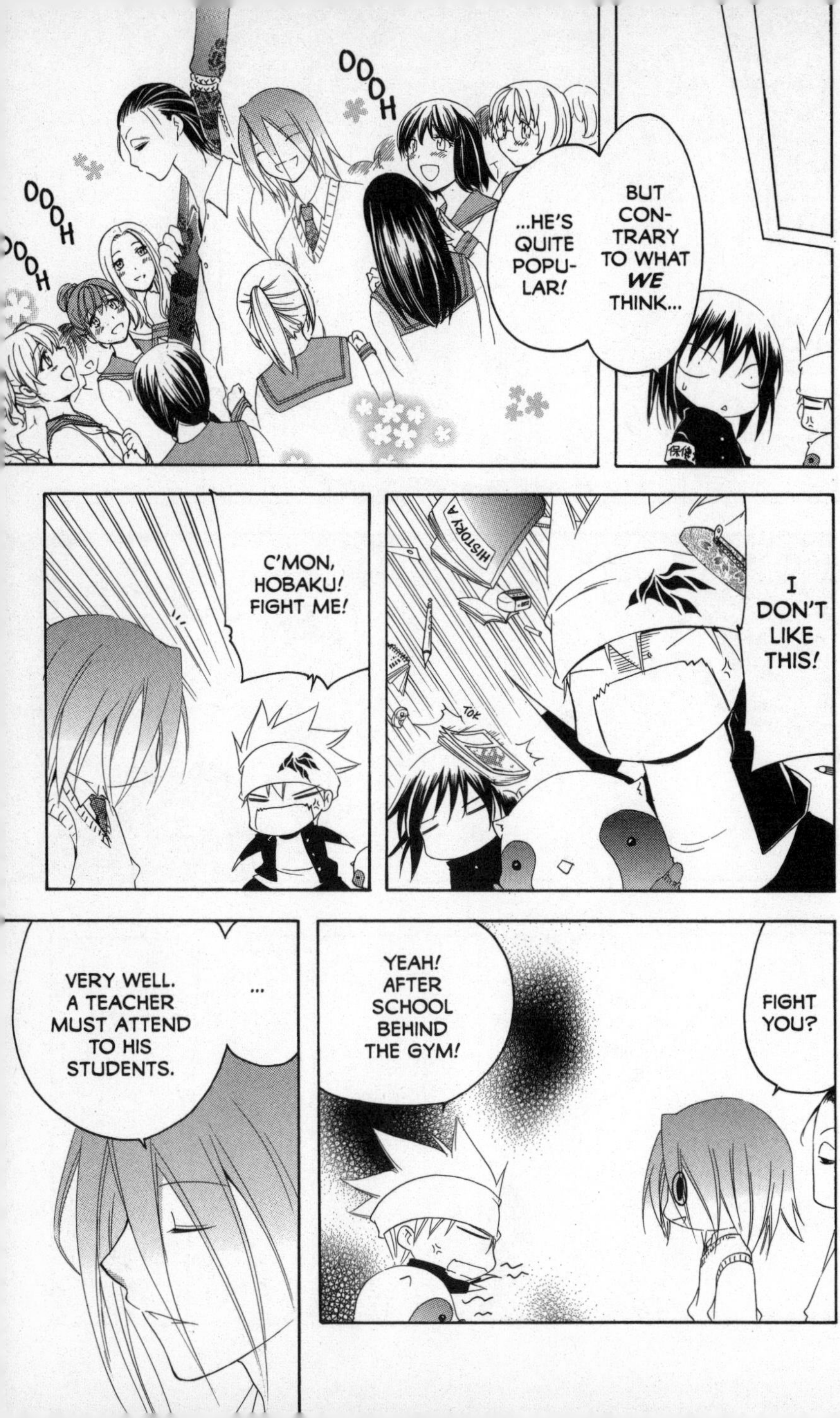
BUT CONTRARY TO WHAT WE THINK...
...HE'S QUITE POPULAR!
OOOH
OOOH
OOOH
I DON'T LIKE THIS!
HISTORY A
TOK
C'MON, HOBAKU! FIGHT ME!
FIGHT YOU?
YEAH! AFTER SCHOOL BEHIND THE GYM!
...
VERY WELL. A TEACHER MUST ATTEND TO HIS STUDENTS.

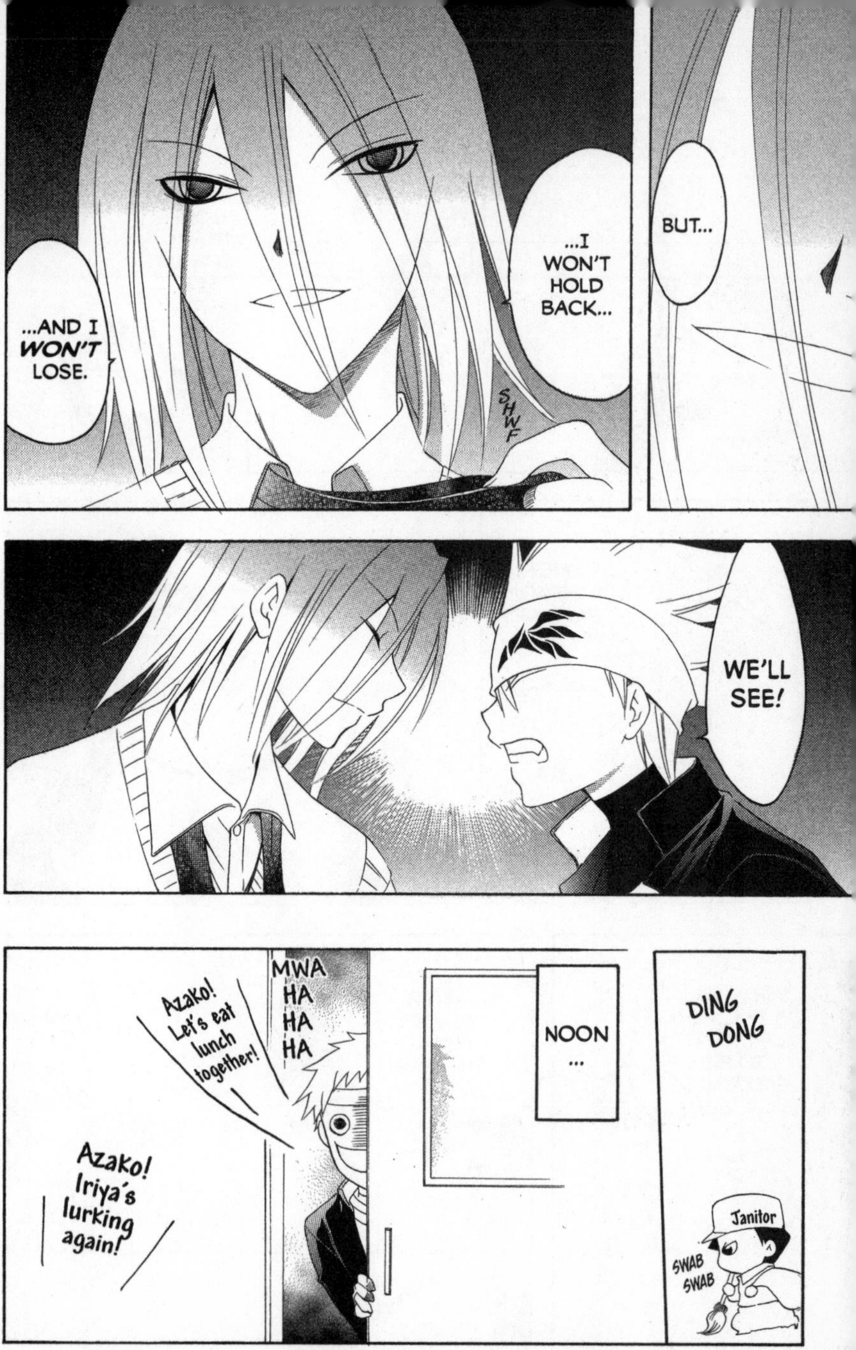
BUT...
...I WON'T HOLD BACK...
SHWF
...AND I *WON'T* LOSE.
WE'LL SEE!
DING DONG
Janitor
SWAB SWAB
NOON ...
MWA HA HA HA
Azako! Let's eat lunch together!
Azako! Iriya's lurking again!

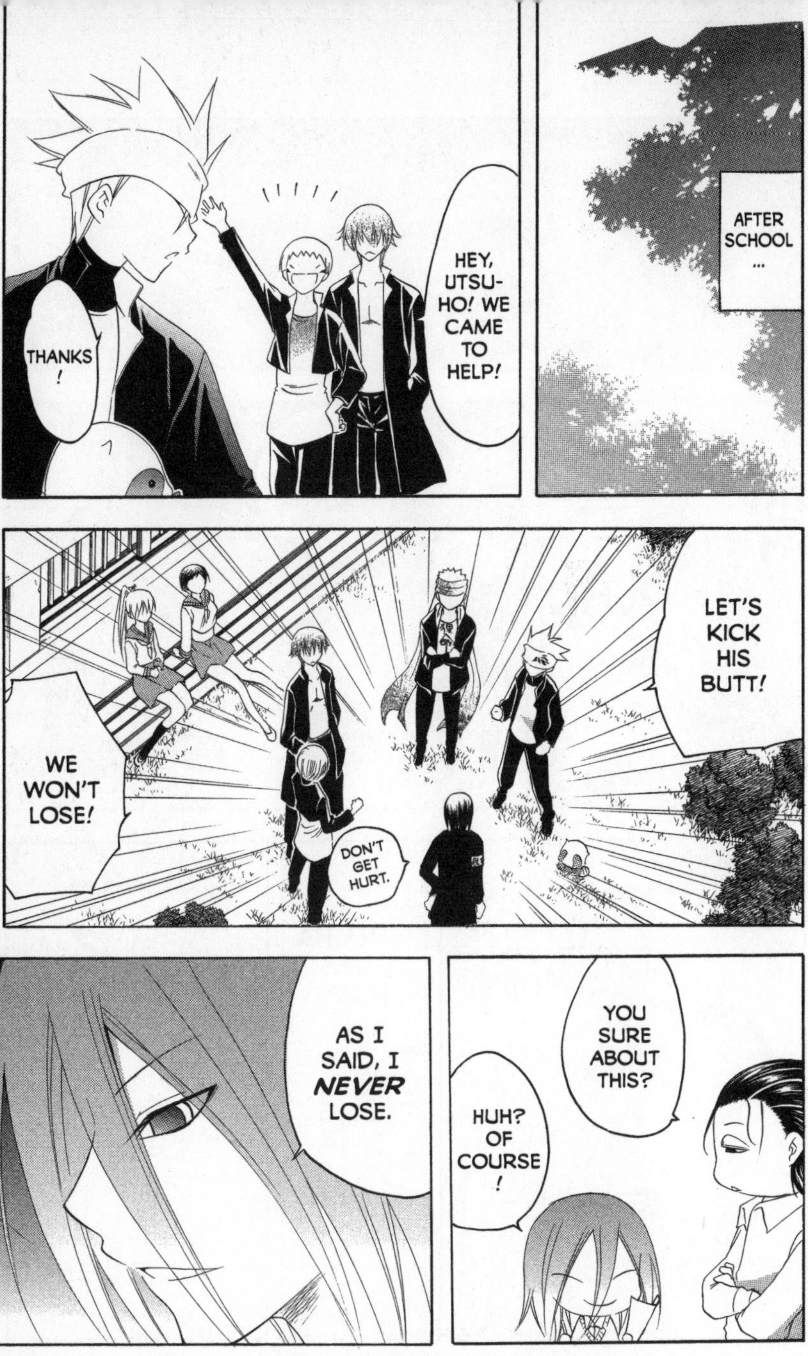
AFTER SCHOOL ...
HEY, UTSU-HO! WE CAME TO HELP!
THANKS!
LET'S KICK HIS BUTT!
WE WON'T LOSE!
DON'T GET HURT.
YOU SURE ABOUT THIS?
HUH? OF COURSE!
AS I SAID, I NEVER LOSE.

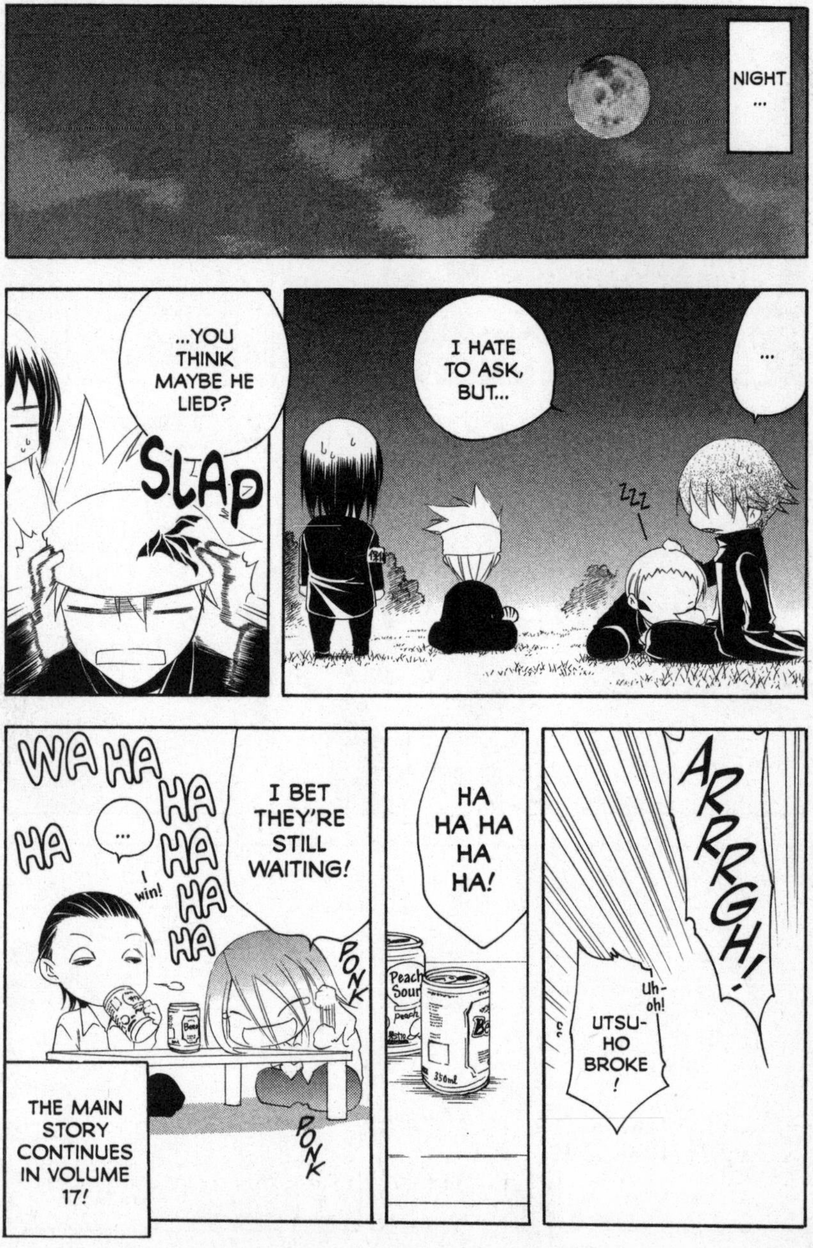
NIGHT...
...
I HATE TO ASK, BUT...
...YOU THINK MAYBE HE LIED?
SLAP
ARRRGH!
Uh-oh!
UTSU-HO BROKE!
HA HA HA HA HA!
Peach Sour
350ml
I BET THEY'RE STILL WAITING!
WA HA HA HA HA HA HA HA
...
I win!
PONK
PONK
THE MAIN STORY CONTINUES IN VOLUME 17!

ITSUWARIBITO
Volume 16
Shonen Sunday Edition

Story and Art by
YUUKI IINUMA

ITSUWARIBITO ◆ UTSUHO ◆ Vol. 16
by Yuuki IINUMA
© 2009 Yuuki IINUMA
All rights reserved.
Original Japanese edition published by SHOGAKUKAN.
English translation rights in the United States of America and Canada
arranged with SHOGAKUKAN.

Translation/John Werry
Touch-up Art & Lettering/Susan Daigle-Leach
Design/Matt Hinrichs
Editor/Gary Leach

The stories, characters and incidents mentioned
in this publication are entirely fictional.

Printed in Canada

Published by VIZ Media, LLC
P.O. Box 77010
San Francisco, CA 94107

10 9 8 7 6 5 4 3 2 1
First printing, December 2015

www.viz.com   WWW.SHONENSUNDAY.COM

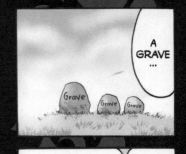

A GRAVE ...
Grave
Grave
Grave
IT'S NOT LIKELY...
...BUT IF I DIE, I WANT MY GRAVE TO READ...
"HERE LIES HIKAE NIBYO, THE COOLEST, NICEST, BESTEST GUY EVER."
SOUND GOOD ?
WILL SOMEONE BE IN THERE WITH YOU?

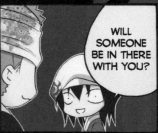